With Willful Intent

Intent

A Theology of Sin

With Willful Intent

Intent

A Theology of Sin

DAVID L. SMITH

A
BRIDGEPOINT
BOOK

Copyediting: Robert N. Hosack
Cover Design: Scott Rattray
Cover Painting: *Eve and the Serpent* by Liandi Su,
    courtesy of the Billy Graham Center, Wheaton, Illinois.

Library of Congress Cataloging-in-Publication Data

Smith, David L. (David Lorne)
    With willful intent: a theology of sin / by David L. Smith
        p.   cm.
    ISBN: 1-56476-265-3
    1. Sin.   2. Sin—History of doctrines.   I. Title.
BT715.S658   1994
214'.3—dc20   93-39474
                                                              CIP

BridgePoint is the academic imprint of Victor Books.

1 2 3 4 5 6 7 8 9 10 Printing/Year 98 97 96 95 94

Dedicated to the memory
of my father and mother,
Benjamin George Smith
and
Evangeline Doleman Smith,
who from my birth taught me
both the horror of sin and
the means of its conquest
through Christ Jesus.

Contents

Preface

Those who teach writing as an art tell their students that the would-be author should write about something with which he or she is familiar or has had considerable experience. When it comes to sin, I have had substantial amounts of both. I have been a practitioner for as long as I can remember. I can also say, however, that I also fairly early on discovered the cure for the disease of sin and have taken advantage of that many years past.

This volume on sin came about as the result of a dearth of texts for the theological study of sin and its conquest. I had for some time used Bernard Ramm's excellent little volume *Offense to Reason* (Harper and Row, 1985). But when I ordered it for a recent theology class, I was told that it was out of print. Nor was there anything else on the market at that time that would suffice for my purposes.

I offer this volume, which is as complete a coverage of the topic of sin as I could make it, in the hope that Christian leaders and students at the advanced undergraduate level or graduate level in theology will find it of use in determining their theology of sin. I have attempted to formulate it in such a fashion that my methodology is clear and that students, following a similar methodology, may prayerfully and carefully work out their own doctrinal position on this important aspect of the human pilgrimage. It is "a" theology of sin, and not "the" theology thereof.

I wish to thank my colleague, Dr. August Konkel, chairman of the Biblical Studies Department at Providence Theological Seminary, for reading the chapters on Old Testament theology and making several constructive suggestions for changes and additions. Much credit for the first chapter of the book, on the patristic and scholastic theologies of sin, must go to my research assistant and student, Terry Kaufman. He spent considerable effort on that area, and I am grateful. I am also thankful to Providence Theological Seminary for its provision of time and facilities for this work; and, as always, to my wife, Gail, who has allowed me to spend most of my free time in research and writing. Most of all, I give the praise to my Lord, Jesus Christ, without whose sacrifice on Calvary writing such a volume would have been an exercise in futility.

David L. Smith
June 1993

Introduction
The Problem of Sin

About two decades ago an eminent American psychiatrist, Karl Menninger, wrote a book in which he extensively surveyed the evil and inhumanity of modern society.[1] He lamented the apparent loss of the one word which so aptly described the tragic state of contemporary life.

> It was once a strong word, an ominous and serious word. It described a central point in every human being's life plan and life style. But the word went away. It has almost disappeared—the word along with the notion.[2]

That word was *sin*.

The years since Menninger's book have been no more optimistic. Events in society—whether international in scope, like the Gulf War; or national, like the interracial conflicts in Yugoslavia; or on a personal level, such as the horrendous increase in child sexual abuse—offer abundant testimony that evil continues unabated. Whatever aliases under which it may be skulking, sin still totally saturates every facet of human existence.

What is the source of evil? Has it always existed? How did it enter the world to infect humanity? Must all human beings sin? Or is sin a matter of the human will? If all human beings must sin, how can anyone condemn them? Is the propensity for evil hereditary? If not, why is it so pervasive? These and scores of

11

other questions present themselves for our consideration.

We are reminded by James L. Garrett that sin per se is a theological conception. "Sin presupposes the existence of God as a personal being, as the Holy One."[3] What evil is committed may be an offense against a corporate body (e.g., the state) or against an individual, but it is a sin against God.

Because sin affects our relationship with God, great care must be taken to work through and answer the above questions as thoroughly and accurately as possible. Our eternal destiny hangs in the balance. This volume will seek to develop such a theology.

The book is divided into three main sections—historical, biblical, and systematic theologies of sin—which reflect the methodology and process being undertaken. The work concludes with a practical theological application which draws the other sections together.

Section One, "A Historical Theology of Sin," provides a detailed overview of the thinking of Christian people about sin from the early church to our own day. Chapter 1 sets out the views of the church fathers during the first 500 years of the church's existence. It was during this period that most of our ideas on sin were developed. The concepts of the patristic era are foundational to most doctrines of sin.

Chapter 2 delineates the revision and consolidation of the doctrine of the Fall of humankind by the Roman Catholic Church in the millennium following the fathers. Chief among the theologians of this Medieval period were Thomas Aquinas and the Scholastics.

The Protestant Reformers rejected much of the theology of Medieval Catholicism, preferring to build on Pauline and Augustinian foundations. The doctrinal thinking of Martin Luther and John Calvin form the basis of chapter 3. Also included are the conclusions of the theologians of the Catholic Counter-Reformation.

The fourth chapter examines the ideas of sin elucidated by post-Reformation Protestantism in the seventeenth through early twentieth centuries. The theologians of the Enlightenment and Romantic periods were less confident of the Bible than were their predecessors. They redirected their thinking about sin toward the scientific method. This trend deepened under the liberals of the nineteenth century. Early in the present century there was a reaction against such liberal thinking on the part of both fundamentalism—which sought to go back to pre-Enlightenment theology—and neo-orthodoxy, which proclaimed a reinterpreted Reformed theology which held to Scripture as interpreted by modern biblical studies.

Chapter 5 concludes the historical section by investigating the concepts of sin held by church thinkers in our own time. Consideration is given to the views of evangelicalism, secularism, and some of the other contemporary theologies.

Section Two, "A Biblical Theology of Sin," sets forth the biblical teaching on the Fall of humankind and its ramifications. Because the Bible is held by Christians to be the fully inspired Word of God sufficient in all matters of faith and practice, what it says about sin should be determinative in our development of a theology.

Chapter 6 examines the Old Testament teaching of the Pentateuch. A key component of this chapter is an exegesis of Genesis 3, the origin of human sin. An explication of the Hebrew words for sin helps to shed light on the nature of the problem being explored.

In chapter 7 the prophetic theology of sin is examined. This study includes both the Former and Latter Prophets. Important considerations are the Deuteronomic history of Israel, and how the writer uses the last book of the Pentateuch as a paradigm for his theological reflection, and the convictions of the major and minor prophets, especially on Israel's persistent sins which led to her destruction as a nation.

Chapter 8 concludes the Old Testament examination with a study of the theology of the Writings. The chief areas of concern here are the Psalms, Wisdom literature, and the Chronicler's theology of sin (and how it differs from that of the Deuteronomist). The chapter concludes with a summary of the Old Testament understanding of sin.

In chapter 9 the New Testament teaching on sin is divided into the Synoptic teaching, the theology of the Pauline epistles, the concepts of sin developed by John, and the teaching of the other writers. Special attention is devoted to an exegesis of the locus classicus on sin, Romans 5:12-21. A summary of the theology of sin in the New Testament concludes the chapter.

Section Three, "A Systematic Theology of Sin," seeks to systematize the teaching of Scripture while using the insights of history, science, and the social sciences. Chapter 10 begins with an investigation of the nature of sin, attempting to define it in regard to the human relationship to God. It divides the topic into two broad categories—sin (primarily) as ungodliness, and sin (secondarily) as unrighteousness—in an effort to analyze its nature. Tied in closely to the nature of sin is its universality. Sin and its resultant guilt are collective, infecting every aspect of humanity and human society.

Chapter 11 examines both the origin of sin (with Adam and Eve in the Garden of Eden) and what has been termed original sin. How does the transgression of our first parents affect us today? Or does it?

Is sin inherited? Chapter 12 attempts to answer that question as it investigates the transmission of sin.

In chapter 13, we examine the relationship between sin and the fallen supernatural world. It is because Satan and his demonic cohorts are the initiators and agents of sin in the world that human beings may find forgiveness and must not of a necessity be punished for eternity if they will repent.

The final chapter of this section tells us how sin may be conquered and will be destroyed. Jesus Christ holds the key to ultimate victory over evil.

If a theology does not "preach," it is of little worth. The conclusion, "A Practical Theology of Sin," demonstrates how the theology we have formulated may be applied in the life of the individual and in the ministry of the church.

As we examine the material following, let us keep in mind that the only absolute is the Bible. While church tradition and the pronouncements of councils, bishops, and theologians are significant, none is inerrant or infallible. It is essential to keep Scripture and tradition separate if we are going to construct an accurate and meaningful theology of the Fall and sin of humankind. We must accept all that the Bible teaches; we need accept only that tradition or church teaching which conforms to the biblical standard. These premises will become manifestly clear as our theology unfolds.

Section One
A Historical Theology of Sin

Chapter One
The View of the Church Fathers

The development of a full-blown theology of sin was slow in coming to the early church, for the writings of the apostolic fathers were not systematic but occasional. And while they took it as a given that sin is universal, they made no concerted attempt to discover why.

That such a systematic formulation did not occur at once should come as no surprise for, in the formative years of the church, there was a tendency to theologize largely in response to questions, problems, or heresies. Because these fathers did not address the theology of sin directly, we must consider other areas through which their positions become evident. Their primary spiritual problem was Gnosticism, and so it will prove worthwhile to examine that heretical philosophy.

The Role of Gnosticism

Much of the theologizing of the second and third centuries was done in response to the teachings of Gnosticism, of which there were several varieties. One branch of this heresy, borrowing from Platonic idealism, taught that everything in the material realm is a more or less imperfect copy of a perfect immaterial idea in the mind of God.[1] Since humankind was said to be created in the image of God, they were therefore imperfect (i.e., sinful) copies of the divine concept of the "heavenly man."

Another Gnostic system, popularized by the Christian heretic, Valentinus, posited a "pleroma" of gods, or "aeons," one of whom — Sophia, or Wisdom — lusted after a full knowledge of the godhead and was expelled from heaven. In her despair she gave birth to the Demiurge, who was known as Yaldabaoth, Yao, or Yahweh; in his conceit and self-deception, he believed himself to be the "high God." He created a series of fallen spirit beings who, in turn, created this world, not perfectly, but as a distortion of the higher world.[2] They also aided in the creation of man who came to life when the Demiurge was tricked by the higher powers into breathing divine light into him. This set the stage for a battle between good and evil for possession of this light. The powers of evil placed man in a human body to keep him imprisoned; they also created woman and implanted sexual desire within him so that he would procreate and further spread these light particles about, making it more difficult for them to ascend back to the pleroma and be reunited with the godhead.[3] Thus, whichever branch one followed in Gnostic thinking, humans were under the control of higher forces, sin was to be expected, and only isolation from the material realm might bring escape.

In response to such thinking,[4] the anti-Gnostic fathers stressed the free will of humankind and the resultant personal assignment of blame. It has been noted that "it was a natural consequence of this polemic attitude toward Gnosticism, that the anthropology of the second and third centuries of both the Western and the Eastern Church was marked by a very strong emphasis of the doctrine of human freedom."[5]

The Second-Century Apologists

The second-century apologists were unanimous in proclaiming that sin is a willful act of each individual; what was inherited from Adam was not a corrupt nature but mortality. Some of them spoke of sin, and even its universality, but it was not tied to Adam's transgression. Their tendency was to regard him as a child who developed along the wrong path; "subsequent generations are free to associate themselves with Adam's guilt or not."[6]

18

Justin Martyr

Justin (ca. 100–ca. 165) is representative of the early emphasis on free will. He took an individualistic view of human sinfulness and death.[7] In his *Dialogue with Trypho, A Jew* (88.4), he stated that each person is responsible for his own sin. Though sin is individual, it is still universal, but Adam's role in this universality is simply that he brought death to all. Adam's sin is shown as the beginning of the spread of evil.

Again, it was the free will given to humankind by God that was the cause for evil. All the human race "ever since Adam's time had fallen under the power of death and of the serpent's deceit, as each person committed sin on his own responsibility."[8] But Justin, like many of his contemporaries, assigned some blame to demons for the existence of evil. He believed that malevolent demons, the result of a union between fallen angels and the daughters of men, were responsible for human corruption, swarming everywhere and obsessing human bodies and souls.[9]

Justin also drew a parallel between Eve and Mary in much the same fashion as Paul compared Adam and Christ (Rom. 5:12ff). Eve, an undefiled virgin, through disobedience brought forth death; but Mary, also an undefiled virgin, through obedience brought forth life in Christ.[10] But Justin assigned no blame directly to Eve for the sins of future generations. Although disobedience may have been introduced by Adam and Eve, it was passed on by example, for we are "brought up in bad habits and wicked training."[11]

Clement of Rome

Clement, bishop of Rome (ca. 96), in his work *1 Clement* (3:4), was concerned with the evil human heart. It has been said that this passage is representative of the belief of all the apostolic fathers. It gives to Adam no role in either the derivation of the wicked heart or the entry of death into the created order.[12] At the same time, one cannot therefore assume that Clement denies original sin.[13] The second-century fathers did have some idea of original sin, but they had not worked through all of its implications.

In his *Epistle to the Corinthians,* Clement railed against those who are disobedient to God's commandments: ". . . but each one goeth after the lusts of his evil heart, seeing that they have conceived an unrighteous and ungodly jealousy, through which also *death entered into the world.*"[14] He seemed to find jealousy and its related attitudes to be a cardinal sin, responsible for murder, sedition, spousal estrangement, and the persecution of the righteous. He called upon Christians to observe these attitudes and wicked behaviors in the lives of the sinful and "fix our eyes on the blood of Christ and understand how precious it is unto His Father, because being shed for our salvation it won for the whole world the grace of repentance."[15]

Tatian

Tatian (110–172) was more thorough in his consideration of the original state of humankind. He held that human beings were not created either mortal or immortal. Rather, a life of good or evil would determine one's destiny.

> We die by our own fault. Our free will has destroyed us: we who were free have become slaves; we have been sold through sin. Nothing evil has been created by God; we ourselves have manifested wickedness; but we, who have manifested it, are able again to reject it.[16]

As with his contemporaries, Tatian held that the blame for sin in this world is humanity's, with each individual responsible for his own wrongdoing. People were originally created capable of a special union of the Spirit with the soul.[17] It is this special spiritual union that was lost by the Fall. While that original relationship may be renewed by repentance and reconciliation, the fact that it is missing weakens humans and makes them susceptible to demonic assaults and, therefore, to sin.

Theophilus

Theophilus (d. 181) held that humanity was originally capable of either mortality or immortality. Human destiny was dependent on how people exercised their free will. His theology of sin was one which became popular among early church leaders: Adam was an immature child in the Garden. "But Adam, being yet an infant in age, was on this account as yet unable to receive knowledge worthily."[18] Had he obeyed God consistently, he would have achieved immortality, but his disobedience led instead to mortality and death.[19]

Theophilus further declared that the tree in Eden was not evil, but the evil was the disobedient act of partaking of the forbidden fruit. Consequently, Adam brought sin on humanity, but it was a philosophically universalist consideration and not an assignment of seminal guilt. We see this from his letter to Autolycus:

> But the sin in which man was concerned brought evil upon them. For when man transgressed, they also transgressed with him. For as, if the master of the house acts rightly, the domestics also of necessity conduct themselves well; but if the master sins, the servants also sin with him; so in like manner it came to pass, that in the case of man's sin, he being master, all that was subject to him sinned with him. When, therefore, man shall have made his way back to his natural condition, and no longer does evil, those also shall be restored to their original greatness.[20]

According to Theophilus, then, Adam's sin put the world in its present state with his expulsion from the Garden of Eden, but his disobedience was linked to his progeny only by type and not by guilt.

Summary

The second-century Apologists affirmed the universality of human sin. Any sense of original sin, however, was limited to this universal sinfulness and the entrance of mortality. No guilt was inherited by Adam's progeny because of his sin. If there were any assignment to be made, it was on the demons who beset human beings with temptation and lust. In the theology of these church leaders, human freedom of will reigned supreme.

The Eastern Fathers

As one moves into the latter part of the second century and toward the third, a dichotomy may be seen developing between

Eastern and Western positions in theology. While some may hold that this "theological polarization" did not occur until the fourth century,[21] a distinct divergence may be noticed earlier than that.

One area of widening separation was thought on original sin. The Eastern theologians generally viewed original sin to be a matter of nature, not guilt. The Latin theologians, on the other hand, saw original sin as an inheritance of guilt. But the Western concept of human physical solidarity with Adam — and so of its participation in his actual sinful deed — was not a part of Greek thought.[22]

Irenaeus of Lyons

In Irenaeus (ca. 140–ca. 200) the doctrines of the Fall and sin began to take on importance; at least, Irenaeus was the first church father to be concrete and systematic in his approach.[23] He held that the Fall marked an interruption of what should have been a period of growth for humans; like Tatian and Theophilus before him, Irenaeus felt that Adam prior to the Fall was undeveloped and imperfect.[24] His concern, however, was less to show that Adam brought sin into the world than to demonstrate that Christ brought salvation. Accordingly, he used several key dialectics, the first being Adam/Christ.

> For as by one man's disobedience sin entered, and death obtained [a place] through sin; so also by the obedience of one man, righteousness having been introduced, shall cause life to fructify in those persons who in times past were dead.[25]

Hints of his theology of sin are also evident in the Mary/Eve pairing, about which he states that "it was that the knot of Eve's disobedience was loosed by the obedience of Mary. For what the virgin Eve had bound fast through unbelief, this did the virgin Mary set free through faith."[26] And so, "Eve, by her disobedience, brought death upon herself and on all the human race: Mary, by her obedience, brought salvation."[27]

Because of a Platonic bent, Irenaeus saw original sin as the result of human solidarity which had turned to evil. While we think in terms of humanity as individuals, he held that all humankind was a single body of which Adam was head. All humans, then, shared in Adam's offense, which had a twofold consequence: death and a loss of the *imago Dei*.[28]

The Alexandrian school

In Alexandria a catechetical school was opened under the leadership of Pantaenus from which would come several prominent theologians. Its distinctive mark was the tendency to interpret the Bible allegorically.

Clement of Alexandria (ca. 150–215) was an early leader of this school. If Irenaeus made some progress toward a doctrine of sin, Clement did not. He felt that the account of the Fall, though true, should be taken allegorically, and so he did not extract from it any theory of original sin.[29] He believed that the account of the first couple's disobedience in Eden was a symbol demonstrating that all people sin on their own account, and so sin is both personal and universal.[30]

Adam is not the head of humankind, but the type. Every person eventually becomes like Adam; he is the symbol for what happens in every person.[31] Like Irenaeus, Clement believed that Adam was born in childlike innocence and was intended to grow toward perfection, but fell with the first sin.[32] The difference between Clement and Irenaeus is the absence in the former's writing of any corporate representation in Adam of all humanity. Clement believed that sin is not a substance, but an action.[33] Because of this understanding, he felt that Adam's sin is inherited by example and not by procreation.[34] Thus, an infant cannot fall under the curse of Adam because it cannot sin of its own accord.[35]

For Clement of Alexandria, then, the existence of sin in the world was fully explained by the freedom of human will. While such a concept of free will is by no means original with him, "there is much truth in the statement that the Alexandrines, and Clement in particular, first defined it and made it the foundation of a system."[36]

Origen (ca. 185–254) followed Clement in Alexandria. He was a very creative theologian, particularly in his anthropology. Like the Latin, Tertullian (whom we shall consider later), Origen proposed two "incompatible" ideas concerning original sin, one

23

based on Scripture and the other on Platonic speculation. He attempted to combine Christianity and Platonism.

Consistent with such a synthetic approach, Origen held to the preexistence of the soul. He believed that God had created a fixed number of rational beings, all exactly the same, all possessing free will. As a result, they had the ability to follow God or to abandon Him. With the exception of the preexistent soul of Christ, all of these rational beings chose to abandon God. Thus, they sinned.

> Those rational beings who sinned and on that account fell from the state in which they were, in proportion to their particular sins were enveloped in bodies as a punishment; and when they are purified they rise again to the state in which they formerly were, completely putting away their evil and their bodies. Then again a second or third or many more times they are enveloped in different bodies for punishment.[37]

Since Origen posited a pre-cosmic Fall, he held Genesis not to be historical but cosmic myth, one which clearly and fully explained universal human sinfulness. He also saw biblical texts such as Psalm 51:5 ("Surely I was sinful at birth, sinful from the time my mother conceived me.") and Psalm 58:3 ("Even from birth the wicked go astray; from the womb they are wayward and speak lies.") as teaching that children are born into the world already stained with sin. As a consequence, children need to be baptized in infancy.[38]

Athanasius (ca. 296–373) depicted the Fall as a human lapse into the "natural" state; that is, it was seen as the loss of the supernatural endowments.[39] But this natural state did not include immortality, "for man is by nature mortal, inasmuch as he is made out of what is not. . . ."[40]

The result of the Fall from that natural state was that death gained a legal hold on human beings. It was a hold impossible to evade, for God had brought it into being because of sin.

> But man, having despised and rejected the contemplation of God, and devised and contrived evil for themselves, received the condemnation of death with which they had been

24

threatened; and from thenceforth no longer remained as they were made, but were being corrupted according to their devices; and death had the mastery over them as king. For transgression of the commandment was turning them back to their natural state.[41]

And so, "when Adam had transgressed, his sin reached unto all men. . . ."[42] Sin introduced to humankind the movement from the supernatural preferred state to a natural one of death and corruption. Only a new work of creation could undo the damage; only an "unalterable One" could change what Adam had "altered."[43]

For Athanasius, Adam was somehow the sum of all people, but he never suggested that we receive from Adam any guilt or moral blame. Nor did he rule out the possibility of someone living sinlessly.[44] Unfortunately, people are prone to repeating the sin of Adam and Eve, and so

the soul, departing from the contemplation of what is good and from moving in its sphere, wanders away and moves toward its contraries. Thus seeing, as I said before, and abusing her power, she has perceived that she can move the members of the body also in the opposite way: and so, instead of beholding the Creation, she turns the eye to lusts, showing that she has this power, too . . . not knowing that she is made not merely to move, but to move in the right direction.[45]

The powers of depravity in human life became so great that the weakened human nature became insufficient in its ability to know its Creator. Indeed, declared Athanasius, in their perversity humans "so wholly rejected God, and so darkened their soul, as not merely to forget their idea of God, but also to fashion for themselves one invention after another." And so they gave themselves over to idols, not only to graven images but also to sticks and stones. "And, in a word, everything was full of irreligion and lawlessness, and God alone . . . was unknown, albeit He had not hidden Himself out of men's sight. . . ."[46]

Athanasius' emphasis was much more heavily on God's redemptive plan to save humans than on their sinful state, trusting Christ who is the image of the Father to renewing fallen humanity once created as His likeness. Rondet tells us, "As in Irenaeus, the sin of Adam appears less than an appalling catastrophe than as an initial fault that unloosed, with all sorts of evils both physical and moral, the multitude of sins from which Christ redeemed us."[47] The Fall, in other words, brought deprivation, not depravity.

The Cappadocian school

Basil of Caesarea (d. 379, also called "the Great") was the first theologian of the Cappadocian school. He supported the idea that the Fall of Adam brought sin and death into the world. At the same time, he does not seem to have envisioned some kind of inherited guilt accompanying these ills, for he held that newborn infants were free from sin.[48] Elsewhere, however, he asserted that Adam's sin has been imputed to all humanity and makes all persons actual sinners, but failed to demonstrate in what way this happened.[49] Basil's ideas do not seem to have been either complete or entirely logical.

Gregory of Nyssa (ca. 330–ca. 394), Basil's younger brother, was the most capable theologian among the Cappadocian fathers, and he had a more fully developed theology of sin. He did not agree with Origen's teaching on the preexistence of the soul, nor with his idea of prenatal sin. Human sin was an historical act by which the whole nature of humankind was weakened and human understanding was darkened.[50] Sin also brought mortality, which Gregory saw as symbolized in the coats of skin which God made for the hapless first couple.[51] But there was no guilt attached to original sin. The Adamic nature is *hamarteitikein,* or "prone to sin."[52] But even though humans receive a mortal and polluted nature, it is possible to live outside of this sinful nature. "Nature gets the pollution of evil necessarily mingled more or less with his life," wrote Gregory, "or, if he is to be quite outside this contagion, it will be at the price of much painful effort."[53] To avoid evil is possible because sin is of the free will. He noted that "evil is in some way or other, engendered from within, springing up in the will at that moment when there is a retrocession of the soul from the beautiful."[54]

Gregory went on to say that one cannot assign evil to the nature, for in the end that would assign evil to the nature's

Creator, God.[55] And so he strongly denied the existence of any evil outside of the will,[56] and it is the free choice of the will, both male and female, to choose between evil and good, which are set before them equally.[57] Gregory probably came closest of any of the Eastern fathers to a strong theology of sin.

Gregory Nazianzus (ca. 330–ca. 390) held much the same views as Gregory of Nyssa. While he had a doctrine of original sin, in that what occurred in Eden affected human nature, he did not demonstrate any linkage of that sin to guilt; that was determined by human free will. We see his views on sin in his teaching on infant baptism.

> Some have not been able to receive baptism because of their tender years or because of some completely involuntary accident. . . . They will receive neither glory nor chastisement, I think, at the hands of the just Judge; since, while they have not been sealed, they are void of offense, and they have incurred this defect involuntarily. But it does not follow that one who does not deserve punishment deserves honor; nor that one who does not deserve honor deserves punishment.[58]

The Antiochan school

The school of the church of Antioch took a somewhat more literalistic approach to the Bible. Its most famous member, John Chrysostom (ca. 347–407), provides for us a lucid portrayal of the thought of this area of the Eastern Church. As with the other Eastern fathers, John did not consider sin as a completely separate doctrine, but rather saw it as a foil to redemption.

Chrysostom believed that Adam's sin brought mortality into the world; it was our inheritance from Adam.[59] "But what means 'for all have sinned'?" he asked. "This: he having fallen, even they that had not eaten of the tree did from him, all of them, become mortal."[60]

Although the Fall had no effect on human free will, it did cause humans to experience certain passions since they had no longer an upward urge toward God.[61] Chrysostom speculated that God is not unjust in imparting consequences on one for the deeds of another, saying that we are so far from taking any harm from this death and condemnation, if we are sober-minded, that we are the gainers even by having become mortal, first, because it is not an immortal body in which we sin; secondly, because we get numberless grounds for being religious.[62]

The consequence of Adam's sin was to make humans mortal and incline them to sin.[63] Chrysostom seemed to indicate that partnership with penalty does not necessitate partnership in the fault.[64] It has been suggested that he "nowhere allows that the Fall had any effect upon man's freedom of will," nor that "concupiscence is of the nature of sin."[65] According to Kelly, however, Chrysostom's position was that the mortality imposed as a punishment on humanity necessitates concupiscence.[66] Certainly, free will is the basis for each person's sin. In fact, no sin was ever committed in ignorance, "for if they sinned through ignorance, then they did not deserve to be punished,"[67] and punishment would not be meted out to one who had not actually committed sin.[68]

Chrysostom believed that the teaching of original sin should be presented alongside of the teaching of the work of Christ, which can undo the consequences of the former: "For that one man should be punished on account of another does not seem to be much in accordance with reason. But for one to be saved on account of another is at once more suitable and more reasonable. If then the former took place, much more the latter."[69] Adam, therefore, is a "type" of Christ, and so original sin should be considered along with redemption.

Chrysostom did not condemn pedobaptism, although he considered infants not to have any sin. "We do baptize infants," he said, "although they are not guilty of any sins."[70] Only personal sins deserve punishment, "for unless a man becomes a sinner on his own responsibility, he will not be found to deserve punishment."[71]

Theodore of Mopsuestia (ca. 350–428) rejected much of the tradition of the Eastern Church in regard to sin. As Tennant says, "He stands out in a somewhat isolated position in that he repudiates the practically universal belief that Adam's transgression was the cause of mortality to all mankind."[72] Theodore asserted that the first man and woman were not created immortal, but mortal, and it was on this belief that he built his unique views of the Fall and sin. Quasten has aptly summarized Theodore's teaching as follows:

> Man was not created immortal, but mortal; Adam and Eve harmed only themselves by their sin; universal mortality is not a chastisement of Adam's sin; the effects of the sin of Adam—the present condition of man—are not penalties, but a test, an experiment instituted by God. The tortures of the damned will come to an end.[73]

Adam, then, is our type, not our ancestor, and we inherited the consequences of the first sin, but not the guilt.[74]

The Latin Fathers Prior to Augustine

In the West the sense of sin as open guilt was more strongly developed than in the East, as was evident as early as the third century in the work of Tertullian.

The catalysts to the development of this doctrine in the West do not lie in pure speculative thought, but rather in the direction of the church's life and practice.[75] That is, convention determined creed. The primary concerns of the Latin fathers were the practical matters of the church. One may therefore use the practice of the church, particularly infant baptism and penance, to provide some direction in an investigation of the development of the doctrine of sin.

Tertullian

Tertullian of Carthage (ca. 160–ca. 220) is a major figure in the development of a theology of sin. The Western interpretation of the Fall may be said to have originated with Tertullian (although there is certainly an earlier debt to Irenaeus, cited previously).

Tertullian's thought was influenced by his Stoic background, where there was a somewhat indifferent attitude about individual immortality and rather a concern with "absorption into the divine substance."[76] But particularly important for Tertullian—and quite visible throughout his thought—was the Stoic understanding of the soul as material.

Tertullian was the first to promote traducianism, declaring that "we indeed maintain that both [body and soul] are conceived, and formed, and perfectly simultaneously, as well as born together."[77] He insisted that both life and the soul begin with conception and that the two kinds of seed, soul and body, are inseparable. In graphic illustration he supported his theory of traducianism by talking about the physical effect of the male's seminal discharge showing a departure of some "soul."[78]

> The consequences of traducianism are quite clear: Every soul, then, by reason of its birth, has its nature in Adam until it is born again in Christ; moreover it is unclean all the while that it remains without this regeneration; and because unclean, it is actively sinful, and suffuses even the flesh with its own shame.[79]

Tertullian's dictum became famous: *Tradux animae, tradux peccati,* "the propagation of the soul implies the propagation of sin."

His theory of soul generation and his rejection of the preexistence of the soul harmonized with his literal interpretation of Genesis 3. The historical Fall was responsible for the entry of death into the world, condemning all humanity.[80] It is therefore entirely conceivable that Tertullian should be viewed as founder of the doctrine of the hereditary sinfulness of nature derived from Adam.[81]

At the same time, Tertullian asserted that humans have the complete freedom to choose good or evil. He wrote, "Thus it is a volition of our own when we will what is evil. . . ."[82] Original sin did not utterly destroy the ability to do good or to choose evil.[83] Flesh of itself remained neutral; it was only "reproached" in Scripture because it is an instrument of the evil will.[84] But in *Against Marcion* he also asked, "If the blessing of the fathers was destined to be transmitted to their posterity before that posterity had done anything to deserve it, why should not the guilt of the fathers flow down to their sons, so that the transgression as well as the grace should spread through the whole human race?"[85]

To add to this interesting dichotomy Tertullian proposed a somewhat surprising position regarding infant baptism, suggesting that a delay to later age was preferable. Young people should

30

come to be baptized while they are receiving the balance of their education. Baptism, he believed, returns one from Satan's power to a "pre-Fall" state.[86] God's grace in Christ takes away the corruption heaped by sin on human nature. That grace can bestow upon humans the power necessary for the living of a transformed life.[87]

Cyprian of Carthage

Cyprian (ca. 200–258) presented an interesting, albeit peripheral, doctrine of sin. He is an example of how church practice is used to support a theological position. He held that original sin was not as culpable as actual sin, but it nonetheless needed remission.[88] Such remission might be achieved in the waters of baptism.

> If then even to the most grievous offenders, and who had before sinned much against God, when they afterwards believe, remission of sins is granted, and no one is debarred from baptism and grace, how much more ought not an infant to be debarred, who being newly born has in no way sinned, except that being born after Adam in the flesh, he has by his first birth contracted the contagion of the old death; who is on this very account more easily admitted to receive remission of sins, in that not his own but another's sins are remitted to him.[89]

Hilary of Poitiers

Hilary (ca. 315–ca. 371) did not deviate substantially from Tertullian's view on sin, except in his idea of its transmission. He believed that original sin was transmitted by the soul's contact with the flesh. Basically, however, he maintained the tradition, asserting that while all humans sinned in Adam, this sin did not completely corrupt human will.[90]

Ambrose of Milan

Ambrose (ca. 340–397) marks an important development in the progress of the theology of sin, especially as it regards original sin. In fact, he has been termed "theologically the most impor-

31

tant forerunner of Augustine,"[91] and the last link before Augustine in the doctrine of sin.[92] The basis for such distinction is the emphasis Ambrose placed on the human sinful condition and how he understood sin to be a state rather than an act.[93] Like Hilary before him, he felt that all human beings sinned in Adam and, as a consequence, all have inherited guilt as well. "Adam was in each of us, for in him human nature sinned, because through one man sin passed over into all."[94]

Ambrose believed that the original sin of Adam in which all humanity has shared was one of pride. He also held that while human beings have been infected with original guilt, such hereditary guilt may be washed away in baptism.[95] While hereditary sin causes people to stumble, it does not hold them culpable on judgment day when they will answer only for their own personal sins.[96]

In regard to the transmission of sin, Ambrose tended toward the creationist theory of the soul's origin, but was unclear as to how sin was passed along. He was unsure whether a child inherited sin from its parent or was born with sin. One thing, however, was sure: "not even a day old child is without sin."[97]

Augustine of Hippo

Augustine (354–430) stands head and shoulders above all the other church fathers when it comes to the theology of sin. It is not so much that his ideas were original, but he synthesized and systematized them more than anyone before him. Rondet notes that "he rendered explicit a tradition which . . . was slowly coming to the surface."[98] Gerald Bonner suggests that Augustine's doctrine of original sin was not really his, but a doctrine from Africa which — while he did not originate it — he defended as catholic teaching.[99] Certainly, no abler defender could be found.

Augustine is widely known as the doctor of grace. But grace cannot be discussed without also discerning why it is needed, and so Augustine spent substantial time on the sinfulness of humankind.

Augustinianism may be summed up in three ideas: original righteousness, original sin as inherited moral weakness, and original sin as original guilt. In modern thought, it has been said, the first and third ideas are "worthless," and the second — the con-

1.1: THE DEVELOPMENT OF PATRISTIC THINKING ON SIN

Clement of Rome   *ca. 30–ca.100*
Adam had no special role in entry of sin into world. Jealousy is basis for most human sin.

✠

Justin Martyr   *ca. 100–165*
Adam brought death to all and began spread of evil, but each individual is responsible for his or her own sin.

✠

Tatian   *100–172*
Strongly emphasized free will of every human being. The Fall cost humans capability of a special union of Holy Spirit with human soul.

✠

Theophilus   *d. 181*
Had Adam obeyed God consistently, he would have achieved immortality. By his sin, he brought evil to all humanity because he was master of the race.

✠

Irenaeus of Lyons   *140–200*
All humankind a single body of which Adam was head. Thus, in Adam's sin all humans sinned.

✠

Clement of Alexandria   *ca. 150–215*
The Fall, though true, is allegorical of humans. Adam is the type, not head, of all human beings. Sin in the world is the result of free will, not of Adam.

✠

Tertullian   *ca. 160–220*
Originated Western view of sin. Since every soul has its nature in Adam, when he sinned, so did all humanity (traducian view of the soul).

✠

Origen   *ca. 185–254*
The Fall was a cosmic myth explaining universal human sinfulness. Held to "preexistent souls" all of which sinned against God; thus, all humans are sinful.

✠

Cyprian of Carthage   *ca. 200–258*
Original sin not as culpable as actual sin, but needs remission nonetheless through baptism.

Athanasius   *ca. 296–373*
The Fall was a lapse into the natural state which was also
mortal in nature. While Adam is the sum of all people, we do
not receive guilt from him.

✠

Basil the Great   *d. 379*
Adam's transgression brought sin and death into the world, but
the newborn are free from sin.

✠

Gregory of Nyssa   *ca. 330–394*
Sin brought mortality, but no guilt was attached to original
sin.

✠

Gregory Nazianzus   *ca. 330–390*
What occurred in Eden affects human nature, but guilt is a
matter of individual freedom.

✠

Ambrose of Milan   *340–397*
All humans sinned in Adam and all share Adam's guilt. The
original sin is pride.

✠

John of Antioch (Chrysostom)   *ca. 347–407*
The Fall had no effect on humans other than the bringing of
death, but it did incline them toward sin.

✠

Theodore of Mopsuestia   *ca. 350–428*
Adam and Eve harmed only themselves by their sin, for humanity was mortal from the outset. Adam is our type, not our head.

✠

Augustine of Hippo   *354–430*
Chief proponent of original sin as inherited guilt. Linked Adam's
sin (and that of human race as a whole) to concupiscence. Even
babies must be purged by baptism of original sin or they cannot
enter heaven.

✠

Cyril of Alexandria   *376–444*
People fall into sin, not because they sinned in Adam, but because Adam's sin created a corrupt human nature.

cept of original sin as an inbred disease of human nature — possesses a certain degree of truth.[100] Each of these ideas must be considered in order to understand Augustine's theological thought. A consideration of the personal factors in Augustine's life which shaped his theology will aid in this understanding.

Behind Augustine's doctrine

A major part of Augustine's conviction came as the result of his own overwhelming sense of guilt, particularly in regard to sexual sin and lust. As a youth he had pursued a licentious lifestyle. After conversion he had continued to struggle with these sins. And so his own unworthiness was ever uppermost in his thoughts. Elaine Pagels observes that, given the intense inner conflicts with lust and his battle to control his sexual impulses, as revealed in his *Confessions,* "Augustine's decision to abandon his predecessors' emphasis on free will need not surprise us."[101] Roy Bettanhouse has been more generous, stating that "Augustine's personal experience of human weakness was providential. But equally so was the challenge posed by Pelagius; for heresy is, proverbially, a theologian's whetstone."[102] Like many before him, Augustine also continued to combat Gnostic heresy, in this case, the "third invasion of dualism in the form of Manicheism."[103]

Augustinian theology was also formed by a literal interpretation of Scripture. He simply grafted on to the supposedly historical facts a spiritual explication which continued in the wholehearted patristic heritage.[104] This literal interpretation depended heavily on the Latin Vulgate rather than the original Greek; since the former was an inaccurate translation, it rendered his interpretation equally inaccurate.

He was also concerned, in his formulation of a theology of sin, to demonstrate that God cannot be the author of evil.[105] And undoubtedly, Augustine's acceptance of the church's practice of infant baptism (a longtime practice) also colored his interpretation of original sin.

When one considers the chronological order of some of these factors, it is probable that Augustine's doctrine took time to find its full form. Much of his ideas of humankind, the Fall, and sin were developed early as he wrestled with Manicheism and his own moral convictions; other portions were articulated later, particularly in the battle against Pelagianism. Our concern is with its final form, for it is this which has had such a strong impact on the Western world for a millennium and a half.

Augustine on original sin

The nature of sin was the basis for Augustine's doctrine of original sin, for he held sin to be a condition rather than just an act. Adam's sin plunged humanity into a new and tragic state.

A basic ingredient contributing to original sin was free will. Adam, as he was created, was in a state of justification and freedom. His will was good and oriented to virtue. His freedom was of the ability not to sin.[106]

In spite of such advantages, Adam sinned. Augustine insisted that his fall was completely because he chose to do wrong. "Thus, from a bad use of free choice, a sequence of misfortunes conducts the whole human race ... from the original canker in its root to the devastation of a second and endless death."[107] Indeed, Adam's sin—given his absolute liberty—was so damnable that it resulted in the downfall of all humankind, sinners begetting sinners.[108]

All sin, in Augustine's mind, was voluntary. Even original sin, which was passed on to infants, was voluntary because it resulted from the free will of our first parents. Augustine's personal guilt evidently guided his theology on free will, for he noted that, "since I am a son of Adam, I was suffering from his freely committed sin."[109]

Thus, Adam's sin placed his progeny's will (in this specific case, Augustine's) in a state of constant conflict. "I was bound, not with another man's chains, but with my own iron will. . . . Because of a perverse will, desire was made; and when I was enslaved to desire it became habit; and habit not restrained became necessity. . . . a very hard bondage had me enthralled."[110]

The root of original sin was pride, which is the beginning of sin and the chief sin. At the same time, the nature of sin is best evidenced in concupiscence. For Augustine, all sexual activity is sin-stained. Even marital sex, though forgivable, is tainted. In his view the sexual act in pre-Fall Eden was much like a handshake, the sexual members merely carrying out their functions. But the Fall changed all that. Harnack writes that, though "Augustine desires to retain the *'amor sui'* [love of self] as the principle conception of sin, in reality he ranks concupiscence above it."[111]

The effects of original sin

The effect of the Fall is that humankind is no longer *posse non peccare* (able not to sin), but is *non posse non peccare* (not able not to sin). Now, along with the culpability of original sin humans add their own personal sins to their accounts. This inability to do good "is part of the desserts of original sin."[112]

The primary universal effect of original sin, Augustine asserted, is guilt. All humanity is stained and guilty, and thus must bear punishment. He declared that even unbaptized infants are condemned to hell because of the guilt they have inherited from Adam, although he believed that their punishment will be light.[113]

This guilt may, however, be negated by baptism, which will wash away the guilt of original sin, though the corrupt nature (concupiscence) will remain. "In baptized infants, [concupiscence] is deprived of guilt, is left for the struggle [of life], but pursues with no condemnation, such as die before the struggle."[114] But baptism removes only the liability of hereditary sin; it cannot destroy the hereditary sin itself.[115] Death is also a concomitant. Thus, original sin has a universal effect on humankind in the passing on of mortality, a weakened and polluted nature, and guilt.

The transmission of original sin

As to how the effects of Adam's sin were transmitted to his descendants was not left unanswered by this paramount theologian, even though he struggled with the problem of soul generation. Augustine denied the preexistence of the soul, but waffled between traducianism and creationism, tending toward the latter.[116]

It has been said that "when it came to connecting Adam's sin with the sins of his descendants Augustine fell into serious inconsistency."[117] Nevertheless, even if he were not sure about soul generation, he was certain about how original sin was passed from generation to generation. Since even in wedlock consummation cannot occur without lust, it is therefore in the sexual act that the nature of the new soul is stained and damaged. And so all human beings are conceived in sin and then born with a sinful nature. Part of that nature is guilt. All human beings, furthermore, were literally in Adam, for all came from his semen. Thus, Augustine confirmed that "Adam was one man, and is yet the whole human race."[118] He denied that sin could enter into the world from Adam by imitation.

> But if the apostle had wished to assert that sin entered into the world, not by natural dessert, but by imitation, he would have mentioned as the first offender, not Adam indeed, but the devil, of whom it is written, that "he sinneth from the beginning"; of whom also we read in the Book of Wisdom.[119]

And so sin was transmitted by carnal generation to all humanity. It remains until remitted by spiritual regeneration.[120] Even those who are righteous cannot bear righteous children, because the very act of conception is due to the overpowering of the will by lust *(libido)*.[121]

Augustine believed that by positing libido as the proof and penalty of original sin he encompassed all human beings excepting, of course, Christ. Of all of Adam's progeny, only He was born apart from libido, for Mary was impregnated by the action of the Holy Spirit, and so Christ was not affected by male semen which is the medium for the transmission of original sin.

The proofs of original sin

Augustine found support for his views from several different sources. One determining factor for him was the practice of infant baptism. Augustine wondered why the church would baptize infants unless there were some sin to cleanse. He declared that infant baptism proves the sinfulness of the flesh.[122] After all, if Jesus is the Savior of all, then He must be the Savior of children; if He is the Savior of children, then they must need saving.[123]

Augustine also looked to human nature as proof of his concepts on sin. He held that libido is in control of the human will, thus proving that even the will has been tarnished by the Fall. It was therefore incapable of overcoming the taint of the Fall. Pagels makes an interesting observation that since "each of us experiences desire spontaneously apart from will means, Augustine assumes, that we experience it against our will."[124]

Augustine asserted, therefore, that since sexual intercourse is carried on only in private—even by shameless people—it must be sinful.[125] He declared emphatically that, had humans not fallen, the genitive organs would still be in subjection to the will, as are the other parts of the body. That Jesus was born of a virgin must say something about sexual union; sexual congress must be where evil nature and weakness are propagated.[126]

On election and reprobation

Augustine contended that because of the Fall, God had rightly predestined some human beings to perdition and some to grace. Those who are elected to persevere to salvation may be known in individual cases only by observing their perseverance to the end.[127]

> Whosoever, therefore, in God's most providential ordering, are foreknown, predestinated, called, justified, glorified, I say not, even although not yet born again, but even although not yet born at all, are already children of God, and absolutely cannot perish. . . . From Him, therefore, is given also perseverance in good even to the end; for it is not given save to those who shall not perish, since they who do not persevere shall perish. . . .[128]

Indeed, predestination was so precise that God had an exact number who would be saved, no more, no less.[129]

While he did not clearly teach that God had purposefully created humankind so that all might become involved in sin and that He might elect some through His grace to salvation and leave others to reprobation to demonstrate His justice, Augustine came very close to it by making the existence and castigation of the wicked integral to the harmony of God's purposes.[130]

Augustine's influence

Any survey of the development of the theology of sin will show the impact of Augustine's thought. But this impact deserves a few observations. As one scholar has said, "Astonishingly, Augustine's radical views prevailed, eclipsing for future generations of western Christians the consensus of more than three centuries of Christian tradition."[131] For better or worse, his formulations would hold sway for several centuries, and have been influential in theology to the present day.

Augustine's opponents

Reception of Augustine's position was by no means positive in every case. The keys to contrary arguments were human free will (decisive in the thought of the early church) and the justice of God, namely, that God would not punish one person for the sins of another.

Chief among those viewpoints challenging Augustine's was Pelagianism, named after the British monk Pelagius, who arrived in Rome about 400, before moving on to North Africa. The Pelagians held that humanity came into the world neutral, with neither virtue nor vice. Adam's sin affected only Adam. Disobedience is not the result of physical descent, but of custom and imitation.[132] Newborn infants are in the same state that Adam and Eve were in their innocence.[133] As far as Pelagius was concerned, since sin was a result of the will and not of the human nature, original sin made no sense. One could even strive toward sinlessness. The assumption that a person could not help sinning was an insult to the Creator.[134] Adam's sin passed on disobedience through example. The baptism of infants provided only illumination and heavenly citizenship, not forgiveness.[135] Pelagius concluded that

> Adam was created mortal, and would have died whether he had sinned or not sinned; that Adam's sin injured only himself and not the human race; that the law no less than the gospel leads us into the kingdom; that there were sinless men previous to the coming of Christ . . . that the whole human race does not, on the one hand, die through Adam's death or transgression, nor, on the other hand, does the whole human race rise again through the resurrection of Christ.[136]

Bishop Julian of Eclanum (d. 450), a disciple of Pelagius, was a determined opponent of Augustine. The latter wrote several treatises against Julian. Julian believed that Augustine's great error was to accept the present state of nature as punishment.[137] Suffering and difficulty in childbirth cannot be taken as proof of sin, for even animals suffer and some "barbarian women" give birth while they are traveling with barely a pause.[138] Julian determined that Augustine's proposals made God give to infants what was not their due, that they should be punished for the sins of others. Such a view created a cruel, unjust God. Augustine did not know how to respond, and wrote to Jerome desperately seeking an answer to the suffering of infants and the justice in the imputation of punishment to those not seemingly deserving of it.[139] He found a partial response to Pelagianism in the existence of the suffering of infants. How can one, in Julian's system, explain the suffering of the "innocent"?

Julian's arguments may be summed up in five points:

If man is the creature of God, he must come from the hands of God good; if marriage is in itself good, it cannot generate evil; if baptism remits all sins and regenerates, the children of the baptized cannot inherit sin, and also righteousness must be propagatable; if God is righteous, he cannot condemn children for the sins of others; if human nature is capable of perfect righteousness, it cannot be inherently defective.[140]

Augustine responded by insisting that evil is not a substance, but a perversion; baptism removes guilt only, and not the sin itself; carnality came after marriage in the beginning; and that humankind is a Neoplatonic unity.[141]

Extreme Pelagianism found a spokesman in Celestius, who declared that Adam was created mortal and would have died regardless; infants, therefore, who died prior to baptism, were still eligible for eternal life.[142] Extreme positions were fairly easily dismissed, but the main tenets of Pelagianism remained as a problem for orthodox Christian theology.

Latter Patristic Thought

Little was done following Augustine by way of original theological thinking. In the East there was a much greater diversity of thought than in the West. Among the Eastern fathers there was the barest and most basic consensus: that human beings have inherited ruin, passion, and mortality because of Adam's sin (requiring a doctrine of the passions as the primary basis for sinful actions), and further, an emphatic denial of the "sin nature" or a transmission of guilt, together with an insistence that any guilt possessed by an individual is the result only of his or her own thoughts and actions.[143]

In the East, then, the assertions of earlier centuries were sustained. Only a free, personal mind can practice sin and acquire accompanying guilt; sin for these fathers was always an individual act, and not at all one of nature.[144]

Cyril of Alexandria

Cyril (376–444) was one prominent churchman who did not hold closely to the Augustinian tradition, probably because of his strong Eastern heritage. He taught that Adam, because of his fall, lost both the incorruptibility and rational nature which made up God's image in him. As a result, he fell victim to concupiscence. Because of his transgression, death and corruption established a bridgehead in the world; Adam's progeny sinned as did he, prey to carnal passions. Cyril taught that people are prone to sin, not because they have sinned in Adam (how could one not living in Adam's time participate in his sin?), but because Adam's transgression caused the corruption of the nature we inherited. Nor was the image of God in humankind destroyed (not even nearly!). Free will, as part of that image, is still active. At the same time, the image cannot be fully restored (in the sense of incorruptibility) apart from God's grace in salvation.[145] David Weaver declares that "it is generally recognized that Cyril did not subscribe to a doctrine of original sin because he did not attribute the universal penalty to a common culpability in Adam, which is really the crux of the issue."[146]

The Council of Carthage

In the West, there was little original thought, for most theologians merely confirmed Augustinian doctrinal teaching. The councils of this era reveal the strong influence of Augustine's theology. At the second Council of Carthage in 418, North African bishops passed a number of Canons rejecting Pelagian views and affirming Augustinianism. They declared that "original sin inherited from Adam is present in every man, and even newly born children need baptism if they are to be cleansed from this taint of sin."[147] Specifically, the council rejected the following:

1. That Adam would have died whether he sinned or not;
2. That babies are not baptized for the remission of sins, and do not contract original sin from Adam;
3. That there is an intermediate state for babies between heaven and hell.[148]

The council also condemned Celestius for his Pelagian teachings. Pope Zosimus issued an epistle affirming fully the action of the church in North Africa. All Latin bishops were compelled to assent to Zosimus' letter. Eighteen bishops, including Julian of Eclanum, refused to go along, and a majority of these took refuge in the East where opinions on sin were not as emphatic.[149]

The Council of Orange

At Orange, in the province of Arles, a Synod of fourteen bishops who had gathered for the consecration of a church, adopted a collection of formulations quoted largely from Augustine. The council declared the need for prevenient grace and for grace at each level of the soul's transformation. It asserted that all good which occurs to human beings is the unmerited gift of God's grace, even to the unsaved.[150]

Contrary to Augustine, while affirming that death and sin were passed on to Adam's descendants as the result of his sin, the council denied predestination to sin.[151] It determined that because of sin human free will has been so distorted that one can neither believe in nor love God unless aided by His grace. Baptism confers salvific grace when the believer makes appropriate efforts.[152]

Conclusions

As one reflects upon the history of Christianity during the first five centuries or so of the church's existence, one is struck by the variety of theological viewpoints. Such diversity was certainly demonstrated among concepts of the Fall and its results. There was little accord, even among "orthodox" theologians.

The earliest fathers did not address the doctrine of sin directly, but rather in reaction to various problems which cropped up in the church's life. In opposition to Gnosticism, for example, which emphasized the inevitability of sin at the hands of higher powers, they stressed the individual's freedom of choice and personal responsibility. They were also insistent that God was not the cause of sin, but that it entered the world as the result of human free choice. At the same time, Adam's sin brought death to all and was the beginning of the spread of sin to all of humankind. They made it clear, however, that rebellion against God was passed on by example, not heredity.

Theophilus was exemplary of the second-century fathers, holding that the Garden of Eden was probationary. Had Adam been obedient consistently, he would have achieved immortality; instead, his rebellion incurred mortality and spiritual death. Though Adam brought sin into the world, it was only by type and not by seminal guilt.

In the latter second century and early third century a more formal shape began to take place in the theology of sin and a gap began to appear between the Greek and Latin fathers. In the East, a number of schools were founded, each with its own special theological emphasis. Collectively, however, they held that Adam introduced mortality into humanity along with the example of rebellion. But sin remains a matter of individual human choice. Many of these fathers believed that it is entirely possible for some people to rise above sinful tendencies and live righteous lives through the exercise of their will. The Western fathers relied more on church practice rather than philosophy to formulate their theology of sin. Tertullian set the direction with his theory of soul-generation coupled to a literal interpretation of Genesis 3. Adam's transgression allowed sin and death to enter the world, polluting all humanity. Baptism, though, will return one to a pre-Fall condition. Ambrose built on Tertullian by adding original guilt by inheritance to permeate the race, albeit he did not believe that such guilt held one culpable in the day of God's judgment.

Augustine, a disciple of Ambrose, was also deeply influenced by his pre-conversion licentious lifestyle and its accumulated guilt. He asserted that sin was a condition, not an act. Through a free act of his will Adam chose to sin, thus making the will free to exercise sin but not righteousness. This enslavement to sin was passed on to his children through sexual intercourse. Thus, all humanity is guilty and must be punished. The guilt of original sin, however, may be washed away by baptism, but the sin itself and concomitant death remains.

Augustine had many opponents. Chief among those in his own day were the Pelagians, who held that all humans were born innocent and sin was a matter of free choice. Like the earlier Greek fathers, they believed that Adam's sin brought mortality to humanity and served as a bad example for them. Infant baptism did not wash away what was not there. Nor would God punish people for what they did not do.

Pelagianism was declared a heresy by several church councils of the time (such as Carthage). Augustinianism ruled the West. But while it would be the predominant mode of thought in Roman Catholicism until the time of the Scholastics, whether that great theologian would have been happy with it is dubious for, as we shall see, it underwent a substantial reworking at the hands of succeeding churchmen and was a very much different product by the end of the first Christian millennium.

Chapter Two
The Classical Catholic Period

The classical Catholic period saw the development of a theology of sin over a period of several centuries, reaching its high point during the scholastic era in the thirteenth century with the thought of the "angelic doctor," Thomas Aquinas. Scholasticism (its proponents came to be termed "schoolmen") was a systematic effort to harmonize classical Greek philosophy with the Scriptures and with patristic theology; Aristotelian philosophy was generally used as a paradigm for scholastic theology.

While the theology of Augustine was the major doctrinal inheritance of the theologians of this period, it underwent many revisions at their hands. Pelagian theology, although condemned by earlier councils, was revived and reshaped. It was then combined with a radically reinterpreted Augustinianism to form what was really a "third kind," Semi-Pelagianism.

Gregory the Great

Gregory, bishop of Rome from 590–604, took Augustinian theology and added to it the superstitions current in his day about angels, demons, and the devil. His interpretation of the great theologian's thought, however, involved an essential change of its meaning.

Sin entered the world because of human weakness. Adam's sin was a free act of his will, "and then he with all his progeny went on to enslave himself. . . ."[1] Like Augustine, Gregory held that through Adam's sin all humans became sinners. This original sin is transmitted by conception, "for conception itself is impurity on account of its carnal delight."[2] Thus, any infant dying without benefit of baptism would be damned for eternity.

At the same time, Gregory did not view original sin from Augustine's perspective. He believed that Adam's sin caused human beings to be born into the infirmity of sickness rather than into the utter incapacity of death (as Augustine believed). This weakness leads to a dulling of the understanding and a captivity of the mind to desire so that the sinner willingly surrenders to physical temptation. But prevenient grace is available (along with subsequent grace) to make the free will into a good will. "Thus [God's] wisdom refreshes the mind with hope and . . . lights up the darkness of the heart . . . knowledge overcomes the emptiness of ignorance."[3]

Gregory conceived of grace as irresistible; he accepted predestination, some being chosen and others left to their evil. He based this predestination, however, on foreknowledge. As a consequence, there was a place for human merit, because there was room for human cooperation with God.[4]

The Controversy on Augustinian Predestination

Augustine had taught a double predestination of the elect to salvation and the godless to perdition. But Augustinians in the ninth century saw that doctrine in much the same sense as had Gregory the Great.[5] They disagreed, as well, with the great theologian's belief that one can do no good unless in receipt of God's grace; they held that both God's grace and human efforts have an important role in salvation.[6]

A Saxon monk, Gottschalk, who was cloistered at Orbais in France, had read some of Augustine's theology and had come to reject the contemporary interpretation of the latter's thought. He determined that he should proclaim double predestination in its narrowest form, and so he focused on the immutability of God who, in His sovereign choice, either elects or rejects human beings:

For just as the unchangeable God, prior to the creation of the world, by His free grace unchangeably predestined all of His elect to eternal life, so has this unchangeable God in the same way unchangeably predestined all of the rejected, who shall be condemned to eternal death for their evil deeds on judgment day according to His justice and as they deserve.[7]

A logical ramification of double predestination was the inability of human beings to use their free will for anything but evil. "None of us," insisted Gottschalk, "is able to use free will to do good, but only to do evil."[8]

Gottschalk set forth his doctrinal views at a religious conference in Mainz, where he was opposed by Rabanus Maurus, a leading theologian of the day, who accused the former of making God the author of evil, and of saying that God forced humans to sin against their will. At the first Synod of Chiersey in 849, Hincmar, bishop of Reims—in whose diocese the monastery of Orbais was located—condemned Gottschalk's theology and confined him to house arrest until such time as he should recant. The latter, however, stuck resolutely to his interpretation of Augustine's theology and so languished in chains, spending the next twenty years in monastic imprisonment.[9]

The council declared a single predestination. Christ died for all humankind, and even though God has predestined punishment for those who reject Him, He did not predestine the reprobate who will be punished. It established the election of the righteous on the divine foreknowledge of their right use of the gifts of grace, although the second Council of Chiersey in 853 affirmed somewhat illogically that "in the first man we lost our freedom of will."[10]

In spite of the council's decision, the debate widened for Gottschalk's views were not without supporters. Prudentius of Troyes, Remigius of Lyons, Servatus Lupus of Ferrières, Ratramus of Corbie, and other theologians propounded double predestination as standard Augustinian doctrine, while Rabanus, Hincmar, and John Scotus Erigena contended for a single predestination to life. The two sides were able to reach a compromise at the Councils of Savonières (859) and Toucy (860). By the time of the latter Synod, however, the controversy was moot, for Gottschalk had been removed by death.[11]

The Early Scholastic Era

Prior to the Scholastic era, the general consensus in the West was that the sinful nature of humanity was generated from Adam, not received by example.[12] Most theologians held the root of original sin to be pride. But the firm grip of Augustinian theology began to loosen, partly because the idea of penance forced the church to move from pure Augustinianism to Semi-Pelagianism. It has been said that the history of the doctrine of sin during the Scholastic period "is the history of the gradual decline of rigid Augustinianism."[13] Such decline was evident in several key figures, especially Anselm of Canterbury and Thomas Aquinas. In the twelfth century, at least, the theology of Augustine would hold on, while other definitions of original sin struggled for acceptance.

Anselm of Canterbury

Anselm (ca. 1033–1109) was the first major contributor to the discussion on sin since Augustine. His ideas on sin and the atonement were distinctive.

Humankind as a rational creation has an obligation to obey the will of God, Anselm asserted. That is its debt. Anselm defined sin as nonpayment of this debt. It is the redirecting of the total human personality away from God. It is the utter alienation of humans from the One whom by reason of creation and of the essence of their being they should adore and obey.[14]

Anselm accepted the idea that disobedience to God has caused death. That death is both physical and spiritual, although his grounds for such thinking are not clear.[15]

Humans are culpable for their sins because Adam initially sinned of his own free will. Having failed to pay this original debt, they are blameworthy. "Man's present sin has thus a double character—as failure here and now to pay the debt owed to God, a debt greatly increased by reason of that first sin, and as guilt in consequence of previous nonpayment of debt."[16] Some might hold the idea that God in His mercy will remit their sins, but they are in error, remonstrated Anselm, because such nonpayment of sin not atoned for would render God's kingdom chaotic, and "it is not proper that God should overlook anything disorderly in his kingdom."[17] The honor of God is at stake here. The honor withheld must be supplied, or punishment must follow. Either satisfaction or punishment must pursue every transgression. Anselm declared that God has not taken the avenue of punishment, but rather the way of satisfaction; otherwise, His purposes would be ruined.[18]

Because humanity was morally bankrupt, Christ made the necessary satisfaction for human sin. This idea of sin, nonetheless, did not rule out original sin. Rather, Anselm tied it to his notion of original justice, which entailed the rectitude of the will, that is, of its submission to God's purposes. Original sin was, therefore, "essentially the privation of this rectitude."[19] Because of this stress on the loss of original righteousness, even infants carried the taint of original sin, which is what each obtains with his nature in his own origin; thus, one may refer to it as natural in addition to original.[20] This "nature" did not belong to "human nature," but rather to nature since creation, and it had its source in Adam, for each person is an individualized part of the whole human nature which derived from Adam. As W.T. Shedd states, "In the case of Adam, an individual transgression resulted in a sin of nature; while in the case of his posterity, a sin of nature results in individual transgressions."[21] Thus, the consequences of the first sin were ignorance, loss of the gift of integrity, and the state of unrighteousness.[22]

Anselm believed that original sin is present in infants, but it does not possess the same level of guilt (or condemnation) as personal sin. It is rather a state of injustice for which satisfaction is required. Thus, regarding infants, Anselm could not "understand this sin [he was] calling 'original' to be anything else than that same deprivation of the required justice."[23] He doubted whether the sins of ancestors passed on to the fourth and fifth generations are really a part of the original sin and denied sin any ontological existence. Sin, therefore, was a state of nonbeing which he relegated to the will.

At the same time, satisfaction was required for original sin. "It is necessary that every human being born in it be condemned unless it is remitted,"[24] he insisted. Baptism remits this original sin and, in fact, all sins prior to the administration of the sacrament. The baptized are not condemned until they reach the place where they recognize the need for repentance.

Peter Abelard

In Abelard (1079–1142) one finds a further disintegration of strict Augustinian theology. He was opposed to all compulsion in doctrinal formulation. No one, he declared, should be obliged to accept any belief he thought untrue. Little was more important to him than freedom of investigation.[25] At the same time, he has been wrongly accused of being a free thinker, for he held to the foundational Scholastic principle of the precedence of the faith and accepted the Bible as divine revelation.[26]

In his treatise on ethics, Abelard removed desire and concupiscence from the status of sins, insisting that "the seat of sin is the intention, which is the root, bearing good and bad fruit."[27] Sin is to be found, that is, not in the deed carried out, but only in the motive which led to its perpetration (although there is no sin unless the intention comes to fruition in action). No deed is sinful unless it goes against one's conscience. Indeed, said Abelard, as long as they thought they were doing right, those who martyred the early saints were free from the imputation of sin.[28]

Abelard was quite radical in his approach to the remission of sins. True repentance, he taught, was a matter of heartfelt contrition. When this occurs, God readily grants forgiveness of sins. Such forgiveness, however, applies only to the eternal consequences of sin. If the sinner would find release from the temporal consequences of sin (either in present life or in purgatory), sufficient works of merit or repentance must be effected.[29]

Original sin for Abelard was not a sin in itself, but only a consequence. It is an obligation to pay a penalty because of Adam's sin. Infants cannot be said to be guilty since they have never committed any personal deeds. But they will nevertheless be condemned because they are jointly accountable with their first parents. Abelard struggled with the dogma of original sin. Because of this unease with Augustinian teaching, he made a strong effort to separate original sin from actual sin.[30]

Abelard's teachings in all areas tended to be innovative for his time and were opposed by many more traditional Catholics. In 1141, his teachings were condemned by the Council of Sens, and he was sentenced by Pope Innocent III to permanent confinement in a cloister, but died of illness in 1142 before it could be carried out.

2.1 A CAPSULE VIEW OF THE CLASSICAL CATHOLIC THEOLOGIANS ON SIN

Pope Gregory the Great   *540–604*
Magna Moralia Dialogues

From a noble family.

First (Benedictine) monk to ascend Peter's throne.

Exalted authority of Roman See over whole church.

Saved Rome from Lombards.

Held that original sin was transmitted by conception which in itself is concupiscence.

Believed in irresistible, prevenient, and subsequent grace to make the free will into a good, not corrupt will.

✠

Gottschalk   *805–868*
The Ecologue of Theodolus

Was committed to a monastery as a child and not allowed to leave.

Defended Augustinian ideas of original sin and double predestination in narrowest form.

Condemned by Hincmar of Reims at First Synod of Chiersey in 849 as heretic and died under house arrest.

✠

Anselm of Canterbury   *1033–1109*
Monologium Proslogium
Cur Deus Homo

Joined a French monastery.

Appointed Archbishop of Canterbury in 1093.

Known especially for his "ontological argument" for the existence of God.

Defined sin as nonpayment of debt to obey God's will and as utter alienation from Him.

God's honor is at stake and must be satisfied, or punishment will follow sin. Christ has made the necessary satisfaction for sin on the cross.

Peter Abelard   *1079–1142*
Sic et Non

Innovative teacher who delighted in radical views.

Became head of cathedral school in Paris.

Fathered illegitimate child with a student, Heloise, and was castrated by her uncle.

Removed concupiscence from the status of sin.

Root of sin is intention, but there is no sin unless intention becomes action.

Remission of sins is a result of contrition, not baptism.

Condemned as a heretic in 1141 by Council of Sens, but died before he could be imprisoned.

✠

Thomas Aquinas   *ca. 1225–1274*
Christian Theology
Summa Theologica
Summa Contra Gentiles
Contra Errores Graecorum

From noble family in Aquino.

Became a Dominican monk.

Student of Albert Magnus.

Taught in Paris, Cologne, and in Italy.

Combined Augustinian theology and Aristotelian philosophy.

Saw original sin as privation of original justice, the state in which humans were created.

Original sin in soul and so humans cannot escape it.

All humans sin in Adam because of transmission of semen from father to child.

Original sin has clouded human reason; while baptism removes its guilt, sinful nature remains.

Divided sins into venial (easily forgiven) and mortal (forgivable only by God's grace).

✠

Duns Scotus   *1266–1308*
Quadlibetal Questions

Native of Britain who was trained at Oxford and at the Sorbonne.

Opposed Aquinas' views.

Original sin is the absence of original righteousness, for the human will is always free to sin.

Sin is inherent only in the will and does not pass to one's progeny by way of infection.

Actual sin is a defeat of the will.

It settles for a lesser end than the supreme love of God.

Christ did not have to die to satisfy God; Adam could have done so by any righteous act.

Sacraments are symbolic.

✠

Desiderius Erasmus   *1469–1536*
In Praise of Folly
Enchiridion Militis Christiani
De Copia Verborum

Born in Netherlands.

Taught by Brethren of the Common Life, and attended University of Paris.

Compiled Greek text of NT.

Saw life as spiritual warfare engineered by Satan.

Had little regard for efficacy of the sacraments apart from repentance and renewal.

Believed that all who turned to the Lord in repentance would be forgiven.

The High Point of Scholasticism

With Anselm and Abelard one approaches the high point of the Scholastic era. During this period theologians were concerned with systematizing existing material. They saw their primary task as reconciling two anthropological principles: the concept of the absolute grace of God, on the one hand, and the reality of human merit (the legal implication of which was human freedom), on the other. Such a feat was impossible; even the appearance of a solution could be achieved only by the use of deceitful distinctions, largely verbal, which masked a concurrent use of two levels of thinking.

Thomas Aquinas

Thomas (ca. 1225–1274) was undoubtedly the premier theologian of the Scholastic era. He resolved the problem of the absolute supremacy of grace and the merit of human righteousness through an interchange of levels of thought. He recognized the doctrine of predestinating grace and, when that was out of the way, dealt with the secondary causation of the human will as an adequate basis for freedom and consequent merit.

Thus, one has psychological freedom combined with metaphysical determination. While God allows some to fall short of eternal life, He does not cause sin, which derives from the human will. God is, however, the cause of the action which becomes formally sinful when one departs from Him.

Aquinas saw original sin as the privation of original justice, which was the state in which humanity was created.[31] Their lower faculties were subject to their higher faculties which were, in turn, subject to God. "This state was granted to man, not just as to a private individual, but as to the first principle of human nature, so that through him it was handed down to his descendants together with human nature."[32]

Original sin does not reside in the flesh but in the soul.[33] Human beings, therefore, cannot escape it, for it is an integral part of them. It is transmitted along with human nature. Though creationist regarding the origin of the soul, Aquinas taught that "the semen by its own power transmits the human nature from parent to child, and with that nature, the stain that affects it."[34] As a consequence, all human beings born of Adam may be considered as a single individual, since they have a common nature which they derive from their initial parents.[35]

One may also deduce that all humans receive original sin in a similar proportion: "Original sin has no degrees, since the gift of original justice is taken away entirely; and privations that remove something entirely . . . cannot be more or less."[36]

When in the state of original justice, the body was sustained by the soul which was subject to God. But when Adam transgressed, his soul was no longer capable of sustaining his body with the gift of life, and so he became subject to death.[37] This subjection to death was inherited by every human being from Adam. And so death is the result of original sin.

Original sin also led to the clouding of human reason. People now allow their lower faculties (or, desires) rather than reason to control their choices.

Since original sin affects one at birth, infants should be baptized immediately. Baptism removes the guilt of that first sin, but its nature remains and can be passed on to progeny.[38] "Original sin incurs everlasting punishment, since children who have died in original sin through not being baptized, will never see the kingdom of God. . . ."[39] Without God's grace to deal with original sin, humankind is hopelessly lost.

Aquinas dichotomized between original and actual sin. Original sin, with which one is born and over which one has no control, is a disorder of the moral constitution which presents itself through concupiscence or irrational desire.[40] Actual sin—whose cause was an inordinate love of self—is a matter of personal choice. Though original sin has clouded one's reason, one continues to have choices. People choose to do wrong and cannot place the blame on original sin. Since the reason is corrupt, it no longer controls one's behavior, and leads to a propensity for sin.

The angelic doctor dichotomized between sins of commission—sins of action which arise from the will—and sins of omission—failure to do the right—though he saw no difference in their essence. He observed that

> omission and commission are found in the same species of sin. For the covetous man both takes what belongs to others, which is a sin of commission; and gives not of his own to whom he should give which is a sin of omission. Therefore omission and commission do not differ specifically.[41]

There is a similar impetus behind both types of sin. Intimately, "sin denotes an inordinate act,"[42] whether of omission or commission.

Are all sins of equal gravity? Since actual sin, according to Aquinas, is the inability of reason to regulate the lower faculties, "therefore it matters much to the gravity of sin whether one departs more or less from the rectitude of reason: and accordingly we must say that sins are not all equal."[43] Thus, the further one moves from reason, the more serious is the sin.

Aquinas divided all sins into two categories according to their gravity: venial and mortal. Venial sin may be easily forgiven. Its gravity is not great, but will require some type of restitution. Mortal sin, on the other hand, cannot be forgiven and consigns the perpetrator to perdition.[44] Only God's grace can forgive mortal sin.

There are a number of steps, said Aquinas, which one may take to receive forgiveness for sins. The first is in the sacrament of baptism. "The Church's intention in baptizing men is that they may be cleansed from sin. . . ."[45] Only those who are baptized have right faith. The combination of baptism and faith achieve forgiveness, whether of original, venial, or mortal sin. All are forgiven in the sacrament of baptism.

Confirmation also confers grace on its recipient, giving him the power to live the Christian life, along with a cleansing for sin. Eucharist and penance also have cleansing aspects. Indeed, the sacramental system as a whole provides some relief from sin or its consequences.[46]

Who is to blame for sin? There are three options frequently discussed: (1) God is responsible; (2) Satan is to blame; (3) Adam and Eve are culpable. In his *Summa Theologica*, Aquinas dealt with each possibility. Because of who God is, it would be contrary to His nature to cause, condone, or accept sin. "Now God cannot be directly the cause of sin, either in Himself or in another, since every sin is a departure from the order which is to God as the end. . . . In like manner neither can He cause sin indirectly."[47]

In some places in Scripture there seem to be indications that God has given some people over to sin. Is He then responsible for their sin? Not at all, said Aquinas, "For if God delivered some up to a reprobate sense, it follows that they already had a reprobate sense, so as to do what was not right. Accordingly He is said to deliver them up to a reprobate sense, in so far as He does not hinder them from following that reprobate sense. . . ."[48] God does not cause a person to sin, but rather permits him/her to continue in sin. God, therefore, is not responsible for human sin.

Is Satan then responsible? Satan is the father of lies and so it is logical to blame him for humankind's wayward nature. According to Aquinas, however, the devil is limited to influencing people to make wrong choices: "the operation of the devil seems to be confined to the imagination and sensitive appetite, by moving either of which he can induce men to sin."[49] And so, "it follows that the devil is a cause of sin, neither directly nor sufficiently, but only by persuasion, or by proposing the object of appetite."[50] Satan does not control, he merely influences.

What of humankind, then? Aquinas held that people possess both the desire for good along with the propensity for wrong. "Even in the lost the natural inclination to virtue remains, else they would have no remorse of conscience."[51]

Since Satan can only influence, and sin is abhorrent to God's nature, humanity must be culpable for its own wrongdoing. every individual is accountable for the wrong decisions he or she makes. And, if not subjected to God's grace, the human will continues to err.[52]

Thomas Aquinas was a modernist for his time. Because of his novel ideas he was attacked by conservative churchmen. Within a few years of his death much of his theology had been condemned as heresy. But these detractors were eventually overcome, and in 1323 he was canonized by John XXII. Since that time he has been revered as one of Catholicism's foremost theologians.

Duns Scotus

The devolution of traditional Augustinianism continued with the theology of John Duns Scotus (ca. 1266–1308). From Aquinas and Scotus originated rival schools, the Thomists and the Scotists.

The salient aspect of Duns Scotus' theological system was his emphasis on the will.

> The entire inner and outer man, with all his thoughts, words, works, and impulses is subject to the will. It is the will alone which makes human conduct good or bad (*Sent.* i.d.42, q.4). The will, and not the thought, is the organ for the appropriation of the highest objects and values. Faith does not arise without the consent of the will (iii.d.29, q.1.11).[53]

According to Scotus, human sinlessness in Eden was only potential, for the will is always free to sin. The sinlessness of Adam and Eve was due only to their possession of a supernatural endowment of grace. The only change in human nature wrought by the Fall was the loss of this supernatural gift. Original sin, then, for all practical purposes consists only in the absence of original righteousness. Concupiscence—which was integral to human nature, but held in check by the divine gift—cannot possibly be a part of it and so is not in any meaningful sense sinful. Sin is inherent only in the will; it does not pass along to Adam's progeny by way of infection.[54]

Actual sin, for Duns Scotus, was a defeat of the will. The will either settles for a lesser end than that of supremely loving God, or it seeks as an end an object intended to be used as a means.[55] Sin is an offense against revealed divine law.[56]

In regard to the forgiveness of sins, Scotus rejected Anselm's idea of satisfaction. Christ did not have to die to satisfy God's wrath against sin. Any righteous act by Adam could have provided such satisfaction. The object offered is irrelevant; what counts is acceptance by God. According to Scotus:

> God will not forgive the sins of the transgressor unless something to be offered to him which pleases him more than the sins of mankind displease him. This could only be the obedience of a person more fervently loved by God than mankind would have been loved by him had they not sinned. This was the person of Christ. . . .[57]

Love for Christ compels God to dispense grace to humankind.

What part do the sacraments play in dealing with sin? They are primarily symbols which show the infusion of God's grace into a sinful individual and which, as the result of the new covenant, effect in the human soul a creative work of God concurrent with its redemption.[58]

John Duns Scotus won the intellects of many scholars. The Scotists saw him as the leading theologian of the Franciscan Order. As far as they were concerned, he was greater than Thomas Aquinas. For several centuries both Scotist and Thomist theologians graced the faculties of the leading universities and generated substantial controversy.[59]

Erasmus: Humanist Theologian

Desiderius Erasmus (ca. 1466–1536) represents the pinnacle of Renaissance humanism. Born in the Netherlands, he was taught by the Brethren of the Common Life (who also taught Luther, Calvin, and Loyola at various points in their formative years), the leading educators of the Low Countries and much of Germany. In 1493 he secured the patronage of the Bishop of Cambrai, which allowed him to attend the University of Paris. There he formed associations with young English humanists Thomas Grey, Robert Fisher, and William Blount. Later, he traveled to England where he became firm friends with John Colet and Thomas More.[60] While he was best known for his edition of the New Testament, he was also a keen moralist and theologian, writing such works as *In Praise of Folly,* the *Enchiridion Militis Christiani,* and the *De Copia Verborum.*

In his *Enchiridion* Erasmus described life as spiritual warfare where "the vices, our armored enemies . . . are prepared to attack us with a thousand stratagems and, evil demons that they are, they concentrate on wounding our minds with inflammable and poisonous weapons."[61] Behind this warfare is "that slimy snake, the first betrayer of our peace and the father of restlessness. . . ."[62]

While one would expect humans — especially Christians — to be wary of the enemy, Erasmus accused his audience of slumbering in self-indulgence. He warned them that "anyone who concludes a treaty with vice violates the agreement made with God in baptism."[63] They should remember what Christ saved them from in baptism — from death, the "wages of sin." Not only does the body perish because it cannot live forever, but there is greater misfortune because the soul is wounded to death by sin.[64]

Erasmus observed that individual sins — such as adultery — were major wounds to the soul. To take pleasure in recalling such sin is sure evidence of the soul's death. "No cadaver is so dead as that soul that has been abandoned by God."[65]

He held to Origen's doctrine of the threefold division of humankind: the body or flesh, the soul, and the spirit. The flesh is the lowest part. Because of original sin, Satan is able to incline this part toward evil. "Failure to overcome this inclination brings us completely under his control."[66] The spirit is the highest part, reflecting the nature of God. "This is that part of us that binds us to God and makes us one with Him."[67] The third part, the soul, lies between the flesh and the spirit. It is neutral and is pulled between the two parts. "If, holding the spirit in contempt, she turns to the harlot, that is, to the flesh, she will be one body with it. On the other hand, if, spurning the flesh, she rises to the spirit, she will be transformed into the spirit alone."[68]

Unlike many of his contemporaries, Erasmus had little regard for the efficacy of the sacraments apart from repentance and a transformation of one's life. "If you are filled with ambition and envy, even though you offer the sacrifice yourself, you are far from the real significance of the Mass."[69] He also noted, "The ceremony [of baptism] consists of washing the body with water, but for you this is not a cleansing of the soul."[70]

Erasmus steadfastly believed, however, in the mercy and forgiveness of God. Whoever turns to the Lord in repentance will be forgiven, no matter how heinous his transgression.

> The clemency of God is ready for all, not just those who have committed a few venial sins. For the Lord clearly promises: "Whosoever the sinner bewails his sins, I will not at all remember his iniquities." He does not make exception to any particular type of crime, nor to the number, nor the magnitude. Only repent of your sins and forgetfulness of all past crimes awaits you.[71]

Erasmus was not a systematic theologian and so what he had to say about sin was not carefully systematized. He was more concerned with calling backslidden or false Christians to repentance than he was in evangelizing the unsaved. It is clear, however, that he believed unquestionably in the mercy and willingness of God to forgive any sin should the perpetrator repent.

Conclusions

During this Catholic period which we have been examining, political, ecclesiastical, and social factors along with personal agendas, philosophical orientations, and exegetical methodologies deeply affected the theological position of the Roman Catholic Church. Gregory the Great based his theology of sin on Augustine's teachings, but he revised aspects of it, shifting the results of original sin from the incapacity of death to the infirmity of sickness. He also accepted predestination, but based it on foreknowledge and thus left space for human cooperation with God.

Some, like Gottschalk, reacted against this revision of Augustinian theology, emphasizing immutable divine double predestination and utter human inability. Such attempts to reinstall the past, however, were doomed, and Gottschalk was condemned as a heretic.

Under the Scholastics the doctrine of sin moved from Augustinianism to Semi-Pelagianism. Anselm held to original sin but maintained that it does not incur the same level of guilt as does actual sin. He also denied sin any ontological existence, seeing it as a state of nonbeing connected to the will. Abelard deleted concupiscence from the category of sin and moved the locus of sin to the intention, declaring sin to be not act but motive.

The high point of Scholastic thought came with Thomas Aquinas who cast off the long-time philosophical paradigm for sin of Neoplatonism for Neo-Aristotelianism. He held much of Augustine's views on original sin, but believed that actual sin was a matter of personal choice, although humans possess a strong propensity for sin. He also divided sins into two categories, venial and mortal, the former forgivable, but not the latter.

Duns Scotus continued to revise Augustinian theology. His stress was on the human will. Human sinlessness was never any more than potential, even in Eden, for there it was held in check only by supernatural endowment. The Fall was the loss of that divine gift. Duns rejected the traditional view of sin as concupiscence. Nor did it pass on from Adam to his kin by way of infection, for it is inherent only in the will. Actual sin was a defeat of the will.

The downward trend in Augustinian thought continued in the Renaissance. Erasmus, the greatest of the Catholic Renaissance theologians, had little use for the Roman Catholic sacramental system in and of itself. Repentance was the key to all remission of sins. Nor were there categories of sins, some of which could be forgiven and others not; God would forgive the truly penitent regardless of the enormity of the sin committed.

By the end of the fourteenth century, "the religious view of sin as guilt, jeopardized already by Augustine and Thomas, fully disappeared."[72] Sin became subject to the human will. The Humanist emphasis was more on divine forgiveness than on human transgression. The mantle of rigid Augustinianism had been rejected by Catholicism. It remained to be donned and maintained by the Reformers, especially John Calvin and his followers.

Chapter Three
The Response
of the Reformers

The salient aspect of medieval theology was its ecclesiastical system, in particular the sacrament of penance. In 1215 the Fourth Lateran Council had decreed: "All believers of both sexes who have attained the age of discretion must faithfully confess their sins in person at least once a year to their own priest, and must make the effort to carry out the imposed penance according to their ability."[1]

In order to help the faithful to deal with the consequences of sin, namely, the temporal punishment for sins which was not covered by the sacrament, the church had instituted indulgences. These indulgences covered not only temporal punishments in present life, but also those borne in purgatory. One might even secure indulgences for this purpose on behalf of those already departed. The idea of indulgences was based on the church's belief that it had the power to bind and to loose sins (Matt. 16:19). And in so doing, it held that it also had the power to take from the merits of Christ and His saints (which far surpassed their own needs) and apply it to those who had a deficiency of merit.

It was in reaction to this system of penance and indulgences that Martin Luther (1483–1546) nailed his Ninety-Five Theses to the Wittenberg Church door in 1517. These theses declared that only God can forgive the guilt of sin; indulgences are unnecessary and even dangerous because they may lead a sinner to a false assurance of salvation.[2] All forgiveness and mitigation of guilt is the result of God's grace, which is apprehended only through faith in Jesus Christ.

The concept of justification by faith, which serves as the keystone of Reformation theology, greatly modified the whole body of anthropological belief and led to the systematization of Protestant doctrine in an orientation other than Catholic. The postulation of Christ as the only way to God depicted sin as a moral and spiritual barrier, thus doing away with its ecclesiastical emphasis. This was the fundamental basis of agreement for many of the Reformation leaders. From this point, with variations based on national, cultural, social, and political factors, came what is now termed Protestant orthodoxy.

The Views of Martin Luther

Martin Luther's views on sin were essentially those of the Latin Fathers of the Ante-Nicene and Nicene eras. He found the Bible to teach that the root of sin is unfaith.[3] To the biblical data he added the teaching of Augustine that egocentricity is the "beginning of all sins," for it "takes from God and from men what belongs to them and gives neither God nor men anything of that which it has, is, and is capable of."[4]

Original sin

Luther's doctrine of humankind was very much opposed to the medieval concept. It is said that he held to a "whole person" concept of humanity; rather than the scholastic dualism between body and soul, he stressed a view of wholeness within the theological milieu, the results of which may be seen in his theology of sin.[5]

Luther asserted that original sin is not just the lack of the supernatural endowments, but a genuine pattern of depravity which has placed its stain on the whole individual. As a result of Adam's transgression, human beings lost the image of God. Luther understood the image to signify that the first couple knew

65

God intimately and lived fully godly lives without fear of death or other danger. All of that was lost because Adam and Eve transgressed. It was replaced in them and their descendants by death, lust, blasphemy, and a hatred for God: "These and similar evils are the image of the devil, who stamped them on us."[6]

The foundational sin, Luther held, is unbelief, a deviation from the path God has set. The first transgression—in which all others are contained—was a questioning of God's Word and a turning away from His commands.

Luther was Augustinian in his treatment of original sin. Its corruption is congenital, being passed from parent to child through the act of generation. It is therefore found in humans before all their experiences and all their conscious expressions of the will. Original sin is an insoluble enigma which in some inscrutable way shapes human existence.[7]

From Adam and Eve on, the nature and essence of humanity are utterly corrupt.[8] The sin we inherit from our first parents is imputed to us just as if we had committed it ourselves. It is a legacy of the Fall.[9]

Sin and God's sovereignty

If God created Adam and Eve righteous, how did they fall into sin? Luther believed strongly in the sovereignty of God, and so he tried to bring Him as close to sin as he dared without making Him the author of it. God did not cause Adam and Eve to transgress, but He permitted it. When Satan rebelled, God abandoned him. Because the devil was inclined to evil, the Lord incited him to increasing evil; He has even incited him to cause human beings to sin.[10]

Thus, Satan and the human will combine to lead people into sin. If God incites Satan to bring humans to sin, it is so that He can demonstrate both justice and mercy to humankind. "At the end of the day God is to be glorified; to recognize this is salvation."[11]

Luther acknowledged that the idea of God willing humans to sin seemed clearly to suggest that He was, therefore, the cause of sin. To continue to insist that God had also made the law and expects humans to keep it creates intense conflict. Luther's response to such a dilemma? "This is too deep for us. God's will is involved, but I am not supposed to know how this all happens."[12]

The human will and sin

Because of sin, human reason has been blinded. It cannot recognize what is sin and what is not. "So it goes its way, regarding its illness as strength, its sin as virtue, its evil as good; and never getting anywhere."[13]

Humans have lost their free will, declared Luther, in that they are no longer free to obey God. Consequently, they fall under divine judgment. Had they retained free will, the results would have been an irresponsible universe. Salvation would have rested on sinful humanity's rash decisions. Chronic instability would be the norm. God could not permit the world to run in such a fashion.[14]

Free will is not a reality for human beings, for the human will is in bondage to evil. Only God has truly free will (and in that aspect of his theology, Luther was a Scotist). The human will is passive in relation to God. God has imposed on human beings the imprisonment of their will. Only He can free that will and enable them to come to Him. Why He wills to save some and deigns to leave others to destruction is a matter of His sovereign grace.[15]

Baptism and sin

The wrath of God rests on sinners. Since He punishes sin, the fault is obviously the sinner's. The punishment for sin is death. Even infants who die unbaptized, Luther asserted, are lost.[16]

"Baptism is an external sign or token, which . . . separates us from all men not baptized. . . ."[17] It is a personalization of God's forgiveness for its recipient. It is God's work from beginning to end. Luther rejected the Roman Catholic view of baptism as a good work rewarded by God with new life.[18]

Baptism symbolizes dying to sin and being resurrected in God's grace through Christ, "so that the old man, conceived and born in sin, is there drowned, and a new man, born in grace, comes forth and rises . . . in this washing a person is born again and made new . . . sins are drowned in baptism, and in the place of sin, righteousness comes forth."[19]

Luther taught that baptism is a sign of the new covenant between God in Christ and the recipient. Under this covenant God does not impute sins against the believer, but blots them out.

3.1: A MIGHTY FORTRESS

No passage from Martin Luther's mind more clearly illustrates his theology of sin and its conquest than does this hymn, still popular in one form or another today:

A mighty fortress is our God,
A bulwark never failing;
Our helper He amid the flood
Of mortal ills prevailing;
For still our ancient foe
Doth seek to work us woe—
His craft and pow'r are great,
And arm'd with cruel hate,
On earth is not his equal.

Did we in our own strength confide,
Our striving would be losing;
Were not the right man on our side,
The man of God's own choosing;
Dost ask who that may be?
Christ Jesus, it is He—
Lord Sabaoth, His name,
From age to age the same;
And He must win the battle.

And tho this world, with devils filled,
Should threaten to undo us,
We will not fear, for God hath willed
His truth to triumph through us;
The prince of darkness grim,
We tremble not for him—
His rage we can endure;
For lo, his doom is sure;
One little word shall fell him.

That word above all earthly powers,
No thanks to them, abideth.
The Spirit and the gifts are ours,
Through Him who with us sideth:
Let goods and kindred go,
This mortal life also—
The body they may kill,
God's truth abideth still;
His kingdom is forever.
—Martin Luther,
trans. Frederick H. Hedge (1805—1890)

Through faith the baptismal covenant is implanted. God will not count sins against the person who is baptized if that person fights against them. But those who do not, "God will not forgive their sin. For they do not live according to their baptism and covenant. . . ."[20]

Ulrich Zwingli on Sin

Ulrich Zwingli (1484–1531) was a founder of the Swiss Reformation. Ordained as a Roman Catholic priest in 1506, he became a disciple of Erasmus a few years later, studying that humanist's edition of the Greek New Testament and following his program for the reformation of the church, namely, an attempt to return to simple New Testament faith and practice. In 1523 the city of Zurich, in whose cathedral he had become a catalyst for reform, chose officially to adopt Zwingli's new views and began to pursue Protestant practices under his guidance. Within a few years, the other major German-speaking cities of Switzerland had joined the new movement.

Zwingli's doctrine of sin was essentially Augustinian, but markedly modified to his own tastes. Initially formed in God's image, Adam and Eve transgressed His commandment not to eat of the tree of knowledge and, in conformity with God's law, they died. Obviously their death was not physical (although physical death did ultimately occur as a result); it must, therefore, be a death of the soul. On the basis of Romans 5:12, declared Zwingli, the death suffered by the soul was sin.[21]

Not only did Adam and Eve die through their sin, but all of humankind died with them. Original sin for Zwingli was "the infirmity and defect of shattered nature."[22] In this defective nature the flesh holds ascendancy over the spirit, so much so that one may say that humans have become flesh by the Fall. Accordingly, they think in fleshly orientations and so have become God's enemies.[23]

Thus, all human beings have been tainted by sin, for Adam — being dead — could not generate progeny untainted by death. In this regard, death for Zwingli was synonymous with sin, for he defined death as that inordinate self-love which is the essence of sin.[24]

His biographer tells us that Zwingli was unique among the

major Reformers of Protestantism for the clarity with which he made the fundamental dichotomy between the corruption of human nature and what is rightfully sin. He observed two kinds of sin: the disease which we inherit from our first ancestors, through which we have become addicted to self-love; and the transgression of God's law. In fact, Zwingli insisted that sin inherited from Adam should not properly be termed sin. Sin-enslaved Adam, and all his descendants have been born into that same slavery.[25]

Zwingli saw original sin in a vastly different light from Catholics and Lutherans. Early in his career he had held that infants sinned unconsciously and therefore were not condemned. Later, however, and during the theological discussions with Luther at Marburg, he tried to avoid the term "original sin," but agreed that children were born with an unavoidable tendency toward sin, with a spiritual defect.[26]

What relationship does baptism have to sin? Baptism in water is an external rite. Baptism in the Spirit occurs only when the person baptized receives faith. Zwingli did not object to the practice of infant baptism, for it led to confirmation through which children were helped to come to a grasp of the faith. What would happen to an infant who died whether baptized or not he was uncertain. He felt that a child of Christian parents who died unbaptized was more likely not to be damned than to be. In any event, God would judge each situation.[27]

The Lord has provided for human sin from before creation, said Zwingli. Christ's sufferings have provided us with a sacrifice which satisfied God's requirement of justice. Jesus' sacrifice covers not only original sin but all sin. His redemptive act becomes ours as we acknowledge Him as our Head.[28]

Melancthon on Sin

Philip Melancthon (1497–1560) was a German scholar who was trained by the famous humanist Reuchlin and who attended the Universities of Heidelberg and Tübingen. In 1518 he was appointed first professor of Greek at the University of Wittenberg. In his inaugural address he spoke on behalf of the humanist program and made a plea for renewed attention to the ancient disciplines of rhetoric and Aristotelian philosophy. In the audience was Mar-

3.2: JOHN BUNYAN

John Bunyan (1628–1688) is revered for two notable writings (though he wrote others): *Grace Abounding to the Chief of Sinners* (1666) and *The Pilgrim's Progress* (1678). The latter work has been called the greatest piece of English literature ever written (next to the *King James Version* of the Bible).

Bunyan was born in Bedfordshire, England, to a tinker (or, mender of pots), and learned his father's trade. He served for a time in the "roundhead" (parliamentary) army during the English Civil War, during which time he became involved with a group of Baptists in Bedford. Their influence, coupled with his wife's encouragement, brought him under spiritual conviction and, after some period of despair because of his sinful condition, he experienced a full assurance of Christ's salvation.

He united with the Bedford church and soon was elected their preacher. When the Stuart kings were restored to the throne (1660), Bunyan was imprisoned for about a dozen years because of his refusal not to preach (all preachers were required to be licensed by the Church of England). During this prison period he wrote *Grace Abounding,* an account of how the Holy Spirit worked in his life to bring him to a full and confident salvation.

The Pilgrim's Progress followed some twelve years later. An allegory of the Christian pilgrimage from pre-conversion days to death (and ultimate eternal life), the book has as its hero, Christian. In his travels from the City of Destruction to the Celestial City, he encounters many obstacles, some personal and some material. These include Pliable, the Giant Despair, the Slough of Despond, and Doubting Castle. But he receives help and encouragement from others, such as Evangelist, Faithful, and Valiant-for-Truth.

Bunyan's doctrine, as illustrated by these two works, is grounded in Scripture. His interpretation of the Bible, however, was clearly molded by his Calvinistic-Baptist background.

The following quotation demonstrates much of Bunyan's view of sin and its defeat.

As for my own natural life, for the time that I was without God in the world, it was, indeed, according to the course of this world and the spirit that now worketh in the children of disobedience. Eph. ii.2, 3. It was my delight to be "taken captive by the devil at his will," 2 Tim. ii.26; being filled with all unrighteousness. . . . Yea, and so settled and rooted was I in these things, that they became as a second nature to me; the which, as I have also with soberness considered since, did so offend the Lord, that even in my childhood he did scare and affrighten me with fearful dreams, and did terrify me with fearful visions. . . .

Wherefore, one day, when I was in a meeting of God's people, full of sadness and terror; for my fears again were strong upon me; and, as I was now thinking, my soul was never the better, but my case most sad and fearful, these words did with great power suddenly break in upon me; My grace is sufficient for thee, My grace is sufficient for thee; My grace is sufficient for thee, three times together; And oh! methought that every word was a mighty word unto me; as My, and grace, and sufficient, and for thee; they were then, and sometimes are still, far bigger than others be.

—*John Bunyan,* Grace Abounding to the Chief of Sinners (London: Religious Tract Society, n.d.), 18, 117.

tin Luther, who responded to Melancthon's speech with admiration and enthusiasm. Shortly afterward, Melancthon became a wholehearted supporter of Luther.

Melancthon wrote a number of books. Of them all, his finest was *Loci Communes Rerum Theologicarum,* published in 1521. It was intended to be an analysis of sin, law, and grace in the light of the Scriptures. It set out the basic teachings of Lutheranism and established him as that tradition's foremost theologian.

Melancthon defined original sin as "a native propensity and an innate force and energy by which we are drawn to sinning. It was propagated from Adam to all posterity."[29] The Bible does not differentiate between "original" sin and "actual" sin; it is all simply "sin," which may be defined as "a depraved affection, a depraved activity of the heart against the law of God."[30]

In their pre-Fall state the first humans were sinless and were guided by the Holy Spirit to do right. Had Adam not transgressed, he would have guided his progeny in the same manner. When Adam sinned, the Holy Spirit no longer led him; his soul was blinded and, as a result, human beings—following in Adam's train—have become lovers of self and seekers of the carnal. Thus, those who say that original sin is the lack of original righteousness are correct.[31]

Melancthon, like Luther, was Augustinian in his doctrine of original sin. He interpreted Psalm 51:5 ("Surely I was sinful at birth, sinful from the time my mother conceived me.") and Genesis 6:5 ("every inclination of . . . [man's] heart was only evil all the time") to mean that human beings are born with sin. He also reversed Romans 5:12ff to observe that if all are being blessed in Christ, then all must first been cursed in Adam. "But what is it to be cursed but to be damned because of sin?"[32]

Melancthon refuted the teaching of the Pelagians that people are capable of goodness on their own. To teach so is to deny original sin. But a bad tree cannot bear good fruit, and a person tainted by sin can do nothing good. Some may speak of doing meritorious works, but human nature is incapable of any merit.[33]

Only an act of God can affect a change within a human being. He causes persons to turn to Him: "God himself invites us and draws us to himself, and when he has drawn us, he takes away our punishment and declares that he is pleased with us and reconciled to us."[34] Without the light of the Spirit of Christ one can neither recognize the loathesomeness of sin nor the desirability of righteousness.

The Hamartiology of John Calvin

John Calvin (1509–1564) was the prime mover in the French and French-Swiss Reformations and undoubtedly the greatest theologian since Augustine. His thought is detailed in his magnum opus, *Institutes of the Christian Religion,* at which he worked most of his life, constantly editing and rewriting it.

Calvin's theology began and ended with the sovereignty of

God. "Since God's will is said to be the cause of all things," he wrote, "I have made his providence the determinative principle for all human plans and works."[35]

On the Fall

Calvin described the first couple's context in Eden as one in which "Adam was denied the tree of the knowledge of good and evil to test his obedience and prove that he was willingly under God's command."[36] Tragically, Adam failed the test, thus causing disaster to himself and all of his posterity.

The reformer cited several factors as contributing to the Fall and did not isolate a single cause. He affirmed Augustine's view that pride was the source of sin. He also observed that Eve was led away "through unfaithfulness," and that disobedience initiated the Fall.[37] He drew a distinction, however, between Adam and Eve.

> Yet it is at the same time to be noted that the first man revolted from God's authority, not only because he was seized by Satan's blandishments, but also because, contemptuous of truth, he turned aside to falsehood. And surely, once we have held God's Word in contempt, we shake off all reverence for him. . . . Unfaithfulness, then, was the root of the Fall.[38]

Calvin was convinced that, had Adam and Eve not been possessed by inordinate ambition, they could have remained in their original condition. Pride was the stalk which grew from the roots of unfaithfulness and disobedience and, since this plant had no support in the order of God's universe, the Fall occurred.[39]

This original transgression not only had serious consequences for Adam, but for all of his descendants. Based on the words of Paul in Romans 5:12ff, Calvin concluded that "Adam, by sinning, not only took upon himself misfortune and ruin but also plunged our nature into like destruction."[40]

The chief result of the Fall was death — the death of the soul. Adam's rebellion resulted in God's curse, as a result of which all of his progeny have moved from life into death. God ordained that the whole human race should share in his corruption.[41]

On original sin

Original sin, according to Calvin's *Institutes of the Christian Religion*, is the "hereditary depravity and corruption of our nature, diffused into all parts of the soul, which first makes us liable to God's wrath, then also brings forth in us those works which Scripture calls 'works of the flesh' (Gal. 5:19)."[42] Original sin is humanity's "inherited corruption."[43] Even unborn children "carry their condemnation along with them from the mother's womb. . . . Indeed, their whole nature is a seed of sin."[44]

The Swiss reformer leaned heavily on several biblical passages to demonstrate the credibility of the doctrine. He held that Psalm 51:5 talks of original sin and that it is an imposing witness giving ample evidence of the original sin inflicted by Adam upon all humanity.[45] Job 14:4 dictates that the whole human family is born of impurity; it too is speaking of the doctrine of original sin.

Like so many others before him, Calvin also turned to Romans 5:12ff for support. Paul says that we all sinned. "But," insisted Calvin, "to sin in this case, is to become corrupt and vicious; for the natural depravity which we bring from our mother's womb, though it brings not forth immediately its own fruits, is yet sin before God, and deserves his vengeance."[46]

While Calvin held firmly to original sin, he did not explain how Adam's sin was extended to all humans, nor how all of humanity incurs guilt as a result. Berkouwer observes that "Calvin himself was aware of the impossibility of seeing this dogma in a way that makes clear the reality of our guilt."[47]

There was some connection between Adam's transgression and his progeny, but Calvin refused to explain what kind of relation there was. Undoubtedly, he was cognizant of the impossibility of uncovering a solution because of his strong emphasis on God's sovereignty. He rejected all rational attempts to explain and instead took refuge in God's will. He stated that it had been ordained by God "that the first man should at one and the same time have and lose, both for himself and for his descendants, the gifts that God had bestowed upon him."[48] Thus, declared Calvin, because it was the will of God, humans should be content with inheriting original sin (or, a depraved nature) and its condemnation in Eden.

75

On actual sin

Calvin agreed with the church fathers who saw sin as the deprivation of a nature formerly pure and holy. Sins are the by-product of original sin; he referred to them as "works of the flesh."[49] He defined sin as "rebellion against the will of God, which of necessity provokes God's wrath, and it is a violation of the law, upon which God's judgment is pronounced without exception."[50] Sin, then, is at the same time the cause and expression of human depravity and alienation from God, the antithesis of obedience.

Sin, observed Calvin, issues in pride and self-love. Human beings admire themselves to the point of self-delusion. Pride is a disease needing to be cured, for as long as humans are allowed to stand upon their own judgment, they determine hypocrisy to be righteousness. Their pride prevents them from seeing evil in themselves and leads to the denial of any defect.[51]

Closely associated with pride was ambition. Adam refused God's generous provision in the garden because of ambition and pride. Ambition has so sullied any virtue or thought in human beings that "before God they lose all favor."[52]

Humankind possesses insufficient resources to remedy the sinful tendencies which arise because of self-love and pride. Left to their own devices, people can do nothing but sin. Human nature will permit no other choice.[53]

On human will

Calvin agreed with Chrysostom that from head to toe human beings are wholly sin.[54] Sin has left the human will enslaved to evil and deprived of freedom of choice. The French reformer used a multitude of expressions to illustrate his view. He described humankind as "fettered by sin,"[55] "bound in servitude to the devil,"[56] and "held under the yoke of sin."[57] That freedom from sin and sinning originally possessed by Adam had been lost as a result of his transgression. Freedom not to sin is therefore no longer a part of human experience.

Calvin recognized a close association between Adam's transgression and the ongoing condition of human sinfulness. Humanity is subject to "the necessity of sinning" because the will, originally free in Adam, "made itself the slave of sin."[58] Men and women sin of necessity because their wills are in bondage.

Once there existed three kinds of freedom. Freedom not to sin was lost when Adam fell. Freedom from necessity "so inheres in man by nature that it cannot possibly be taken away."[59] Calvin saw confusion, however, between compulsion and necessity. Human will remains, although virtue has been lost through the Fall.[60] Calvin's conclusion was that "the will bereft of freedom is of necessity either drawn or led into evil."[61]

Necessity for Calvin meant that one sins necessarily because of one's nature, but at the same time one sins voluntarily and willingly.

> The chief point . . . must be that man as he was corrupted by the Fall, sinned willingly, not unwillingly or by compulsion; by the most eager inclination of his heart, not by forced compulsion; by the prompting of his own lust, not by compulsion from without. Yet so depraved is his nature that he can be moved or impelled only to evil.[62]

Calvin pictured human beings as slaves, not forced reluctantly and unwillingly to obey their master, Satan, but slaves who of necessity obediently follow his every command.[63]

On predestination and reprobation

We have already indicated that Calvin formulated all of his theology — the doctrine of sin and the Fall included — to conform to his view of the sovereignty of God. Whether a person is saved from the consequences of his sin or suffers perdition because of his sin is determined by God's election. In His divine and absolute authority God has predestined some sinners to salvation and others to perdition.

Calvin defined predestination as "God's eternal decree, by which he compacted with himself what he willed to become of each man . . . eternal life is foreordained for some, eternal damnation for others."[64] This election is irrevocable and it has absolutely nothing to do with human merit.

Calvin admitted that he found the idea of some being predestined to damnation a terrible one to contemplate. It was especially so in view of his foundational statement that God had preor-

3.3: THE MAJOR PROTESTANT REFORMERS AND THEIR VIEWS ON SIN AND THE FALL

Martin Luther   1483–1546
Eisleben, Germany (Birthplace)   Leipzig (Education)
95 Theses
The Babylonian Captivity of the Church
The Bondage of the Will
Large Catechism
Small Catechism

Facts	Doctrine of Sin
In 1506 began teaching at Wittenberg.	Root of sin is unfaith
Hated sale of indulgences.	
In 1517 posted ninety-five theses on church door.	Humans inherit original sin and their will is in bondage to Satan until liberated by faith in Jesus
Was excommunicated in 1520.	
Translated Bible into German.	
In 1525 married former nun, Catherine von Bora.	
Bitterly opposed Peasants' Revolt.	

✠

Ulrich Zwingli   1484–1531
Upper Toggenburg, Switzerland (Birthplace)
Vienna, Basel (Education)
Concerning Freedom and Choice of Food
Sixty-Seven Conclusions

Facts	Doctrine of Sin
Was influenced by Humanist teaching, especially that of Erasmus.	Did not believe in inherited guilt, but in inherited tendency to sin.
Entered priesthood and in 1518 came to Zurich.	
Initiated many reforms and led the canton to embrace reform principles.	Jesus' sacrifice covers both original and actual sin.
He and Luther could not agree.	
He was killed in battle against the Catholic cantons.	

✠

John Calvin   1509–1564
Noyon, France (Birthplace)   Paris, Orleans (Education)
Institutes of the Christian Religion
Commentaries (on various books of the Bible)

Facts	Doctrine of Sin
Became a reformer under influence of Nicholas Kopp.	Pride the root of sin.
Forced into exile in 1533.	Original sin inherited.
In 1536 was persuaded by Guillaume Farel to aid in reform at Geneva.	God predestines both the damned
Was ousted in 1539, but returned in 1541 for remainder of life.	and the saved (the latter through
Established theocracy in Geneva.	Christ).

---

dained the Fall, a logical extension of his belief that the will of God is "the necessity of things."[65]

Considering that God's will is determinative of all things, one might wonder why God had not elected all human beings to salvation. Calvin responded, quoting Augustine to the effect that God did not choose to save the damned because "he did not want to, and why he did not want to, is his own business."[66]

Reactions to the Reformation

Luther's unhappiness with conditions in the Roman Catholic Church aroused dissatisfaction in others, not only with Catholicism but with the existing Reformation movements of the time. As a consequence, a variety of radical movements ensued. Some of these, reacting against the strong objective emphasis of Luther and Calvin, opted for a mystical approach to Christianity. Others, with similar reactions, moved toward a liberal rationalism.

Mysticism

The evolution of the Schwenkfelders in the latter half of the sixteenth century was one of the most interesting aspects of the

3.4: THE RADICAL REFORMERS AND SIN

The Radical Reformation has also been termed the "Third Reformation" and may include those reformers not associated with either the Protestant or Catholic Reformations. The mainstream of this Reformation was a pacifist group which came to be known as "Anabaptists."

The Anabaptists began with the Swiss Brethren during the Reformation under Ulrich Zwingli in Zurich. Some of Zwingli's followers, upon studying the Bible, determined that his reforms were not going far enough in their allegiance to Scripture. Chief among these was his slowness in achieving reform and especially his failure to eschew infant baptism in favor of the baptism of (adult) believers only. On January 21, 1525, a group felt led to seek believers' baptism, even though they had been christened as infants. These Swiss Brethren, as they came to be known, proclaimed their view of the church as taught by the Bible, in spite of official opposition. The result was persecution and, for many, exile or death. In spite of ferocious opposition, under the leadership of men like Conrad Grebel, Balthasar Hubmaier, and Michael Sattler, the movement grew quickly.

Anabaptist missionaries spread the Gospel wherever they went and thousands across Europe accepted their message and were baptized upon profession of their faith in Christ. Persecution threatened the survival of the movement, for tens of thousands were massacred by Protestants and Catholics alike, who saw them as a great threat to the established church and to stable government. Under the leadership of Menno Simons, however, in a Netherlands more tolerant than the rest of Europe, the Anabaptists regrouped and became more established. Eventually, this pacifist group of separatists took their leader's name, becoming known as Mennonites.

While borrowing from Catholics and Protestants alike, Anabaptist theology was neither. Balthasar Hubmaier *(On Free Will)* taught that before the Fall, humanity possessed body, soul, and spirit that were all righteous. By sin Adam lost free will for himself and his descendants. Human flesh became utterly corrupt, but the spirit remained upright and whole, untainted by the flesh. The soul, however, was wounded and powerless (but not irreparable), a prisoner of the flesh. Through Christ, the spirit may become happy and vibrant; the soul may recover its freedom to choose good and reject evil; the flesh, unfortunately, remains hopelessly carnal.

Michael Sattler, former of the Schleitheim Confession (a statement of faith uniting most Anabaptists), rejected Martin Luther's concept of salvation by *sola fide*. Confession of sin and acceptance of God's forgiveness in Christ are necessary, but not enough in and of themselves. Sattler identified with St. Benedict, who connected salvation to personal sanctification. Not faith alone, but "the obedience of faith" is necessary to salvation. One must live a Christlike life in the community of saints. Thus, a permanent defeat of sin was the result of a progressive sanctification rather than of the forensic justification stressed by Luther and Calvin.

mystical reaction. These were followers of a Silesian noble named Caspar Schwenkfeld (1489–1561). Strongly influenced by Meister Eckart, Johann Tauler, and other earlier mystics, he had initially been a follower of Martin Luther, but came to believe that the Lutherans were too objective in their theologizing. They made too much of the external Word of God and too little of His indwelling presence. The latter is what humankind truly needs, and it is what was missed in the initial creation (regardless of human sin). It may, however, be attained in the new creation effected by Christ, a human being who—because of His miraculous virgin birth—was able to enter into a union with God. Believers receive the divine nature through participation in the Eucharist which, in its true form, is not merely an external rite but an inner feeding of the soul on the heavenly bread which is the divine flesh of Christ Himself.[67] Fisher notes that

> Schwenkfeld did not reject the doctrine of the death of Christ, which effaces guilt; but this was only the stepping-stone to the higher life which Christ makes the possession of His followers through a real, spiritual communication of it. The true believer can live without sin.[68]

Socinianism

Whereas the chief Reformers based their theology on a foundation of Scripture as interpreted in the orthodox ecumenical creeds of the ancient church, a group of Italian Protestants rejected the trinitarian basis of the faith as irrational. Two of their leading lights were Laelius Socinus and his nephew, Faustus.

Laelius Socinus (1525–1562) was a brilliant Italian Protestant who had sought refuge from Roman Catholic persecution by fleeing to Switzerland. He had had deep theological conversations with Calvin, Bullinger, and Luther. Upon his death, his papers were bequeathed to Faustus Socinus (1539–1604), who had also been active in Zurich and Basel and who—based on his uncle's ideas—founded the system which came to be known as Socinianism.[69]

The Socinian position declared that the content of Scripture must be justified by human reason and it rejected as inspired any doctrines which it considered to have failed its rationalistic criteria. The Socinians were Pelagian in their doctrine of sin. Adam was not intended to receive immortality. They denied original sin and asserted that human beings possess free will to obey God. They did not believe that God's holiness demanded an atonement for sin, and they rejected the idea that Christ's crucifixion furnished satisfaction for human guilt. His work served simply to demonstrate to humans how to live a right life in God's sight.[70]

All in all, Socinianism was a rational critique of orthodox theology in general and Reformed theology in particular. Even though it came to an end in its organized form in the mid-seventeenth century, it prepared the way for the theology of the Enlightenment and more recent liberal doctrinal concepts.

Arminian Teaching on Sin

Calvin's teaching on predestination made an increasing impact on the Reformed churches of Europe, especially in the generation following. Theodore Beza, a successor to Calvin, developed Calvin's doctrine even more rigidly, referring to election and reprobation as the "mirror" of the glory of God. Calvin's theology, however, was formulated in its most stringent aspect by Franciscus Gomarus, a supralapsarian, who determined that predestination had not even considered the human Fall; both eternal perdition and the Fall had been foreordained by divine decree.[71]

Not all Reformed theologians, however, approved of Calvin's approach. Particularly opposed to his view of double predestination and irresistible grace were Jacob Arminius and his associates. A professor (from 1603) at Leyden in Holland, Arminius collected and synthesized the works of writers of the early church (those who had been prominent prior to Augustine). To this mix he added the thought of Protestant theologians such as Melancthon, Hemmingius, and Latimer. The resulting system, conditional in opposition to absolute predestination and general in opposing particular redemption, he defended with vigor.[72] Though he died in 1609, his views were championed by Dutch theologians James Uytenbogaart and Simon Episcopius.

Arminius' theology was sharply attacked in many of the Reformed churches and branded as heretical. A Synod was summoned at Dort in 1618–19 to consider these charges. In 1610 Arminius' followers united together to protest these attacks. The defense of the Remonstrants was presented at Dort, but was condemned.

Arminius rejected the Augustinian-Calvinistic doctrine of double predestination, declaring it "repugnant to the nature of God, but particularly to those attributes of His nature by which He performs and manages all things, His wisdom, justice, and goodness."[73] Nor does such a doctrine conform to the biblical description of the nature of eternal death, "for it is called 'the wages of sin' . . . God, therefore, has not, by any absolute decree without respect to sin and disobedience, prepared eternal death for any person."[74]

Arminius held that the double predestination makes God the author of sin. If God foreordained that humankind should fall from grace, then He has denied to them even before they sinned the grace they needed to avoid sin. Such an act would make God a sinner. "As a legitimate consequence it also follows, that sin is not sin, since whatever that be which God does, it neither can be sin, nor ought any of his acts to receive that appellation."[75]

Instead, Arminius set forth a doctrine of predestination based on God's foreknowledge. God has chosen to save those He foreknew would accept His grace and believe and persevere. He has allowed to reprobation those whom, in His foreknowledge, He knew would not repent and believe.[76]

In regard to original sin, Arminius held that, while the human race participated in Adam's sin insofar as all existed in him, "God has taken the whole human race into the grace of reconciliation, and has entered into a covenant of grace with Adam, and with the whole of his posterity with him."[77] Since infants have not transgressed this covenant they will not be condemned. If God condemned them to perdition for Adam's sin, He would be treating them with much greater severity than even the demons who committed terrible sins that were unnecessary.[78]

The first sin (of Adam) was a transgression of the law, Arminius taught, for God had commanded him not to eat of the tree of the knowledge of good and evil. The commandment not to eat was a test of his obedience. Through his sin Adam both offended God and became liable to two deaths, spiritual and physical. He also lost the primitive righteousness and holiness with which God had endowed him.[79]

The effects of our first parents' sin are not limited to them, but are common to the whole human race. All humanity was in Adam's loins when he transgressed. "Wherefore, whatever punishment was brought down upon our first parents, has likewise pervaded and yet pursues all their posterity. So that all men 'are by nature the children of wrath.' . . . With these evils they would remain oppressed forever, unless they were liberated by Jesus Christ. . . ."[80]

Arminius categorized actual sins in many ways. There were sins of commission and sins of omission; sins *per se* and sins *per accidens;* sins of ignorance, infirmity, malignity, and negligence; sins contrary to conscience and not contrary to conscience.[81]

Though the Bible says that "the wages of sin is death" (Rom. 6:23), not all sins are therefore equal. A crime against God is more serious than one against a human being. One that is perpetrated willfully is worse than one committed as the result of error.[82]

Sins may also be divided into pardonable and unpardonable. A pardonable sin (also known as a "sin not unto death") is one which may be repented of and so forgiven. An unpardonable sin (a "sin unto death") is one which can never have repentance, such as the sin against the Holy Spirit.[83]

The Catholic Reformation

Although fifteenth- and sixteenth-century Catholic religious reformers such as Erasmus had been agitating for reform within the Roman Catholic Church, it was the energy of the Protestant Reformation which forced the Catholic hierarchy to reexamine every facet of church faith and practice. Many leaders acknowledged problems in areas such as fasting, penance, celibacy, and monasticism. Jaroslav Pelikan reflects on the effect of the Reformation on the Roman Church.

> By "boldly passing judgment" on such abuses, the Reformation had performed a useful service, but its demand for "pure doctrine and uncorrupted morals" was no justification for "overthrowing all the authority of all the ages of history." The removal of an abuse must not involve removal of "the substance of the matter" that had been subject to abuse.[84]

3.5: IGNATIUS OF LOYOLA

One of the leading figures in the Roman Catholic movement for reform was Ignatius of Loyola (ca. 1491–1556). Born at Loyola in Spain, he was a professional soldier whose career was terminated by a serious leg wound in 1521. While convalescing he read a number of works on the lives of the early saints and determined that, if he could not be a soldier in the army of Spain, he would be a soldier for the Lord. The following year he spent in meditation at the monastery of Manresa and, while there, recorded his spiritual disciplines in a work entitled *The Spiritual Exercises.*

Over the next ten years he trained for his Christian vocation at the Universities of Barcelona, Alcala, Salamanca, and Paris. While Luther's training and spiritual experience led him away from the established church, Loyola's led him to a renewed devotion to Roman Catholicism. Along with a small group of friends, he established The Society of Jesus (of which he became general), devoted to complete and unthinking obedience to the papacy for the purpose of spreading and defending the Catholic faith. Their lifestyle was to be based on Loyola's *Spiritual Exercises.*

Approved by Pope Paul III in 1540, the Jesuits grew rapidly, even though standards for admission were high and training (both spiritual and intellectual) was rigorous. By the time of Loyola's death, the Society numbered more than a thousand "soldiers" throughout Europe, all of them fanatically loyal to the pope and to their general.

Their chief objectives in these early years included the giving of a high-quality education (to influence the molders of society for Catholicism), counter-reformation (to blunt the thrust of Protestantism in Europe), and mission work (to expand Catholicism throughout the world). They were very successful in all these areas.

A quotation from Loyola's work will give some idea of his view of sin and dealing with it.

By an effort of my memory, I will recall the first sin, that of the angels; next, I will use my reason to think about it; then my will, striving to remember and think about all this in order to develop in myself a sense of utter shame, as I compare my numerous sins with the angels' one sin; that one sin brought them to Hell; how often have I deserved it for all my sins.

. . . Let me picture Christ our Lord hanging on the cross before me, and speak to Him in this way: how has He, the Creator, come to be man? Knowing eternal life, how has He come to this temporal death, this death for my sins? Then, turning to myself, I will ask: What have I done for Christ? What am I doing for Christ? What must I do for Christ?

—Ignatius of Loyola, The Spiritual Exercises,
trans. Thomas Corbishley (Wheathampstead, U.K.: Anthony Clarke, 1973), 30, 32.

Protestant reformers had raised all sorts of accusations against the faith of Rome which required defense. It began with Luther's Ninety-Five Theses, which called into question the doctrines of purgatory, human merit, and penance. All three of these areas had an unbreakable connection with the doctrine of sin.

The Council of Trent

The Council of Trent (1545–63) was the vehicle by which the Roman Catholic Church marked out its course in the light of events in the fifteenth and sixteenth centuries. It also sought a mediating position between opposing factions in Catholicism. While the Popes had no real desire to call a council, the interference of princes and governments in church affairs along with strident demands by the Emperor Charles V gave them little choice. In December of 1545, Pope Paul III called for a church council to meet at Trent in Germany. Its initial colloquium numbered about 112, mostly Italians, and it adjourned in 1547. It was reestablished by Julius III in 1551, only to disband the following year. After two years, it was reassembled by Paul IV in January of 1562, and met until December of 1563. There were 255 persons at this final convocation, some two thirds of whom were Italian.[85]

The Pope determined the council's direction from the start to its finish. Papal legates presided at the sessions and set its agenda by permitting no proposals to be made to the convocation except through themselves. Papal approval was always obtained for proposed doctrinal assertions prior to seeking the council's sanction. Topics were considered by groups of theologians and sometimes by the whole assembly. When they were approved, they were proclaimed in the general sessions of the council.[86]

The fifth session of the council determined the official position on original sin. One faction held that original sin should be located in concupiscence; the other held it simply as a lack of righteousness. The council declared that Adam, by his own volition, lost the righteousness and holiness with which he had been endowed at creation, and so came under God's wrath and Satan's power. The result was his deterioration in both body and soul. And yet, his free will was not completely extinguished, although it was weakened and perverted.[87]

Adam's transgression, asserted the council, along with its resultant guilt was inherited by the whole race. Because they were received by propagation and not imitation, it is impossible by human means to be free of them. Even infants can be cleansed of original sin and guilt only by baptismal regeneration.[88]

Even though the individual is forgiven and renewed in baptism, concupiscence remains. While concupiscence is spoken of by the apostles as sin, the church decided that in the regenerate it was not truly sin, but rather that it is the result of sin and tends toward sin.[89]

The sixth session discussed the sinner's justification. Baptism imparts grace, imputing Christ, who remits our sins. Human beings, consenting to God's working in them and cooperating with Him, prepare themselves for justification. Justification is preserved by obedience to God's law and the laws of the church. It may be lost, however, through unbelief or any mortal sin. But renewal may occur by the sacrament of penance. Absolution will remove both the guilt and the eternal penalties. Temporal penalties, though, may be removed only by works of satisfaction.[90]

Jansenism

A moving force within Catholicism for reform was the bishop of Ypres, Cornelius Jansen (d. 1638). His belief was that the best curative for the lax morality of Roman leaders — especially the Jesuits — was a revival of Augustinian doctrine. To this end he spent some twenty-two years on a work on Augustinian thought, *Augustinus*, which was published posthumously in 1640 by his followers.

The work set forth and defended Augustine's theology in its purest form in regard to original sin, the Fall of humankind in Adam, human inability, irresistible grace, and connected concerns.[91] It declared that original sin has fully sated humanity. The sinner is completely under the domination of sin. He can do nothing toward achieving salvation until Christ brings the "medicinal aid" of grace. Only this grace, which is irresistible, can work good in human beings. Grace has love as its object, and love is sufficient to remit sins.[92]

Shortly after the book's publication, it was prohibited by the Inquisition and condemned by Pope Urban VIII in 1642. Several French theologians known as the Port Royalists, and including

Blaise Pascal and the Abbot of Saint-Cyran, rejected the papal ban
and fiercely supported Jansen's thought, but to little avail. Innocent X in 1653 condemned five papal propositions, including the
view of grace as irresistible. In 1656, Alexander VII anathema-
tized those holding papal views, and the Jesuits persuaded Louis
XIV of France to authorize the destruction of the Port Royal
cloister. The much longed for Augustinian revival fell with Jan-
senism under the rule of Semi-Pelagianism, never to rise again.

Conclusions

The Semi-Pelagianism espoused by the Catholic Church of latter
medieval times contributed to the immense dissatisfaction with
the church on the part of the humanists, resulting in the Protestant Reformation. In opposition, the Reformers embraced Augustinian theology, which had fallen out of favor beginning with
Thomas Aquinas, albeit without much of the sacramental trap-
pings accompanying it.

Martin Luther adopted Augustine's doctrine of original sin —
that all humanity has become utterly corrupt as an inheritance
from Adam and Eve — but preferred to go beyond Augustine to
the Latin Ante-Nicene fathers in his broader theology of sin.
Because of sin humans have lost their freedom of will and have
become enslaved to Satan. Because of his emphasis on justification by faith, Luther did not accept the Catholic concept of merit
in regard to dealing with sin.

Ulrich Zwingli also followed an essentially Augustinian path.
Adam and Eve broke God's law in regard to eating of the tree of
the knowledge of good and evil and so died spiritually. All of
humanity died with them and have become God's enemies. At
the same time, Zwingli did not like the term "original sin" and
viewed it as a spiritual defect which led humans into a tendency
toward sin. Baptism was not truly efficacious in removing sin
unless the recipient of the sacrament possessed faith in Christ.

Philip Melancthon believed that the Bible did not differentiate
between original and actual sin. It was all sin. As the result of
Adam's transgression, his soul was blinded. Adam's progeny inherited this blindness and are enslaved to sin. All are damned
because of what the first human couple did. Only an act of God
can cause a transformation of human nature. Only the light of

Christ can cause a sinner to recognize the horror of sin and change his or her ways.

John Calvin was probably the most Augustinian of the Protestant Reformers. His whole theology was formulated in the light of his view of the absolute sovereignty of God. Pride was the root of Adam's transgression, with serious results not only for the first couple but for their descendants. The fallout from that sin was death, spiritual and physical. Even though sin was the fault of Adam and Eve, the Fall was ordained by God as was the condemnation of all human beings henceforth. Calvin built on an Augustinian foundation in crafting his doctrine of double predestination. God has predestined some people to salvation and others to damnation. His grace is lavished upon the former and is irresistible.

Among Reformed church leaders following Calvin's era, there was not unanimity. Jacob Arminius rejected much of Calvin's theology, viewing double predestination as repugnant to God's nature since it ultimately makes Him the author of sin. He did, however, accept the basic premise of Augustinian teaching on original sin, namely, that all of humanity were in Adam's loins when he sinned, and so share in his punishment. All are children of wrath until liberated by Christ.

While a reformation occurred in Roman Catholic practices and doctrines, Semi-Pelagianism was confirmed over Augustinian theology by the Council of Trent. The sacramental system remained in place virtually unchanged. Efforts by Cornelius Jansen to revive doctrinaire Augustinian theology met with failure. The sacramental system remained in place virtually unchanged. Indeed, Roman Catholic theology would remain the same until the latter half of the twentieth century. Protestant views of sin, however, would become increasingly fractured and divergent as the decades progressed.

Chapter Four
The Ideas of
Latter Protestantism

Immediately after the Protestant Reformation, as we have not-ed, the dynamic teaching of the Reformers had been concret-ized into inflexible dogma. A reaction to the rigidity of Protes-tant Scholasticism came in the Pietistic movement of the early eighteenth century; the latter represented a stress on a conver-sion experience, personal faith, and a strong commitment in daily life to the cause of Jesus Christ. In Britain, Pietism led into the Evangelical Revival, spearheaded by John Wesley.

John Wesley on Sin

John Wesley (1703–1791) was a son of the High Church of En-gland who trained at Oxford for the priesthood. After a rather unsatisfying missionary stint to the American natives in Georgia, he came under the influence of the Moravians and had a remark-able conversion. He became an open-air preacher and, ultimately, the founder of the Methodist tradition (all without ever leaving the Church of England). Though initially rejected by the English religious establishment, some fifty years of unselfish ministry won him the respect of his peers and almost all of his country-men.

While not a systematic theologian, Wesley was a capable scholar well-versed in the Bible, Patristics, and the theology of the English Reformation. He was also indebted to the works of the Puritans, the Moravians, and William Law. We are told that "the shape of Wesley's theology was affected by certain historical influences—patristic, Reformed, and Caroline—but its substance was determined by its Biblical sources."[1]

Original sin

Wesley held that humankind was initially created righteous. They related to their Creator in love and obedience. God had created them in His image and likeness, which consisted of a spiritual and immortal nature, dominion over the rest of creation, goodness and true holiness. But the first human couple also possessed freedom; their love and obedience were completely voluntary. Had they continued to obey, they would have been rewarded with eternal happiness.[2]

Adam and Eve, tragically, used their freedom to disobey God. In that disobedience they fell from God's favor, losing His image. Their love for Him was replaced by dread. When given the opportunity to confess their sin, they instead prevaricated, "which proves, not only their having sinned, but their being as yet wholly impenitent."[3] Nor did they retain their original righteousness.

Wesley avowed that this first transgression had devastating effects. When the first couple sinned, they died spiritually.

> Hereby [Adam] incurred death of every kind; not only temporal, but also spiritual and eternal. By losing his original righteousness, he became not only mortal as to his body, but also spiritually dead, dead to God, dead in sin; void of that principle which St. Paul terms, "the life of God" (Eph. 4:18); St. John, "eternal life abiding in us" (1 John 3:15).[4]

Adam's first sin, insisted Wesley, was that of a public person. He was representative of all humanity. "And, as such, St. Paul shows it is imputed to us and all his descendants."[5] Thus, the consequences of Adam's sin were transmitted to his children through all ages. "The fact I know, both by Scripture and experience. I know it is transmitted; but how it is transmitted I neither know nor desire to know."[6] To prove the fact, Wesley surveyed history from the very earliest times up to his own day, an account of corruption, war, want, and utter misery.[7]

John Wesley believed that the doctrine of original sin was absolutely essential to the intent of the Gospel, namely, to humble vain humanity, and to clearly demonstrate that it is God's free grace and not human free will which is responsible for salvation from sin.[8]

The nature of sin

Wesley was Augustinian in his view of the nature of sin. The root of sin is pride. It causes human beings to replace God with idols, to love themselves more than Him, and to give themselves honor which rightly belongs to God. "And although pride was not made for man, yet where is the man that is born without it? But hereby we rob God of his unalienable right, and idolatrously usurp his glory."[9] Sin, therefore, manifests itself in atheism. The natural person, Wesley asserted, has no more "idea of God than any of the beasts of the field . . . no fear of God at all, neither is God in all his thoughts."[10]

Why did Adam transgress? Wesley rejected John Calvin's view that God in His sovereignty planned sin and incited the Fall. To the contrary, Wesley laid the blame squarely on human freedom of choice.[11] The first human, Adam, made a willful decision — knowing what God had clearly commanded — to eat the fruit of the forbidden tree.

The cure for sin

The only cure for sin, Wesley declared, is God's salvation in Jesus Christ. He emphatically rejected Calvinistic predestination, finding it contrary to the biblical doctrine of salvation by grace through faith.

> Those who maintain absolute predestination, who hold decrees that have no condition at all, cannot be consistent with themselves, unless they deny salvation by faith as well as salvation by works. For, if only "he that believeth shall be saved," then faith is a condition of salvation. . . .[12]

4.1: JOHN WESLEY'S DOCTRINE
OF THE CONQUEST OF SIN

John Wesley was strongly influenced in his views of sin and its defeat by the Moravian Brethren, and even though he parted company with them and many of their doctrinal positions, he owed them much, as is evident in this hymn of Count von Zinzendorf (their chief patron and early leader) which Wesley translated into English.

Jesus, Thy Blood and Righteousness

Jesus, Thy blood and righteousness
My beauty are, my glorious dress;
'Midst flaming worlds, in these arrayed,
With joy shall I lift up my head.

Bold shall I stand in Thy great day,
For who aught to my charge shall lay?
Fully absolved through these I am,
From sin and fear, from guilt and shame.

Lord, I believe Thy precious blood,
Which at the mercy seat of God
Forever doth for sinners plead,
For me, e'en for my soul, was shed.

Lord, I believe were sinners more
Than sands upon the ocean shore,
Thou hast for all a ransom paid,
For all a full atonement made.

Just as faith is a condition of salvation, so unbelief is a condition of reprobation.

He condemned unconditional rejection as a hindrance to the inward work of God at every level. Such unconditionality means that no warning or exhortation can help those who live carelessly. If one is reprobate, one is lost no matter what. Then too the believer who feels assured of salvation will grow more and more slack until he falls into the sin from which he had escaped. Believing himself to be in grace, "he sins on, and sleeps on till he awakens in hell."[13]

Nor would Wesley accept the idea that original sin could be the basis for condemnation. The Bible nowhere says that one will be damned for that alone.[14]

Sin and believers

Because Wesley tended toward an Arminian theology of sin, he believed wholeheartedly in human free will, both prior to salvation and following it. When combined with original sin—which is active in every person, even in the regenerate—freedom of will leads Christians toward sinful behavior. In opposition to Count Zinzendorf, who claimed that true believers are saved not only from the dominion of sin but also its being, Wesley declared that sin remains in the believer even though it may not reign. "That believers are delivered from the *guilt* and *power* of sin we allow; that they are delivered from the *being* of it we deny."[15] While Christians have been reconciled to God through the blood of Christ and the flesh has been conquered, it nonetheless continues to exist and to battle against His Spirit.

The common Christian experience, Wesley asserts, is that

while they feel this witness [of Christ] in themselves, they feel a will not wholly resigned to the will of God. They know they are in him; and yet an heart ready to depart from him, a proneness to evil in many instances, and a backwardness to that which is good.[16]

Wesley's response to such a predicament was all the more earnestly to "put on the whole armour of God" and so to continue to withstand Satan and his wiles.[17]

On Christian perfection

Wesley taught that Christians might attain a level of maturity where they are so dedicated to God that He becomes all in all to them. In such a state they are perfect; that is, they no longer commit sin.[18] "It remains, then, that Christians are saved in this world from all sin, from all unrighteousness; that they are now in such a sense perfect, as not to commit sin, and to be found freed from evil thoughts and evil tempers."[19]

In response to those who questioned whether one could be human and not sin, Wesley conceded that — while Christian perfection excluded sins — "I do not expect to be freed from actual mistakes, till this mortal puts on immortality . . . we cannot avoid sometimes thinking wrong, till this corruptible shall have put on incorruption."[20] His defense was that "where every word and action springs from love, such a mistake is not properly a sin. However, it cannot bear the rigor of God's justice, but needs the atoning blood."[21]

Wesley saw sin as a voluntary transgression of a law. Those involuntary transgressions of law were what he held to be "mistakes." A person filled with God's love will still be heir to the latter.

Schleiermacher's Views on Sin

Friedrich Schleiermacher (1768–1834) was the son of a German Pietist clergyman. As a youth he was sent to a Moravian school where he developed a keen sense of sin, and of the need for grace. At seminary, when faced by the arguments of religious skepticism, he lost his faith in the deity of Christ and in atonement through His blood. Later, at the University of Halle, he was immersed in Kantian philosophy and began to redevelop a sense of Christian doctrine. Ordained in 1794 as a Reformed pastor, he served in Berlin, where he was influenced by the Romantic movement. Four years later he published *On Religion: Speeches to Its Cultured Despisers,* which demonstrated the influence of Romanticism on his theology, still in formation. In 1821 and 1822, he published his matured theology, *The Christian Faith.*[22]

Schleiermacher held the essence of religion to be experience. Likewise, the essence of experience is the believer's sense of absolute dependence. "The common element in all howsoever diverse expressions of piety, by which these are conjointly distinguished from other feelings, or, in other words, the self-identical essence of piety, is this: the consciousness of being absolutely dependent, or, which is the same thing, of being in relation with God."[23] The feeling of dependence became for him the cornerstone of all Christian doctrines.

On human consciousness

Schleiermacher posited three levels of human self-consciousness. The first, back in the early period of human life, is a state of consciousness little differentiated from that of animals; "the spiritual life [is] as yet entirely in the background."[24] There is no distinction at this level between self and the world.

As children grow, however, feeling and perception become increasingly distinct from each other. Both our sense of the world and our sense of self develop in the same measure. As this sense progresses, the sense of our ability to affect the world increases, but so does our sense of dependence on the world.[25] This is the second level. At this point, value judgments are decided by the antithesis of the depressing and elevating, of pleasure and of pain.[26] This second stage replaces the first.

Although the second level is a permanent one, there is also a third level, one of religious consciousness. While the former splits into partial feelings both of dependence and freedom, the latter involves absolute human dependence. In this third level, antitheses have been superseded by self-consciousness of the feeling of absolute dependence on an Other which is totally unaffected either by the human will or the world, an Other which possesses absolute freedom.[27]

Justo Gonzalez says of this third level:

> The religious self-consciousness thus determines the fact that systematic theology will have to deal with three main themes: the self, the world, and God. Since the second level of consciousness is never overcome, and at that level all is based on the antithesis of pleasure and pain, the third level — within the Christian faith — now judges the previous existence and the continuation of that second level is sin.[28]

On perfection

Perfection in Schleiermacher's vocabulary was defined very much differently from Wesley's view. In *The Christian Faith*, the former discussed the original perfection of humankind.

Schleiermacher defined the doctrine of the original perfection of the world as "the implication that the world offers to the human spirit an abundance of stimuli to develop those conditions in which the God-consciousness can realize itself."[29] In other words, God has made the world in such a fashion that it is adequate to bring human beings to an awareness of Him. Just as the world is active toward humans, so they are active toward it: "The knowability of the world would be empty if it did not include in itself the expression of its being known."[30] We have the responsibility to shape it on the basis of our awareness of God. Our failure to develop God-consciousness prior to doing so is sin, as is our failure to mold the world into the form of God's kingdom.[31]

The original perfection of humankind refers to "the predisposition to God-consciousness, as an inner impulse, [which] includes the consciousness of a faculty of attaining, by means of the human organism, to those states of self-consciousness in which the God-consciousness can realize itself. . . ."[32] In other words, human beings have always possessed the capability of God-consciousness, our lack of which is sin.[33]

On sin

Schleiermacher insisted that sin cannot be considered solely by itself. It must be seen as the antithesis of grace. "Thus since in our statements about sin we are to keep in view those still to be made about grace, we may regard sin on the one hand as simply that which would not be unless redemption was to be; or on the other hand as that which, as it is to disappear, can disappear only through redemption."[34] We may say, then, that sin is anything which interferes with our God-consciousness or inhibits the redemptive process which delivers us whole God-consciousness.

The problem lies in the second level of our self-consciousness. The flesh, or sensuous aspect of self, militates against the spirit. Were the flesh (i.e., the totality of the lower powers of the soul) directed completely by impulses from the sector of God-consciousness, there would be no conflict and we would exist in a sinless state. But the two have not become one.

> Since, however, the consciousness of sin never exists in the soul of the Christian without the consciousness of the power of redemption, the former is never actually found without its complementary half . . . and, if taken by itself alone, represents only that state of a hopeless incapacity in the spirit, which prevails outside the sphere of redemption.[35]

Schleiermacher considered that his definition of sin as a stalling of the determinative power of the spirit, because of the autonomy of the sensuous functions, was entirely compatible with explanations portraying sin as a departure from God. He did not, however, see it as a violation of divine law. But then, he said, law is not really a Christian term. "An interpretation more Christian in its origin, and at the same time directly in keeping with our own, is that which says that sin consists in our desiring what Christ contemns (sic) and *vice-versa.*"[36]

On original sin

Schleiermacher observed that sin in a person seems to have its source in something outside of and prior to himself or herself. And yet, he noted, the sensuous excitation which conflicts with the higher self-consciousness is indubitably the act of an individual, and every individual's sin necessarily has its source in the perpetrator.[37]

The theologian saw this dichotomy, which occurs universally, as those forms of sin described by the teaching of the church as "original sin" and "actual sin."

> Thus under one head the state of sin is considered as something received, something we bring with us, prior to any act of our own, yet something in which our own guilt is latent; under the other, it is set forth as becoming apparent in the sinful acts which are due to the individual himself, but in which the received element brought with us is revealed.[38]

But he did not care much for either term. The latter term

depicts the real act of sin, but the qualifying adjective "actual" suggests that original sin is not real, a misleading idea. In the former term, the qualifier "original" correctly explains the bond of later generations with earlier ones, but the noun "sin" is misleading, for it is evidently being used in a sense similar to that of the other expression. Original sin, however, is a prior condition to all actual sins.[39]

Schleiermacher defined original sin as "the sinfulness that is present in an individual prior to any action of his own, and has its ground outside his own being, [and] is in every case a complete incapacity for good, which can be removed only by the influence of Redemption."[40]

Original sin always issues in actual sin. It may not be evident, but it is always present internally. Schleiermacher saw original sin as "the corporate act and the corporate guilt of the human race."[41] Bernard Ramm observes that

> historically the church has tied the transmission of sin into the fact that all humans derive from the same biological stock even though sin is not to be defined biologically. Schleiermacher breaks with that tradition and interprets the transmission of sin in terms of its social dimensions among people.[42]

All sins are interrelated. An individual's sins ultimately affect the world, which in turn affects the individual.[43]

The remedy for sin

Schleiermacher noted that almost all religions in the world seek through sacrifices, penances, and the like to rid human beings of the misery of sin. Whether these rituals are intended to avert punishment or relieve guilt, they obviously fail to bring peace of mind. Such things simply serve to highlight the need for human redemption.[44]

Jesus is the supreme Redeemer because of His absolute God-consciousness, which never came into conflict with His second stage of consciousness. Jesus was totally passive in His humanity, allowing God to be totally active in Him. That Jesus was wholly passive — that is, absolutely dependent — is evidence of His

sinless perfection. As human beings are passive in relation to
Him, God works through Him to bring them redemption. They
become unconscious of their own life and utterly conscious of
God. As transformed persons they become part of a new creation
and so return to original perfection. Evil is no longer punishment
for sin, but an occasion for ethical activity in the world.[45]

The Social Dimensions of Sin

Schleiermacher moved the concept of original sin away from the
biological unity of humanity to the social sameness of humans.
Out of this view grew a theology of societal sin which stressed
the corporate or collective nature of sin. The emphasis of the
advocates of this idea was as much ethical as theological.

Albrecht Ritschl and the kingdom of sin

Ritschl (1822–1889) was a German theologian who rejected the
Hegelian interpretation of Christianity which he had been taught
at the University of Halle. He believed that Christian doctrine
could never be found by intellectual speculation. Since religion is
fundamentally practical, its locus is not metaphysical knowledge,
but moral value.

Ritschl was both attracted and repelled by Schleiermacher's
theology. He detested the mysticism in the latter's doctrine; he
liked the teleological view of Christianity and the emphasis on
"fellowship" in religion. He saw his own theology as a corrective
to Schleiermacher's. In fact, he confessed, "He is, in respect of
method, my predecessor; I have learned my method partly from
him. . . ."[46]

The general tenets of Ritschl's theology may be found in his
major work *The Christian Doctrine of Justification and Reconciliation,* which was published starting in 1870. In it he contended
that Christianity is like an ellipse with two foci, redemption and
the kingdom of God. These two are so closely related as to be
inseparable. Some theologians have tried to describe the former
as foundational to theology, and the latter to ethics. But they are
mistaken, for each one can properly be understood only when
seen in its proper relation to the other.[47]

Ritschl saw sin as a "value notion" which could be fully known only in the context of the Christian community and over against its antitheses such as the kingdom of God and the Christian style of life as evidenced in the life of Christ. David Mueller tells us that

> such a position allows for an extra-Biblical awareness of sin when measured in the light of the good or the moral law, and a still deeper knowledge thereof in the light of the law of the Old Testament. Yet attempts to comprehend the meaning of sin along avenues that bypass the knowledge of sin that derives from the Christian apprehension of the norms just enumerated are . . . unable to establish a true apprehension of the essence of sin.[48]

First and foremost, declared Ritschl, sin is a fracturing of the human relationship with God, which ultimately shows itself in sinful behaviors. He broke with Augustine's idea of sin as concupiscence, insisting that it was the failure to maintain the original, harmonious relationship Adam and Eve enjoyed with God.[49]

He also rejected the Augustinian concept of original or inherited sin. Sin, he suggested, originates in the will and consists only of acts of the will. Infants are not brought into the world in a sinful state, and the universality of sin among human beings is the result of ignorance. He did admit, however, that sinful behavior reacts against the will producing it, and creates a propensity to sin, ultimately a habit from which issue additional sins.[50]

Ritschl further saw sin as opposite to the *summum bonum* elaborated in the kingdom of God.

> Now sin is the opposite of the good, so far as it is selfishness springing from indifference or mistrust of God, and directs itself to goods of subordinate rank without keeping in view their subordination to the highest good. It does not negate the good as such; but, in traversing the proper relation of goods to the good, it issues in practical contradiction to the good.[51]

He taught that there was a corporate kingdom of sin paralleling the kingdom of good. Such an idea naturally comes to light as one progresses from a consciousness of personal sin to one of corporate sin. Sin, he maintained, must be seen as the selfish behavior of all humanity because each person is in illimitable action with all others. This kingdom of sin is a pejorative influence, motivating human beings to sin. "The fact of universal sin on the part of man is established, in accordance with experience, by the fact that the impulse to the unrestrained exercise of freedom, with which everyone comes into the world, meets the manifold attractions to self-seeking, which arise out of the sin of society."[52]

Forgiveness of sins for Ritschl meant the removal of the penalty of separation from God. But this does not mean that Christ became the expiation for our sins. Rather, the consciousness of guilt for failing the moral destiny appointed for us by God no longer has power to alienate us from God.[53] Thus, we are reconciled to Him.

Reconciliation brings a new relationship to God. It is, like sin, both individualistic and corporate, corporate because it derives from the faith community and is oriented toward the kingdom of God. One must not consider the kingdom an eschatological affair; it is the new order established by Jesus, a corporate state of life dominated by the Holy Spirit where human beings exist in loving, mutual, unselfish service.[54]

Walter Rauschenbusch and the Social Gospel

The Social Gospel did not begin with Rauschenbusch (1861–1918), but he is recognized as its primary advocate. Trained in theology in the liberal schools of Germany, Rauschenbusch spent eleven years as pastor of a German Baptist church in New York City's Hell's Kitchen area. Here he came to the realization that the troubles of the world were not caused by the personal sins of individuals so much as by societal and institutional sins. His theological reaction—and efforts to combat—these evils were set forth in his book *A Theology for the Social Gospel* (1917).

The Social Gospel for Rauschenbusch was an expanded and intensified gospel of salvation. He complained that while the individualistic gospel had allowed people to realize the sinfulness of every human heart and the efficacy of faith in bringing the grace and power of God to save all who seek Him, it had failed to deliver a reasonable understanding of the fallenness of the social order and its participation in the sins of all those within it. Nor has it inspired confidence in God's desire and ability to redeem institutions from their inherited guilt of oppression. "The social gospel seeks to bring men under repentance for their collective sins and to create a more sensitive and more modern conscience."[55]

The Social Gospel, Rauschenbusch contended, is nothing novel in theology, nor is it alien to Christian belief. It is an integral aspect of the Christian faith in salvation from sin and evil. As one matures in belief, one begins to look beyond individual sins to how they relate to the social groups with which one is involved. Indeed, the Social Gospel is the oldest gospel of all, for it is inextricably linked with the kingdom of God as proclaimed by Jesus and John the Baptist. It looks forward to an earthly social order ruled by Christ.[56]

Rauschenbusch accepted both the theory of evolution and the documentary hypothesis as expounded in his day, and accordingly he rejected the traditional doctrine of the Fall. The original object of the Genesis account, he asserted, was not to explain the entry of sin into the world, but rather the entry of death and evil. It played virtually no role in the work of the prophets who were very much aware of sin. It was not until post-biblical Judaism that any great interest in Adam's fall was shown. Only Paul made any serious use of Adam's transgression. But it was the patristic theologians who built up the story of Genesis until it came to signify what it does today.[57]

The Social Gospel has "no motive to be interested in a doctrine which diverts attention from the active factors of sin which can be influenced, and concentrates attention on a past event which no effort of ours can influence."[58] The Augustinian teaching of inherited sin has made the catastrophe of the Fall so overwhelming that any inheritance of sin since seems minimal. Thus, present-day theology has had virtually nothing to say about the contributions of contemporary people to the wretchedness of humankind. The Social Gospel prefers to deal with modern developments of evil, such as sexual vice, graft, war, and despotism. "It is hard to see how the thought of Adam and Eve can very directly influence young men and women who are to be the ancestors of new generations."[59] As far as Rauschenbusch was concerned, the biblical account of Adam's transgression cannot bear "the tremendous weight which the theological system of the past has put upon it."[60]

Rauschenbusch was able to agree with the theological definition of sin as selfishness, for it supplied a solid foundation for a social idea of sin and salvation. He did feel, however, that the Social Gospel would go a long way to socialize and vitalize the doctrine.[61]

Contrary to most theologians, he rejected the concept that sin is only against God. He wrote:

Sin is not a private transaction between the sinner and God. Humanity always crowds the audience-room when God holds court. . . . We love and serve God when we love and serve our fellows, whom he loves and in whom he lives. We rebel against God and repudiate his will when we set our profit and ambition above the welfare of our fellows and above the Kingdom of God which binds them together.[62]

The ultimate example of sin may be seen, not in a person who blasphemes or denies the Trinity, but in social groups who have stolen the inheritance of the common people for their own private gains, those who have trampled on the rights of others. "When we find such in history, or in present-day life, we shall know we have struck real rebellion against God on the higher levels of sins."[63]

Rauschenbusch scored the Christian church and its theologians for what he saw as their failure to preserve the biblical doctrine of the kingdom of God. By losing sight of the kingdom, theology also lost its understanding of organized sin and, as a consequence, the power to teach humanity about the subject. "Theology has not been a faithful steward of the truth entrusted to it. The social gospel is its accusing conscience."[64]

How is sin passed on from one generation to the next? While Rauschenbusch rejected the theology of the Fall, he defended the doctrine of original sin because it depicted the human race as united through all the centuries by origin and blood. "Depravity of will and corruption of nature are transmitted wherever life itself is transmitted."[65] He believed that there was scientific corroboration for the biological transmission of evil from parent to child.

The problem with original sin, he felt, was that the doctrine had been overworked. The "old theology" sought to involve all of us in Adam's guilt along with the corruption of his nature and his condemnation to death. By so doing it has trivialized each person's own sins and made them appear irrelevant. Rauschenbusch refused to accept the idea that the will had been corrupted by and enslaved to sin by Adam's transgression.

> If our will is so completely depraved, where do we get the freedom on which alone responsibility can be based? If a child is by nature set on evil, hostile to God, and a child of the devil, what is the use of education? For education presupposes an appetite for good which only needs awakening, direction, and spiritual support.[66]

In addition to the biological transmission of sin, Rauschenbusch posited a transmission via social tradition. He found this latter mode of equal importance to the former. And it is much more liable to religious domination. He cited as examples of social tradition evils and crimes such as alcoholism, drugs, sexual deviation, and blood feuds; all of these are socialized, not inherited. It is clearly evident that sin is embedded in social customs and institutions, and is passed on to the individual by his/her social group. "A theology for the social gospel would have to say that original sin runs down the generations not only by biological propagation but also by social assimilation."[67]

While Rauschenbusch preached against a "kingdom of evil" which stands over against the kingdom of God, he did not hold to the existence of literal demons or of Satan. "Popular superstition, systematized and reinforced by theology . . . built up an overwhelming impression of the power of evil."[68] Not even the Reformation applied a corrective; it was left up to the dawn of modern science to save humankind from a distorted theology.[69] His modern kingdom of evil replaced a demonic kingdom of Satan. He acknowledged a debt to Schleiermacher and Ritschl for this solidaristic concept of sin.[70]

The remedy for sin was found in Jesus Christ. Just as Rauschenbusch's emphasis on the doctrine of sin was corporate rather than individualistic, so was his emphasis on salvation. Individual redemption occurs as the result of repentance. Even so, the redemption of institutions and organizations must be the result of conversion; this is accomplished by giving up power in

4.2: THE MAJOR FIGURES OF LATTER PROTESTANTISM

John Wesley   1703–1791
Works

Humans were created free, but used their freedom to disobey God, losing His image and dying spiritually.

Adam was representative of all humanity and his sin was imputed to all his posterity.

Humans remain free to reject or accept God both prior to and after conversion.

They may attain to a level of sinless perfection in Christ.

Friedrich Schleiermacher   1768–1834
On Religion: Speeches to Its Cultured Despisers
The Christian Faith

Sin is that which interferes with God-consciousness. It is the result of our self consciousness conflicting with God-consciousness.

Every individual's sin has its source in the perpetrator.

All sins are related.

Each person's sin affects the world and the world's sin affects the individual.

Victory over sin comes through absolute dependence on God.

Albrecht Ritschl   1822–1889
The Christian Doctrine of Justification and Reconciliation
Theology and Metaphysics

Sin is the fracturing of the human relationship with God.

He rejected original or inherited sin.

He saw a corporate kingdom of sin paralleling the kingdom of God.

Forgiveness is God's removal of the alienation of sin.

Søren Kierkegaard   *1813–1855*
The Concept of Dread
Either — Or

Genesis 3 not literal, but an existential cross section of the primal act of sinning.

Original state of humanity was ignorance. In sinning Adam became spiritual.

Sin comes about through a voluntary "leap" into evil.

It is alienation from God. While all humans share in a universal guilt, each is responsible for his own sin.

Forgiveness comes as a result of a "leap" into faith.

Walter Rauschenbusch   *1861–1917*
A Theology for the Social Gospel

Adam's sin affected only himself (although it acted as a bad example).

Sin is basically selfishness.

Sin is not biologically, but socially, transmitted.

He saw a "kingdom of evil" set over against the kingdom of God, but held Satan and demons to be superstition.

Both individuals and institutions must be converted to Christ.

Paul Tillich   *1886–1965*
Systematic Theology

Sin is existential estrangement of a person from the "Ground of his being" (i.e., God).

Genesis 3 is a symbol for the human predicament and should not be taken literally.

He rejected any concept of original sin.

In Christ estrangement from God may be conquered. Christ is the Bearer of the "New Being" who is reconciled to God.

Karl Barth   *1886–1968*
Epistle to the Romans
Church Dogmatics

Genesis 3 is "saga," not literal history.

Adam did not pass any "disease" of sin to his progeny. At best he is "first among equals."

Every person sins on his own.

Jesus is the perfect "first among equals" of whom Adam is the negative side.

All human beings have become elect (saved) in Jesus just as they were lost in Adam.

Emil Brunner   *1889–1966*
Dogmatics

Genesis 3 is myth and must be applied to the contemporary situation.

Sin can be understood only in the light of Christ's redemption.

Sin is apostasy or rebellion, an open defiance of God.

Sin is universal and evil is contagious.

He held to the universality of sin, but not to a biological transmission through Adam.

There is a devil, but the cross of Christ marks his defeat.

Christ is the key to victory over sin.

Reinhold Niebuhr   *1892–1971*
The Nature and Destiny of Man

Genesis 3 is myth, teaching that evil is extrinsic to humanity.

The combination of human finiteness and freedom leads to anxiety which, in turn, may lead to sin.

Sin is primarily pride or self-love.

The Augustinian concept of original sin is a logical absurdity.

The solution to sin (pride) is in the *agape* of the cross.

favor of honest service. By so doing, these groups move out of the kingdom of evil and into the kingdom of God.[71]

Conclusions

Both Ritschl and Rauschenbusch, influenced by Friedrich Schleiermacher's teaching on the social dimensions of evil, advanced the theology of sin by moving beyond an individualistic notion of sin to a corporate concept. Both depicted a kingdom of evil standing over against the kingdom of God. What was suggested by Ritschl was delineated by Rauschenbusch. The former noted that selfish behavior is not confined just to individuals but extends to whole societies; the latter delved deep into an understanding of the nature and structure of organized corporate sin. Both argued, however, that movement away from the evil kingdom to the heavenly one is accomplished by reconciliation to God through the agency of Jesus Christ.

The Existential View of Sin

Schleiermacher's emphasis on original sin in connection with the social unity of humankind led to the formulation of a theology of corporate or institutional sin by the advocates of the Social Gospel. Interestingly, his influence led in the opposite direction, as well, back to an emphasis by existentialism on the individual. We shall examine that school's view of sin as represented by Søren Kierkegaard and Paul Tillich.

Kierkegaard, father of existentialism

Søren Kierkegaard (1813–1855) was a Danish Lutheran philosopher and theologian who stressed the need for a deeper relationship with God based on personal decision rather than abstract reasoning.[72] His family context and upbringing undoubtedly played a significant part in the way he related to God. His father, Michael, was tormented by the belief that he was damned forever because—as a cold and hungry child—he had cursed God. Michael also believed that his offspring were doomed because he had married Søren's mother, his housekeeper, shortly after his first wife's death, out of necessity. Søren shared in the family sense of doom, and it made him despairing and melancholic. He fell in love with and became engaged to Regine Olsen, only to conclude that he would cause her to suffer, and so he broke the engagement.[73]

Kierkegaard had a problem with Genesis 3 as a literal account of the Fall. He felt that such a literal interpretation moved Adam beyond the context of human history. Our first parent is portrayed in a sinless condition in Eden. Upon transgressing he fell into depravity. But such a portrait is not representative of any other human beings, for none have commenced life or sinning in such a fashion. Ramm tells us that Kierkegaard insisted that

> Adam must be put back into history. This is done by understanding Gen. 3 not as a myth nor as literal history but as an existential cross section of the primal act of sinning. This is not a superficial rerun of the old maxim that we are each our own Adam, but a profound existential analysis as to why as a matter of fact and necessity we do sin.[74]

In his work *The Concept of Dread,* Kierkegaard asserted that the original state of humankind was ignorance, not knowing good from evil. Adam was seemingly pre-human in this state, for he was composed only of soul and body but lacked spirit. It was in transgressing that he became spiritual. As spirit, he became pulled between the finite and the infinite, and was filled with anxiety and dread, both seeking God and drawn to the world.[75]

Sin—whether in Adam or in modern human beings—is effected by a free and voluntary "leap" into evil. This state, while incurring ethical guilt, is not sin unless and until it results in a rejection of eternal responsibility. Such denial brings sin and total alienation from God. And Adam is representative of all humans in that all lose their innocence by personal guilt in their own plunge into sin. Kierkegaard emphatically denied that Adam caused his posterity to sin.[76]

At the same time, while every human being is liable for his own behavior, Adam did leave a legacy for all. "What is received from Adam is dread, spirit, sexuality, knowledge of good and evil, and oneness with the human race."[77] While he recognized that all human beings share in a universal guilt, he was intent on stressing the personal responsibility of every individual.

110

Dread may not only lead into sin, but also to repentance and faith. Faith overcomes sin. Faith is a direct relationship with the Absolute. When a person "leaps" or plunges faithward, the faith received—and the accompanying knowledge of divine forgiveness—brings victory over despair.[78]

Paul Tillich, radical existentialist

Tillich (1886–1965), the son of a German Lutheran pastor, received his doctorate from the University of Breslau and, after teaching positions at Berlin, Marburg, Dresden, and Leipzig, became Professor of Philosophy in 1929 at Frankfurt. As National Socialism became increasingly prominent, Tillich's open antagonism to Adolf Hitler forced him to leave Germany. In 1933 he accepted an offer from Union Theological Seminary in New York to become Professor of Philosophical Theology, where he taught until his retirement in 1955. From there he went to Harvard and, in 1962, to the University of Chicago.[79] A prolific writer, his theology is contained in his three volume *Systematic Theology,* begun in 1951.

Tillich's theological approach was termed the "method of correlation." He held that philosophy and theology should be mutually complementary. Philosophy should pose questions of "ultimate concern" (humanity's ultimate concern is what commands its total commitment); theology dialogues with philosophy, understands the questions posed, and formulates satisfactory responses.[80]

There has been some debate as to Tillich's theological position, some scholars associating him with Schleiermacher and some with Bultmann. Alexander McKelway alleges that

generally, Tillich may be called an existentialist insofar as his system of thought begins with the supposition that being can only be understood in the light of an analysis of man's existence. But Tillich must be distinguished from the mainstream of existentialism, because he proceeds from an analysis of existence to essence. . . . There is no doubt, however, that Tillich's thought is close to existentialism. . . .[81]

In his magnum opus, Tillich referred to God as the Ground of

Being, "the name for that which concerns man ultimately."[82] God is "Being-itself, in which we participate by the very fact of existing."[83] In actual fact, the term "God," according to Tillichian thought is really only a symbol of the Abyss, or the Other, the most universal concept.

Tillich believed that sin is a matter of existential estrangement of a person "from the ground of his being, from other beings, and from himself."[84] As a result, humans are hostile to God. And yet, it is this very hostility that demonstrates the relationship between God and humankind. "Man's hostility to God proves indisputably that he belongs to him. Where there is the possibility of hate, there and there alone is the possibility of love."[85]

While estrangement is not a biblical word, it is suggested throughout the Bible, said Tillich. It is implied in the Genesis account of the Fall, in the account of Cain's murder of Abel, and in the diatribe of the prophets against those who turn to idols. It is also implied in Paul's accusation that humans have perverted God's image into that of idols.[86]

At the same time, Tillich did not hold estrangement and sin to be synonymous. The church has used sin, for the most part, in the plural, as deviations from the moral law. Such connotations have little to do with the idea of estrangement from God.

> Nevertheless, the word "sin" cannot be overlooked. It expresses what is not implied in the term "estrangement," namely, the personal act of turning away from that to which one belongs. Sin expresses more sharply the personal character of estrangement over against its tragic side. . . . Man's predicament is estrangement, but his estrangement is sin. It is not a state of things . . . but a matter of both personal freedom and universal responsibility.[87]

Like Kierkegaard, Tillich determined the Fall to be "a symbol for the human situation universally, not as the story of an event that happened 'once upon a time.' "[88] He found a literal interpretation of Genesis 3 an absurdity which removed from the account the symbolism of every person's individual action that actualizes the universal fact of estrangement: "the combination of man's estrangement with a completely free act by Adam is inconsistent as well as literally absurd. It exempts a human individual from the universal human character by ascribing freedom to him without destiny. . . ."[89] The freedom humans have to choose sin (when they exercise it) results in self-loss, "the loss of one's determining center, the disintegration of the unity of the person."[90]

To speak, therefore, of "Adam before the Fall" is not to speak of an actual state, but a state of potentiality. The actual state is the present state in which persons find themselves; nor has it ever been otherwise. "The notion of a moment in time in which man and nature were changed from good to evil is absurd, and it has no foundation in experience or revelation."[91]

Tillich, then, rejected the Augustinian concept of original sin as "too simple to be true,"[92] for it omits the tragic element in the human predicament. Human beings exist (and always have existed) in a state of estrangement from the Ground of their Being. Actualized creation and estranged existence are synonymous. While creation is good in its basic character, when it is actualized, it declines into universal estrangement as the result of freedom and destiny.[93]

In Jesus Christ, declared Tillich, the human estrangement from the Ground of Being may be conquered. Christ is the symbol of "New Being," "a reality in which the self-estrangement of our existence is overcome, a reality of reconciliation and reunion."[94] He is the Bearer of the New Being. Salvation is healing, the reunion of what is estranged, the overcoming of the split which exists between humankind and God. It is "the fulfillment of the ultimate meaning of one's existence."[95]

Neo-orthodoxy on Sin

Existentialism invested orthodox Christian terminology with new meaning. Its transformation of the doctrines of sin and salvation into psychological symbols removed it a substantial distance from traditional theology.

Like existentialism, neo-orthodoxy sought to renew orthodox Christian belief. It wanted to keep traditional doctrines while making the faith more relevant and believable for contemporary humans. The result was a considerably different emphasis on the doctrine of sin, more after the image of Søren Kierkegaard than that of orthodox Christianity.

Karl Barth, father of the movement

Born in Basel, Switzerland, Karl Barth (1886–1968) embraced liberal theology in his early twenties. As a young pastor caught up in the chaos of World War I, he discovered that his training had not prepared him to minister effectively to people seeking solutions. In his frustration he turned to the Bible and found in it the help he had sought. Paul's Epistle to the Romans revolutionized his preaching and his theology. His commentary on Romans was a great success and led to his appointment as a professor at Gottingen in 1921. In 1935 he was expelled from Germany because of his outspoken opposition to Adolf Hitler and Nazism. Returning to his native land, he began a long and distinguished career at the University of Basel.[96]

Although he never acknowledged the debt, Barth owed much to Kierkegaard for his view of Genesis 3. The account of Adam and Eve, Barth declared, must never be taken as literal historical fact. It is not history, but saga.

> We miss the unprecedented and incomparable thing which the Genesis passages tell us of the coming into being and existence of Adam if we try to read and understand it as history, relating it either favorably or unfavorably to scientific paleontology. . . . The saga as a form of historical narrative is a *genre* apart. . . . [It] is the form which, using intuition and imagination, has to take up historical narration at the point where events are no longer susceptible as such of historical proof.[97]

Adam came into being in this sphere of saga.

Like Kierkegaard, Barth understood Adam to be an existential symbol for every person. Adam is that name given by God to the whole of world history. The scene in Eden is reenacted by every human being. "There never was a golden age. There is no point in looking back to one. The first man was immediately the first sinner."[98]

Barth did not feel that any special blame should be laid at Adam's door. At best he is *primus inter pares* ("first among equals"). He did not pass onto us any disease. We are not irresistibly overthrown because of his transgression. If we are Adam, we are so on our own responsibility and of our own volition.[99] "Adam is not a fate which God has suspended over us. Adam is the truth concerning us as it is known to God and told to us. . . . It is God who establishes it. . . . It is God's Word which fuses all men into unity with this man as *primus inter pares.*"[100]

Barth pointed to Romans 5:12ff as evidence that Paul understood Adam as representative of all of sinful humanity. But he pointed out another Representative of humankind. He was not, however, "the *primus inter pares* in a sequence. He represented them as a genuine leader, making atonement by His obedience, covering their disobedience, justifying them before God."[101] In fact, Barth declared, Jesus is the original and true Adam, of whom the Genesis Adam is the negative side. Because of what He has done, all humans have become elect in Him.[102]

Barth believed in double predestination, not surprising considering his Reformed background. But predestination for him did not mean that some people have been elected to be saved and others to be damned. Rather, it refers to Christ who signifies both God's election and rejection of humankind. Barth argued that the fate endured by Christ mirrors the inner-Trinitarian process by which the Father elected the Son, and through Him, all humankind. Through that same process He also rejected Christ and allowed Him to endure the cross so that He might be exalted in and through the Resurrection. Predestination, then, originated in the mind of God; it is a demonstration that all human beings are qualified for salvation, while God the Son takes upon Himself all the punishment for sin.[103]

Emil Brunner, crisis theologian

Emil Brunner (1889–1966), virtually the cofounder of neo-orthodoxy, was born in Switzerland and educated at Zurich, Berlin, and Union Seminary in New York. In 1924 he became professor of theology at Zurich.

Because he was more widely accepted among British and North American theologians than was Barth, English speakers came to understand neo-orthodoxy primarily as rendered by Brunner. He became first known in Anglo-American circles for his "crisis theology." When God in Christ confronts human beings, a crisis or turning point occurs as one realizes the possibility of two divergent paths, one leading toward God and life, the other leading away from God into death.[104]

Brunner, like Barth, had turned away from both liberalism and traditional orthodox theology to construct upon a Kierkegaardian foundation a "new orthodoxy." His belief system was set forth in his magnum opus, the three-volume *Dogmatics,* finished shortly before his death.[105]

Emil Brunner chastised those who would try to defend the historicity of the Genesis story of Adam and Eve as "quixotic and reactionary."[106] Modern science has clearly proved the evolutionary development of humans from lower life forms. At what point the actual "humanization" took place, we do not know. But as human, humanity is wholly new, over against the whole of nature. Since the Genesis account is a mythical one, the Fall must be brought to contemporary humankind apart from an historical "Adam in Paradise."[107]

Sin can be understood, contended Brunner, only "in the light of the Christian revelation, which effects the transition from the state of 'being a sinner' to that of 'being redeemed.' "[108] The focus of that light must be on the sinner in need of redemption, not on the justified sinner.

Sin, biblically defined, is apostasy or rebellion, "the break with that which God had given and established."[109] It is forsaking Him. It is an open defiance of Him, a breach in communion with Him. "The story of the Fall reveals the fundamental cause for this breach in communion; the desire to be 'as God.' Man wants to be on a level with God, and in so doing to become independent of Him."[110]

When one looks at sin as the attempt to achieve autonomy, a decisive act is implied, one which determines the totality of existence. Since sin involves the whole person, and the symbol of the whole personality is the heart, therefore sin originates in the heart. The entire person rebels against God; included in this rebellion is his whole ego, every individual power of his mind and body are mobilized against God.[111]

The world at large, Brunner confessed, declares sin to be universal. Experience demonstrates that evil is contagious, moving from one person to another until it has infected all of society. It also spreads to institutions and environments, and moves from these to "reinfect" individuals. A collective evil emerges, which assumes demonic proportions. Brunner acknowledged his debt to Albrecht Ritschl's concept of a "kingdom of evil."[112]

Thus, there exists a duality of sin. The Christian revelation demonstrates that every individual is confronted by God. At the same time, before God all humans become one in Christ, and so we become aware of the universality of sin. "Before Christ we are one indivisible humanity. The act of rebellion which I see in Christ as my sin, I see there as the identical act of all."[113]

Following Kierkegaard, Brunner believed that, even though every individual is created a separate and distinct person, God made all with the same divine destiny. As a result, the action of one person affects all.

> We can go further, and say that the destiny for which each of us was created includes as its τέλος [ultimate end] the fellowship of all — each of us is destined for the Kingdom of God, not only for an individual divine Telos — and, therefore, the fact that I am a sinner concerns everyone else.[114]

While Brunner was sympathetic to Augustine's aim in formulating the doctrine of original sin (namely, the demonstration of sin as a dominant force and the solidarity of human guilt), he nonetheless considered the latter's emphasis on the transmission of sin through sexual procreation to be a perversion of the biblical teaching on that subject. He noted Augustine's misinterpretation of Romans 5:12ff and contended that, while Paul stresses the solidarity of human sin, he does not discuss how this Adamic "unity" originated. Nor does he even mention a biological transmission of sin from Adam to his posterity. Bad qualities may be inherited (along with good ones) from our parents, but sin — that is, abandonment of, or alienation from, God — cannot.[115]

If human beings inherited sin biologically, then it could rightly be said that human beings are sinners in the same way as we say that they are mammals. God has made them that way and they cannot help it. But when we say "man is a sinner" then we say the exact opposite: God did not make man so; man can help it, indeed this is his great, and his only guilt. . . . Sin and guilt are co-extensive."[116] Tragically, once one sins, one falls under the power of sin and no longer is able to move back into innocence. Since sin alienates one from God, and since one cannot forgive one's own sin, communion with God is gone. Not only has the sinner lost this vital personal connection, but he has also irretrievably lost existence as God intended it to be. "This is what the doctrine of Original Sin really means . . . that the *peccatum* [sin] involves the *non posse non peccare* [not able not to sin]."[117]

In rebelling against God, Brunner maintained, the sinner is fighting his own nature as God created it. Sin is not only a matter of being alienated from God, but also of existing in self-alienation. The whole orientation of human life becomes misdirected. Instead of craving God, the sinner craves the pleasures of this world. "Since, however, even as sinner man does not cease to be destined for God, sin manifests itself as a perpetual state of conflict, in which man oscillates between the desire to escape from God and the longing for him. . . ."[118] This conflict is demonstrated both in Kierkegaardian despair of the soul and in Augustinian restlessness of the heart. It is further evidenced in the "bad conscience," or a sense of guilt.

The consequence of human sin is death; not simple mortality, but an immediate death of fear and agony. Brunner cites Paul's use of the Greek word *thanatos* (death) to include "another element, namely, the fact that sin is a destructive force, an element of disintegration, in the whole of human life."[119] It is something that manifests itself in psychological and physiological suffering. It is a poison which infects institutions and society.

In reflecting on the possibility of a doctrine of supernatural beings other than God (i.e., angels, demons, Satan), Brunner admitted some difficulties. Since he refused the doctrine of the verbal inspiration of Scripture, he held ultimate authority to be not what the Bible says, but rather its relation to God's purposes as revealed in Christ Jesus. Since the Bible says relatively little about such beings, one cannot really formulate a doctrine of spirits without going beyond biblical teaching. And he questioned the existence of benevolent angels, for they "are only mentioned as it were on the outskirts of Biblical truth." Much teaching on Satan and demons he blamed on medieval mythology.

At the same time, Brunner conceded that "what the Bible has to say about Satan has a direct connection with the heart of biblical revelation."[121] Both Jesus and Paul speak of Satan, or the power of darkness. Furthermore, "the devil is partly a psychological and partly a sociological reality."[122] Nor can one envision the advent of Christ who came to save us from the works of the devil apart from the context of satanic power.[123]

Brunner's conclusion was that there is indeed a power of darkness. It is a superhuman force which militates against humankind. But the most important thing to realize about the devil is that Christ has vanquished him. The cross marks his defeat and is a continuing sign of the One who conquered him. Christ is the key to victory, whether over the external evil of Satan or the internal sin which alienates a human being from God.

Reinhold Niebuhr and ethical neo-orthodoxy

Reinhold Niebuhr (1892–1971), born in Missouri to a German Lutheran pastor and his wife, is generally regarded as the premier American neo-orthodox theologian. Upon graduation from Yale University, he had an experience similar to Walter Rauschenbusch's as he served a pastorate among the lower working class in Detroit. The liberal theological training he had received was ineffective in alleviating the pain of his people. As a result, he became heavily involved in social and political activism. In 1928, Union Seminary of New York appointed him professor of Christian Ethics; there he developed and promoted "realistic" theology.[124] Niebuhr's theology was set forth in his two-volume *The Nature and Destiny of Man,* the first volume of which contains a clearly delineated doctrine of sin and the Fall.

Like his neo-orthodox peers, Niebuhr eschewed a literal interpretation of Genesis 1–3, holding it to be myth. It teaches that, while sin is not the consequence of any element intrinsic to the human situation, humankind was tempted by an external principle of evil. "Man is tempted . . . to break and transcend the limits which God has set for him. The temptation thus lies in his situation of finiteness and freedom."[125] This situation arises from the contradiction of humanity's being both part of nature and part of the spiritual realm beyond nature.

Niebuhr was much more definite in his belief in Satan than was Brunner. Christians, he maintained, have correctly identified the serpent of Genesis 3 with the devil. "To believe that there is a devil is to believe that there is a principle or force of evil antecedent to any evil human action."[126] The biblical doctrine of Satan holds a twofold importance: (1) he was not created evil, but fell as the result of an act of rebellion against God; (2) Satan's fall occurred before that of Adam and Eve; thus, the human transgression is not an act of total perversity, nor does it unalterably occur as a result of the situation of finiteness and freedom in which humans are positioned. Such a situation "becomes a source of temptation only when it is falsely interpreted. This false interpretation . . . is suggested to man by a force of evil which precedes his own sin."[127]

The human situation arouses within all human beings a deep anxiety, which is at the same time both the inner precondition of sin and the factor underlying all human creativity. Humans are anxious because their lives are limited, but yet they are aware of these limitations. Nor do they know the limits of their possibilities. No matter what they achieve, higher possibilities lie beyond. "There is therefore no limit of achievement in any sphere of activity in which human history can rest with equanimity."[128]

The primary sin, the Bible teaches, is pride or self-love. Niebuhr's concern was to relate this idea of sin to observable human behavior. He categorized pride into three types, which are nonetheless interrelated: pride of power, pride of knowledge, and pride of virtue.[129]

The pride of power comes in various forms. There is that pride in which the ego fails to realize how dependent and frail is human life and so believes that it has control of its own existence and destiny. And yet, it does not feel completely secure and so lusts for power in an effort to attain that security. There is, as well, that pride of power spurred by greed. Our own culture is immersed in the continual attempt to attain total physical comfort as security from the ravages of nature. There is also that will-to-power which "seeks a security beyond the limits of human finiteness and this inordinate ambition arouses fears and enmities which the world of pure nature, with its competing impulses of survival, does not know."[130]

Pride of knowledge often is merged into the pride of power in such a way that the two seem virtually inseparable. Niebuhr saw intellectual pride as being closely related to ignorance of the finiteness of the human mind. He believed it is also related to an effort to rationalize and obfuscate the stain of self-interest on human truth.[131]

This pride has forgotten that it is concerned with a temporal process and believes itself in utter transcendence over history. Many ideologies, for example, claim to have the final word on life. "But the real fact is that all pretensions of final knowledge and ultimate truth are partly prompted by the uneasy feeling that the truth is not final and also by an uneasy conscience which realizes that the interests of the ego are compounded with this truth."[132]

Pride of virtue, or moral pride, is interconnected with intellectual pride. It establishes standards of righteousness to which the self adheres and, at the same time, condemns all others who fail to measure up to them. It is, in fact, a form of self-righteousness. Very often that self confuses its standards with God's. Standards which fail to measure up are judged evil. The terrible sin involved here is that this self believes its relative moral standards to be absolute and therefore denies any need of salvation.

Niebuhr saw spiritual pride as the offspring of moral pride. "The ultimate sin is the religious sin of making the self-deification implied in moral pride explicit. This is done when our partial standards and relative attainments are explicitly related to the unconditioned good, and claim divine sanction."[133] He regarded religious intolerance as a premier form of spiritual pride. When a religious person—whether of Christian or other faith—assumes that, because of the revelation he possesses, he enjoys a higher standing with God than others, then he is guilty of making the forms of that religion an instrument of his pride.[134]

Group pride derives from individual pride, but then proceeds to gain authority over the individual. Too often he bows to the group's demands even when it conflicts with his moral standards.[135] Niebuhr held the prime example of this "collective egotism" to be national states.

He agreed with the orthodox Christian interpretation of the biblical proposition that all human beings are equally sinners in God's sight. But he did not agree that all are equally guilty. "It is important to recognize that Biblical religion has emphasized this inequality of guilt just as much as the equality of sin."[136] It has been especially quick to condemn the rich and powerful who oppress the poor and needy. Nor should that be surprising, for the pride of the powerful or the wealthy is likely to be more productive of evil than that of the less so. Niebuhr makes it clear that when the poor or weak or oppressed gain a social victory over those who have dominated them, they tend to "exhibit the same arrogance and the same will-to-power which they abhorred in their opponents and which they were inclined to regard as a congenital sin of their enemies."[137]

The traditional doctrine of original sin as expounded by Augustine and Calvin was found by Niebuhr to be a logical absurdity. How can original sin, when it is defined as an inevitable corruption, not be viewed as belonging to essential human nature? Is it not absurd to suppose that sin should be regarded as natural in the sense that it is universal but not in the sense that it is necessary? The difficulty of the doctrine of original sin, Niebuhr observed, is its elaboration of free will. Both Calvin and Augustine insisted that human will is enslaved to sin, but at the same time declared the reality of free will in regard to human responsibility.[138]

And yet, while it may seem absurd, the classical Pauline doctrine of original sin serves to throw light upon very complex aspects of human behavior. Niebuhr asserted that one cannot always make a distinction between original sin and actual sin.

> The actual sin follows more inevitably from the bias toward sin than is naturally assumed. On the other hand the bias toward sin is something more than a mere lag of nature or physical impulse or historical circumstance. There is, in other words, less freedom in the actual sin and more responsibility for the bias toward sin (original sin) than moralistic interpretations can understand.[139]

Actual sin flows from the enticement of anxiety in which all of life finds itself. But sin does not originate necessarily from it. The tendency toward sin from which actual sin results is anxiety plus sin. "Or, in the words of Kierkegaard, sin presupposes itself. Man could not be tempted if he had not already sinned."[140]

Why a person sins inevitably but without evading personal responsibility for that sin lies in the human situation itself. Human freedom is the basis of one's creativity while also being one's temptation. Because a person is concerned with the contingencies and necessities of the natural process, but at the same time stands beyond them and realizes their dangers, he becomes anxious. That anxiety causes him to attempt to escape his finiteness and weakness by seeking autonomously to rise above these perils instead of obediently subjecting himself to God's will.[141]

The solution to humanity's anxiety and sin is to be found in the cross. The *agape* of the cross provides a context of meaning in which the self can achieve satisfaction. The cross is particularly significant to victory over sin because it is indissolubly connected to the Resurrection. And the Resurrection attests that "the self in its final freedom transcends the conditions of nature-time and cannot be fulfilled in them."[142] It also attests to the forgiveness of human sin. "The Gospel, in short, both guards the dignity of the self which transcends death and recognizes the misery of the self, which faces the problem of sin, as well as the fact of death."[143] The Resurrection brings forgiveness not only to the individual in his sin, but to the corporate sin, as well.

Conclusions

While retaining certain aspects of the Enlightenment and existentialism, neo-orthodoxy has redirected its doctrine of sin back toward a more orthodox approach, but incorporating into it certain features designed to make it more relevant to contemporary human beings. Its insistence that sin can be understood only in light of the Christian revelation is particularly noteworthy. While initially developed by Karl Barth, this emphasis was expanded by both Brunner and Niebuhr. The definition of sin as rebellion against God also maintained the orthodox connection, and neo-orthodox attempts to explain in a psychological manner how this occurs are helpful. A valuable corrective against much existential teaching is the assertion of the traditional teaching that the solution to sin is to be had in the death and resurrection of Jesus Christ. While not going as far as many conservative Christians would like, neo-orthodoxy was a step back in the right direction.

Some Observations

Latter Protestantism held a multiplicity of views of sin, springing from the theologies of sin which developed out of the Reformation era. Most were predicated on either the Augustinian/Calvinist or Arminian concepts.

John Wesley, while Augustinian in his view of the nature of sin, was firmly Arminian in holding to human free will. Because of original sin, human freedom leads even believers to sin. As the Christian matures in the faith, however, one may come to that point of perfection where he or she will no longer commit sin.

Friedrich Schleiermacher, strongly influenced by pietistic thought, rejected a rationalistic theology in favor of experiential religion (the "religion of the heart"). He maintained that experience should be grounded in one's awareness of absolute dependence. Sin in that which inhibits one's consciousness of relating to God. Schleiermacher's definition of terms was a radical reinterpretation of traditional ones. Original grace he took to mean a predisposition to God-consciousness; original sin was sinfulness inherent in a person prior to any transgression of his own. He tied original sin to the corporate sin and guilt of the entire race.

Ritschl, like Schleiermacher, held to a corporate view of sin. He rejected Augustinian original sin, declaring sin to be an act of the will. He saw a kingdom of evil standing in opposition to the kingdom of God. This kingdom of sin motivates human beings to sinful behaviors.

Rauschenbusch also followed Schleiermacher in propounding social sin. Sin militates not only against God, but against His creatures. By adhering to a view of individual sin, the church has lost sight of organized corporate sin and so the power to teach people about it. He too rejected traditional concepts of original sin, for they made personal sin irrelevant.

Schleiermacher's theology of experience led to the foundation of existentialism by Søren Kierkegaard, and its propagation by latter theologians such as Paul Tillich. Sin is the state of alienation from God, a natural state from birth for all persons. Reconciliation in Christ is the reunion of that estrangement.

Neo-orthodoxy sought to return theology to its orthodox roots, while making it relevant to contemporary humanity. Defining sin biblically, this movement sought to explain its nature and occurrence in psychological terms. Sin is rebellion against God; its detrimental effect may be remedied only through the death and resurrection of Christ.

While neo-orthodoxy was the primary theological development of the first half of the present century, many more would follow in the latter portion. They, like this great predecessor, would attempt to make the theology of sin relevant to contemporary human beings.

Chapter Five
Contemporary Approaches to Sin

The latter part of the twentieth century has spawned a variety of schools of theological thought. The result is a diversity of views of sin, each diverging to a greater or lesser extent from traditional Christian views. In this chapter we shall examine some of the better known theologies in respect to their teaching on sin.

The Theology of Hope

The theology of hope, a product of the late 1960s, is grounded in Albert Schweitzer's eschatology. It seeks to relate faith to history, but stresses that the significance of history can be determined only at its consummation. This system extends beyond the traditional theological limits, merging into the areas of politics, sociology, ethics, and biology. The best known representatives of this futurism include Jürgen Moltmann and Wolfhart Pannenberg.

Jürgen Moltmann

Moltmann (1926–), a German systematic theologian of the Reformed tradition, may be termed the father of the theology of hope. He formulated his ideas in the context of post-war Germany in which capitalism and communism were in open conflict, and he was influenced by both. He presented his Christian doctrine, securely anchored in eschatological hope, in a trilogy: *Theology of Hope* (1955), *The Crucified God* (1974), and *The Church in the Power of the Holy Spirit* (1977).

While Moltmann does not deny that sin is the proud rejection of God in favor of self, he sees it as only one aspect. "The other side of such pride is hopelessness, resignation, inertia, and melancholy. From this arise the *tristesse* and frustration which fill all living things with the seeds of a sweet decay."[1] He points to Revelation 21:8 which places the "fearful" before all other categories of the sinful whose end is eternal death and notes the warning of Hebrews that the horrific sin which threatens the faithful is to fall away from the living hope. "Temptation then consists not so much of the titanic desire to be as God, but in weakness, timidity, weariness, not wanting to be what God requires of us."[2]

These sins of hopelessness, Moltmann contends, are those sins of omission which the Middle Ages termed *tristitia* and counted among those sins against the Holy Spirit which end in death. They take two forms, presumption and despair. "Presumption is a premature, self-willed anticipation of the fulfillment of what we hope for from God," while "despair is the premature, arbitrary anticipation of the non-fulfillment of what we hope for from God."[3] They are both forms of hopelessness, for one impatiently insists on present fulfillment and the other has no hope whatsoever.

Real living takes place only when hope is present. Moltmann says:

> Where in faith and hope we begin to live in the light of the possibilities and promises of this God, the whole fullness of life discloses itself as a life of history and therefore a life to be loved. . . . In love, hope brings all things into the light of the promises of God.[4]

The expectation generated by this hope makes life worthwhile. "That is why it can be said that living without hope is like no longer living."[5] Moltmann sees hell as hopelessness and the abandonment of hope.

Obviously, the solution to the sin of hopelessness is the inges-
tion of hope. Jesus has become hope's embodiment.

> In this crucified Jesus men have again and again been able
> to see themselves in the course of history. . . . They have
> also lost their resignation and given up their well-justified
> despair about themselves, because they have found in his
> solidarity with their misery the humanity of God, and a love
> which takes away from them shame, anxiety, and self-
> accusation.[6]

In this hope and love is found reconciliation, which is the
beginning of redemption in a despairing world. One who has been
reconciled cannot remain satisfied with the world as it is, but
looks ahead in hope to the glorious possibilities held out by God.[7]

Wolfhart Pannenberg

Pannenberg (1928–) was born in Stettin, Germany (now part of
Poland) and, although baptized a Lutheran, spent his younger
days in the company of those outside the church. As a student of
philosophy, however, he studied for a time at Basel under Karl
Barth, which forced him to consider the claims of the Christian
faith and aroused an interest in the historical disciplines, to a
study of which he turned himself in 1951 at Heidelberg. There,
under the tutelage of professors such as Gerhard von Rad and
Gunther Bornkamm, he moved away from Barth's concepts to a
new consideration of the relationship of faith and history.[8]

Like Moltmann, Pannenberg views Christianity from an eschatological perspective. God reveals Himself to human beings
through the events of history. But it is only in the consummation
of history in the future that the real Person and nature of God
will be understood.[9] Pannenberg has been a prolific writer, but
some of his major works include *Jesus — God and Man* (1968),
Theology and the Kingdom of God (1969), *Anthropology in Theological Perspective* (1985), and *Systematic Theology* (1988).

In regard to the root or basis of sin, Pannenberg is Augustinian. Egotism or pride is the center for all sin. "When the ego
which is proud . . . wills itself to be the center and ultimate end,
it usurps the place in the order of the universe that belongs

127

solely to God, its creator and supreme good."[10] Closely related to egotism is concupiscence for, contrary to nature, the perverse will deviates from the higher and better to the lower and poorer. Thus, with Augustine, Pannenberg claims that concupiscence is so closely linked to pride (egotism) that it may be described as sin and the cause of sin.[11]

> The Augustinian presentation of human sinlessness as a corruption of desire has two important advantages that still make it superior to other forms of the Christian doctrine of sin. The first advantage is the empirical orientation of Augustine's psychological description. The other advantage also depends on this psychological approach and has to do with the relevance of sin to the relation of human beings to themselves.[12]

Pannenberg denounces Karl Barth's denial of such a connection between human sinfulness and empirical data in favor of a judgment based on Christian faith. After all, even those who deny Christ are continually confronted in their experience with the brokenness which characterizes human existence. He does agree, however, that only through the eyes of faith is one able to see that perverse behavior is a turning away from God.[13]

Pannenberg also agrees with Augustine that, in their perversity of will, human beings of their own volition reject their own happiness, which can come only from God. He uses this point as a springboard to Kierkegaard's analysis of dread and despair. The latter described the despairing will's attempt to "ground the self in the self instead of in God. The attempt brings despair, because precisely by making it, human beings fall short of their true selfhood."[14] Thus, human beings fail in their relation to themselves.

If one assumes the Augustinian conception of sin as unbridled egotism, then sin would seem to be anchored in the natural aspects of human existence. But Pannenberg argues that, though "human beings are in this sense sinners by nature, this does not mean that their nature as human beings is sinful."[15] He arrives at such a conclusion by observing that it is in the nature of humans to seek to transcend what they are by nature (that is, their natural condition).[16]

But why should egocentricity be regarded as sin in humans and not in other higher animals who are also centrally organized? He answers that human beings have a special character exclusive of the other creatures. Only they know that they are selves. "Only because the destination of human beings is exocentric and finds fulfillment solely in the radical exocentricity proper to them as religious beings can the egocentricity that is analogous in them to animal centrality turn into a failure of their existence, their destination as human beings."[17]

If sin, however, is anchored in the very foundations of human existence, why should we be held accountable for our behavior? The response is that nothing can be sinful which is part of our natural and original condition. The idea of responsibility has always been connected to the idea of volition. Any action which is involuntary can be neither praiseworthy nor blameworthy.[18] But all humans are accountable when they choose as good what is objectively bad for them, when they fail to harmonize their behavior with their destiny, believing a lie in place of the truth. Such a wrong choice is what Luther termed "bondage of the will."

This seemingly inherent structure in all human beings which leads to bondage is, contends Pannenberg, what Christian theology refers to as "original sin."[19] The will's enslavement here

is due to an addiction that is not merely partial but is connected with the egotism of human beings, inasmuch as the ego experiences itself as the center of its world and wills itself to be this center, even though it must then come into inevitable conflict with other such self-appointed centers and, above all, with the one real center of all reality.[20]

Pannenberg makes three observations on original sin (as opposed to sin as act). First, human beings do not become sinners either by choice or imitation; they already are sinners prior to any action. Secondly, sin has a locus far deeper than any individual transgression. Thirdly, the universality of human sin is a presupposition for the universality of human redemption as effected by Christ Jesus.[21]

The Genesis account of Adam and Eve is seen by Pannenberg in a light similar to the neo-orthodox and existential schools. It is a myth which demonstrates the universality of sin. Adam is the Primal Man. He is "the prototype of all human beings, as their embodiment, as the Human Being pure and simple. In every individual, Adam's journey from sin to death is repeated as in a copy."[22]

Pannenberg questions Augustine's use of Adam as the progenitor of sin. He dismisses Augustine's idea of Adam's having biologically transmitted the disease of sin to his posterity. He holds that all sinned in Adam only "to the extent that Adam is regarded not as the historical ancestor of the race but as a mythical prototype and embodiment of the entire race."[23] When one tries to make Adam into the historical ancestor of humankind, then his situation no longer is a paradigm for the human situation because, historically, he would have been in a position categorically different from that of any human being since. In such a case, the individual sin of Adam could hardly be imputed to his descendants. One cannot be held jointly culpable, as though one were a joint cause, for a deed committed by someone else millennia ago and in a circumstance fundamentally unlike one's own. Augustinian original sin, Pannenberg concludes, cannot accomplish its intended purpose.[24]

Nor does he find Protestant efforts to provide a substitute for original sin much more satisfying. He surveys the various alternatives, from the "kingdom of evil" posited by Kant, Schleiermacher, and Ritschl,[25] to the supra-historical mythical Fall of existentialists such as Mueller and Althaus.[26] He feels that Brunner more accurately dealt with the problem of the universality of sin when he observed that before God all humans are one in Christ "and it is the unity of our destiny as revealed in Christ that explains the unity and solidarity of all human beings in Adam."[27] With the aid of God's revelation in Christ, we can look back and see us all as a tightly knit group of humans under the condemnation of death, and we can look forward to see all of us as a group of redeemed persons who share Christ's life; "the universality of redemption presupposes the universality of sin."[28] Pannenberg argues that this universality may be empirically verified in concupiscence. It may be recognized as guilt before God in the light of the human destiny disclosed in Christ.[29] The Adam story of the Genesis narrative is merely an antitype of the unity of human destiny in Jesus Christ.

Summary

Theologians of hope seem to have formulated a doctrine of sin tending toward existentialism more than anything else. Jürgen Moltmann sees hopelessness as a root of sin. It appears in a twofold manner: as presumption, which is the attempt to achieve the promises of God without waiting for Him to act, and as desperation, which is acting in the expectation that God will not act in the future. Wolfhart Pannenberg posits sin as egocentricity. Humans fail to recognize that they are exocentric and so do not achieve the destiny that God has intended for them.

Process Theology

The process movement, a "theology of becoming," came to prominence in the late 1960s. Developed by a group of theologians from the University of Chicago, it built upon the thought of process philosopher Alfred North Whitehead (1861–1947), who held that reality is always in process, and Jesuit paleontologist Pierre Teilhard de Chardin (1881–1955), who taught that all of creation is progressing according to an evolutionary process designed by God. Process theology emphasizes that God both acts upon the world and is acted upon by it. Neither is static. Both are in flux. Both are becoming. It is a theology which attempts to harmonize Christianity with present-day experience and a contemporary scientific worldview.

Daniel Day Williams

Williams (1910–1973), originally one of the University of Chicago theologians who developed process theology, and then a professor of systematic theology at Union Theological Seminary in New York, based his theology of sin on his view of humankind as the image of God. "In the biblical faith man's greatness is understood in the light of the image of God which he bears. If God is love the image of God in man defines the forms of love in human existence."[30] He contended that modern theology has agreed that the *imago dei* is not a set of attributes or qualities humans possess, but rather the relatedness God created between Himself and human beings, and to which they are capable of responding. The best way to express such an idea is to posit love as the significance of the image.[31]

This thesis that the *imago dei* is the form of creation for life fulfilled in love gives us our basis for the interpretation of sin. The root of sin is failure to realize life in love. The cleft in man which results from sin is more than the loss of a supernatural endowment. It is the disaster resulting from twisted, impotent or perverted love.[32]

While Williams agreed with orthodox theology that sin affects the entire person, he was not as traditional on exactly what those effects are. Sin does not necessarily destroy the power of reason. Nor does it eliminate human creativity (although it may cause that creativity to become demonically self-destructive). While it may lead humans away from God and toward the worship of idols, they still retain a sense of God and of the holy. Within every individual is some aspect of love which points him or her to the love of God, for all love originates in Him.[33]

God's love is the power of creation and re-creation. His image is His invitation to humanity to participate in His creativity. Humans have the ability to reshape life and society. If they choose to go the opposite direction, using their creative abilities demonically or self-destructively, that is sin. Or creativity may be redemptive and productive.[34]

Norman Pittenger

Norman Pittenger (1905–) is another pioneer in process thought. A professor at General Theological Seminary in New York for thirty-three years and then (from 1966) senior resident at King's College in Cambridge, and a member of the divinity faculty of Cambridge University, he is best known for his work in process Christology, but has published a number of works on ethics, in which he presents a process theology of humankind and sin.

Pittenger derides what he sees as the traditional concept of a static view of God, humanity, and morality. God has not created human beings with a particular nature, nor has He revealed immutable laws by which they are to live. "Knowledge of evolution in its narrower biological sense and evolution in its wider significance of development cosmically and physically, as well as psychologically and sociologically, has altered things."[35] Consequently, he proposes an alternative viewpoint, that there is a basic sense of "ought" in human experience, "a deep, if dim, awareness that the cosmos itself is on the side of humankind's forward thrust toward self-actualization in society."[36] Unless existence really is "a tale told by an idiot, full of sound and fury, signifying nothing" (Shakespeare), then people must act in such a way as to attempt at least to achieve human self-realization along with others.[37]

Like Williams, Pittenger finds the significance of humankind as God's image in responsible relationships. Every person is called to be a fellow-laborer with God who is absolute Love, "to be with that Love as a 'co-creator' . . . in all the relativity of our human situation, and with the probability that mistake and failure will be part of our lot."[38] He sees Jesus as the epitome of love "so far as human existence allows."[39]

Pittenger associates the terms "original sin" and "concupiscence" with the inclination of people to act selfishly with little concern for their fellows. "The former points to a situation in which human insight is distorted and human energy is enfeebled; the latter has to do with a persistent drive in people to get their own way without bothering about the consequences."[40] He rejects the orthodox view of sin in terms of radical evil from which humans need to be redeemed for a life "beyond the skies." Because process thinkers view creation as a dynamic process which progresses toward fulfillment by the mutual demonstration of love, they can see redemption in broader terms, seeing human sinfulness as misdirection and a failure in love.[41] Redemption is the reorienting of human life toward genuine fulfillment by identifying with the loving activity of Christ.

Conclusions

Process theology does not hold to the orthodox view of sin. It espouses an evolutionary — albeit theistic — development of humankind. Humans, the world, and even God Himself are all in process. Sin is the failure in process to follow the intrinsic "oughtness" of humans which directs all of us to loving interaction for the universal good. Redemption is the reorientation of behavior to conformity with the model of absolute love as presented and modeled by Christ.

Liberation Theology

Liberation theology is essentially a Two-Thirds World movement. Since it is not monolithic, it is better to speak of "theologies" of liberation, although there are common elements which link them together.

Liberation theology maintains a consummate concern in the political implications of the human relationship to God. It grounds itself in the Old Testament prophetic notions of injustice, oppression, and alienation. It acknowledges that God is able to confront the sordidness of societies, but it proclaims that human beings act as mediators of divine aid.[42]

Gutiérrez: Latin American liberationist

Latin America is the cradle of liberation thought. Its foremost formulator is Gustavo Gutiérrez (1928–), a Roman Catholic priest and professor of theology, whose book *A Theology of Liberation* is a classic text for the study of liberation thought.

Born in Lima, Peru, of mixed parentage, Gutiérrez experienced racial discrimination early in life. Graduating with a doctorate in theology in 1959 from the University of Lyons in France, he became priest of a Roman Catholic parish in Lima in the early 1960s and an instructor in theology at the Catholic University. But he found his European theology insufficient for effective ministry to the terrible poverty of his parish. And so, during the latter 1960s, he began to develop his liberation principles. Gutiérrez holds to a traditional doctrine of personal sin, asserting that sin is a rejection of the gift of God's love. The rejection is a personal, free act. It is a refusal to accept God as Father and to love others as the Lord loves us. Only the action of God can heal human beings at the root of the self-centeredness that prevents them from going out of themselves.[43]

He freely admits, however, that he is more concerned with the social dimensions of sin and, in this regard, he tends toward the views of Walter Rauschenbusch and Reinhold Niebuhr. Because it is "the absence of brotherhood and love in relationships" among people, sin permeates societal structures and results in the exploitation of people by others, and in the oppression and enslavement of certain people groups. "Sin appears, therefore, as the fundamental alienation, the root of a situation of injustice and exploitation."[44]

There is no question, however, that the sin at the heart of unjust situations is the result of the personal, free act of individuals. While society per se does not engage in these free acts, it is affected by what they do. Gutiérrez cites Pope John Paul II to the effect that social sin exists by virtue of human solidarity. There is a "communion of sin." Sin does not occur in a vacuum. It always in some way affects other people.[45]

Sin clearly occupies a very important place in Gutiérrez' theology. "To sin is to refuse to love, to reject communion and fellowship, to reject even now the very meaning of human existence."[46]

Just as social sin is caused by a human solidarity, so it may be excised through human solidarity. The construction of a just society necessitates a communion of love which opposes the negation of love, namely, sin. But sin, being radical evil, can be vanquished only by the radical liberation bestowed by God in His grace. This grace may be seen in each act of genuine human love. "The relationship between grace and sin is played out in the inmost depths of the human person."[47]

Radical liberation from sin is virtually synonymous with political liberation. Christ is the Son of God who has come to liberate all human beings from all oppression to which sin has subjected them. As individuals are transformed by the Holy Spirit, they will begin to identify with the poor and persecuted in their distress and will be impelled to strive to eliminate such horrendous conditions. Gutiérrez contends that "the historical, political liberating event is the growth of the Kingdom [of God] and is a salvific event. . . ."[48] At the same time, salvation and the kingdom in their fullness are eschatological.

Cone: Black theology

Raised in a small African-American community in Arkansas, James H. Cone studied at Garrett Theological Seminary and

135

earned his doctorate from Northwestern University. A pioneer in the black theology movement, he teaches systematic theology at Union Theological Seminary in New York.

Black theology is the theological form of "black power," which Cone defines as "black people taking the dominant role in determining the black-white relationship in American society."[49] It is the achievement of black liberation from white racist oppression by whatever means necessary, whether by strikes, boycotts, or even armed rebellion. It is affirming freedom before all else, even before life itself. Black theology, similarly, is "a theology whose sole purpose is to apply the freeing power of the gospel to black people under white oppression."[50] And Cone quite frankly admits that it initially was the theological arm of black power which permitted black theologians the freedom to express their theology in independence of white theology.[51]

Cone bases black theology on a dual footing of existentialism and liberationism. He notes the absurdity between the equality for all human beings expressed by the American Declaration of Independence and the treatment accorded black Americans by white Americans — even those noted as black liberators — as being less than human, asserting that "to this day, in the eyes of most white Americans, the black man remains subhuman."[52]

Cone approaches sin in much the same way as Gutiérrez, acknowledging its pertinence to individuals, but emphasizing its collective application, that is, its relevance to race, class, and society in general: "it is clear from divine revelation as witnessed in Scripture that authentic liberation of self is attainable only in the context of an oppressed community in the struggle of freedom."[53] Cone describes the meaning of sin in his book on *The Spirituals and the Blues*,[54] where he asserts that these two forms of black music express the soul of black people in a liberation paradigm as they attempt to achieve authentic personhood.

Sin, Cone declares, is closely connected to death and Satan. By denying Christ, one embraces Satan and follows a course which ends in death and perdition. Satan is the embodiment of sin, but the two are not synonymous. Sin is a universal concept which expresses that human beings are separated from God. "It means that the creature is not what the Creator intends."[55] Sin is, furthermore, a term which describes the state of the person who has disregarded the salvific event of the cross. How can one hear the liberating Word of God and refuse to follow the freedom road set out by Jesus Christ?[56]

Cone regards both the white system of slavery from the past and the present white system of racial oppression as essentially dynamic. His description of the black slaves' view of their white masters emits strong overtones of his view of what he sees as white racist oppression of blacks, Native Americans, and other nonwhite people groups: "Black slaves expected nothing. White people are, after all, Satan's representative on the earth and you don't make deals with devils. The responsibility of Christians is to strive against evil.[57]

Cone's concept of liberation is that it can occur only in the community of the oppressed. "No one can be truly liberated until all are liberated. . . . In an unjust society, freedom for Christ can be found only among those who are in chains."[58] At the same time, the paradox is unavoidable that "freedom is the opposite of oppression, but only the oppressed are truly free."[59] He asserts that Christ has connected liberation with the persecuted, the poor, and the unfortunate of this world, and so the Christian community willingly becomes oppressed and identifies with the oppressed.

How does black theology define oppression? Cone acknowledges that all are oppressed, including those who are oppressors. The problem arises when "oppressors claim to be victims, not for the purpose of being liberated but for their own social interests in retaining a 'Christian' identity while being against Jesus Christ."[60] Such a state is hypocrisy and blasphemy. If oppressors are to be truly liberated, then they must be freed from engaging in political, social, and economic oppression, and be turned to works of service.[61]

C.S. Song: Asian narrative theology

Choan-Seng Song, one-time president of Tainan Theological College in Taiwan and now professor of theology and Asian cultures at Pacific School of Religion in Berkeley, California, is one of Asia's foremost theological minds. In the early 1980s he began a crusade to extricate theology from traditional methodology and make it applicable to his own Asian context. The vehicle he selected for this endeavor was story—narrative, poetry, parable, and so forth.

Song is somewhat syncretistic in his theological outlook. Theology must be informed, he declares, by those of other faiths as well as by those within the church.

> Theology in Asia must be a theology of the church. But it must also be a theology of Asia. It ought to listen to a cloud of witnesses within the church. But to a cloud of witnesses out in the world of Asia it must also listen . . . listen with our hearts, our souls, and our might. Then we may be able to say in our theology, as that man cured of blindness by Jesus did, "All I know is this: once I was blind, now I can see." Theology is not debate. . . . It is not reasoning. Theology is confession. It is witness to the truth wherever it manifests itself.[62]

Song, therefore, willingly incorporates stories from Buddhist and other non-Christian sources to teach theological truth.

Sin is explicated through the Parable of the Rich Fool (Luke 12:16-20). The rich farmer was a fool because he had no room in his life for God. He was also a fool because he was heartless and made no provision for his tenant farmers who had families to feed and debts to pay and who had toiled diligently to make the good harvest a reality. Nor would he consider sharing with others in need.[63]

Jesus also made much of the fool in the Parable of the Rich Man and Lazarus (Dives) (Luke 16:19-31). Had Jesus stopped the story in the realm of this life, Song declares, His hearers would have believed that the wealthy man deserved his luxurious lifestyle, that it was his karma. But by depicting the rich man suffering in Hades while Lazarus relaxed in comfort with Abraham in Paradise, Jesus destroyed karma.

> Good karma or bad karma, what moves God is the miserable life of those who go hungry, naked, and homeless through no fault of their own. And the rich are fools if they have no feeling for the wretched of the earth, their brothers and sisters. They are fools because they say there is no God — if not with words, then with what they do not do for persons like Lazarus. This is sin . . . indifference to the plight of others. . . .[64]

According to Song, Jesus radically reinterpreted the meaning of sin. It is not the breaking of some legalistic ritual. It is self-righteousness which denounces the faults of others but exonerates itself from its own flaws. Sin is not a matter of breaking canon law but of hardening one's heart against loving others and identifying with their suffering.[65]

Sinners are fools—not because of stupidity, for they are often very clever—for "they proclaim by their deeds that there is no God, even though they may go to church every Sunday and observe every possible requirement as faithful church members."[66] Because they have no heart for God, they have no heart for their fellow human beings and their pain.

We must not think that Jesus was a long-faced ascetic. He enjoyed eating and drinking with outcasts, those outside the religious community. But while He was at home with the poor and harassed, He could not suffer wealthy fools.[67]

Summary

Liberation theology of all types stresses the collective aspects of sin. All liberation theologies would agree with Gutiérrez who says that "in the final analysis the root of social injustice is the rejection of love—that is, sin—which you rightly call 'opposition to God.' "[68] But the social injustice which concerns them is not individual. Liberation theologians are much more prone to speak of the "sinful structures of society."[69]

Creation Spirituality

The most recent theology to come to the fore in North America, creation spirituality is an effort to regain the radical and mystical church of yesteryear. Its founder and prime mover is Matthew Fox, a Dominican priest. A disciple of Thomas Merton, Fox holds a doctorate in the history and theology of spirituality from the Institut Catholique de Paris. In 1977 he founded the Institute of Culture and Creation Spirituality in California to encourage and promote his principles.[70]

In defining creation spirituality, Fox splits the term into its two component parts. Creation, he says, "is us in relationship with all things."[71] "All things" implies all space and time, past, present, and future. It is "a trace, a footprint, an offspring of the Godhead. Creation is the passing by of divinity in the form of isness."[72] Spirituality is "a spirit-filled way of living,"[73] a movement away from the individualistic to the solidaristic. Creation spirituality is a spiritual journey into the deeper things of our common human existence.

Fox has categorized the creation spirituality tradition into a spiritual journey of four paths, according to "what matters": "We are told in Path One that awe and delight matter; in Path Two that darkness, suffering, and letting go matter; in Path Three that creativity and imagination matter; and in Path Four that justice and celebration, which add up to compassion, matter."[74] God will be found in and through each of these four paths.

As far as Fox is concerned, each of the paths holds a different perspective, including a different outlook on sin and what it signifies. In the First Path, which he calls the Via Positiva, one learns that sin is ecological. "It represents the most basic injustice, that of humanity to its own source, the earth."[75] Sin is dualistic here, involving the abuse of others in a subject/object fashion, as well as abuse of the rest of creation.

There are also sins of omission on the Via Positiva. The worst of these, Fox seems to feel, is the sin of limiting pleasure or Eros. "By sinning in this way we refuse to fall in love with life, to love what is lovable, to savor life's simple and non-elitist pleasures, to befriend pleasure, to celebrate the blessings of life, to return thanks for such blessings by still more blessing."[76] An integral part of this particular sin of omission is the failure of adults through their spiritual and educational institutions to pass on to the coming generation an awareness of the cosmos, a love of beauty, and how to appreciate both.

Forgiveness for and redemption from this sin may be received as the offender works to bring healing and justice back to human relationships with fellow humanity and other damaged sectors of creation; "harmonious living and lifestyles of simplicity represent salvific action on humanity's part."[77]

In the Via Negativa (Path Two), sin consists of the refusal to empty oneself and develop receptivity.

Clinging to ego and therefore refusing to let it go for deeper and more transcendent experiences, clinging to control, to will power, even to religious control, to ascetic control in the name of spirituality, clinging to our sacred images of our sacred selves — all this can be sin . . . our spirit wants to be set free. It wants to let go.[78]

Fox also suggests here that sin has a legitimate place in people's lives. We can and should allow sin to instruct us. "Not to do this is to multiply the sin."[79]

Salvation on this road comes through forgiveness — not the forgiveness of God, but through ourselves. We have the power, Fox insists, to forgive ourselves, to forgive others, and to allow others to forgive us. It is largely a matter of letting go of guilt and fear. "There is no healing, no salvation, without forgiveness. And with forgiveness all things become saved and healed once again."[80]

In his section on the Via Creativa (Path Three), Fox decries the traditional definition of sin, that it is the privation of good. He sees sin, rather, as the misuse of good. The latter is a deeper understanding of sin.

The Via Creativa lays bare the immense demonic power that is coiled up in the very divine power, namely, the imagination of humanity. The divine and the demonic are very close together; only a thin line separates them/us. . . . And the deepest of all demonic activity is the use of our divine imaginations to invent destruction.[81]

Pornography is an obvious example of this misuse of good or, as Fox terms it, sadomasochism. But it is only "the tip of the iceberg" when pitted against the "boardroom sadomasochism" which seeks power in the many institutions of our society from government to the church. "Sadomasochism prevails wherever humans exploit the earth, the animals, the fishes, or one another."[82] It is an effort to misuse creativity, imagination, and the artistic in order to attain security and power (to have power over other people or things makes one feel secure).

One avenue of salvation on this third path is the awakening to the divine power within us. Creation spirituality is panentheistic and sees the image of God in humankind as inner divine power. God is in us and we are in Him. He has granted humans the capability "of growing into their divinity by way of divine imagination."[83] As this growth is realized, humans become co-creators with God.

Sin in Path Four, the Via Transformativa, is coldness of heart, apathy, an uncaring spirit. Because God is passionate for life, celebration, and justice, "to settle for a heart that is indifferent to the sufferings of others is to refuse to imitate the Creator."[84] It is essentially a rejection of God.

Sin as injustice, argues Fox, is not trivial. It kills people and even destroys entire nations and cultures; "it is the use of creativity to lord over others, to kill, to be sadistic, to refuse to celebrate."[85] Behind this sin lies the basis of all sin, namely, the attempt to seek isolation and privatization, and to eschew interdependence. "Privatized salvations sin against the cosmos itself. They blind us to the levels of ecological justice as well as human justice that we must be about."[86]

Just as injustice is sin, so justice is salvation. As one dispenses justice both to other humans and to creation, God will grant salvation, for He is God both of salvation and justice.

Fox declares that "there is no such thing as privatized or individualized salvation."[87] Our task in achieving salvation is the reclamation and transformation of society. The Fourth Path beckons people to regain their roles as agents of corporate justice and renewal.

Observations

Fox obviously has a radical concept of sin. He eschews traditional views, particularly of original sin. He prefers instead to talk about "original blessing." Far more important are love and desire. "Our origin in the love of our parents . . . and the celebration of creation at our birth, are far, far more primeval and original in every sense of that word than is any doctrine of 'original sin.' "[88] He holds that, though human beings sin, they are not obliged to. They may refrain from sin and regain their original state of blessing through actions which are sensual and creative.

Fox admits that sin is a reality, but he insists that it is overstressed. He holds Augustine of Hippo responsible for having seduced the church away from its biblical heritage. Sin, for Fox, is not that type of behavior which the church condemns as morally wicked, but rather wrong thinking about God and His creation.

Like Rauschenbusch and Reinhold Niebuhr, he finds evil in institutions which maintain and promote false ideas about ecology, women, and native people groups.[89]

Western Christian tradition, asserts Fox, with its teaching of Fall/redemption theology as the foundation of sin, is "the way of idolatry."[90] He sees its idea of God as "a vengeful, sadistic deity . . . a God of guilt."[91]

Contemporary Catholicism

Since Vatican II (1962–65) the Roman Catholic Church has undergone a theological transformation, becoming more oriented toward the thinking and methodology of Protestant higher criticism. While the changes which occurred were particularly relevant to the church's teaching on salvation, they included the doctrine of sin.

Karl Rahner

Among those Roman Catholic theologians who led the way in the fight for change within the church was Karl Rahner (1904–1984). Born in Germany, Rahner was ordained a Jesuit priest in 1932. He was a student of Martin Heidegger, graduating with his doctorate in 1936. He spent his life teaching dogmatic theology at Innsbruck, Munich, and Münster. He was a prolific writer; his major work was the sixteen-volume *Theological Investigations,* comprising some 8,000 pages, published from 1954 to 1984.

Because Christianity is a religion of redemption, it is only natural to expect it to deal extensively with human sin and guilt.

> Christianity understands man as a being whose free, sinful acts are not his "private affair" which he himself can absolve by his own power and strength. Rather, however much man's free subjectivity is responsible for them, once they are done they can be really overcome only by God's action.[92]

The average common individual today, according to Rahner, poses a problem generally not encountered in the church's previous history. The normal person does not at a conscious level fear

God because of his sin or worry whether He is merciful. This is because "the modern social sciences have a thousand ways and means to 'unmask' the experience of man's guilt before God and to demolish it as a false taboo."[93] If anything, people see sin and guilt as part of the preexisting state of the world and that humans are a sacrifice to this condition and not its cause. Even when moral evil is caused by a human being of his own volition, it is assumed that the perpetrator is really a victim of his nature and social environment. Such a situation, declared Rahner, should serve as a challenge to persons to investigate whether the message of Christianity may possess truth in its understanding of the human condition.[94]

Unlike traditional theologians, Rahner held that all human beings possess freedom. But that freedom has to do with God. "Freedom is the freedom to say 'yes' or 'no' to God."[95] Because they are beings of freedom, humans can really say "no" to God Himself, and not merely to some distorted conception of God. It is indeed possible that this "no" to Him "can become a reality in him [that is, the one saying 'no'] in the sense that . . . he really is evil, and he understands this evil as what he is and what he definitively wants to be."[96]

But Rahner held that Christianity does not inform us on whether people have come to that point where evil defines the net end result of their lives. "In real theology we do not have to break our heads over such questions as whether anyone, and if so how many people suffer eternal loss, or whether anyone, and if so how many people really in fact decide against God in their ultimate and original freedom."[97] The Bible does tell us, however, that we have the freedom to close ourselves into the absolute and ultimate loneliness of a "no" to God. It also allows us to comprehend the depiction of hell as a representation of this final loneliness.[98]

Nor did Rahner believe that one can know with absolute certainty whether the objectively guilty aspect of his behavior is the result of a genuine decision of freedom telling God "no." And while we cannot know with absolute certainty if we are sinners, we do know that we can be sinners, in spite of the praise we give ourselves in everyday living.

Rahner also had a different view of original sin. It does not mean, as Augustine and Calvin propounded, that the transgres-

144

sion of Adam has been imputed to us, whether biologically or in some other way, as our ethical quality. "Personal guilt from an original act of freedom cannot be transmitted, for it is the existential 'no' of personal transcendence toward God or against him."[99] Such a personal situation is unique and cannot be conveyed to another.

An understanding of what "original sin" means, then, is based on two factors. First of all, it is based on the universality of the determination by guilt of *every* person's situation, and this factor includes the original nature of this determination by guilt in the history of the human race. . . . Secondly, it is based on the reflexive insight . . . into the nature of the relationship between God and man. This factor includes the specific nature of the conditions of possibility for this relationship which are implied in the relationship, and also the special depths of guilt if and when there is guilt. . . .[100]

Original sin expresses the historical origin of the contemporary and unchangeable state of our freedom as co-conceived by sin. In other words, original sin—or the guilt of our historical situation—taints all of the individual elements within the context of this freedom. Without the guilt which co-determines this situation, one's whole, free encounter with others would be different. In a state without guilt, sorrow, illness, pain, and death would not exist in the same manner as we now experience them. Seeing original sin in this perspective, there is no longer "any need to think of man in his innocence living in a historical paradise for a longer period of time, and to reject what is really meant in Genesis as a mere myth."[101]

Summary

Rahner's theology of sin appears to be not unlike that of Piet Schoonenberg, where original sin is akin to the world's sin.[102] The latter has to do with the accumulation of sin in history; such is the situation into which every human being is born. This sinful situation precedes the exercising of freedom and helps to decide the orientation of the choices of all persons.[103]

In spite of the situation in which they find themselves, humans possess freedom, freedom to say "yes" or "no" to God. To say an ultimate "no" to God is to close ourselves into ultimate loneliness, which is what is symbolized by the biblical picture of hell.

Rahner decried original sin as portrayed in Genesis 3. The biblical account is myth, symbolizing freedom's emergence in history. To suppose that Adam's sin has become the inheritance of all future generations is to misread the account's intent. To assume that all humanity has been made culpable for his sin is equally wrong. There was no paradise, nor innocence.

Contemporary Evangelicalism

One might expect modern evangelicals to be quite traditional in their approach to the theology of sin. Some, however, have attempted to "resolve past conflicts" by a radical use of biblical hermeneutics.[104] These include Donald Bloesch and Millard Erickson.

Donald Bloesch

Donald Bloesch (1928–), whose doctorate is from the University of Chicago, teaches systematic theology at Dubuque Theological Seminary in Iowa. He borrows from neo-orthodox theology in his efforts to achieve a harmonious and consistent doctrine of sin.

In examining original sin as depicted in Genesis 3, he notes with approval Reinhold Niebuhr's comment that the account "must be taken seriously but not literally."[105] One does so by positing "the correct hermeneutical procedure for understanding the 'myth' of the fall."[106] Using the historical critical method, he comes to the conclusion that Genesis 3 is symbolic, but he rejects Niebuhr's view that the Fall is a passage from anxiety to prideful self-affirmation. Rather, it is indicative of a movement from communion with God to a fracture of that communion. "Moreover, it is our conviction that this story indicates a first fall before recorded history as well as a universal fall."[107] Adam is both the first man and Representative Man. Thus, it is not just the first human beings who fall in Genesis 3, but human nature itself.

Bloesch also sides with Emil Brunner in regard to the relationship of the primal sin to the numerous individual sins. It is "a relation *sui generis*" that is devoid of analogies. "Sin is not a natural necessity but a historical inevitability. The sinner can avoid any particular sin, but he cannot escape the taint of sin in all his actions."[108] Along with Kierkegaard, Bloesch attempts to explain the paradox of original sin and human freedom; he asserts that, while original sin is a spiritual and not a biological disease, it is nonetheless transmitted biologically. But it does not become fixed in human beings until they acquiesce to it and permit it to overshadow their entire beings.[109]

Back of sin is the devil, representative of the kingdom of Satan, also known as the kingdom of this world. Bloesch notes in Genesis 1 in the separation of light from darkness what he considers to be evidence of a conflict between that kingdom and the kingdom of God. He demonstrates that the idea of a kingdom of darkness is a theme in the Old Testament which becomes more strongly emphasized in the intertestamental and New Testament periods. "God has set up his kingdom in the midst of a fallen world, but antigod powers, angels of violence, have tried to overthrow it by force (Matt. 11:12). In attacking the kingdom of Christ, the demonic powers sealed their ultimate destruction."[110] Nonetheless, they continue to maintain a hold on the unbelieving world, and to wage war on believers.

Millard Erickson

Millard Erickson (1932–), former dean and professor of theology at Bethel Theological Seminary, now research professor of theology at Southwestern Baptist Theological Seminary, is one of evangelicalism's favorite and more prolific writers. In his theology of sin he makes a broad distinction between depravity and guilt, between original sin and original guilt.[111]

Erickson understands the Bible to teach that, because of Adam's sin, all humans receive a flawed nature and God's condemnation. All humanity is adjudged guilty before Him. Erickson confesses to being Augustinian—seeing Adam as the head of the human race—in regard to the imputation of original sin. In our first two parents all of us sinned.

The relationship of Adam and Christ as taught by the Apostle Paul in Romans 5 is foundational for Erickson's theology of sin.

Each one has in some parallel manner influenced all of human-kind (Paul tells us that, just as Adam has brought us to death by his sin, so Christ has brought to us life by His obedience). But one must be careful in determining exactly what that parallel is. If one decides that Adam's sin has led to universal condemnation regardless of individual decision, one must—in order to maintain the parallel—also accept that Christ's righteousness will lead to universal salvation regardless of personal decision. Evangelicals would, of course, refute this second premise because the Bible reveals "abundant evidence that there are two classes of persons, the lost and the saved, and that only a decision to accept the work of Christ makes it effective in our lives."[112] Therefore, suggests Erickson, the imputation of Adam's guilt to humans must require some kind of personal free choice by all humans.

Until such a choice is made, any imputation of guilt will be only conditional. Nor can one experience condemnation unless and until one attains to the age of accountability. Should a child die prior to that point, he or she will receive the same salvation as those who did achieve that age and who made a free decision to commit their lives to Christ in faith.[113]

Erickson sums up his case by saying that we become accountable and culpable when we embrace our depraved nature. There is a point in our life when we become conscious of our proclivity for sin.

> At that point we may abhor the sinful nature that has been there all the time . . . and might even, if there is an awareness of the gospel, ask God for forgiveness and cleansing. . . . But if we acquiesce in that sinful nature, we are . . . approving or concurring in the action in the Garden of Eden so long ago.[114]

Conclusions

The aim of these evangelical theologians is to provide a systematic explanation of sin as set forth in Scripture. In order to make this explanation cohesive, however, they must make some leaps in logic which cannot be substantiated by the Bible. While these explanations sound reasonable, they have spliced together the biblical aspects with materials from existentialism and higher

5.1: A SUMMARY OF CONTEMPORARY APPROACHES TO SIN

Theologians of Hope

Jürgen Moltmann   *Wolfhart Pannenberg*
Johannes B. Metz

Sin is both rebellion against God and hopelessness, the latter perhaps more deadly than the former.

Jesus Christ is the Bringer of hope.

In a perversity of will, humans voluntarily deny their own happiness. Their attempts at autonomy induce despair.

Genesis 3 is a myth illustrating the human predicament. Adam is Primal Man, the human prototype.

Emphasize the solidarity of humanity in Adam (to loss) and in Christ (to salvation).

Process Theologians

Charles Hartshorne   *John Cobb*
Schubert Odgen   *Norman Pittenger*
Henry Wieman   *Daniel D. Williams*

Sin is perverted love, misdirection.

Original sin is a term suggesting the distortion of human insight.

There is no such thing as radical evil.

Redemption from sin is the reorienting of human life toward real fulfillment by identifying with the love of Christ.

Liberation Theologians

Gustavo Gutiérrez   *Jose Miguez-Bonino*
Leonardo Boff   *James Cone*
Deotis Roberts   *Desmond Tutu*
Alan Boesak   *Lee Jung Young*
C.S. Song   *Matthew Fox*

Sin is the rejection of the gift of God's love. It is a personal, free act.

Liberation theology places greater stress on social sin than on personal: sin is the absence of love for one's fellows. It has corporate dimensions.

Victory over sin can come for the individual only through relief of corporate oppression, whether institutional, economic, or national.

Liberation theology tends to identify redemption with political liberation.

Contemporary Catholic Theologians
Karl Rahner   *Hans Küng*
Edward Schillebeeckx

All humans possess freedom. Sin is the human saying "no" to God.

Personal guilt from an original act of freedom cannot be transmitted to another human being. Original sin, therefore, is the universality of the conviction by guilt of every individual's situation.

Redemption from sin lies in the decision to imitate Christ in His saying "yes" to God.

Contemporary Evangelical Theologians
Donald Bloesch   *Millard Erickson*
Clark Pinnock   *Bernard Ramm*

Genesis 3 is not necessarily to be taken as literal history in the sense that we hold. It is representative of the fracture of human communion with God.

Sin is rebellion against God.

Back of sin is Satan.

Sin is transmitted biologically, but it cannot be imputed until the individual transgresses by a free act of his will (evangelicals have varying views on the transmission and imputation of sin).

Redemption comes through submission in faith to Jesus Christ as personal Savior and Lord.

criticism which are fraught with presuppositions and assumptions.

Bloesch's assertion, for example, that Genesis 3 is symbolic and not literal (a neo-orthodox position) can neither be proved nor disproved, but it is not the typical evangelical stance on this issue and smacks somewhat of Brunner's early belief in a pre-creation cosmic Fall. In order to avoid a Calvinistic predestining of all human beings to sin, therefore, Bloesch must necessarily place sin within the realm of human free will (albeit a will inevitably tainted by evil).

Erickson faces much the same difficulty as Bloesch. If all human beings sinned in Adam, then it is reasonable to assume that all are guilty before God and worthy of condemnation because of that original sin. Not desiring to accept such a conclusion, however, Erickson is compelled to intimate that the imputation of Adam's sin is not carried out until a personal sin is effected by an individual. He faces the same difficulty in regard to the parallelism of Romans 5:12ff.

Final Observations

Recent times have seen the development of a diversity of teachings upon sin. The intention of the theologians involved has been benign: they have attempted to explain sin in ways which are relevant to contemporary humankind. None, however, have adhered completely to biblical materials (and it may even be argued that it is impossible to present a completely systematic theology of sin without some assumptions and leaps in logic!). These views range from an existential foundation (such as presented by the theologies of hope, liberation, and contemporary Catholicism) to those with a panentheistic and mystical orientation (such as process and creation spirituality). We must conclude that contemporary evangelical theology (which attempts to bear the mantle of traditional orthodox Christianity) has adhered more closely to a *sensus literalis* than have other schools of thought cited. Sin is viewed by evangelicals as a fracture of communion with God which leads to personal guilt and alienation. This continuing estrangement is nourished by demonic cosmic beings who are also in rebellion against their Creator. The theology of hope, liberation theology, and contemporary Catholic theology do, however, have valuable contributions—largely based in Scripture—to make to an understanding of sin, although they tend to lean more heavily on existentialist thought than the former. Process theology, because of its extreme dependence on evolutionary panentheistic thought cannot be of much help, for sin is simply a failure in the continuing process of becoming. In creation spirituality we come the farthest afield from orthodox belief, for at best, sin is simply "wrong thinking" about God and His creation.

Section Two
A Biblical
Theology of Sin

Chapter Six
The Old Testament Teaching on Sin

For Christian believers the proper substance of any doctrine is grounded in the biblical teaching on the matter. Both the Old and New Testament are absolute truth, the latter the completion of the former. We shall examine the teaching of the Old Testament on the human Fall and sin in this and the following two chapters and, in chapter 9, the teaching of the New.

The Teaching of the Pentateuch

In his book *In the Beginning*, Henri Blocher notes that "the human race quite rightly feels that it cannot find its bearings for life today without having light shed on its origins."[1] A crucial part of those origins concern the beginning of sin in the human race. Commenting on the opening chapters of Genesis, Francis Schaeffer declares

[that] in some ways these chapters are the most important ones in the Bible, for they put man in his cosmic setting and show him for his peculiar uniqueness. They explain man's wonder and yet his flaw. Without a proper understanding of these chapters we have no answer to the problems of metaphysics, morals, or epistemology. . . .[2]

Genesis 3: An exegesis

Genesis 3 is the classic Old Testament text in regard to sin. It is a narrative known universally, which suggests that it goes back beyond Israelite tradition, far older than can be traced. But it is in Scripture that we learn its significance.

The majority trend today is for scholars to reject the traditional title of "The Fall." Blocher sees the idea of a fall as "contamination from Greek and Gnostic themes."[4] Westermann suggests that it does not accord with the intention of the passage, but is a determination of later Judaism.[5] A better title for it, according to Blocher, might be "the deviation" or "the breaking of the covenant."[6]

The context

The account finds the first man and woman living in Eden, the garden of delight. They were put there by God to tend the garden. The key verses in setting the context are Genesis 2:16-17: "And the Lord God commanded the man, "You are free to eat from any tree in the garden; but you must not eat from the tree of knowledge of good and evil, for when you eat of it you will surely die."

To make much of the prohibition of a single tree here is to miss the real thrust of this passage, which is the abundance of God's provision for humankind. Out of all the trees of Eden only a single one was forbidden. And we may learn from this prohibition that it was assuredly for human good, once again the result of divine providence.[7]

There is clearly a choice posed here, a choice to obey or not. Schaeffer notes that "there is nothing intrinsic about this tree that is different in any other way from the other trees."[8] It could as easily have been something else; the point was to leave human beings with an alternative. If they were obedient, they would continue to enjoy the garden and their Creator. But if they decided to disobey, they would die. Indeed, the Hebrew is emphatic, literally, "dying, you will die."

Enter the serpent

"Now the serpent was more crafty than any of the wild animals the Lord God had made" (3:1a). The serpent is introduced into the Genesis narrative with little fanfare or information. We are told that it was made by the Lord God and that it was more wily than other creatures. Other than that we are told nothing. Von Rad insists that "the mention of the snake here is almost incidental . . . because the narrator is obviously anxious to shift the responsibility as little as possible from man."[9] The whole focus of the story is to be on Adam and Eve and their disobedience.

Though the Genesis author gives little explanation in regard to the serpent, the Christian church from earliest times supplied its identity. It was either Satan in disguise or possessed by Satan. In Revelation 12:9, John has picked up on the Genesis theme: "The great dragon was hurled down—that ancient serpent called the devil or Satan, who leads the whole world astray."

The temptation

The serpent and the woman occupy center stage. The serpent posed a seemingly sympathetic question, "Did God really say, 'You must not eat from any tree in the garden'?" (3:1b) It exaggerated God's command not to eat of the one tree and thus cast suspicion on His words.

The woman sprang to the Lord's defense: "We may eat fruit from the trees in the garden, but God did say, 'You must not eat fruit from the tree that is in the middle of the garden, and you must not touch it, or you will die' " (3:2-3). Some people make much of the woman's addition to the Lord's command (God did not say not to touch it),[10] but we do not know enough to attach any special significance to it. It may even be that Adam in relaying God's command to Eve added that admonition as a safeguard!

The serpent's seeming concern was now exchanged for an attitude of derision: "You will not surely die. . . . For God knows that when you eat of it your eyes will be opened, and you will be like God, knowing good and evil" (3:4-5). Here was a suggestion that God was really a liar, that He was jealous that Adam and Eve might—if they ate of the forbidden tree—learn something that would make them just like Him. Thus, a choice was placed before the woman—to take the serpent's word and eat the forbidden fruit, or to be obedient to God.

What was involved in the knowing of good and evil? Various

suggestions have been offered. C.F. Keil has suggested that it was a matter of moral discernment.[11] Hermann Gunkel and J.A. Soggin (among others) emphasize this knowledge as sexual, including the ability to procreate.[12] Von Rad declares that this knowledge had to do with "the independence that enables a man to decide for himself what will help or hinder him"[13]; Blocher observes that, in calling the tree one of "the knowledge of good and evil," the Genesis author has created a merism, a figure of speech which symbolizes completeness by using two opposite poles. In this case, the merism signifies the totality of knowledge. To eat of this tree is to possess all knowledge, that is, to be like God.[14] Thus, the serpent was leading the woman to believe that she and her husband would be on a level with God.

"When the woman saw that the fruit of the tree was good for food and pleasing to the eye, and also desirable for gaining wisdom, she took some and ate it" (3:6). As she mulled over God's seeming unfairness, she gazed upon the fruit dangling from a nearby branch and noticed how luscious it seemed, how delectable it would taste and, above all, how knowledgeable she would become.

Ray Stedman notes in regard to her actions:

Eve did not realize that her mind had played a trick on her. It had taken the apparent facts which the enemy had set before her and had justified them, so that they looked reasonable, rational. The thing to do then, of course, was to give in. After all, anything that is good for food, pleasant to the senses, and satisfying to the ego must be all right. . . .[15]

And so the woman took the fruit and ate it, perhaps almost anticipating that she might be immediately struck dead by God. But nothing happened, and so she gave some to her husband — who apparently had been with her all this time — and he ate some too.

Adam's disobedience seems to have been much easier to occasion than Eve's. After all, he was the initial human creation, and he was the original receiver of God's revelation in regard to the garden and its trees. But while the serpent had spent considerable energy to tempt Eve to disobedience, it had taken only a simple offering of the fruit to the man by his wife. Paul, in commenting on this first sin, notes that "Adam was not the one deceived" (1 Tim. 2:14). He obviously sinned knowledgeably and willingly, thus absolutizing the triumph of sin.

The results

The man and woman did not achieve the high heights they had hoped: "Then the eyes of both of them were opened, and they realized that they were naked; so they sewed fig leaves together and made coverings for themselves" (3:7). The serpent's promise that their eyes would be opened came true. They had changed, but not for the better. The writer tells us that "they realized they were naked." A loss of innocence had occurred; they felt a sense of guilt and shame at their mutual nakedness. And so they covered up with fig leaves.

Westermann informs us that

breaking God's command means being ashamed before another person. . . . Being ashamed is a reaction to being unmasked, and such an unmasking is possible only when the relationship between man and God is ruptured. . . . Being ashamed . . . always has reference to something like sins, failures, or wrong doings.[16]

"Then the man and his wife heard the sound of the Lord God as He was walking in the garden in the cool of the day, and they hid from the Lord God among the trees of the garden" (3:8). Previous to this episode the first couple seemed to have had a regular, open, personal communication with God. But after having consumed the forbidden fruit, they suddenly felt fear at the sound of His approach and so they hid from Him.

"But the Lord God called to the man, 'Where are you?' He answered, 'I heard you in the garden and I was afraid because I was naked; so I hid' " (3:9-10). Here we see God's taking of the initiative in ferreting out what had occurred. When the couple did not appear at the usual time, He looked for them. "The God who punishes people is the God who cares for people."[17]

The man confessed that he had been hiding because he was afraid. Just as he had been ashamed of his nakedness before his wife, so he and his wife were now ashamed of their nakedness before God. Von Rad notes that "fear and shame are henceforth the incurable stigmata of the Fall in man. This is the first thing of which the man speaks, of emotions, which exist objectively and not yet consciously completely beyond and before any rational reflection."[18]

"And he said, 'Who told you that you were naked? Have you eaten from the tree that I commanded you not to eat from?' The man said, 'The woman you put here with me – she gave me some fruit from the tree, and I ate it.' Then the Lord God said to the woman, 'What is this you have done?' The woman said, 'The serpent deceived me, and I ate' " (3:11-13).

When God confronted the sinful pair, they evaded personal responsibility for their sin by seeking to blame someone else. Adam blamed Eve, and there was a bit of waspishness in his response as he suggested that God was responsible for his disobedience because, after all, He put the woman to be with him. Eve, for her part, blamed the serpent. One might have supposed that God would confront the serpent too, but He did not. The writer had intended it so in order to demonstrate the inexplicability of the origin of evil.[19]

When God meted out the sentences upon the three perpetrators, He crafted each to fit the individual offender. "So the Lord God said to the serpent, 'Because you have done this, cursed are you' " (3:14a). The serpent was cursed by being condemned to crawl on its belly and eat dust all of its life. One should not presume that prior to this event the snake had legs; rather, the writer was symbolically demonstrating the absolute debasement of the creature.[20]

Furthermore, "I will put enmity between you and the woman, and between your offspring and hers; he will crush your head, and you will strike his heel" (3:15). God frustrated the intention of the serpent to enlist human beings as allies in his fight against the Lord by causing permanent enmity between the snake's seed and the woman's. The picture is graphically clear: the man attempting to stomp on the serpent's head, while the snake slithers up behind the man and sinks his fangs into his heel.

Christianity, at least since the time of Irenaeus of Lyons, has seen this passage in a Christological light. Christ is the offspring of the woman who has crushed the serpent's (Satan's) head, though the serpent struck at Him on Calvary. While the interpretation of Genesis 3:15 as a "proto-evangelium" is logical and almost inescapable in a canonical context, whether the passage solely in its Old Testament context carries the weight of such an argument is dubious.

"To the woman he said, 'I will greatly increase your pains in childbearing; with pain you will give birth to children. Your desire will be for your husband, and he will rule over you' " (3:16). God's punishment here of the woman was descriptive, not prescriptive. He did not curse her as He cursed the serpent, but told her the ramifications of her disobedience. She would bear children in pain. Even worse, there would be a separation between her and her husband. Susan Foh has suggested that the concept of "desire" here is not simply a matter of the woman's sexual desire for her husband, but of her desire to control or manipulate him.[21] From a linguistic point of view such an interpretation must be questioned. The point is being made that the relationship has now changed; in the pre-Fall economy it was one of mutuality, but now the husband would seek to dominate his wife. No longer would the oneness of Genesis 2:24 be complete.

"To Adam he said, 'Because you listened to your wife and ate from the tree about which I commanded you, "You must not eat of it," cursed is the ground because of you; through painful toil you will eat of it all the days of your life. It will produce thorns and thistles for you, and you will eat the plants of the field. By the sweat of your brow you will eat your food until you return to the ground, since from it you were taken; for dust you are and to dust you will return' " (3:17-19).

As with the woman, the man's punishment was not a curse on him, but descriptive of what he had brought on himself. The man had been put on the earth to tend it, but no longer would the ground cooperate. He would toil at his work until he returned to the dust whence he came.

"The Lord God made garments of skin for Adam and his wife and clothed them" (3:21). Prior to imposing the final punishment — banishment from the garden — God made a telling symbolic gesture. He fashioned clothes for the sorry pair from animal hides. "How could he better demonstrate that he wishes to remain the God of sinners, for their good and not their ill? . . . God *covers* sin and its degradation."[22]

"And the Lord God said, 'The man has now become like one of

us, knowing good and evil. He must not be allowed to reach out his hand and take also from the tree of life and eat, and live forever.' So the Lord banished him from the Garden of Eden to work the ground from which he had been taken" (3:22-23). The Lord's statement about the man having "now become like one of us" was somewhat ironic, for it confirmed the snake's promise to Eve (in 3:5). Certainly, humans had not become exactly like God, but there were similar points. The chief one was human autonomous knowledge and will. They had determined to disobey God and become independent.[23] There is a further irony in that these humans had declared themselves to be what they could never be (autonomous), and yet what they must nonetheless be if they continued on the path of rebellion.

Because of their sinful disobedience, Adam and Eve could not be allowed to eat of the tree of life. Living forever in their sinful condition would not have been good for them, nor for future humankind. It was also a confirmation of God's original sentence (in 2:16ff) of death. That death was spiritual, and this passage denies to human beings immortality. Because of sin, humanity is not inherently immortal. Instead, Adam was forced to till the ground whence he came until he returned to it in death.[24]

To prevent them from eating of the tree of life, Adam and Eve were banished from the garden. Nor could they return, for God had placed cherubim at the gate with a flaming sword to deny them entrance (3:24).

Summary

The Genesis account of the first human sin is constructed on an historical foundation. The first man and woman were created sinless and placed in an earthly paradise called Eden. They were not, however, spiritual robots. Their continuance in the garden was dependent upon right choices with which they were confronted. God had placed in the garden a tree—of the knowledge of good and evil—from which they were forbidden to eat. Would the first couple decide to fall in line with God's will and live forever in paradise? Or would they go their own way and sample the fruit in defiance of God's command?

We know their decision; Eve listened to the serpent, ate the fruit, and gave some to Adam. The results were tragic: their eyes were opened to shame and a realization of innocence lost, accompanied by alienation from God. When confronted by the Lord, this pitiful couple attempted to evade personal responsibility for what they had done by shifting the blame elsewhere—Adam onto his wife and God, Eve onto the snake.

The result of this sin was punishment. The serpent was cursed above all other creatures, and God created a setting of hostility between it and the woman's descendants. While the man and woman were not cursed, their sin brought some very negative results. They had become alienated from each other; gone was any unity. Henceforth, the woman would seek to control her husband by manipulation, and the man would dominate her. The woman would bear her children in pain. The man would have to scratch and toil in the earth to make it produce.

Even more tragic, God's warning in 2:16ff came true. Spiritual death occurred with their sin. Adam and Eve began to die physically, as well. Their expulsion from the garden ensured both.

The Genesis author demonstrates that the three beneficial relationships of chapter 2 have now become ones of conflict. (1) Creation is in conflict with God's purposes as seen in the judgment on the serpent. The latter has brought a curse on all creation, and for that he will find himself in conflict not only with God, but with all creation (in particular, the humans he deceived), which is now under a curse. (2) The good relationship of male and female is now cursed. What might have been responsible loving mutuality now falls under male domination which will often prove to be autocratic and harsh. (3) The man *('adam)* who was made from the ground *('adamah)* as indicated by Genesis 2:7 will now find that it is resistant to his efforts and he must live by the sweat of his brow. The key word for each of the curses seems to be conflict. This is then developed in the next section where the conflict escalates from the murder of one to the philosophy of Lamech to the cause of the flood where violence is everywhere.

Genesis 4–11

Chapters 4–11 of Genesis are an integral part and logical completion of the account of humanity's disobedience. They delineate the progression of sin in the affairs of human beings over a period of at least two millennia.

Chapter 4

After their banishment from Eden, Adam and Eve had children. Their two oldest sons, Cain and Abel, grew up to be a farmer and shepherd respectively (4:2). Both of them offered a sacrifice to the Lord of their labors, Abel from his sheep and Cain from his produce. While we are not told why, God honored Abel's sacrifice but rejected Cain's (4:4-5).

Cain reacted with envy and rage, "and his face was downcast" (4:5). Von Rad tells us that being downcast signified alienation from community relationships.[25] Such a reaction suggests, further, that Cain's demeanor was similar prior to this event and may even have played a part in God's refusal to accept his offering.

God confronted Cain about his anger in a seeming attempt to cause him to reflect on his behavior: "Why are you angry? Why is your face downcast? If you do right, will you not be accepted? But if you do not do what is right, sin is crouching at your door; it desires to have you, but you must master it" (4:6-7). In effect, God was trying to help Cain to reject temptation; He was unwilling to leave him to face the power of the serpent by himself. God was present with him, in spite of having rejected his sacrifice.[26]

But Cain did not heed the Lord's advice, and sin did indeed master him, for he became a fratricide (4:8). Westermann tells us that "what is so shocking about the whole event is that a man like him [Cain], who does his work and presents his offering to God, is capable of this. It is not Cain, but everyone who can become the murderer of one's brother."[27]

Immediately, upon completion of his dastardly deed, Cain was again confronted by God: "Where is your brother Abel?" (4:9) By his answer Cain compounded the murder with a lie: "I don't know. . . . Am I my brother's keeper?" (4:9) One sin had begotten another. Von Rad says that Cain deflected the opportunity God gave him to confess his sin by indulging in a witticism: "Shall I shepherd the shepherd?"[28]

But Cain's sin could not be concealed. God reacted in horror: "What have you done? Listen! Your brother's blood cries out to me from the ground" (4:10). The murderer might attempt to dismiss an embarrassing question, but he could not so easily still the cry of his brother's spilt blood which loudly called upon God for justice.

Nor could he evade God's swift and terrible punishment. The Lord banished Cain from the very ground into which he had spilled Abel's blood (4:11). "The relation of the fratricide to the mother earth is disturbed much more deeply. It is so shattered, in fact, that the earth has no home for him. What remains for him is an unstable and fugitive life."[29]

Cain's sentence caused him great anxiety: "My punishment is more than I can bear. Today you are driving me from the land, and I will be hidden from your presence. I will be a restless wanderer on the earth, and whoever finds me will kill me" (4:13-14). He was not sorry for his sin, but he was terrified of its consequences, for he realized that a life God does not oversee is a life unprotected. He was terrified that when he was banished both from his homeland and from God's presence he would be killed.[30]

Despite Cain's sin and its punishment, God was still there to protect him. "If anyone kills Cain, he will suffer vengeance seven times over" (4:15). And so, before he was banished, the Lord placed a protective mark on him (what kind of mark, we have no idea).

Cain's descendants were more learned and articulate in the expression of their sins (4:17-24). Blocher tells us that

> with its efficiency, the Cainite civilization provides sin with institutional consolidation. Lamech formulates a rule which his tribe will observe and which will secure it in an interminable vendetta. This violence takes its place in the social code. . . . Sin becomes formally a part of the human tradition.[31]

The "Saga of the Sword," as it is called, set out the increasing depravity of humankind—from Adam's sin to Cain's fratricide to Lamech's terrible vengefulness in multiple murders.

Genesis 6–11

The remaining chapters of this section delineate a new and more horrific stage in the development of human depravity. It began as "the sons of God" took wives from "the daughters of men" (6:1-3). As to who these former types might be is a matter of scholarly debate. One viewpoint is that they were a type of divine being in the class of a god who discovered female human beauty, had sexual intercourse with these beautiful women, and sired a race of Nephilim, or mighty ones.[32] Another idea is that the "sons of God" denote the descendants of the godly line of Seth, who intermarried with those in the ungodly line of Cain (4:26), which resulted in the virtual demise of the former as their offspring grew to be wicked people.[33] While the latter would seem a more reasonable idea (the former would necessarily be myth), both have the same conclusion, namely, the extreme deterioration of the human race.

As God looked on the human race He saw "how great man's wickedness on earth had become, and that every inclination of the thoughts of his heart was only evil all the time" (6:5). Indeed, human degradation had increased to such a degree that the earth was totally corrupt except for a single family: "Noah was a righteous man, blameless among the people of his time, and he walked with God" (6:9).

God determined to judge this wickedness: "I am going to put an end to all people, for the earth is filled with violence because of them. I am surely going to destroy both them and the earth" (6:13). But because of Noah's righteous life, He would preserve him and his family. God told Noah, "So make yourself an ark" (6:14).

Here we have a reversal of creation as God took steps to undo what He had done. Just as the land had emerged from the waters, now they would cover it up again and all of sinful humanity with it (7:4). Blocher notes that, "so exceedingly evil and harmful is sin, both intensively and extensively, that there is no moderate therapy that can cure it, so satisfactory amendment of life can be expected from the old earth. The flood denounces the perversion of sin as a 'radical evil,' as total depravity."[34] In the ensuing deluge "every living thing on the face of the earth was wiped out.... Only Noah was left, and those with him in the ark" (7:23).

So the flood cleansed the earth and humanity started afresh with the family of righteous Noah. The sinners had been expunged. God began the new order of humanity with a fresh covenant, the sign of which was a rainbow (9:8ff). Interestingly, prior to so doing, He gave the new first family a warning which harkened back to Cain: "And for your lifeblood I will surely demand an accounting. I will demand an accounting from every animal. And from each man, too, I will demand an accounting for the life of his fellow man. Whoever sheds the blood of man, by man shall his blood be shed; for in the image of God has God made man" (9:5-6).

One may well ask why, having purged the earth of all the corrupt, God felt it necessary to caution the righteous against the sin of Cain, the taking of a human life. The obvious answer is that He saw the definite possibility of such an act occurring again. The sinners might have been excised, but sin seemingly had not.

Nor was sin long in coming to the fore. Noah got drunk on wine he had produced from his own grapes. In a stupor he lay in his tent unclothed. His son Ham immodestly looked upon his father's nakedness, but the other two sons covered up their father without looking at him. As a result, Ham's line was cursed, while Shem and Japheth were blessed (9:18ff). Thus, we find sin arising in Noah and coming to fullness in Ham. Sin was far from extinct.

We find the ultimate experience in human sin (certainly, in corporate human sin) at Shinar (Babylonia) where the descendants of Noah settled (11:2). There, they decided to build a memorial to themselves, a tower (likely a ziggurat, a temple dedicated to astrology) "that reaches to the heavens" (11:4). Speiser says that this phrase means "to rival the heavens."[35] Why? "So that we may make a name for ourselves and not be scattered over the face of the whole earth" (11:4). The idea of making a name, we are told, stands apart from the usual idea of memorializing oneself through outstanding deeds and signifies rebellion against God in pride and presumption.[36] It is clear that these people were engaged in one of the oldest and original sins of humankind, an attempt to be autonomous.

God acted immediately to frustrate their plans, noting that, "if as one people speaking the same language they have begun to do this, then nothing they plan to do will be impossible for them" (11:6). There is a striking similarity to 3:22, where God ejected the first couple from the garden so that they could not eat of the tree of life and live forever. But this time He set people at odds with one another by frustrating their language (11:7). And so they scattered over all the earth, the heavenly tower left uncompleted.

"Thus another division has emerged . . . between the men of the earth in their nations with implications that reach into racial and cultural divisions, linked to linguistic differences. And all of them are rooted in the same source—the sin of man."[37] And so Babel, intended by the inhabitants of Shinar to be "the gate of heaven" (the Babylonian sense of the word), became instead "confusion" (the Hebrew meaning).

Other pentateuchal examples

As the Book of Genesis continues and then gives way to Exodus and the other books of the law, the focus narrows to another righteous man—Abraham—and his family. But once again we find God's people ensnared by the enemy.

Abraham

Abraham's obedience to God's command to leave home and kin to go to a new land is well known (Gen. 12:1ff). Shortly after his arrival in Palestine, however, the land was hit by a famine, "and Abram went down to Egypt to live there for a while because the famine was severe" (12:10). There is no evidence that God led him to this foreign land; the evidence indicates that he went on his own initiative.

Evidently Abraham's wife Sarah was a great beauty, and he was afraid that her attractiveness could lead the Egyptians to make her a widow in order to possess her. "Say you are my sister, so that I will be treated well for your sake and my life will be spared because of you" (12:13). And things occurred much as Abraham envisioned. The Pharaoh saw Sarah and, finding out that she was the patriarch's sister, took her into his harem and gave Abraham gifts (perhaps as a *mohar*, or bride-price). There is no evidence that Abraham made any effort to right this monstrous evil which he had allowed to be perpetrated on his wife. The reader of the narrative has to be prepared for the worst.

God, however, intervened to protect Sarah: "But the Lord inflicted serious diseases on Pharaoh and his household because of Abram's wife Sarai" (12:17). The monarch discovered the cause behind his affliction and confronted Abraham over his lies. "What have you done to me? . . . Why did you say, 'She is my sister,' so that I took her to be my wife? Now, then, here is your wife. Take her and go!" (12:18-19) And he banished Abraham from Egypt.

While the intention of the narrator is to show how God intervenes to protect His people, we get a glimpse of other things, as well. We find out that even those who are on an intimate basis with God are tainted with sin which will cause them to abandon their dependence on Him in favor of an independent course of action. The results of such autonomy are disastrous and lead to many potential evils.

But we do not have the end of the story. Abraham got into a somewhat similar situation (this time in Gerar rather than in Egypt), and did precisely the same thing (Gen. 20:1ff). Many interpreters insist that this episode is simply a reduplication of the Genesis 12 story as recounted by a different redactor.[38] Perhaps they feel that a genuine historical repetition of such a faux pas would be ludicrous. But does not our own personal experience of sin tell us that, to the contrary, people frequently commit an utterly foolish evil and, only a short time later—given a similar circumstance—do exactly the same thing again.

Abraham relocated to the kingdom of Gerar. Once again, fearful of the local people, "Abraham said of his wife Sarah, 'She is my sister' " (20:2). As one would expect, the king (the name Abimelech may well be a title, just like Pharaoh) learned of Sarah's great beauty and took her as his wife. And, once again, God had to intervene to protect her from the consequences of Abraham's sin: "But God came to Abimelech in a dream one night and said to him, 'You are as good as dead because of the woman you have taken; she is a married woman" (20:3).

Abimelech responded in righteous indignation that he had not touched Sarah. He maintained that he was innocent in spite of Abraham's deception. "I have done this with a clear conscience and clean hands" (20:5). We find this pagan coming out very well by comparison with the guilty man of God!

God was gracious to Abimelech. He told him that He was aware of his innocence, "and so I have kept you from sinning against me. That is why I did not let you touch her" (12:6). He commanded him to return Sarah to Abraham and he would live. To refuse would bring death to the king and all his people.

Abimelech was obedient to God's direction. Once again Abraham stood humiliated as a pagan monarch upbraided him for his sinful actions: "What have you done to us? How have I wronged you that you have brought such great guilt upon me and my kingdom? You have done things to me that should not be done" (20:9). Abraham's only excuse was that he was in fear of his life, and besides, he really hadn't lied because Sarah and he had the same father. Abimelech heaped coals of fire on Abraham's head by giving him all sorts of gifts and, unlike the Pharaoh, inviting him to settle anywhere in Gerar he wished. Once again God had interceded to protect His people from the terrible consequences of their sins.

Lot

The Apostle Peter describes Abraham's nephew as "a righteous man" (2 Peter 2:7) but, as one examines the Genesis narrative, one must wonder why. Sin seems to have constantly overwhelmed Lot.

When a quarrel arose between the herdsmen of Lot and those of Abraham because the grassland where they were camping would not support both, Abraham generously gave his nephew the choice of which lands he would take to graze his animals. Instead of acknowledging the position of his uncle as head of the clan and offering him the best lands, Lot took the choice region for himself (Gen. 13:5-13). In so doing, he relocated near the cities of the plain.

Two of these cities were particularly wicked. "Then the Lord said, 'The outcry against Sodom and Gomorrah is so great and their sin so grievous that I will go down and see if what they have done is as bad as the outcry that has reached me" (18:20-21). When two angels investigated Sodom, they met Lot who offered them his hospitality. He had settled in Sodom and had married into its population. When the angels entered his home, some of the local inhabitants surrounded it and demanded that he send them out. "Where are the men who came to you tonight? Bring them out to us so that we can have sex with them" (19:5). Lot remonstrated with them and attempted to protect his visitors by offering the Sodomites his two virgin daughters instead. As it worked out, the angels had to protect Lot and his family: "they struck the men who were at the door of the house, young and old, with blindness so that they could not find the door" (19:11).

The angels told Lot that he and his family must flee the city because "the outcry to the Lord against its people is so great that he has sent us to destroy it" (19:13). But when Lot spoke to his daughters' fiancés, they thought that he was joking and paid no attention to him. Ultimately, the angels had to take Lot, his wife, and two daughters by the hand, and force them from the city, warning them to flee to the mountains without stopping or looking back. "But Lot's wife looked back, and she became a pillar of salt" (19:26) as the Lord rained burning sulphur upon the evil cities.

Lot's righteousness paled against the events which occurred immediately following the destruction of Sodom and Gomorrah. Undoubtedly afraid that God might decide to unleash further devastation on the cities of the Jordan plain, Lot would not remain in the city of Zoar where he had taken refuge, but took his two daughters to the shelter of a cave in the mountains nearby. "One day the older daughter said to the younger, 'Our father is old, and there is no man around here to lie with us. . . . Let's get our father to drink wine and then lie with him and preserve our family line through our father" (19:31ff). And so Lot allowed himself to become drunk and, in an incestuous liaison with their father, his two daughters were impregnated with sons. Reason and the account together suggest that what happened was not a single episode but transpired over time.

While the narrator does not explicitly pass judgment on Lot's actions, he does depict the evolution of a moral and spiritual ruin. And indirectly, by the story's conclusion, severe condemnation is made of the incestuous affair and Lot's utter bankruptcy.[39]

Jacob and Esau

Depravity continued to manifest itself in Abraham's direct line through his grandsons, Jacob and Esau. The narrator gives us a number of pictures which show the character of both—Esau, the elder (twin) brother, who had a complete disregard for spiritual concerns; Jacob, the younger twin, whose life was founded on deceit.

We are given an accurate portrait of both in Genesis 25:29-34. Esau had been off hunting, but without success. Famished, he dropped in on Jacob who was cooking lunch. "He said to Jacob,

'Quick, let me have some of that red stew! I'm famished!' . . . Jacob replied, 'First sell me your birthright.' 'Look, I am about to die,' Esau said. 'What good is the birthright to me?' " (25:30-32) Jacob made him swear an oath giving over to him the right of inheritance, thus making the transfer completely binding.[40] Then he gave Esau some of the stew, and he consumed it. "So Esau despised his birthright" (25:34).

One must wonder about Esau's disregard for his birthright. It may well have been that he had no confidence in the covenant promises that God had given to his father Isaac and his grandfather Abraham. Jacob, on the other hand, obviously trusted these promises.[41] Esau's sin was his disdain for spiritual things; Jacob's, his selfishness and cruelty toward his brother.

Jacob's deceitfulness was highlighted in his theft of his brother's covenant blessing. It was not enough to deprive Esau of his birthright; he had to steal the blessing too. What was even worse, their mother was his active accomplice, coaching him on how to deceive his father into thinking that he was Esau. So Isaac gave Jacob the blessing intended for Esau. When Esau discovered that he had lost the blessing, "he burst out with a loud and bitter cry and said to his father, 'Bless me—me, too, my father!' But he said, 'Your brother came deceitfully and took your blessing' " (27:35ff). There was nothing left for him.

Esau planned to kill Jacob. But their mother, Rebecca, sent him to stay with her brother Laban in Haran. There, the deceiver was deceived by his uncle, who made him work for seven years for the love of his life, Rachel, only to pawn off on him her ugly elder sister; then he made him work another seven years for his intended. "That Laban secretly gave the unloved Leah to the man in love was, to be sure, a monstrous blow, a masterpiece of shameless treachery, by which he for the time being outmaneuvered Jacob, who was not exactly dubious either."[42] But Jacob was not outmaneuvered for long. Shortly after marrying Rachel he tricked Laban out of hundreds of cattle and made himself wealthy (30:25-43).

Joseph and his brothers

The Joseph narrative in Genesis 37–50 serves as a balance and contrast to the primeval record of the first eleven chapters of the book. The author seems to have deliberately depicted it as an antitype to Adam and to the remaining principle characters in that first section of Genesis.[43] Joseph's brothers had committed a sin against God and an evil against their brother almost as heinous as that of Cain against Abel by selling him into slavery in Egypt (37:26-28). When God exalted Joseph as prime minister of Egypt and placed his brothers in his power, they were very fearful (45:3) and were especially so when their father died, feeling that Joseph might now seek retribution for their wicked deed (50:15). But their brother quieted their apprehensions: "Don't be afraid. Am I in the place of God? You intended to harm me, but God intended it for good to accomplish what is now being done, the saving of many lives" (50:19ff). Here we come full circle, from the division of brothers in Genesis 4 because of sin, to the using of sin by God to bring reconciliation to brothers. "And in Joseph there is in fact explicitly fulfilled for the first time the promise to the patriarchs of their being a blessing to the peoples of the earth (12:3; 28:15)."[44] The sin of Joseph's brothers and its satisfying resolution becomes not only a foil to the primeval history, but provides linkage to the Book of Exodus and the liberation of Israel under Moses.[45]

Moses

Moses is reckoned by the Scriptures to be the greatest of the Old Testament prophets. Surely if anyone should have been free of sin, it would have been Moses. But when we examine the record we find him starting off by murdering a fellow Egyptian (Ex. 2:12). His career as a leader of Israel went along blamelessly, but ended on a sour note.

During the wanderings of the Israelites in the wilderness, they camped at Kadesh in the Desert of Zin. But there was no water to be had, and so the people began to rail at Moses and complain about poor treatment. "The Lord said to Moses, 'Take the staff, and you and your brother Aaron gather the assembly together. Speak to that rock before their eyes and it will pour out water' " (Num. 20:7-8). Moses did as the Lord ordered, and assembled the people together before the rock. But then, "Moses said to them, 'Listen, you rebels, must we bring you water out of this rock?' Then Moses raised his arm and struck the rock twice with his staff. Water gushed out, and the community and their livestock drank" (Num. 20:10-11). Moses had allowed his anger to get the better of him and had disobeyed God, striking the rock instead of speaking to it. There was, furthermore, an element of pride evident in his question, "Must *we* bring you water out of this rock?"

Moses' punishment was severe: "Because you did not trust in me enough to honor me as holy in the sight of the Israelites, you will not bring this community into the land I give them" (Num. 20:12).

Aaron

Aaron was Moses' brother and the first high priest of Israel as well as the head of a line of priests by appointment of the Lord God Himself (Ex. 28:1ff; Num. 8:10ff). One would expect the high priest of God to be exemplary in his behavior. Alas, it was not to be!

When Moses went up on Mount Sinai to receive God's law, he was away so long that the Israelites became restive. "They gathered around Aaron and said, 'Come, make us gods who will go before us. As for this fellow Moses who brought us up out of Egypt, we don't know what has happened to him" (Ex. 32:1). Aaron did as they asked, taking their gold and jewels and fashioning a golden calf. He built an altar in front of it and announced a festival to the Lord the following day. "So the next day the people rose early and sacrificed burnt offerings. . . . Afterward they sat down to eat and drink and got up to indulge in revelry" (Ex. 32:6).

Up on the mountain, God told Moses what was happening below, suggesting that He would destroy the Israelites and make Moses a great nation in their place. Moses remonstrated with God on Israel's behalf. "Then the Lord relented and did not bring on His people the disaster He had threatened" (Ex. 32:14).

When Moses came down the mountain and saw the golden calf and the revelry of the Hebrew people, he became extremely angry. He took the calf, ground it to a powder, mixed it with water, and forced the people to drink it. Then he directed his anger at Aaron: "What did these people do to you, that you led them into such great sin?" (Ex. 32:21) Aaron responded, "You know how prone these people are to evil. . . . they gave me the

174

gold, and I threw it into the fire, and out came this calf!" (32:22, 24) Rather a lame excuse!

The result of this terrible sin was the death of some 3,000 of the guilty. Moses again interceded for Israel before the Lord, but "the Lord replied to Moses, 'Whoever has sinned against me I will blot out of my book.'. . . And the Lord struck the people with a plague because of what they did with the calf Aaron had made" (32:33, 35).

One wonders how Aaron escaped death. It may be that, while he made the calf, he did not worship it. But he certainly facilitated the Israelites' disastrous orgy.

Nor was this the only such episode. Some time later, as the Hebrews wandered through the desert, both Aaron and Miriam tried to incite an insurrection against Moses because of his Cushite wife, whom they hated. " 'Has the Lord spoken only through Moses?' they asked. 'Hasn't he also spoken through us?' " (Num. 12:2)

But God was aware of what they were up to, and He punished Miriam by striking her with leprosy. Aaron appealed to Moses to forgive their foolishness and the latter interceded with the Lord to heal their sister. Miriam was excluded from the Israelite camp for seven days, at which time she was whole again (Num. 12:14-15).

Once more we may ask why no punishment was meted out to Aaron. He was certainly a co-conspirator with his sister. There is no answer to such a question. We may only suppose that he was a pawn in Miriam's plot. At least, the scenario would suggest such a case.

Aaron's sins seem to have come out of a weak character. All of these episodes demonstrate how easily he was led by others, whether the Hebrew people, his sister, or his brother.

Leviticus: Atonement and forgiveness

Leviticus, the third section of the Pentateuch, is known by rabbinic Judaism as *tôrat kōhanîm*, "law of the priests." It deals almost completely with cult, the overseeing of which was the province of Aaron and his descendants, a part of the tribe of Levi.[46] The basis of the Hebrew cult was the sacrificial system. While sacrifice was a prominent aspect of Near Eastern religions and Israel shared many of their features, the practices of the latter were securely ensconced in the context of divine revelation from Sinai.[47] Two of the offerings of the sacrificial system—the sin and guilt offerings—concern the covering over of the people's sin.

The sin offering

Leviticus 4:1–5:13 discusses atonement for unintentional sins. The passage speaks to four different categories: the priest (4:3-12), the whole community (4:13-21), the tribal leader (4:22-26), and the individual Hebrew (4:27–5:13).

When God's representative—"the anointed priest"—sinned, there was danger of his infecting the entire community with guilt. Thus, it was particularly important that he make atonement for his sin. To do so, he must bring to the Lord "a young bull without defect as a sin offering for the sin he has committed" (4:3). A set ritual was to be followed, where the blood was taken into the Tent of Meeting and sprinkled seven times in front of the curtain of the sanctuary. Then some of it was spread on the horns of the altar of incense, and the remainder poured out at its base.

If the entire Hebrew community became guilty of breaking God's law unintentionally, a similar ritual (as with the priest) was to be followed, except that the elders—as representatives of the community—would lay hands on the bull's head prior to its being slaughtered.

The sin offering for the leader and the ordinary Hebrew were essentially the same. The former was to offer a male goat (4:23) and the latter a female goat (4:28). Only a very small amount of blood was used; it was not spread on the horns of the altar of incense, but only on the altar of burnt offering. The rest was poured out at the altar's base. Noordtzij notes that

> the blood from these individual sin offerings was never brought within the sanctuary. This indicates that an unintentional transgression committed by a leader or a common Israelite was considered to be less serious than the cases discussed previously, since the guilt here applies only to the individual.[48]

In 5:1-6, three cases are set forth which concern sins resulting from thoughtlessness. The first involves one who witnessed a misdeed by another but failed to testify about it (5:1). The second dealt with one who touched something—animal or human—ritually unclean and so was defiled and potentially able to make others unclean (5:2). The third concerned one who thoughtlessly swore an oath to do something without due regard to its sanctity (5:4). "When anyone is guilty in any of these ways, he must confess in what way he has sinned and, as a penalty for the sin he has committed, he must bring to the Lord a female lamb or goat from the flock as a sin offering; and the priest shall make atonement for him for his sin" (5:5-6). Allowances were also made for those too poor to afford the specified animal. They could give instead a pair of doves or pigeons (5:7-10) or a tenth of an ephah of fine flour (5:11-13).

Noordtzij summarizes this offering by observing that

> except in the sin offering of the high priest who, in being both the guilty person and the person performing the ritual of atonement, occupied a unique position, the assurance was at all times given that the presenting of the sin offering would be followed by atonement and forgiveness (4:20, 26, 35; 5:6, 13). Whoever confessed his sin and presented an offering in accordance with his means received forgiveness, and no one was excluded from this possibility.[49]

The guilt offering

Leviticus 5:14–6:7 sets out a second sacrifice of expiation, the guilt offering. It is distinct from the sin offering in that it concerns a "breach of faith," or some offense against property.[50] Wherever this offering was required, not only was the sacrifice of a ram or its equivalent demanded, but also restitution. The offender "must make restitution in full, add a fifth of the value to it and give it all to the owner [of the property taken] on the day he presents his sin offering" (6:5). It is obvious that the law for the guilt offering was the consequence of two separate prescribed acts, which concerned respectively the allocation of what was holy to the Lord (5:15-19) and the allocation of what was the property of one's fellow Hebrew (6:1-7).[51]

177

6.1: LEVITICAL SACRIFICES

Burnt Offering
Atonement for sin in general
Male of herd or flock without flaw
All was offered
Leviticus 1

Meal Offering
Thankfulness for firstfruits
Unleavened, salted cakes or grain
Token amount was offered
Leviticus 2

Peace Offering
Blessings, deliverance, general thanksgiving
Male or female without flaw
Fat pieces were offered
Leviticus 3; 22:18-30

Sin Offering
Purification
Priest or group: bull
King: male goat
Individual: female goat
Fat pieces were offered
Leviticus 4:1–5:13

Guilt Offering
Objective guilt or defilement of something holy
Ram without flaw
Fat pieces were offered
Leviticus 5:14–6:7

The Day of Atonement

The great Hebrew fast day known as the Day of Atonement or day of coverings occurred annually on the tenth day of Tishri. Leviticus 16 delineates its rites. It was one of the most determinative rituals in all of Judaism, especially in the few centuries prior to Christianity. Its tremendous vitality serves to explain why that holy day survived the devastation of the Jerusalem temple, despite the fact that its rites symbolized the sacrificial system.[52]

The death of Aaron's sons Nadab and Abihu (10:1ff) provided the context for the initiation of the Day of Atonement. The high priest, on the morning of the sacrifice, was to bathe (16:4) and then don the sacred garments of his office (16:4). "From the Israelite community he is to take two male goats for a sin offering and a ram for a burnt offering" (16:5).

Before beginning the rites of atonement on behalf of the people, he was to select a bull to make atonement for himself and his family. Then he was to take the goats and bring them before the Lord at the entrance to the tabernacle. He would cast lots to see which would be sacrificed as an offering to the Lord and which would be used as a scapegoat to bear the sins of the people into the desert.

The high priest would purify himself by offering the bull as a sin offering. Then he would slaughter the goat for the sin offering on behalf of the people. He would take some of the blood of the animal and enter the Most Holy Place, where he would sprinkle it. "In this way he will make atonement for the Most Holy Place because of the weakness and rebellion of the Israelites, whatever their sins have been. He is to do the same thing for the Tent of Meeting, which is among them in the midst of their uncleanness" (16:16). He would take some of the blood and sprinkle it seven times on the horns of the altars, thus cleansing them from the uncleanness of the Israelites (16:7). "Thus the instruments of the cultus on which the relation between God and Israel depended were once again 'holy' and usable by God."[53]

Whereas the sacrifice of the goat was to achieve the removal of Israel's defilement of its cultus, the idea of the scapegoat was to remove the guilt of the people themselves. Once the high priest had fully atoned for his own sins, he was to bring out the goat.

"He is to lay both hands on the head of the goat and confess over it all the wickedness and rebellion of the Israelites — all their sins — and put them on the goat's head. He shall send the goat away into the desert in the care of a man appointed for the task. The goat will carry on itself all their sins to a solitary place; and the man shall release it in the desert" (16:21-22).

The goat was regarded to be indeed ladened with all the sins of all the people. As it was led off into the wilderness never to return, even so their sins were taken away, never to return. Thus, the people were liberated from all their sins, with the exception, of course, of those sins "with a high hand," that is, sins committed defiantly.[54]

The rites were now completed. The high priest returned to his regular garments and offered burnt offerings for himself and the people (16:24ff).

Rylaarsdam summarizes the significance of this rite by noting that, "According to the Mishna (Yom. 8.8-9) repentance was indispensable if one were to participate in the fruits of the Day of Atonement . . . only the action of God through and by the cultus he himself had instituted could wipe out man's sin."[55]

Deuteronomy

While Deuteronomy is an integral part of the Pentateuch, because of its origins and character it is quite different from the other four books, and so it deserves special consideration. The other books of the Pentateuch purport to be "law codes" given by God to Moses, and then transmitted by him to Aaron or to the assembly of Israel. But Deuteronomy is not a law code; rather, it is a restatement of the law in a hortatory or homiletical context.[56]

The book is part of that group of books ascribed to Moses. It is doubtful that anyone would argue that Dueteronomy was written by Moses in its entirety, for no one would say that he wrote about his own death! What is argued is how much of the material is Mosaic and how much is demonstrably post-Mosaic. The dating of the book is much debated by scholars and ranges from the second millennium (the time of Moses) to as late as the postexilic period (500 B.C.).[57] I would side with conservative evangelical scholarship that Deuteronomy is based firmly and substantially on the historical Moses and the words he gave to Israel in Moab.

On the other hand, some editorial efforts are plainly visible and it would be difficult to give a date for its final form. That form may have taken shape in the general era of the United Monarchy some two or three centuries after Moses' death.[58]

Deuteronomy: a bridge to history

Marvin Tate has stated that the chief concern of Deuteronomy is with the salvation history of Israel, and so it is not only "law preached" but also "history preached."[59] In its present form it appears to have been intended as a guide to the Israelites for a secure existence in the Promised Land.[60]

Over the last several decades scholars have become increasingly aware that this book plays a critical part in the formation of the Old Testament. It undoubtedly began with the realization that the law book found in the temple during its renovation by Josiah must have been this book or a major portion of it. We know from 2 Kings 22–23 that its message led Josiah to foster a spirit of national repentance and initiate sweeping reforms. Along with Hezekiah's reforms (2 Chron. 29), we know of no others during the monarchy period which sought to make Mosaic law the basis of Hebrew life.[61]

Further insight into the importance of Deuteronomy dawned in 1942 with the work of Martin Noth on Old Testament history. Its effect was not felt for several more years, however, because of World War II. He declared that the books of Joshua, Judges, 1 and 2 Samuel, and 1 and 2 Kings were all bound together by a theological interpretation which was based on Deuteronomy. He referred to this work with the abbreviation Dtr.

> To access the work as a whole, it is more important to notice certain aspects of the arrangement of the books Joshua-Kings which can be traced back to the work of Dtr. In particular, at all the important points in the course of the history, Dtr. brings forward the leading personages with a speech, long or short, which looks forward and backward in an attempt to interpret the course of events, and draws the relevant practical conclusions about what people should do.[62]

Research has continued on the importance of Deuteronomy to Old Testament history.

181

Thus, both Deuteronomy and the Deuteronomistic history to which it gave impetus are essentially theological works with theological messages. The former is the closest Old Testament work we have to a systematic theology. "They both display a method to be used to enunciate the faith in a way that speaks to their own particular times, that will give the faithful a doctrinal hold on themselves as they face challenging new situations, and that will help to unify and correlate the elements of faith to withstand assault from without."[63]

The structure of Deuteronomy

To even a casual reader it should be evident that the book has a carefully defined structure. The most apparent aspect is that it incorporates three addresses of Moses to Israel. In the first (1:6–4:40), Moses appeals to Israel to pay attention to God's demands. The second address (chaps. 5–28), the main section of the book, contains instructions in the law. The third (chaps. 29–30) appeals to Israel to accept and keep the covenant. Chapters 31–34 appear to be appendices.[64]

The first address

This first address is strong in its appeal to history. Moses reminded the people of their early days from the Exodus on. He noted how God had commanded them to possess the Promised Land, "but you were unwilling to go up; you rebelled against the command of the Lord your God" (1:26). Because of their lack of faith they were condemned to wander in the wilderness until their generation had died out. In spite of their sin and its punishment, however, God had provided graciously for them (2:7).

The climax to this address is found in the fourth chapter. Having reminded the people of God's goodness and His punishment, Moses now exhorted them to heed His commands. Obedience would bring blessing—life and security in the land of promise; disobedience would result in punishment—death and a loss of security. "The principle here stated has become known as the Deuteronomic principle. It is stated many times in Deuteronomy, but it is also found elsewhere in the Old Testament, either directly or by inference."[65] Moses clearly illustrated this principle by reminding the people what had happened at Baal Peor: "The Lord your God destroyed from among you everyone who followed the Baal of Peor, but all of you who held fast to the Lord your God are still alive today" (4:3-4).

Moses warned them, as well, of the dangers of idolatry. God had taken Israel out of bondage in Egypt to be His own possession. Such a unique status demanded a particular ethical behavior, clearly set forth in the covenant God had made with them.

Moses cautioned them against forgetting that covenant as the years passed by, and turning them away from God to idols. Should that occur, the result would be death, dispossession from the land, and a scattering among foreign nations (4:26ff). Thus, exile was promised. And yet, even under such terrible circumstances, promised Moses, the Lord would not forget them.

But if from there you seek the Lord your God, you will find him if you look for him with all your heart and all your soul. When you are in distress and all these things have happened to you, then in later days you will return to the Lord your God and obey him. For the Lord your God is a merciful God; he will not abandon or destroy you or forget the covenant with your forefathers, which he confirmed to them by oath (4:29-31).

The second address

This second speech by Moses is the substance of what he had learned atop Mount Sinai alone when he had met with the Lord God. Moses here was acting as a mediator between Israel and her God.

Moses had already pointed out to the people (in his previous address) the importance of God's covenant and their obedience to it. Now he reminded them of the Decalogue, the most fundamental of covenant stipulations (5:1-21). These "Ten Commandments" declared that God had set out two broad areas of obligation for His people, relating to Him and to their fellows. To violate any one of them would be to violate one's relationship with God Himself.[66] Von Rad tells us that the Decalogue "speaks of duties towards God and towards man. In the second part the commandment to honor parents comes across first, then follow

the commandments which protect the life, the marriage, the freedom, the reputation and the possessions of fellow men."⁶⁷ Moses
also reminded them of their reaction to the giving of these laws:
"We will listen and obey" (5:27). And he exhorted them to keep
that intention "so that you may live and prosper and prolong your
days in the land that you will possess" (5:33).

He then continued his exhortation to the people, emphasizing
that God was not a pantheon; He was One. Thus, they must
make Him the full and only object of their religious devotion:
"Hear, O Israel: The Lord our God, the Lord is one. Love the
Lord your God with all your heart and with all your soul and with
all your strength" (6:4-5). In Deuteronomy, "love" is almost synonymous with "obedience."⁶⁸ This commandment was to be
transmitted from parent to child on a continuing basis. Adherence
would bring reward, but a failure to obey the Lord would bring
terrible punishment, "for the Lord your God . . . is a jealous God
and his anger will burn against you, and he will destroy you from
the face of the land" (6:15).

Moses observed that God was giving Canaan to Israel as an
inheritance. It would be sumptuously supplied with all good
things (8:7-9). But these very blessings in their abundance might
become a hazard to God's people and so the speaker admonished
Israel not to forget the Lord and become self-confident and
proud: "You may say to yourself, 'My power and the strength of
my hands have produced this wealth for me.' But remember the
Lord your God, for it is he who gives you the ability to produce
wealth, and so confirms his covenant" (8:17-18). In such bountiful
times, the nation must beware of dishonoring the covenant with
God by turning to self-adoration, the ultimate idolatry.

Nor was this the only danger. Moses also warned the people
against thinking — once they had possessed the land — that they
had achieved victory over their enemies because of some righteousness inherent within themselves (9:1-6). To the contrary,
Israel was sinful, but God was working out through them His
own purposes. Indeed, "from the day you left Egypt until you
arrived here, you have been rebellious against the Lord" (9:7).
And Moses digressed upon a lengthy history of that rebellion
noting that, had it not been for his intercession and the Lord's
forbearance, they would have been destroyed (9:25-29).⁷⁰

Most of the remainder of this second address was taken up

with the detailed covenant laws. There are seven major sections: (1) 12:1–14:21, concerning the unity and purity of the nation's worship; (2) 14:22–16:17, concerning various obligations and institutions; (3) 16:18–18:22, concerning the responsibilities of officials and Israel's duties to them; (4) 19:1–21:9, concerning war and death; (5) 21:10–22:30, concerning family relationships and respect for life; (6) 23:1–25:19, concerning purity and compassion; (7) 26:1-15, concerning first-fruit and tithing obligations.[71] In all of these areas, severe penalties were set forth for offenders.

This second address closed with a proclamation of blessings and curses, a natural pattern in ancient covenants.[72] Many interpreters feel that this section was amplified — particularly the segment of curses — in the years following.[73] The Israelites would be richly blessed if they were obedient to the covenant; they would be cursed and destroyed if they failed to observe the covenant and its laws.

The third address

Moses, being mediator between God and Israel, was commanded by the Lord to establish the terms of the covenant with the nation (29:1). The third and final address was the ratification of the covenant, and it followed the traditional Near Eastern treaty pattern, even though it was presented in narrative rather than systematic form.[74]

The ratification began, typically, with a historical review (29:2-8). Thompson notes:

> Alas, Israel, so signally favoured as to have lived in the midst of many evidences of divine favor and power, lacked the deeper understanding . . . to discern behind the external events a deeper significance. . . . Such blindness on the part of those who reject God's revelation is not uncommon. Men may hear but not understand, because of a hardness of heart.[75]

So concerned was the writer with the sin of idolatry that he felt constrained once again to caution the people against this abhorrent practice. He noted how, when traveling through foreign lands en route from Egypt to Canaan, they had observed "among them their detestable images and idols of wood and stone, of silver and gold" (29:17).

In typical treaty form, the speaker posed a series of questions and answers which presupposed the destruction of the covenant people for having failed to be obedient to covenant stipulations (29:22-28). Exile to a foreign land was promised, along with the utter desolation of their homeland.

The preacher seemed to take it for granted (in 30:1) that the Hebrew people would fail to keep the covenant. When that occurred, they would turn back to God in obedience. "Then the Lord your God will restore your fortunes and have compassion on you and gather you again from all the nations where he scattered you" (30:3). Their enemies would be confounded and cursed, and the Israelites would once more be restored to a secure position within the divine economy.

This address was concluded with a clear-cut choice set before the people.

> See, I have set before you today life and prosperity, death and destruction. For I command you today to love the Lord your God, to walk in his ways, and to keep his commands, decrees and laws, that you will live and increase. . . . But if your heart turns away and you are not obedient, and if you are drawn away to bow down to other gods and worship them, I declare to you this day that you will certainly be destroyed (30:15-18).

Conclusion

Several appendices conclude Deuteronomy. They deal with such things as Moses' appointment of Joshua to succeed him, provisions for the reading of the law, and Moses' death. In telling Moses of his impending demise, the Lord also gave him an insight into Israel's future (31:15ff). The people would soon "prostitute themselves to the foreign gods of the land they are entering" (31:15). They would abandon God and break the covenant. When that occurred, He would allow many disasters to come to them "because of all their wickedness in turning to other gods" (31:18). God commanded Moses to write a witness against them for Him. Chapter 32 is a record of the song of witness he wrote and taught the Israelites.

Observations

The major sin against which Deuteronomy inveighs seems to be apostasy, that willful abandonment of God in favor of other gods of one's own choosing. The Israelites were warned that such a turning away would cause their devastation and enslavement by foreign peoples. If they repented, however, and sought the Lord once more, He would restore them and His blessings would be poured out upon them once more, for He was always willing and ready for reconciliation (but only in the context of their obedient devotion). This cycle of obedience and blessing—disobedience and devastation—repentance and renewal would be foundational to Israel's history in the centuries to come.

Summary: The Mosaic Theology of Sin

It has been suggested by one scholar that we should think of the Pentateuch in terms of a novel.

> Not that it is a work of fantasy. . . . Like *War and Peace* and *Adam Bede,* the Pentateuch has its own truth and its own credibility even when it recounts events some people may not think actually happened, like a talking snake or a universal flood. Like a novel, it reports the inner thoughts of its characters . . . and it recounts the dialogue of persons whose actual words have been long since forgotten when the author was writing. Like a novel, it transports its readers through space and time, makes them witnesses to the behaviors and changing motivations of its characters . . . insisting that its readers judge for themselves the persons and the acts they encounter in its pages.[78]

The Pentateuch is largely a narrative in form and is a unity. We should see it not as five separate books, but as a single book in five volumes. The theme of the work is God's relationship with humanity. It details God's goodness to human beings, their betrayal of that goodness, and how He reacted in turn.

Genesis depicts the beauty of God's creation, noting that "God saw all that He had created and it was very good" (Gen. 1:31). The first man and woman were a part of that goodness. The narrator then describes a chain of events precipitated by human sin. It began with the humans' decision to seek parity with their Creator, and so they plucked and ate the fruit of the tree of the knowledge of good and evil. By seeking to amplify their being on the godward side beyond the natural boundaries (in other words, by desiring equality with God), Adam and Eve removed themselves from simple obedience to the Lord. They were rewarded with lives of pain and toil, and a never-ending and futile battle with evil and, ultimately, death.[79] From that point, the quality of human behavior steadily declined until God determined to eliminate all humankind, with the exception of righteous Noah and his family. But even this new start was to little avail, and God eventually destroyed human unity by confounding their language.

In spite of increasing human depravity, God did not give up on His errant creation. Out of all the peoples of the earth, He selected one family and from that family one individual, Abraham. Because Abraham proved faithful, God promised to make him a great nation, to place him and his posterity in a new land which would be their everlasting possession, and to make him a blessing to all nations.

The promise to Abraham and his progeny was the beginning of God's covenant dealings with His special people. By the time of the Exodus, the family of Abraham had become the nation Israel. Upon rescuing them from slavery in Egypt, God formulated a conditional covenant with them. If the Israelites obeyed Him, He would bless them; if they were disobedient, He would punish them. To guide them, God gave them His law, the primary aspect of which was that He was to be Israel's God, their only Lord.

In spite of God's goodness to Israel and the explicitness of His covenant, the Hebrews were disobedient almost from the outset of their release from slavery. Their prepossessing sin was idolatry, the worship of false gods.

The Book of Deuteronomy sums up the theology of the author. Having described both human depravity and God's grace, he presents a straightforward conclusion: God has set forth His covenant with His people; if they obey it, they will receive blessing. Human proclivity toward sin being what it is, however, the Israelites will turn away from Him to other gods. God must and will punish such sin in a terrible fashion. At the same time, He is even more ready and willing to forgive and restore than to punish. If and when His people will abandon their sin and turn to Him in repentance, the Lord will forgive them and reinstate them. This theology would be the framework for Hebrew worship and doctrine for centuries to come.

Chapter Seven
The Prophetic
Teaching on Sin

T he second division of the Hebrew Scriptures is the Prophets. It includes the Former Prophets, or historical books, and the Latter Prophets, or those prophets whose writings were collected and preserved. We shall examine the historical section and then the Latter Prophets in an effort to extract their teaching on sin.

The Deuteronomic History

As was mentioned earlier, scholarly research—both "mainline" and evangelical—has generally come to regard Joshua–Kings as a unified, comprehensive history of Israel from its beginnings in Canaan. To make such a statement is not to imply that all these books were written by a single author, nor that they were written in a time frame far removed from the events which are described, but rather that they were written by Deuteronomic historians, that is, those who saw events in Israelite history unfolding in terms of the theological pattern used in Deuteronomy. Some of these writers may have taken existing historical materials at a latter date and reworded them to conform to the Deuteronomic model.[1] At any rate, because it was so strongly influenced by the

Book of Deuteronomy, this selection of historical books has been given the name Deuteronomic (or Deuteronomistic) History.[2]

This history was probably completed (in its final form) during the Hebrew Exile. Since the last recorded event is the freeing of Jehoiachin from imprisonment in Babylon (561 B.C.), it is probable that the work was completed some time in 560 B.C. or shortly thereafter.

The writer used in the Book of Deuteronomy as a paradigm for a theology for Exile, a period in which the Hebrew people were forced to reformulate their faith, worship, and lifestyle. Consequently, the overwhelming majority of scholars (of all stripes) refer to him as the Deuteronomist. John Watts tells us that the author developed his theology for this terrible time in three parts:

> The first is a theology of history which notes that the era of Moses-Joshua was followed by the disasters recorded in Judges-Samuel. Then he demonstrates a theology of God's initiative or response in which a new chapter opens with David-Solomon only to be followed by the disasters of the Kingdoms. This in turn leaves room for a new response from God.[3]

Mingled in with the history are appeals to the Hebrews to return to God and to call upon Him, with the assurance that if they do so He will return to them.[4]

The Book of Joshua: Hope for the future

This book has taken its title from its principle character. His name is significant, for the Hebrew form, *Yehoshua*, means "the Lord is salvation" and is the name given by the angelic messenger to our Savior (in the Greek, *Iesous*). It gives us some idea of the author's intention in writing.

In his commentary, Marten Woudstra warns against placing a human hero at the center of any biblical account. Scripture is theocentric, not anthropocentric. He observes, "The historical context within which the events are placed by the biblical author tends to be ignored. When a straight line is drawn from the 'then' to the 'now,' the uniqueness of biblical events as instances of

God's self-revelation is in danger of being overlooked."[5] Indeed, the book's purpose lies in recording God's mighty works "so that you might always fear the Lord your God" (4:24).

One aspect heavily emphasized by the author—some would say the central emphasis—is the eternal faithfulness of God.[6] Israel would endure much opposition and undergo considerable difficulty. Apostasy would recur. Enslavement lay down the road. During such times, God's people needed to hear that He was ever loyal to His proclaimed word.[7]

God's Word was mediated to Israel primarily in covenantal form. One would suppose that previous experience would have dictated to the people of Israel the wisdom of obeying it. And yet, only a short time after crossing into Canaan, one finds a blatant disregard for God's commands.

God had promised the miraculous destruction of the walls of Jericho and that city's fall to the army of Israel. Everything in the city, however, was placed under the ban *(herem);* that is, the city was to be totally destroyed and nothing retained (excepting the family of Rahab, because of her kindness to the Hebrew spies, and precious metals which were consigned to the Lord's treasury) as a sign that God had cursed the place (6:17-19). Trent Butler tells us that

> *[herem]* was not only a program for Israel to accomplish. It was a temptation in Israel's way. She could be placed under *[herem]* if she violated the program of *[herem]* set out for her by her leader. The danger was not only individual. The individual's act endangered the entire community.[8]

Despite such clear instruction, we read, "But the Israelites acted unfaithfully in regard to the devoted things *[herem]*" (7:1). Achan, a soldier from Judah, took some booty and hid it under his tent. "So the Lord's anger burned against Israel" (7:1).

The result was that Achan's sin was imputed to Israel as a whole. The author was seeking to demonstrate that Israel must not take God or His blessings for granted. The nation was always bound to God in its covenantal commitment to obedience. When that commitment was disregarded or taken lightly, then His anger flared, and Israel's place and possessions were threatened.[9]

The immediate consequence of God's anger was displayed at

Ai. Not knowing of the violation of the ban, Joshua sent 3,000 armed men against the city, but they were defeated and thirty-six of them were slain (7:3-5). When he approached the Lord in perplexed dismay to ask why this catastrophe had occurred, God was very blunt in His response: "Israel has sinned; they have violated my covenant, which I commanded them to keep. They have taken some of the dedicated things" (7:11). If the Lord was ever to be with the people again, then the violation of the ban would have to be removed. "He who is caught with the devoted things shall be destroyed by fire, along with all that belongs to him" (7:15).

Achan was singled out and exhorted by Joshua to confess fully, thus glorifying God in the truth. Woudstra notes that "the sin is committed against God; it is a violation of his covenant, and only through giving glory to him can the evil be eradicated. Hiding the sin would be a form of self-assertion."[10] Achan complied, admitting the theft of silver, gold, and a Babylonian robe (7:20ff).

Achan's punishment for the violation of God's covenant was death by stoning for him and his family (thus suggesting their collusion in his crime). Their bodies were then burned and stones were piled atop their remains as a memorial of all that had occurred (7:25ff). God's anger against Israel was now terminated and a fresh attack on Ai brought success (8:1-29).

Following Ai's destruction, the whole Israelite encampment was moved into the area. Joshua called a meeting of all the people, built an altar to God on which he carved a copy of the Mosaic law (perhaps the Decalogue), and read to this solemn assembly "all the words of the law — the blessings and the curses — just as it is written in the Book of the Law" (8:34). This covenant renewal ceremony showed the people that even though they had sinned and broken God's covenant, they remained inheritors of His promises and blessings. In repenting of sin and making things right with the Lord, they found new acceptance by Him.[11]

Successive chapters of Joshua record the allotment of territory in Canaan to the various Israelite tribes. The writer notes: "So the Lord gave Israel all the land he had sworn to give their forefathers, and they took possession of it and settled there. . . . Not one of all the Lord's good promises to the house of Israel failed; every one was fulfilled" (21:43, 45). God's word is sure and will always be fulfilled as promised, in spite of His people's sinful disobedience.[12]

The last two chapters concern Joshua's farewell to the people as their leader (shortly before his death). Essentially, it was a call to covenant obedience. They were in many respects a reprise of the opening chapter. Joshua observed that the Lord had kept His promises to drive the other nations from the Promised Land. Time after time He had quite literally saved their lives. And their departing leader warned them (and a direct translation of the Hebrew reads), "Take care for your very souls that you love the Lord your God"[13] (23:11). If they wished to remain secure and have their lives maintained, in other words, they had best love their God. And a corollary of that love was to beware of apostasy, an ever-present possibility. Joshua noted the presence of remnants of the former inhabitants of Canaan in their midst and cautioned the Israelites against adopting their practices or intermarrying with them (both expressly forbidden by the Lord), for if they did, "you may be sure that the Lord your God will not continue to drive out these nations before you. Instead, they will become snares and traps for you, whips on your backs and thorns in your eyes, till you perish from this good land which the Lord your God has given you" (23:13).

Indeed, if they strayed from God into apostasy, Joshua declared, God's promise of wrath against them would be as surely fulfilled as were His promises to bring them into Canaan to possess the land. If they transgressed the covenant, they would certainly perish quickly from the land He had bestowed upon them (23:14-16).

At a solemn assembly convened in Shechem, Joshua provided the Israelites as a whole with a prophetic overview of the salvation history of Israel to this point, beginning with Terah, the father of Abraham (24:2). He reminded them that the Lord "gave you a land on which you did not toil and cities you did not build; and you live in them and eat from vineyards and olive groves that you did not plant" (24:13). He admonished them, therefore, to fear the Lord and serve Him exclusively. In the event that such a thing was not palatable to them, there was an alternative: "Choose for yourselves this day whom you will serve, whether the gods your forefathers served beyond the River, or the gods of the Amorites in whose land you are living" (24:15). But Joshua wanted it clearly understood that his choice and that of his household was to serve the Lord.

The people responded with an adamant declaration of loyalty to the Lord. Joshua accepted their affirmation of the covenant, but reminded them of God's holiness and jealousy. They could not assume that God would automatically forgive their sins. Two words are used here: The first is *pesha* (transgression) which sees sins as a willful breaking of the law. The second is *het*, which denotes sin as a missing of the righteousness required by God.[14] "If you forsake the Lord and serve foreign gods, then He will turn and bring disaster on you and make an end of you, after He has been good to you" (24:20).

So the covenant was renewed, in writing. And on the site of their commitment to the Lord, Joshua erected a large stone as "a witness against us, for it has heard all the words of the Lord which He spoke to us; it will be a witness against you so that you do not betray your God" (24:27).

The Book of Judges: An account of failure

The term from which this book acquires its name has very little relationship to our present idea of the judge as a legal arbiter. The key to the term in Hebrew may be seen in 2:16, "Then the Lord raised up judges who saved them [Israel] out of the hands of these raiders [oppressors]." These judges were essentially the liberators or saviors of their countrymen from tyrants. The Hebrew word for judge is not directly used of any individual except in 11:27 of the Lord. And this is the thought behind the writing of the book, that the Lord is Judge or Deliverer of Israel. He works through men and women of His choice to save His people.[15]

The era of the Judges was a vital time in Israel's history,[16] for it was a time of progression from existence as a number of different groups and tribes, often vying with one another, to national unity. Judges also demonstrates the changes effected as these nomadic peoples, living in relative isolation from others, now settle into a context dominated by the pagan religious culture of the Canaanite peoples. Much of Israel's future history is the result of formation by factors present during the period of the Judges.[17]

Theologically, the point which the author of Judges is trying to make is that the Israelites, called to come out from among the perverted Canaanite peoples surrounding them and be holy to the Lord, in spite of repeated deliverances revert to being Canaanite themselves in their lifestyle and religious practices. Instead of being counterculture in their living out of the covenant, they conform completely to the heathen cultural milieu.[18]

Walter Rast has divided the Book of Judges into four sections: (1) the entry of the Israelites into Canaan (an account differing from that in Joshua), 1:1–2:5; (2) a Deuteronomic introduction to the era being recounted, 2:6–3:6; (3) materials on Israel's liberators (the "judges"), 3:7–16:31; and (4) a series of appendices containing narratives of a number of tribal events, 17:1–21:25.[19]

The first section of Judges is an account of how the Israelite tribes, led by Judah, claimed Canaan in battle from its pagan inhabitants. For various reasons, however, they failed to vanquish completely their opponents in spite of God's commands to do so. Chapter 1, with a few exceptions, is a dreary tale of failure after failure. Consequently, the angel of the Lord came to the Israelites.

> I brought you up out of the land of Egypt. . . . I said, I will never break my covenant with you, and you shall not make a covenant with the people of this land, but you shall break down their altars. Yet you have disobeyed me. . . . Now therefore I tell you that I will not drive them out before you; they will be thorns in your sides and their gods will be a snare to you (2:1-3).

The author tells us that the people wept when they heard these words (2:4), but it was too late. Israel had failed to be faithful to God despite His faithfulness to her; now she would have to pay the price for her disobedience.

The second section (2:6–3:6) is not related chronologically to the former. This passage goes back beyond the first part to Joshua's last days and his death. It provides an overview of, and sets the tone for, the period of the Judges. The author notes that during Joshua's lifetime and even during the time of the elders who outlived him ("who had seen all the great things the Lord had done for Israel"), the Hebrews served the Lord (2:7). But with the passing of that generation, a new generation were spawned "who knew neither the Lord nor what He had done for Israel" (2:10). With this new and ignorant group began a recurring four-phased cycle which spanned the following two centuries.

Whenever the Lord raised up a judge for them, he was with the judge and saved them out of the hands of their enemies as long as the judge lived; for the Lord had compassion on them as they groaned under those who oppressed and afflicted them. But when the judge died, the people returned to ways more corrupt than those of their fathers, following other gods and serving and worshiping them. They refused to give up their evil practices and stubborn ways (2:18-19).

This cycle included more than a dozen judges.

Section three (3:7–16:31) gives detailed information on these cycles of perversity and reformation, beginning with Othniel (3:7ff) and concluding with Samson (13:1–16:31).

The concluding section (17:1–21:25) consists of a number of anecdotes concerning Dan and its migration to northern Canaan, and some about Benjamin. One of the most notable sections is chapter 19, which demonstrates clearly the failure of Israel to become truly the people of God. It is a narrative which is intended strongly to resemble (or even parallel) Genesis 19 (the Sodom and Gomorrah narrative). Indeed, some interpreters have suggested that it is earlier than the latter and that the Genesis narrative is secondary to it, but this is much open to dispute and it should be seen in reverse.[20] The story is crafted to demonstrate that the Ephraimite town in the Judges account is really Sodom and Gomorrah. When discerning Israelites look at themselves, they should see a nation which has not conformed to God's lofty call, but which has sunk to the depths of degradation of those cities God destroyed because of their great wickedness. Indeed, in this story we have the theme of Judges, the Canaanitization of Israel. Every section of the book stresses that horrifying message.[21]

In the last verse of the book, the Deuteronomic historian has both demonstrated the spiritual condition of Israel at this time and provided a link to the following books of Samuel: "In those days Israel had no king; everyone did as he saw fit" (21:25).

The last judge of Israel

The story of the judges extends into the early chapters of 1 Samuel, for Samuel was both the last and greatest of the judges

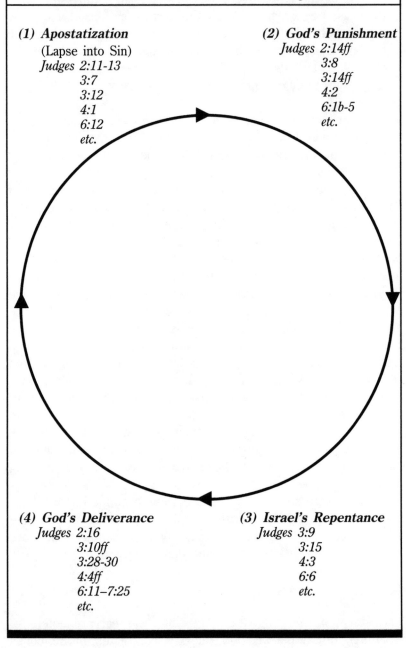

7.1: THE CYCLE OF SIN AND RESTORATION IN DEUTERONOMIC HISTORY AS ILLUSTRATED IN THE BOOK OF JUDGES

(1) Apostatization
(Lapse into Sin)
Judges 2:11-13
3:7
3:12
4:1
6:12
etc.

(2) God's Punishment
Judges 2:14ff
3:8
3:14ff
4:2
6:1b-5
etc.

(4) God's Deliverance
Judges 2:16
3:10ff
3:28-30
4:4ff
6:11–7:25
etc.

(3) Israel's Repentance
Judges 3:9
3:15
4:3
6:6
etc.

of Israel. It was under his guidance that Israel took a king.

First and 2 Samuel, like the other books of the Deuteronomic history, continue the story of the covenant. They are characterized by promise, the promise of a brighter and happier relationship with God as typified by the upward movement of their leadership from the low point of the house of Eli to the high point of God's promise to establish the house of David forever.

Samuel's story begins in the black days of the judges, when chaos reigned. Israel was being led by the priest Eli and his two sons, Hophni and Phinehas. These religious leaders, however, were more jaded than any who had preceded them. The Deuteronomic historian's judgment on them is that "Eli's sons were wicked men; they had no regard for the Lord" (1 Sam. 2:12). They would take from the meat offered to the Lord the fat portions that were supposed to be burnt before Him (2:13-17). They also were engaging in fornication with the women who took care of the tabernacle (2:22). Eli was too old to deal with his sons as he should have. But his words of reproof to them were prophetic: "If a man sins against another man, God may mediate for him; but if a man sins against the Lord, who will intercede for him?" (2:25) These degenerate and unheeding sons serve the author as a foil for Samuel, who "continued to grow in stature and in favor with the Lord and with men" (2:26).

Eli and his house were doubly condemned by the Lord. A prophet was sent to him with words of condemnation for him and his descendants. They would all die young, beginning with his sons who would both die on the same day. God would also replace them with a priest who would be faithful and devoted to Him (2:27-36). The Lord also spoke to Samuel in a vision, telling him that

> I will carry out against Eli everything I spoke against his family—from beginning to end. For I told him that I would judge his family forever because of the sin he knew about; his sons made themselves contemptible, and he failed to restrain them. Therefore, I swore to the house of Eli, "The guilt of Eli's house will never be atoned for by sacrifice or offering" (3:12-14).

When Samuel revealed to Eli what God had said, the old priest meekly accepted his fate: "He is the Lord; let Him do what is good in His eyes" (3:19).

It was not long before Israel was embroiled in a war with the Philistines. When they were defeated in the first battle, the Hebrews decided to take the ark of the covenant into battle with them, "so that it may go with us and save us from the hand of our enemies" (4:3). But it was to no avail. The Israelites were soundly defeated, Hophni and Phinehas were killed, and the ark was captured (4:10-12). When Eli heard the news, he fell off the chair on which he was sitting and died of a broken neck (4:18). Phinehas' wife went into labor and gave birth to a son whom she named Ichabod, "the glory has departed from Israel" (4:21).

With Samuel installed as the judge, however, the glory of the Lord returned. He led the Israelites to reject foreign gods and return to the Lord wholeheartedly (7:2-6). When the Philistines attacked Israel, they were routed. In fact,

> throughout Samuel's lifetime, the hand of the Lord was against the Philistines. The towns from Ekron to Gath that the Philistines had captured from Israel were restored to her, and Israel delivered the neighboring territory from the power of the Philistines. And there was peace between Israel and the Amorites (7:13-14).

The first king

When Samuel grew old, he appointed his sons, Joel and Abijah, as judges. "But his sons did not walk in his ways. They turned aside after dishonest gain and accepted bribes and perverted justice" (1 Sam. 8:3). As a result Israel's elders demanded a king to administer the nation. Initially, Samuel demurred, for the request for a king was simply one more sign of the people's continuing apostasy; they were rejecting God's kingship (8:7ff). Joyce Baldwin observes:

> The Lord had his ideal for his people, but in this far-from-ideal world he adapted his purposes and acquiesced sufficiently to allow Israel a king, even incorporating the monarchy into his revelation of himself to Israel. Kingship was soon to be a major theme of the Old Testament, but so was

the pattern, begun at the exodus, of refusal to obey the Lord's rule.[22]

Thus, when the Lord allowed their request, Samuel anointed Saul, son of Kish, of the tribe of Benjamin (1 Sam. 9). He warned the Israelites that if they and their king obeyed the Lord, all would be well. "But if you do not obey the Lord, and if you rebel against his commands, his hand will be against you, as it was against your fathers" (12:15).

While Saul started well, it was not long before he disobeyed God. He was campaigning against the Philistines and, when hard pressed, retreated to Gilgal. There he awaited Samuel, who had promised to sacrifice to God on the army's behalf. When Samuel did not arrive at the appointed time, the soldiers began to desert. "So he said, 'Bring me the burnt offering and the fellowship offering.' And Saul offered up the burnt offering" (1 Sam. 13:9). He had just finished when Samuel arrived.

"You acted foolishly," Samuel said. "You have not kept the command the Lord your God gave you; if you had, he would have established your kingdom over Israel for all time. But now your kingdom will not endure; the Lord your God has sought out a man after his own heart and appointed him as leader of his people, because you have not kept the Lord's command" (13:13-14).

On another occasion Samuel, on God's authority, commanded Saul to march on the Amalekites. He was to annihilate them and destroy all their possessions. But Saul spared the life of Agag, their king, and kept the best cattle and sheep (1 Sam. 15:1-9). When upbraided by Samuel, Saul suggested that he had kept the livestock to offer to God. But no ritual can atone for a defiant demeanor toward God and His injunctions, because obdurate obstinacy to God glorifies self as the authority, which is God's province alone.[23] Samuel's judgment on Saul was, "You have rejected the word of the Lord, and the Lord has rejected you as king over Israel" (15:26).

Saul had forgotten the Source of his authority. He had forgotten that his throne was utterly dependent upon his reverent and unhesitating obedience. His disobedience to God destroyed his rule beyond all hope of repair.[24] From this point on, Saul degenerated into melancholic madness and ultimately lost his kingdom and his life (1 Sam. 31:1-6).

The Davidic dynasty

With the accession to Israel's throne of David, son of Jesse, of the tribe of Judah, one would have supposed the days of apostasy to be over. After all, David had been termed by God to be a man after His own heart (1 Sam. 13:14), and God had promised him, "Your house and your kingdom will be established forever" (2 Sam. 7:16).

David was the greatest Israelite king of all, creating a powerful and wealthy empire. But his success went to his head, and he evidently came to think of himself as more than he was. One evening, when his troops were in the field and he was in Jerusalem, he saw from his palace rooftop a young woman bathing. Upon inquiry, he was told that she was Bathsheba, wife of one of his soldiers, Uriah the Hittite. Despite her marital status, the king sent for her and had intercourse with her, impregnating her (2 Sam. 11:1-5). When stratagems failed which were calculated to make Uriah appear responsible, David had his general, Joab, place that soldier in the front line of battle, where he was killed. David promptly made Bathsheba his wife, and she bore him a son. "But the thing David had done displeased the Lord" (11:27).

The duty of a prophet of the Lord was to encourage the king to fulfill his covenant responsibilities to God and to rebuke him should he be disobedient.[25] Nathan had succeeded Samuel in this office. When David sinned, it was his task to confront the king. Unlike his predecessor Saul, however, David at once repented and confessed, "I have sinned against the Lord" (2 Sam. 12:13). Baldwin comments, "This was the turning-point in the life of David, and the clearest indication that he was different from Saul in the most essential relationship of all, that of submission to the Lord."[26] God forgave David, although there were consequences to his sin which could not be recalled. The child of their illicit union died (12:15ff). David's family had all sorts of problems. His daughter Tamar was raped by her half brother Amnon (13:14), who in turn, was murdered by her brother Absalom (13:28ff). Even though David forgave him, it was not long before Absalom mounted a rebellion against his father and David was forced to flee Jerusalem (15:13ff). Absalom took his father's concubines as his own (16:21ff), thus heaping offense after offense upon his father. In due course, David's army put down the revolt and, during the fighting, Joab killed Absalom (18:14). David's last days were filled with hardship and sorrow.

Second Samuel 2–8 summarizes the kingdom of David, concluding with the total extent of his empire (in chap. 8). Chapters 9–29 and 1 Kings 1–2 are frequently seen as a source called "the succession narrative." In this account we are taken back to the occurrence of David's sin and the devastating consequences it had for his house, to the point where there was a threat to the rightful heir right up until 1 Kings 2:11. The Deuteronomic historian makes the point that, at the time of great success in his rise to power, David was the most vulnerable to temptation. The result would have been the undoing of all that he had accomplished had it not been for God's grace in forgiving his sin and establishing Solomon as his successor.

Solomon

After some fighting among his sons for power, David was succeeded by his second son with Bathsheba, Solomon (1 Kings 1–2). God covenanted with the new king as with his father, promising him wisdom "and a discerning heart, so that there will never have been anyone like you, nor will there ever be" (3:12). He also told him that he would receive riches and honor. "And if you walk in my ways and obey my statutes and commands as David your father did, then I will give you a long life" (3:14).

In spite of a promising start—building a great temple to the Lord and extending the boundaries established by David—Solomon quickly deteriorated. He married some 700 wives of foreign extraction (to cement political alliances). There were Egyptians, Moabites, Edomites, and so on—they were those whom God had commanded the Hebrews not to marry because they would lead them away from Him. As he grew older, Solomon began to follow the worship practices of his wives, honoring Ashtoreth, goddess of the Sidonians, and Molech, the fire god of the Ammonites. He built altars to the other gods his wives worshiped. He gradually abandoned his devotion to God and became apostate.

203

The Lord became angry with Solomon because his heart had turned away from the Lord, the God of Israel. . . . So the Lord said to Solomon, "Since this is your attitude and you have not kept my covenant and my decrees, which I have commanded you, I will most certainly tear the kingdom away from you and give it to one of your subordinates. Nevertheless, for the sake of David your father, I will not tear it out of the hand of your son . . . but will give him one tribe for the sake of David my servant and for the sake of Jerusalem, which I have chosen" (11:9, 11-13).

Rehoboam

Under Solomon's son, Rehoboam, the Hebrew empire was split into two parts. Judah remained loyal to the Davidic dynasty. The remainder elected Jeroboam, a former servant of Solomon, as ruler.

Rast tells us that

the tragic division of the kingdom which occurred soon after the death of Solomon was understood by the [Deuteronomic] historian as a punishment against the Solomonic household for its failure to do away with the competing cults of Ashtoreth and other deities, and for its failure to follow the commandments and statutes of the old covenant. . . . The religion of the ten northern tribes is seen, along with the end of the northern and southern kingdoms, as an event of special significance in the judgment against the evil period of the kings.[27]

The Northern Kingdom

Jeroboam was afraid that his kingdom would eventually seek to reunite with Judah under Rehoboam. As a result, he directed his people's religious loyalties away from Jerusalem—and so away from the Lord—by constructing two golden calves and telling his subjects, "Here are your gods, O Israel, who brought you up out of Egypt" (1 Kings 12:28). He placed them in shrines at Bethel and Dan. He also installed priests at the shrines and instituted festivals at which he offered sacrifices to the golden calf at Bethel. "This was the sin of the house of Jeroboam that led to its downfall and to its destruction from the face of the earth" (13:34).

Nadab

When Jeroboam died, he was succeeded by his son Nadab. "He did evil in the eyes of the Lord, walking in the ways of his father and in his sin, which he had caused Israel to commit" (1 Kings 15:26). He had reigned only about one year when he was assassinated by Baasha, son of Ahijah of Issachar, who took his place as king. He systematically annihilated all of Jeroboam's family "because of the sins Jeroboam had committed and had caused Israel to commit, and because he provoked the Lord, the God of Israel, to anger" (15:30).

The Deuteronomist wants his readers to understand what happens as the result of apostasy. In Jeroboam and Nadab, he sets out not only a warning as to the consequences of rebellion against God, but he also constructs a paradigm into which the remaining kings of Israel will fit and which demonstrates the reasons for the nation's downfall. Whether king or commoner, one cannot play fast and loose with the Lord God of Israel and emerged unscathed.

The advent of chaos

Baasha was king for twenty-four years, but it is recorded that he too "did evil in the eyes of the Lord" (1 Kings 15:34). Upon his death, he was succeeded by his son, Elah. In the second year of his reign, however, Elah was assassinated by Zimri, one of his military commanders. As Baasha had done to Jeroboam's house, so Zimri did to Baasha's, exterminating the whole line, "because of all the sins Baasha and his son Elah had committed, and had caused Israel to commit, so that they provoked the Lord, the God of Israel, to anger by their worthless idols" (16:13).

Zimri reigned only a short time, however, for when the army learned what had happened, they proclaimed their commander, Omri, king of Israel. He besieged Zimri in the capital city of Tirzah. Zimri committed suicide, perishing in a fire. As with those before him, it was "because of the sins he had committed, doing evil in the eyes of the Lord" (1 Kings 16:19), following after idols.

The Omri dynasty

After some internal fighting, Omri established his supremacy in Israel. Six years into his reign, he bought the hill of Samaria and moved the capital there from Tirzah. But Omri too we read, "did evil in the eyes of the Lord and sinned more than all those before him" (1 Kings 16:25). That he was an extremely successful politician is evidenced from the Assyrian annals, where Israel was mentioned as the "land of Omri" long after his death. But the Deuteronomic historian has no regard for Omri's stellar accomplishments of state, for their luster had been totally darkened by his evil lifestyle.

Omri died after twelve years of rule, and was followed by his son Ahab, who reigned in Samaria for twenty-eight years. The narrative has no use whatsoever for Ahab, noting that he was the worst of Israel's kings, finding Jeroboam's sins too trivial to bother with. He married Jezebel, a daughter of the king of Sidon, and began to serve her god, Baal. He even built a temple to Baal. In fact, "he did more to provoke the Lord, the God of Israel, to anger than did all the kings of Israel before him" (1 Kings 16:33).

God commissioned Elijah the Tishbite as His prophet to confront Ahab. He prophesied that no rain would fall in Israel for several years (1 Kings 17:1), and it was so. Jezebel, in the meantime, was attempting to eradicate the worship of the Lord by killing all His prophets (18:4). The drought culminated in a contest between Elijah and the prophets of Baal on Mount Carmel. When God consumed His sacrifice with fire from heaven, the people acknowledged His lordship (18:39) and, at Elijah's behest, slaughtered all of the prophets of Baal (18:40). Shortly after this dramatic demonstration of the Lord's power, the land is drenched in a downpour (18:45).

Richard Nelson tells us that "the contest on Carmel deals with a critical ideological issue in Kings. Yahweh is truly and exclusively God. God punishes apostasy, in this case by drought; but God also rewards fidelity, as evidenced by the rainstorm that follows the people's return to faith."[28]

When Ahab was killed in a battle against the Aramaeans, he was succeeded by his son, Ahaziah, who reigned for two years. "He did evil in the eyes of the Lord, because he walked in the ways of his father and mother and in the ways of Jeroboam son of Nebat, who caused Israel to sin" (1 Kings 22:52). He died as the result of God's judgment for consulting Baal-Zebub god of Ekron about an injury he had suffered rather than the Lord (2 Kings 1:1-17). The message of the Deuteronomist to the people of his day was clear. In their exile, they might well be tempted to consult the foreign gods of their captors about the future. This account of Ahaziah makes clear the fate of any of God's people who seek direction from any other source but Him.[28]

Ahaziah was succeeded by his brother, Joram, who "did evil in the eyes of the Lord, but not as his father and mother had done" (2 Kings 3:2). While he did away with Baal worship, he nonetheless kept to the idolatrous practices initiated by Jeroboam.

The Jehu dynasty

Because the line of Ahab was polluting not only Israel but also Judah, God through the Prophet Elisha anointed Jehu, commanding him to destroy the house of Omri (2 Kings 9:1ff). The new king obeyed the command, slaughtering some seventy males in the Omri dynasty, as well as Ahab's advisers, friends, and priests (10:1ff). Then he invited the priests of Baal to a great celebration at the temple of Baal in Samaria, killed all of them, and destroyed the temple, effectively ending the worship of that deity. "Yet Jehu was not careful to keep the law of the Lord, the God of Israel, with all his heart. He did not turn away from the sins of Jeroboam, which he had caused Israel to commit" (10:31).

The purpose of the Deuteronomist here is twofold. First, he reinforces afresh the penalty for apostasy. Sooner or later, rebellion against God brings a divine punishment which results in disaster for the offender. Second, he demonstrates that even this drastic operation under Jehu was insufficient to purify Israel; life under the new royal family continued in much the same vein as under the old. God was going to have to act more radically to correct His wayward people in the Northern Kingdom.

After twenty-eight years as king, Jehu died and his son Jehoahaz ascended the throne. Because "he did evil in the eyes of the Lord by following the sins of Jeroboam" (2 Kings 13:2), the Lord kept Israel in servitude to Aram. Nor was Jehoahaz' son, Jehoash, any different.

Even though the next king, Jeroboam II, continued the tradition of idolatry during the forty-one years of his rule (2 Kings 15:23ff), Israel prospered as it had not in decades. It seemed that God was giving the nation one final opportunity to get right with Him.[30] But Israel continued in idolatry.

The fall of the Northern Kingdom

With Jeroboam's passing, turmoil engulfed the Northern Kingdom. Five kings ruled over a period of twenty years. Assassination and rebellion were the order of the day. The last king of Israel was Hoshea, who ruled for nine years. When he was unfaithful to his overlord, Shalmaneser of Assyria, the latter invaded Israel, imprisoned him, and deported large numbers of Israelites.

The Deuteronomist wants to make it clear that the cause of the nation's demise was not just rebellion against the Assyrian overlord. The people had violated the covenant spiritually in idolatrous worship. They had violated the covenant socially and economically in ill-gotten wealth, power, and greed.

> All this took place because the Israelites had sinned against the Lord their God, who brought them up out of Egypt from under the power of Pharaoh king of Egypt. They worshiped other gods and followed the practices of the nations the Lord had driven before them, as well as the practices that the kings of Israel had introduced. The Israelites secretly did things against the Lord their God that were not right (2 Kings 17:7-9).

The Assyrian emperor brought in foreigners to resettle the land. The Deuteronomist makes the point that they and the now deported Israelites were the same kind of people. They both feared the Lord and worshiped other gods at the same time (2 Kings 17:40ff). His point (made for the Jews in Babylonian exile) is that syncretism does not work. One cannot successfully serve both God and idols, for God will not permit it.

The Southern Kingdom

One might have supposed that the loss of a majority of his kingdom would have caused Rehoboam to be more dependent on God. But the Deuteronomist tells us just the opposite: "Judah did evil in the eyes of the Lord. By the sins they committed they stirred up his jealous anger more than their fathers had done" (1 Kings 14:22). They erected pagan shrines and even instituted male prostitution at them; "the people engaged in all the detest-

7.2 KINGS OF ISRAEL

1050	Saul (1050–1010)
1030	
1010 Ishbosheth (1010–1003)›	
990	David (1003–970)
970	Solomon (970–931)
950	
930	Jeroboam (931–910)
910 Nadab (910–909)›	
890	Baasha (909–886)
Elah (886–885)›	
Zimri (885)›	
	Omri (885–874)
870	Ahab (874–853)
850 Ahaziah (853–852)›	Joram (852–841)
830	Jehu (841–814)
810	Jehoahaz (814–798)
790	Jehoash (798–782)
770	Jeroboam II (793–753)

	Zechariah (753-752)›
	Shallum (752)›
	Menahem (752-742)
750	Pekahiah (742-740)
	Pekah (740-732)
730	Hoshea (732-722)
710	
690	Assyrian Conquest and Dispersion
670	
650	

able practices of the nations the Lord had driven out before the Israelites" (14:24). By way of punishment, Shishak of Egypt invaded Judah and took as booty all the treasures of both the temple and palace.

Rehoboam died in the eighteenth year of the reign of Jeroboam of Israel and was succeeded by his son Abijah. Even though he committed the same sins as his father, God blessed Jerusalem because of David, "for David had done what was right in the eyes of the Lord and had not failed to keep any of the Lord's commands all the days of his life" (1 Kings 15:5).

Asa

Asa, Abijah's son, became king two years later and reigned for forty-one years. "Asa did what was right in the eyes of the Lord, as his father David had done" (1 Kings 15:11). He purged the land of male prostitution and got rid of the idols his predecessors had erected. And while he did not remove all the high places of the pagan gods, the writer observes that "Asa's heart was fully committed to the Lord all his life" (15:14). Thus, he became the first of a number of cultic reformers, to be succeeded by Joash, Hezekiah, and Josiah.[31]

Jehoshaphat

Jehoshaphat, Asa's son and successor, ascended Judah's throne in the fourth year of the reign of Ahab of Israel. Although the usual information about Jehoshaphat's age, parentage, and relationship to the covenant is given in 1 Kings 22:41ff, the Deuteronomic writer introduces him earlier, in 22:2ff, as a foil, first to Ahab and then to Ahab's son Ahaziah. Nelson comments:

> The contrast between Jehoshaphat and Ahaziah is sharp. The first walked in the righteous way of Asa; the second in the evil way of Ahab, Jezebel, and Jeroboam. Although he did not eliminate the high places (cf. 15:14), Jehoshaphat did remove the rest of the cult prostitutes (cf. 15:12). Ahaziah, in contrast, served and worshiped Baal, continuing the heritage of divine anger from 16:13, 26, 33; 21:22. Ahaziah stands in the line of stereotypical apostasy (22:52-53); Jehoshaphat enjoyed a long life, ruled over Edom, and was succeeded by his son. Ahaziah ruled a little longer than a year, lost Moab for Israel (2 Kings 1:1), and had no son (2 Kings 1:17). He died ingloriously by falling out of a window.[32]

The decline of Judah

Jehoram, Jehoshaphat's son, began his reign in the fifth year of Joram of Israel (2 Kings 8:16). Unfortunately, he failed to walk in his father's ways. He married a daughter of Ahab and she probably led him into apostasy. "Nevertheless, for the sake of his servant David, the Lord was not willing to destroy Judah" (8:19). There were other consequences, however; the Edomites rebelled against Judaean domination and, in the ensuing battle, Judah's army was routed and Jehoram had to run for his life.

Jehoram was succeeded by his son, Ahaziah, in the twelfth year of the reign of Joram. Probably because of his wicked mother, Athaliah, Ahaziah "walked in the ways of the house of Ahab and did evil in the eyes of the Lord, as the house of Ahab had done, for he was related by marriage to Ahab's family" (2 Kings 8:27). Through marriage the two royal houses became merged in the pursuit of pagan practices. But Ahaziah's life came to an abrupt end in his first year as king when Jehu rebelled against Joram and killed both kings.

Upon Ahaziah's death, his mother Athaliah staged a coup, seizing power by massacring all of the princes royal, except the youthful Joash, who was hidden away by Ahaziah's sister, Jehosheba, who was also the wife of the priest Jehoiada. While she was able to maintain rule in Judah for six years, at an opportune time a party led by Jehoiada and supported by the priests, army, and people placed Joash on the throne, and Athaliah was executed (2 Kings 11:16). Undoubtedly, this popular revolt was encouraged by the success of Jehu's revolt in Israel.[33]

Because Athaliah's usurpation of Judah's throne had broken the Davidic succession, a formal renewal of the Davidic covenant was initiated by Jehoiada "between the Lord and the king and people that they would be the Lord's people" (2 Kings 11:17).[34] They demonstrated their allegiance to the Lord by destroying a temple to Baal which had evidently been constructed in Jerusalem. "Joash was seven years old when he began to reign" (11:21).

Joash's reign as described by the Deuteronomic writer is somewhat ambiguous. He records that the king followed God's ways because of the oversight of Jehoiada. He also collected money to repair the temple which had deteriorated badly. Unfortunately, when Judah was threatened by Hazael of Aram with invasion, Joash robbed the temple of its gold and silver vessels to buy Hazael off. There is no report that he sought God's advice or help. While the Deuteronomic writer does not explicitly condemn the king, he does note that Joash was assassinated by royal retainers (2 Kings 12:20), an unusual end for a king accounted righteous.

Joash's son, Amaziah, ascended the throne of Judah in the second year of Jehoash of Israel. In this account he is damned by faint praise: "He did what was right in the eyes of the Lord, but not as his father David had done. In everything he followed the example of his father Joash" (2 Kings 14:3). During his reign he achieved several successes: he executed his father's killers; he did not kill their sons because the law of Moses forbade it; he also defeated 10,000 Edomites and captured their chief city. But his successes went to his head. He challenged Jehoash of Israel to battle. At Beth Shemesh in Judah the Israelite army routed the Judaeans, captured Amaziah, and pillaged the royal palace and temple of their treasures. Several years later, a conspiracy against the Judaean king took place, and he was assassinated.

Amaziah's teenaged son, Azariah, was placed on the throne by popular demand (2 Kings 14:21). Although "he did what was right in the eyes of the Lord, just as his father Amaziah had done" (15:3), he did not remove the pagan worship centers and the people continued to sacrifice to idols. The narrator advises his readers that "the Lord afflicted the king with leprosy until the day he died" (15:5), but refrains from passing any sort of judgment, allowing them to reach their own conclusions.[35]

Azariah's son, Jotham, became regent and then king. Jotham too followed the Lord in much the same manner as his father and grandfather before him. But, like them, he did not suppress the idolatrous practices of the people.

The Deuteronomist is not as optimistic about Ahaz, Jotham's son. Unlike his immediate predecessors, and very much unlike David, Ahaz "did not do what was right in the eyes of the Lord his God" (2 Kings 16:2). Even worse, he burnt his own son in a pagan sacrifice, thus emulating the practices of those nations God had driven out of Canaan. At the same time, however, he was also a patron of the temple and did extensive renovations to it, including a large new altar. Nelson notes:

The ambiguous figure of Ahaz, partially a success and partially a failure, sometimes faithful to God but quite often not so, reflects Judah's situation precisely. At this point in the plot of Kings, Judah's future is still open. There are still two ways before Judah, the way of obedience and life and the way of idolatrous worship and death (Deut. 30:15-20). Eventually Judah would lose this choice, and death became inevitable (21:10-15).[36]

213

An interlude of revival

Ahaz's son, Hezekiah, became king of Judah in the third year of the reign of Hoshea, final king of Israel. The Deuteronomist is effusive in his praise of Hezekiah. This king was devoted to the Lord throughout his whole life. He followed David in his love for God (2 Kings 18:3). Unlike his predecessors, "he removed the high places, smashed the sacred stones and cut down the Ashera poles. He broke into pieces the bronze snake Moses had made, for up to that time the Israelites had been burning incense to it" (18:4). Indeed, says the writer, he was without peer among the kings of Judah, for he was faithful to the Mosaic covenant (18:6). The result was that, though Israel was destroyed by Assyrian invasion, Sennacherib could not conquer Jerusalem (19:20-37).

The return to apostasy

The account of Hezekiah's son, Manasseh, and his grandson, Amon, is an account of two wretched apostates. In it we see the work of the Deuteronomist who intended it as an introduction to the account of Josiah's reformation (2 Kings 22:3–23:24).

> There is a trace of the Deuteronomic redaction as well as of the first compilation. The original compiler does not visualize the collapse of the kingdom of Judah (e.g., vv. 1-7, 16-22, 25-26). This includes the normal Deuteronomic introductions and epilogues and general appraisal of the respective reigns. The redactor in vv. 8-15, qualifying the last sentence in vv. 1-7, visualizes the destruction of Jerusalem as divine retribution for idolatry.[37]

Manasseh was as evil a king as his father had been righteous. "He did evil in the eyes of the Lord" (2 Kings 21:2), undoing all his father had accomplished against pagan worship practices. He even participated in the actual cults of Baal and Asherah (21:3). He also caused one of his children to be sacrificed in the fire of Molech (21:6). What is more, he took an idol of Asherah, the mother-goddess, and placed it in the temple of God (21:7).

Verses 8-15 of chapter 21 are a Deuteronomic homily on the conditional grace of God. They also recapitulate the sins of Manasseh and his subjects. God had promised to keep Israel secure in the land He had given them, but only if they kept the covenant He had made with them through Moses (v. 8). But the people did not listen, and had allowed their king to lead them into acts which were more vile than those of the original Canaanites whom the Lord had destroyed (v. 7). The same fate, therefore, would befall Judah as had befallen Israel because of Ahab's sin; Judah would fall to her enemies (vv. 12-14), "because they have done evil in my eyes and have provoked me to anger from the day their forefathers came out of Egypt until this day" (v. 15).

The writer records that Manasseh shed innocent blood, so much so that it filled Jerusalem from end to end. It is suggested by some that this refers to his persecution of the prophets (e.g., Hebrews 11:37 records some prophets — and tradition includes Isaiah here — as having been sawed asunder), who would undoubtedly have opposed his vassalage to Assyria.

Upon Manasseh's death after a reign of fifty-five years, he was succeeded by his son, Amon, who "walked in all the ways of his father; he worshiped the idols his father had worshiped, and bowed down to them. He forsook the Lord, the God of his fathers, and did not walk in the way of the Lord" (2 Kings 21:21-22). We are not shocked to learn that "his officials conspired against him and assassinated the king in his palace" (21:23). We do learn, however, that the "people of the land" destroyed the plotters and placed Amon's son Josiah on the throne (21:24).

The Deuteronomic renewal

The Deuteronomist's account of Josiah is a theological puzzle. He records that "he did what was right in the eyes of the Lord and walked in all the ways of his father David, not turning aside to the right or to the left" (2 Kings 22:2). He observes, further, that "neither before nor after Josiah was there a king like him" who followed the Mosaic covenant so devotedly (23:25). It comes then as a terrible shock when we read that "the Lord did not turn away from the heat of his fierce anger, which burned against Judah because of all that Manasseh had done to provoke him to anger" (23:26). And we are a little discomfited when we read that Josiah was killed in battle against Pharaoh Neco of Egypt (23:29). Nelson notes that "Kings provides no theoretical answer to the theological paradox it creates, but Josiah's own behavior exemplifies the only practical solution. He faithfully obeys God anyway, without regard to any hope of reward."[38]

The fall of Judah

God's judgment on Judah proceeds quickly through the remaining chapters of 2 Kings. The people crowned Josiah's second son, Jehoahaz, as king. "He did evil in the eyes of the Lord, just as his fathers had done" (23:32). But Pharaoh Neco deposed him and appointed his elder brother Jehoiakim in his place. His record was no better and he too "did evil in the eyes of the Lord, just as his fathers had done" (23:37).

During Jehoiakim's reign, Nebuchadnezzar of Babylon invaded Judah and the Hebrew king became his vassal. After three years he rebelled, but died prematurely. He was succeeded by his son Jehoiachin who, at only eighteen years of age, was forced to face Nebuchadnezzar's wrath. The young king and his court, and ten thousand of Judah's leading people, were taken into captivity. This was not an unfitting punishment, for the Deuteronomist records that he, like his father, engaged in evil practices (24:9).

Nebuchadnezzar placed Jehoiachin's uncle Zedekiah on Judah's throne. Zedekiah's evil practices, the Deuteronomist tells us, were the cause of the country's final downfall. He rebelled against Nebuchadnezzar just as his brother had done. Consequently, the Babylonians marched against Jerusalem and besieged the city. When the city wall was breached, Zedekiah and his army fled; but Nebuchadnezzar pursued them and captured the king. As a punishment for his rebellion, Zedekiah's sons were killed before him; his eyes were then put out, and he was taken to Babylon in chains (25:7).

The Babylonian army returned to Jerusalem and set fire to the temple, the palace, and all of the houses. Then they broke down the walls surrounding the city. With the exception of a few poor peasants, they carried the population into exile (25:8-11).

Hope for the future

The book ends with an anecdote about the imprisoned King Jehoiachin. Nebuchadnezzar's successor released him from prison

7.3: MONARCHS OF JUDAH	
1050	Saul (1050–1010)
1030	
1010	David (1010–970)
990	
970	Solomon (970–931)
950	
930	Rehoboam (931–913)
910	Abijah (913–911)›
890	Asa (911–870)
870	Jehoshaphat (873–848)
850	Jehoram (853–841)
	Ahaziah (841)›
	Athaliah (841–835)›
830	Joash (835–796)
810	
790	Amaziah (796–767) and Uzziah (790–740)
770	

750		Jotham (750–731)
730		Ahaz (735–715)
710		
690		Hezekiah (715–686)
670		Manasseh (697–642)
650	Amon (642–640)›	
630		Josiah (640–609)
610	Jehoahaz(609)›	
590	Jehoiachin(597)›	Jehoiakim (609–597)
		Zedekiah (597–586)
		Babylonian Exile (586–539)

and gave him a place of honor above all the other exiled monarchs in Babylon. For the rest of his life Jehoiachin received a
royal allowance and ate at the king's table (25:27-30). Thus, the
door remained open for the possibility of a return to the throne of
a descendant of David.

Summary

As we have already noted, the Deuteronomic history came into
being about 560 B.C. (since the record ends about 561 B.C. as

evidenced by 2 Kings 25:27ff). We know little about the author other than his great affinity for the Book of Deuteronomy and his loyalty to its traditions. We also know that he had a wealth of historical material on which to draw for his account of these periods of Israel's existence. He used Deuteronomy as a paradigm for his writing.

Deuteronomy makes a clear demand that the Lord is God and none other. He alone is to be worshiped and obeyed. There is, furthermore, only one place for the worship of the Lord; that is the legitimate sanctuary where He has put His name. A sharp differentiation is made between the worship of the Lord God of Israel and the worship of Canaanite deities. Israel was confronted with a choice: it could worship the former or the latter; but God would not tolerate the attempt to worship both.[39]

The Deuteronomic historian holds this same basic theology, evaluating the kings of Judah and Israel on the basis of their acceptance of the Jerusalem temple as the only legitimate place of worship, or their veneration of the "high places." As a result of this assessment, the kings of Israel were all utterly condemned because they without exception practiced "the sin of Jeroboam" or "the sin of the house of Ahab." The kings of Judah, on the other hand, were a mixed bag: two—Hezekiah and Josiah—met with complete approval; six received conditional approval (Asa, Jehoshaphat, Joash, Amaziah, Azariah, and Jotham); and the remainder were judged as having done "evil in the eyes of the Lord."[40]

In the estimation of the Deuteronomist, these kings sinned because "their heart was not fully committed to the Lord" (1 Kings 8:61; 11:4; 15:3). And it was the result of this commitment of the king's heart (or lack of commitment) that determined whether Israel was to be saved or spurned because, as went the king, so went the people. Von Rad asserts that

this decision, however, did not depend only on the kings' complete devotion to or apostasy from Jahweh, but upon their attitude to the revelation of Jahweh known in Israel from of old, that is, to the law of Moses. . . . Thus the Deuteronomist sees the main problem of the history of Israel as lying in the question of the correct revelation of Moses and David. Did the kings discern and comply with the will of

Jahweh promulgated by Moses? As we know, the answer is NO — the decision of the kings was taken against the revealed will of Jahweh and for evil.[41]

As a result, God's patient waiting for His people to come to their senses and return to Him ultimately came to an end. First, Israel was allowed to meet destruction and exile and, when Judah failed to learn the lesson provided by Israel's ruin, she met a similar fate at the hands of the Babylonians.

But even in exile hope was not lost. The Deuteronomist demonstrated for these wretched captives through their own history how God responds to repentance and a confession of sin. God's intervention in history has a potential for double action: it both punishes sin and, in the judgment of destruction, clears the way for restoration.[42] Watts tells us that the message of the Deuteronomist to exiled Jews

> called for expectation and hope. It documented the course of Israel's apostasy and God's faithfulness to his word. It documented God's presence and work among his people even in the destructive forces of the enemy. So the fault lay with Israel, not with God. It also showed how God had acted in the past, following judgment with new initiative.[43]

Thus, if the people truly repented of their sin and turned afresh to God, there was clear hope that He might restore to them both the relationship they once enjoyed with Him as well as the land that He had given to them.

The Latter Prophets

Because their writings have been preserved, we have a clearer idea of the teaching of the Latter Prophets than of the Former. We also have additional insights into the life of the Hebrew people as they went into decline, were destroyed and exiled, and then were reestablished. These prophets span the years between 750 and 400 B.C.

The prophets dealt with perennial issues of faith. The preexilic prophets were concerned with fidelity to the Mosaic Law and the covenants God had made with Israel. As a result, they were caustic in their denunciation of the kings and people of Israel for their apostasy and idolatry. Frequently, their messages carried hope for repentance and renewal. Their oracles were preserved to teach later generations.[44] The exilic prophets were encouragers of a desolate people, stressing God's continuing goodness and sovereignty; if the captives would devote themselves to Him, He would pity them and restore them to their homeland. Among those restored, the prophets were effective in pushing the people to rebuild the temple and reestablish fully the practices of the ancient faith. In all of these periods a major part of their task was the prevention of sin, the denunciation of sin and the sinner, the promise of punishment for sin, but also the promise of forgiveness and restoration for the repentant sinner.

Amos

Amos, the earliest of the canonical prophets, exercised his prophetic ministry in the Northern Kingdom. He was a native of Judah, a farmer—and not a professional prophet—by trade. He was active during the time of Jeroboam II of Israel (ca. 787–747), a contemporary of Uzziah (also known as Azariah) of Judah (ca. 787–736), and a probable date for his mission to Israel is generally set about 760 B.C.[45]

Amos proclaimed Israel's destruction because of her sins. His message began with harsh words of divine punishment for the nations surrounding the Northern Kingdom, even for Judah. Then it refocused on Israel herself: "You only have I chosen of all the families of the earth; therefore I will punish you for all your sins" (3:2).

Although he never used the word "covenant," a term very common among many of the other Old Testament writers to denote Israel's election by God, the idea of God's having personally elected the Hebrews was certainly implied, not only in the verse cited above, but throughout. Amos 2:9–3:2 shows God's care for His people from their liberation from Egypt on. Therefore, there was a special relationship between Israel and the Lord.[46]

Israel had fractured this relationship. Consequently, declared Amos, God would destroy them. God had repeatedly attempted to reclaim His wayward people by demonstrating His sovereignty over creation. He had brought drought, blight, and pestilence on them (4:7-10). He had even allowed some of them to be conquered (4:11). In spite of these catastrophes Israel had not repented. "Therefore this is what I will do to you, O Israel, and because I will do this to you, prepare to meet your God, O Israel" (4:12). Repeatedly, God had shown the people mercy, allowing them to be punished, but without destroying them (7:1-6). But their stubborn continuation in sin had worn God's patience thin. And so, "I am setting a plumb line among my people Israel; I will spare them no longer" (7:8).

Israel's sins were many. One major sin was injustice. With the increasing prosperity of some people had come an undermining of covenant brotherhood. Instead of supporting their poorer fellow Israelites, they had increasingly oppressed them. Greedy property owners gobbled up the land of their impoverished neighbors (8:4). The wives of the well-to-do were as rapacious as their husbands (4:1). "You oppress the righteous and take bribes and you deprive the poor of justice in the courts" (5:12).

Another major sin was their corruption of religion. The Israelites were a deeply religious people, attending religious festivals and making pilgrimages to various shrines. But their lives did not measure up to their seeming devotion. They were using religious ritual to attempt to manipulate the Lord. Eric Rust observes, "The common belief is that because Israel is God's covenanted people, therefore they are bound to be secure. There is a failure to realize that the privilege of the divine election brings moral obligations in its train."[47]

As a result, Amos attacked the Israelite sacrificial system. Unlike some of his contemporary fellow prophets he did not assail idolatry. He did not suggest that God did not expect sacrifices or celebrations of worship. But he did declare that their religious ritual was worthwhile only when effected in conjunction with moral behavior and ethical action such as God required in the covenant.[48]

Amos held out little hope for Israel's future. Their end was prophesied throughout his ministry. Only a "remnant of Joseph" (5:15) would remain from the nation because of their wickedness.

Hosea

The only native Northerner whose writings have been preserved, Hosea was the last in a line of prophets in Israel, a line which included such stalwart holy men as Elijah and Elisha. Little is known about his origins; nor is there much information on his occupation, although he appears to have been a well-educated person. He is called a prophet in a quoted saying (9:7), and so may well have been a member of a prophetic school or family. He prophesied during the reign of Jeroboam II.[49]

In obedience to the Lord's command, Hosea took to wife an adulterous woman. She was probably a cult prostitute from one of the Canaanite religions. This was analogous to Israel's "vilest adultery in departing from the Lord" (1:2).

Hosea's preaching reveals several important theological principles which relate to the concept of sin. First, Israel was God's people. This is made obvious throughout the book in the analogy of marriage. There are also a number of historical references to Israel's relationship with God, to His covenant with Adam (6:7), to Jacob (12:3ff), to the bondage in Egypt (2:15; 11:1; 13:4), to Moses (12:13), and to the time in the wilderness (2:3; 9:10; 13:5). Such episodes from Israel's history are not mentioned merely with the intention of historical reflection but to "remind the people that they were chosen as Yahweh's own . . . and they were cared and provided for over the years."[50]

Again, Israel had refused God's love by breaking the covenant. They had done so in their personal lives: "There is only cursing, lying, and murder, stealing and adultery; they break all bounds, and bloodshed follows bloodshed" (4:2). They had sinned against God in and through their kings. "They delight the king with their wickedness, the princes with their lies," and "all their kings fall, and none of them calls on me" (7:7). Worst of all, they had rejected God's covenant in their false worship. It was against their heathen practices that Hosea made most of his prophecies. One aspect of this idolatry was the worship of the golden calves erected by Jeroboam I: "Throw out your calf-idol, O Samaria! My anger burns against them. . . . This calf—a craftsman has made it; it is not God. It will be broken in pieces, that calf of Samaria" (8:5-6).[51]

But the real focus of the prophet's denunciation was Baal worship. This Canaanite fertility god was worshiped through the union of people with sacred prostitutes to remind him that his purpose was to make their land fecund. Under Jezebel, the Canaanite wife of Ahab, the Israelites had been led into a wholehearted veneration of Baal. Although Jehu's bloody coup had dampened enthusiasm for this cult, it had evidently become popular again in Hosea's time. In such a context, 2:2 may be seen not just as an appeal to Gomer on the part of a wronged husband, but rather to Israel to abandon its loyalty to Baal and return to the Lord: "Rebuke your mother, rebuke her, for she is not my wife, and I am not her husband. Let her remove her adulterous look from her face and the unfaithfulness from between her breasts."[52]

Because Israel would not heed God's appeals, the nation would be punished. God's compassion and mercy were at an end. The people of Samaria must bear their guilt because they had rebelled against their God. They would fall by the sword; their little ones would be dashed to the ground; their pregnant women would be ripped open (13:16). Undoubtedly, Hosea was well aware of the current situation. Assyria had been swallowing up nations all through the area. It was only a matter of time before it was Israel's turn; without the Lord's protection they would be destroyed.

In spite of the people's apostasy and sure destruction, Hosea continued to call them to repentance. If only they would turn to God:

> I will heal their waywardness and love them freely, for my anger has turned away from them. I will be like the dew to Israel; he will blossom like a lily. Like a cedar of Lebanon he will send down his roots; his young shoots will grow. His splendor will be like an olive tree, his fragrance like a cedar of Lebanon (14:4-6).

He would remember their idolatrous ways no longer, but would restore them fully.

The final verse of the book is an exhortation to the wise person to reflect on and learn from the lessons written there: "Who is wise? He will realize these things. Who is discerning? He will understand them. The ways of the Lord are right; the righteous walk in them, but the rebellious stumble in them" (14:9).

Isaiah

One of the outstanding practitioners of the prophetic ministry in Hebrew society was Isaiah, son of Amoz, who lived in eighth-century B.C. Judah. His book spans a period of two and a half centuries, from the eighth to the fifth centuries. Chapters 1–39 speak to the preexilic monarchy period of Judah, while the remainder addresses the nation's situation after its fall.[53] It is the first section of this work which has so much to say about sin.

Taken as a whole, [it] tells of God's punishment of Israel, particularly the kingdom of Judah; punishment of the nations, for idolatry and injustice; and God's subsequent redemption of the people of Israel. Both the punishment and the redemption begin in Jerusalem/Zion, reaching from there to encompass the nations of the world.[54]

The key to Isaiah's theology may be found in the account of his vision (6:1-13). "In the year that King Uzziah died, I saw the Lord seated on a throne, high and exalted, and the train of his robe filled the temple" (6:1). About Him flew the angelic heralds chanting His holiness: "Holy, holy, holy is the Lord God Almighty; the whole earth is full of his glory" (6:3).

Two basic ideas about God are presented here: His holiness and His glory. The Hebrew word for holy *(qadhosh)* was used by the Semites to distinguish gods from humans. In Isaiah's vision the seraphim praised God as three times holy. Rust declares that

God is the most unique and separate Being who stands apart from men. He is transcendent in his splendor and majesty, towering in his enthroned glory above the Temple, the prophets, and the people. He is not like other holy ones and his holiness takes its unique quality from his own exalted character. Indeed, the other gods are idols. . . . Such deities shall pass away, but men will flee in fear before the terror of Yahweh.[55]

God's otherness (or, holiness) is fundamentally moral. The ultimate gauge of His resplendence is His moral purity, a perfection which sets Him apart from sinful humanity. God's righteousness, then, is closely connected to His holiness. His basic character is expressed in the Sinai Covenant which demands human righteousness.[56]

In his vision, the prophet was convicted both of his own un-

225

righteousness and that of his people. "I am ruined! For I am a man of unclean lips, and I live among a people of unclean lips, and my eyes have seen the King, the Lord Almighty" (6:5). In this situation the Sinai covenant tradition is obvious. The Hebrews by their sinful behavior had caused a gap between themselves and their God. Along with his own guilt feelings, Isaiah encounters the corporate guilt of Israel which drives him to become the Lord's envoy to His rebellious people.[57] The nation had rebelled against God. "I reared children and brought them up, but they have rebelled against me. The ox knows his master, the donkey his owner's manger, but Israel does not know, my people do not understand. . . . They have forsaken the Lord" (1:2-4). Isaiah was quite pointed in his setting forth of the people's sins. These included idolatry (2:8), the oppression of the poor and helpless (3:13-15; 10:2), and the abandonment of reliance on the Lord in favor of political alliances with the heathen nations (28:14-22).

In spite of their sin, God loved His people and was willing to forgive them. Thus, Isaiah proclaimed God's mercy in the "Song of the Vineyard" (chap. 5). In much the same way that a vineyard owner cares for his grapevines and does all in his power to nourish them for superior production, so God had nourished Israel so that they would bring forth the spiritual fruit He desired. They nonetheless produced wild grapes. "The vineyard of the Lord Almighty is the house of Israel, and the men of Judah are the garden of His delight. And He looked for justice, but saw bloodshed; for righteousness, but heard cries of distress" (5:7). Despite God's demonstration of love for Israel, they insisted on doing evil.

Love and privilege involve accountability. God envisioned the exhibition of a life on the part of His people which would coincide with His character and purposes. But the nation instead reciprocated with flagrant unrighteousness and the violation of His covenant.[58] A prophecy follows the Song of the Vineyard in the form of a series of "woes," through which the prophet singles out for reproach and judgment some of the rotting grapes which the vineyard had produced.

> Woe to you who add house to house and join field to field till no space is left and you live alone in the land. The Lord Almighty has declared in my hearing: Surely the great

houses will become desolate, the fine mansions left without occupants. . . . Woe to those who rise up early in the morning to run after their drinks. . . . They have no regard for the deeds of the Lord, no respect for the work of His hands. Therefore my people will go into exile (5:8-9, 11-13).

The woes oracles are indictments against those greedy capitalists who sought to increase their wealth by the acquisition of more houses and property, at the same time expanding the gap between wealthy and impoverished, an essential fracture of God's intention for Hebrew brotherhood. While their tactics may have been "legal," they broke the spirit of God's law. "The land as Yahweh's gift with each family having its inheritance or allotted portion as a basis for existence became less and less the norm."[59] There is also an indictment of libertines, those who indulge themselves in wasteful, luxurious living, but who pay God no heed. The fate of all these sinners will be exile and poverty.

Isaiah's "apocalypse" (chaps. 24–27) expanded his notion of judgment to a universal scope. It served as a summary and conclusion to the judgments against the nations in chapters 13–23. God would judge the nations which He had used to punish Israel, each of these judgments being but an illustration of the final and great judgment against Leviathan (27:1), the great symbolic referent of the nations, and most probably to be related to the serpent of Genesis 3. "See, the Lord is coming out of his dwelling to punish the people of the earth for their sins. The earth will disclose the blood shed upon her; she will conceal her slain no longer" (26:21). All sinners must face God's wrath and condemnation.

While the tone of chapters 40ff is somewhat different because they address a completely different situation from the first thirty-nine, for the theme is redemption rather than judgment, a condemnation of sin persists nonetheless. Chapters 40–48 focus on the folly of idolatry. Once he has finished with his introduction to the theme of redemption (in 40:1-11), the prophet directly alludes to idolatry.

To whom, then, will you compare God? What image will you compare him to? As for an idol, a craftsman casts it, and a goldsmith overlays it with gold and fashions silver chains for it. A man too poor to present such an offering selects wood that will not rot. He looks for a skilled craftsman to set up an idol that will not topple (40:18-20).

Chapter 41 examines both the sovereignty of God and its antithesis, the absolute absurdity of idolatry. The prophet pictures a courtroom scene where the Lord challenges these false gods to present their arguments (41:21) as to why they have any claim to deity. But there is only silence, for what can a god of wood, stone, or metal have to say? The conclusion is clear: "But you are less than nothing . . . he who chooses you is detestable" (41:24).

Isaiah 44:9-20 condemns idolatry in "one of the most incisive pieces of satirical prose in the Old Testament."⁶⁰ It begins with the declaration that idol makers are weak human beings; how can idols they craft be of any aid to anyone? Then it moves us into an idol factory where we learn in some detail how an idol is constructed (vv. 12-13). The crowning touch comes as the writer describes how the craftsman chooses a tree from the forest, allows it to grow to the span he desires, and then chops it down. Part of it he burns for firewood over which he cooks his food and warms himself; when he has met his material needs, then he uses the rest for carving out his "god," which he promptly worships. "He prays to it and says, 'Save me; you are my god' " (v. 17). The prophet concludes with a reflection on the tragedy of idol worship. Green observes:

> The idolater becomes so deluded, so blind, so insensate that he cannot apply reason to his actions. . . . He cannot discern that he is falling down before a mere "block of wood" and that he is feeding on "ashes." A deluded mind has led him astray, and he cannot deliver himself or say, "Is there not a lie in my right hand?"⁶¹

Like so many of his colleagues — particularly those of the exilic and postexilic periods — the prophet is unwilling to let matters rest without offering hope for the future. The "Servant Songs" (42:1-9; 49:1-6; 50:4-9; 52:13–53:12) are an expression of that redemptive hope. The last of these, the vicarious suffering of the Servant for sin, is unquestionably the most appealing to Christians: "But he was pierced for our transgressions, he was crushed for our iniquities; the punishment that brought us peace was upon him, and by his wounds we are healed. We all, like sheep, have gone astray, each of us has turned to his own way; and the Lord has laid on him the iniquity of us all" (53:5-6).

Micah

The introduction to the Book of Micah (1:1) tells us that the prophet's ministry occurred during the reigns of three kings of Judah: Jotham (742–732), Ahaz (732–715), and Hezekiah (715–686). He was, therefore, a contemporary of Isaiah. A number of scholars believe that the center of Micah's ministry was about (and just after) the time of Sennacherib's invasion of Judah and that the conclusion of that campaign in such disarray provided a setting for these words of prophecy which have been preserved.[62]

Micah's book gives us little information about the prophet's personal life other than that he was an inhabitant of Moresheth-gath, located some twenty-five miles southwest of Jerusalem. Nor is there any record of his divine call to prophesy, although there is a brief autobiographical passage with an attestation to it: "But as for me, I am filled with power, with the Spirit of the Lord, and with justice and might, to declare to Jacob his transgression, to Israel his sin" (3:8). There is no indication from his preserved work that he had the qualms about his ministry which burdened Isaiah (6:5) and Jeremiah (1:6). He seems to have been fully committed to the task.[63]

Micah's idea of God was very much like that of Isaiah. Not only is his book similar in structure to Isaiah's (though on a much smaller scale), but his theology is, as well. "Their basic message is the same and can be summarized in the following broad terms: The historic fall of the kingdom of Judah is interpreted theologically as a divine punishment for the sins of the nation, and the eventual restoration of a religious community is prophesied as an act of God's grace."[64]

The oracles of Micah are a biting indictment of the wealthy and powerful: "Woe to those who plan iniquity, to those who plot evil on their beds! At morning's light they carry it out because it is in their power to do it. They covet fields and seize them, and houses, and take them. They defraud a man of his home, a fellow-man of his inheritance" (2:1-2). Their punishment would be the loss of their possessions, their ridicule, and their ruin.

He also lashed out at those false prophets who subverted God's will and prophesied for money what people wanted to hear. They were nothing but liars and deceivers.

> Therefore night will come over you, without visions, and darkness, without divination. The sun will set for the prophets, and the day will go dark for them. The seers will be ashamed and the diviners disgraced. They will all cover their faces because there is no answer from God (3:6-7).

Judah had sinned, and so faced destruction. "Zion will be plowed like a field, Jerusalem will become a heap of rubble, the temple hill a mound overgrown with thickets" (3:12).

The book suddenly turns from a message of condemnation and judgment for sin to one of future blessing. Because of God's love and mercy, there would be a restoration. It concludes on a very optimistic note.

> Who is a God like you, who pardons sin and forgives the transgression of the remnant of his inheritance? You do not stay angry forever but delight to show mercy. You will again have compassion on us; you will tread our sins underfoot and hurl all our iniquities into the depths of the sea. You will be true to Jacob, and show mercy to Abraham, as you pledged on oath to our fathers in days long ago (7:18-20).

Zephaniah

The Prophet Zephaniah was active during the time of Josiah, appearing about 630 B.C. or a short time thereafter. He is regarded by many as a forerunner to the Prophet Jeremiah.[65] The genealogy of Zephaniah is the longest listed for any of the prophets, going back four generations to Hezekiah. In his message and theology this prophet differed very little from his fellows. Along with his emphatic proclamation of the judgment of sin, one can discern a measure of frustration with the widespread oppression of decent, godly people at the hands of the powerful. As a consequence, he declared that in the coming day of the Lord all would see God's vindication of the righteous.[66]

Zephaniah portrayed a morally responsible God who was deeply offended by human sin. The appalling idolatry encouraged by Manasseh which continued into the reign of the young Josiah came in for strong denunciation[67]: "I will cut off from this place every remnant of Baal, the names of the pagan and the idolatrous priests – those who bow down on the roofs to worship the starry host, those who bow down and swear by the Lord and who also swear by Molech" (1:4-5). But those who humbled themselves and were obedient to God's commands might be saved from the coming destruction (2:3).

While the prophet's foremost concern was with the judgment of Judah, his vista broadened to include all creation. The nations surrounding would be destroyed because of their godless behavior (2:5ff). Ultimately, all creation would be affected.

At the same time, the prophet holds out hope for the future. A remnant of Judah will be saved to preside over a transformed humanity. "The Lord, the King of Israel, is with you; never again will you fear any harm" (3:15).

Nahum

We know very little about Nahum other than that he was a native of Elkosh, a village of uncertain location in the countryside of Judah. The Old Testament does not specifically say so, but scholars generally seem to consider Jerusalem the most likely locale for his ministry. It also believed that the time of his work was about the time of the fall of Nineveh in 612 B.C. at the hands of a coalition of Babylonians, Medes, and Scythians.

The book is divided into two poems, the first (1:1-9) in the form of an acrostic, and the second (1:10–3:19) somewhat longer. The theme of the former is that the Lord who is righteous and holy will wreak havoc upon the unrighteous. Nahum stressed that God's anger is not impetuous: "The Lord is slow to anger and great in power; the Lord will not leave the guilty unpunished" (1:3). Nor, noted the prophet, do the righteous need have any fear from God's wrath: "The Lord is good, a refuge in times of trouble. He cares for those who trust in him" (1:7).

The longer poem is a liturgy celebrating Nineveh's overthrow

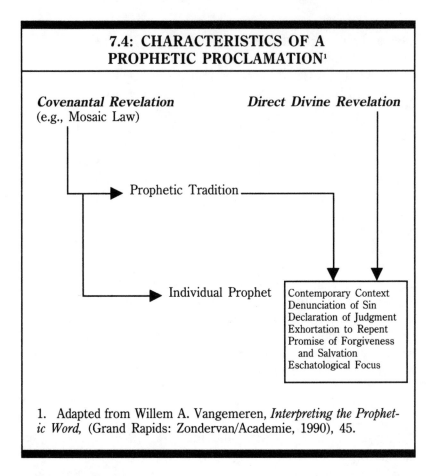

7.4: CHARACTERISTICS OF A PROPHETIC PROCLAMATION[1]

Covenantal Revelation
(e.g., Mosaic Law)

Direct Divine Revelation

Prophetic Tradition

Individual Prophet

Contemporary Context
Denunciation of Sin
Declaration of Judgment
Exhortation to Repent
Promise of Forgiveness
and Salvation
Eschatological Focus

1. Adapted from Willem A. Vangemeren, *Interpreting the Prophetic Word*, (Grand Rapids: Zondervan/Academie, 1990), 45.

and Judah's safety: "Celebrate your festivals, O Judah, and fulfill your vows. No more will the wicked invade you; they will be completely destroyed" (1:15). And the prophet depicted conditions in this city under seige as the surrounding forces broke through its defenses to kill and pillage. The cause without question, Nahum declared, was that the Lord Himself stood against this evil city (2:13).

Jeremiah

The dominating prophet of the time of Judah's decline and fall, Jeremiah's ministry spanned about half a century. He received his call in the thirtieth year of King Josiah's reign (626 B.C.). The great king's reforms would have been proclaimed immediately afterward. He was a member of a priestly family from Anathoth, just outside of Jerusalem.

Jeremiah's description of life in Israel during the preexilic period was one of complete unfaithfulness to the Lord. "Has a nation ever changed its gods? (Yet they are not gods at all.) But my people have exchanged their Glory for worthless idols" (2:11). The nation had further demonstrated its apostasy by relying on foreign, godless nations for its security (2:18). This reliance would be disappointing, "for the Lord has rejected those you trust; you will not be helped by them" (2:37). Ward observes that

> the only possible explanation of the nation's senseless behavior was that it had lost its heart to idolatrous powers. "I have loved strangers, and after them I will go," Israel boasted (2:25). Compelled by passion, the faithless bride of YHWH had given herself to others, believing they could satisfy her desire (4:30; 3:1-2, 6-10). But since passion without discipline is a fickle thing, this devotion too was inconstant. Thus she moved from lover to lover in a futile search (3:28, 36), even turning back to YHWH when she thought she would benefit from it (3:4-5). "The heart is devious above all else, it is perverse—who can understand it?" the prophet asked (17:9).[68]

Because he understood how serious Israel's sin was, Jeremiah stressed the aspect of God as judge. The nation had rebelled against God and had broken His covenant. In illustrating its condemnation, Jeremiah—like Isaiah—used a vine analogy: "I had planted you like a choice vine of sound and reliable stock. How then did you turn against me into a corrupt, wild vine?" (2:21)[69]

Israel's infidelity was further demonstrated in Jeremiah's condemnation of social injustice. He attacked the oppression of the fatherless and the poor. "Their evil deeds have no limit; they do not plead the case of the fatherless to win it, they do not defend the rights of the poor. 'Should I not punish them for this?' declares the Lord" (5:28-29). Two other social evils he attacked were lying and sexual perversity (5:1-3, 7ff). These latter ills fracture interpersonal relationships and destroy the fabric of society.[70]

In spite of their offenses against God, these sinners had a

strong sense of security based on aspects of their temple worship and ritual. Since the temple was God's residence (as per Deut. 12:5, 11) where His presence dwelt, they reasoned that He would never allow it to be destroyed. If the temple could not be destroyed, then neither could Jerusalem. But Jeremiah attempted to counter such ideas: "Do not trust in deceptive words and say, 'This is the temple of the Lord, the temple of the Lord, the temple of the Lord!' " (7:4) In a lengthy sermon during the reign of Jehoiakim, Josiah's son, on the folly of such false assurance, Jeremiah warned the people, "The Lord sent me to prophesy against this house and this city all the things you have heard. Now reform your ways and your actions and obey the Lord your God. Then the Lord will relent and not bring the disaster He has pronounced against you" (26:12-13).[71]

Jeremiah focused his attention not only on the corporate sins of the people, but also the individual sins of each citizen of Israel. His own intimate relationship with the Lord allowed him a depth of understanding of the individual's responsibility before God. The Hebrew people understood the heart to be the center of human volition. And Jeremiah had come to realize, perhaps more keenly than any other prophet, how devious and stubborn the human heart could be: "The heart is deceitful above all things and beyond cure. Who can understand it? I the Lord search the heart and examine the mind, to reward a man according to his conduct, according to what his deeds deserve" (17:9-10).

At the same time, the prophet did not see these people as beyond the power of God's love. Salvation was still a real possibility. If an individual would forsake his or her wicked ways and repent, a new relationship with the Lord might be effected. This possibility is proclaimed in 7:5-7: "If you really change your ways and your actions and deal with each other justly, if you do not oppress the alien, the fatherless or the widow and do not shed innocent blood . . . and if you do not follow other gods to your own harm, then I will let you live in this land." For those who worried that it was too late for forgiveness because of their fathers' sinfulness, he had a word of assurance: "In those days people will no longer say, 'The fathers have eaten sour grapes and the children's teeth are set on edge.' Instead, everyone will die for his own sin; whoever eats sour grapes—his own teeth will be set on edge" (31:29-30).

In fact, declared Jeremiah following the fall of Jerusalem, God will effect a redemptive act in which the individual heart will be transformed and a new covenant will be made with every individual. "I will put my law in their minds and write it on their hearts. I will be their God and they will be my people" (31:33).

Habakkuk

We know nothing about Habakkuk other than his name. A deutero-canonical work, Bel and the Dragon, tells us that he was a Levitical priest. Nor have we any concrete idea of the circumstances under which his prophetic oracles were delivered, although we do know that he worked as God's messenger in late sixth-century Judah.

Habakkuk was much concerned by the violence and injustice which prevailed in Judah during this period of great chaos. "Destruction and violence are before me; there is strife, and conflict abounds. Therefore the law is paralyzed, and ... justice is perverted" (1:3-4). Habakkuk could not understand why God permitted these things to happen.

Nor could he comprehend why the Lord would judge Judah by allowing the Babylonians to conquer them. In spite of their sinfulness, the Hebrews were more righteous than these pagans. In response, God pointed out to the prophet that, while "the righteous will live by his faith" (2:4), all those who are unrighteous will suffer condemnation. Five woe oracles set forth the sins of Babylon—violence, bloodshed, drunkenness, lust, and idolatry (2:6-20)—and Habakkuk was reassured that this mighty pagan power would ultimately be destroyed, although for now, it would serve as God's instrument of punishment against Judah.[72]

Obadiah

Very little can be said about Obadiah. Some scholars have wondered whether the name, which means "servant of Yahweh," should be perhaps seen as a pseudonym of an anonymous prophet; others, whether the author might be the Obadiah of King Ahab's time (1 Kings 18:3-16). The content of the book suggests that the writer experienced the event of his prophecy himself and that he was a Judaean (1:13).[73]

Nor are scholars unanimous on the date of Obadiah's ministry. Some have placed it about 850 B.C. in the time of Jehoram of Judah, because of his prophecy against Edom (see 2 Kings 8:20-22). More interpreters, however, place the book about 586 B.C., at the time of Judah's destruction by Babylon. It is suggested that he may have been one who was left in the ruined Hebrew capital following the exile of most of its populace (2 Kings 25:12, 22).[74]

Obadiah dealt with sins of betrayal and gloating over the destruction of one's enemy. He directed his entire prophecy against Edom for its pride and hatred of Judah: "You should not look down on your brother in the day of his misfortune, nor rejoice over the people of Judah in the day of their destruction, nor boast so much in the day of their trouble" (v. 12). Because of Edom's lack of compassion for Judah, it too would be destroyed without pity: " 'There will be no survivors from the house of Esau.' The Lord has spoken" (v. 18).

> The kingdom of God (Zion) will be exalted when all resistance to God's lordship is put down. The Day of the Lord will bring destruction to the enemies of his children. Any intrusion of divine judgment in the history of redemption is evidence that God rules. The godly may take comfort in the hope that human powers will be brought down and that God's kingdom will come with power and salvation.[75]

Jonah

Jonah the son of Amittai was an eighth century B.C. prophet, a native of Gath Hepher, near Nazareth. We are told by 2 Kings 14:25 that he was active in the reign of Jeroboam II (793–753 B.C.) of Israel. Jonah told the king that he would recover Israel's ancient boundaries. Because Assyria was much concerned with troubles in the East, it could not proceed with its conquest of Palestine, and so Israel was able to pursue aggressively the strengthening of its cities and borders.[76]

Though Jonah was an eighth-century prophet and so a predecessor of Amos, prevalent scholarly opinion is that the book bearing his name was a later composition, perhaps just prior to the fall of Judah. Certainly, the prophet is depicted in a rather uncomplimentary and unprophetic light! It has been said that "the book is a prophetic *māsāl* (proverb) that draws attention to Jonah's folly and encourages a wise response by the self-righteous."[77]

Much debate has taken place over the literary genre of the book. Is it historical, allegorical, or parabolic? An even more important question is whether it really matters. The point of the story is the necessity of recognizing the sovereignty of God, and that He can bless or transform whom He will. "Nineveh has more than a hundred and twenty thousand people who cannot tell their right hand from their left, and many cattle as well. Should I not be concerned about that great city?" (4:11)

> The prophecy contains a strong warning to all the godly. The elect may miss the blessing of seeing God's grace extended outside the immediate covenant community because they impose limits on God. While Jonah was praying anxiously for his deliverance, the sailors had been tasting the love of God for three days! Likewise, the people of Nineveh, who repented of their sin, rejoiced that the impending judgment had not come; at the same time Jonah was a miserable man.[78]

In regard to the theology of sin, Jonah is the one Old Testament book which especially deals with the problem of an unforgiving spirit. It is symbolic of the Jews, who hated their pagan neighbors and simply would not believe that the Lord would extend mercy to these heathens; rather, they should be predestined to fuel the fires of Gehenna. Israel needed to learn that God's mercy is extended to others than themselves.

Ezekiel

Ezekiel's world was very much different from that of earlier prophets, for he was with Israel in exile. Previous prophets had addressed kings, priests, and other leading figures in society— people who enjoyed the power and resources to affect the direction of political and social policy. But the exiles under Ezekiel's ministry had neither power nor resources; they were aliens in a foreign land.[79]

We are told that Ezekiel was a priest whose father was named Buzi (1:3). He was probably born about 622 B.C., during the reformation of Josiah, and was among those condemned to make the forced march from Jerusalem to Babylon after Jehoiakim's unsuccessful rebellion against Nebuchadnezzar. There he lived in the Hebrew community of Tel Abib (3:15), an agricultural settlement by the river Kebar (1:1). In 592 he received a vision of God which led to his prophetic ministry. The account of this vision is contained in chapters 1–3. One important lesson he learned from this vision was that though He was God of Israel, the Lord was not restricted to Palestine nor to the Jerusalem temple. He was a universal God and He was present in Babylon with His exiled people.[80]

Several theological ideas may be distilled from the book. The first of these is that God will judge human sin. Since this was an emphasis of all the other prophets, we should not be surprised to find that Ezekiel stresses it as well. Newsome points out that

> what is unusual, however, is that in the teaching of Ezekiel only one part of the community of God's people is singled out as the object of future judgment. That is, of course, Jerusalem and Judah, while another part, the Babylonian Jews, is described as already having suffered the consequences of the nation's sin.[81]

Ezekiel depicts sin in cultic terms, a picture which goes along well with his priestly vocation. In his view, the conquest of Judah and Jerusalem's destruction were conclusive evidence of God's anger. He was outraged by the worship of idols in the Jerusalem temple revealed to him by God. "He said to me, 'Son of man, have you seen what the elders of the house of Israel are doing in the darkness, each at the shrine of his own idol?' They say, 'The Lord does not see us; the Lord has forsaken the land' " (8:12). In his analogy comparing marriage to God's relation with Israel (chap. 16), Ezekiel condemns the nation's breaking of the covenant; Israel is like a faithless wife gone whoring after idols and participating in their perversion. "This is what the Sovereign Lord says: I will deal with you as you deserve, because you have despised my oath by breaking the covenant" (16:59).[82]

The judgment Ezekiel saw falling upon Judah was not only corporate but also individual. In his vision of the Jerusalem temple (chap. 9), six angelic executioners were summoned, each one holding a weapon of destruction. They were accompanied by a man clad in linen, with a writing kit by his side. The linen-clothed man was instructed by God to mark the forehead of all those Jerusalemites who were agonizing over the perversion occurring in the temple. They would be spared when the executioners began their grisly task. "Thus the judgment is a purging and an individualizing process which is completed in the Exile."[83]

One of the most important individualizing teachings of the Old Testament is found in Ezekiel 18. It is also a major contribution to the theology of sin. The Jews — both in Jerusalem and in exile — had the tendency to blame their forebears for their troubles. They continually cited the old Hebrew proverb: "The fathers eat sour grapes, and the children's teeth are set on edge" (18:2). God then declared that from that point on the people should not quote it any longer; only the person who is personally guilty will be punished for his sin. Thus, "no person or generation is cast off by YHWH because of the sins of his forebears and, further . . . no person or generation is absolved from moral accountability because of the virtue of forebears."[84]

Ezekiel was also quick to point out that God took no delight in punishing sinners. Therefore, He was affording every person the opportunity for daily renewal, and the moral freedom to seize that opportunity. That one had previously fallen morally was not an insurmountable barrier to repenting and living a righteous life (18:21-23). In the same way, the righteous cannot fall into sin and expect to escape judgment because of former meritorious behavior (18:24).[85] In 18:30-32 God calls them to repentance.

> Therefore, O house of Israel, I will judge you, each one according to his ways, declares the Sovereign Lord. Repent! Turn away from all your offenses; then sin will not be your downfall. Rid yourselves of all the offenses you have committed, and get a new heart and a new spirit. Why will you die, O house of Israel? For I take no pleasure in the death of any of you, declares the Sovereign Lord. Repent and live!

Joel

Little is known about Joel other than that he was the son of a man named Pethuel (1:1). The context of his prophetic ministry was Judah and especially Jerusalem. When he was active is a matter of speculation. Scholars have variously placed him during the reign of Joash (Keil), Josiah (König), and Jeremiah (Kapelrud). Majority scholarly opinion in recent years places him in the post-exilic period, perhaps about the time of Nehemiah.[86]

Joel intended his message to be told from generation to generation (1:3). It was placed in the context of a horrendous plague of locusts (1:4-12) which impacted every aspect of life. It was an occasion to remind the people to prepare themselves for God's judgment, for the Day of the Lord might occur at any time: "Let all who live in the land tremble, for the day of the Lord is coming. It is close at hand—a day of darkness and gloom, a day of clouds and blackness" (2:1-2).

What was the proper attitude for God's people as they looked toward that great Day? It was to be one of genuine repentance for sin and not simply external ritual tokenism. The prophet's admonition has become a watchword for all generations.

> Rend your hearts and not your garments. Return to the Lord your God, for he is gracious and compassionate, slow to anger and abounding in love, and he relents from sending calamity. Who knows? He may turn and have pity and leave behind a blessing (2:13-14).

God desired to visit His people with prosperity and all manner of blessings, if only they would look to Him in faithful obedience.

The day would come, the Lord promised, when never again would God's people be subject to plagues, hunger, or shame. And in that day, "I will pour out my Spirit on all people. Your sons and daughters will prophesy, your old men will dream dreams, your young men will see visions. Even on my servants, both men and women, I will pour out my Spirit in those days" (2:28-29).

The Apostle Peter demonstrated to Christians of all time the beginning of the fulfillment of the above promise on the Day of Pentecost. "The Spirit is the eschatological gift of the Father and the Son (Acts 2:16-39). He witnesses concerning the restoration to come and calls on all the members of the new community . . . to look forward to the redemption of creation."[87] All of God's people must look forward to the time of restoration, the New Jerusalem, and the final destruction of evil.

Haggai

Haggai was a postexilic prophet whose ministry took place in Jerusalem in 520 B.C. with those exiles under Zerubbabel, a Davidic prince, who had returned to live in the city and to restore it and the temple. Nothing is known of Haggai other than his name.

Like his prophetic predecessors, Haggai saw a close connection between human sin and God's condemnation. The difference between him and those who had gone before him was his cultic view of righteousness and sin. We do not find here the sense of moral outrage over injustice and oppression expressed by Amos, Ezekiel, and others. Rather, the inhabitants of Jerusalem were being judged for their failure to construct a new temple.[88] "Therefore, because of you the heavens have withheld their dew and the earth its crops. I called for a drought on the fields and the mountains, on the grain, the new wine, the oil, and whatever the ground produces, on men and cattle, and on the labor of your hands" (1:10-11). If they would be obedient, then the Lord would bless them and the temple would be filled with His glory (2:6-9).

Zechariah

Zechariah, the son of Berechiah, the son of Iddo, was from a priestly household (Neh. 12:4, 16) and was a contemporary of Haggai (Ezra 5:1; 6:14). He prophesied during the reign of Darius of Persia. The starting date of his prophecy was 520 B.C.

The prophet called for spiritual renewal. He spoke of a cleansing from sin (5:1-11). The people were reminded of the reason for Judah's destruction by Babylon; it was because of their sins. They indulged in social oppression and would not listen to God.

> They made their hearts as hard as flint and would not listen to the law or to the words that the Lord Almighty had sent by his Spirit through the earlier prophets. So the Lord Almighty was very angry. "When I called they did not listen; so when they called, I would not listen," says the Lord Almighty (7:12-13).

Zechariah's emphasis was eschatological. Jerusalem would be restored to become the center for God's new kingdom. These blessings would occur when Israel repented. "On that day a fountain will be opened to the house of David and the inhabitants of Jerusalem, to cleanse them from sin and impurity" (13:1). Idolatry and false prophecy would be destroyed and God would reign forever.

One of the most important prophecies of this book has been appropriated by the church as pertaining to Jesus Christ, God's Messiah: "They will look on me, the one they have pierced, and they will mourn for him as one mourns for an only child, and grieve bitterly for him as one grieves for a firstborn son" (12:10). He will bring restoration to all who mourn His being pierced.[89] Restoration and renewal are available to all who mourn the cause of Christ's death—the sin of the whole world and their own personal sins.

Malachi

The term *Malaki* (my messenger) is more likely a title than a name. Should it be the latter, however, we know nothing at all about him. His time of prophecy is judged to be after the rebuilding of the temple, perhaps about 400 B.C.

The writer was extremely critical of the people of Jerusalem. They had sinned in their cultic practices, failing to carry out the Levitical regulations for offerings. "When you bring blind animals for sacrifice, is that not wrong? When you sacrifice crippled or diseased animals, is that not wrong?" (1:8) They were profaning God's house.

He was equally critical of the priests. They were, he declared, indifferent to the Lord. " 'If you do not listen, and if you do not set your heart to honor my name,' says the Lord Almighty, 'I will send a curse upon you, and I will curse your blessings' " (2:2). They had violated the covenant (2:8).

Again, Malachi lashed out at those who had profaned the covenant by breaking faith with their spouse. They had forsaken the wife of their youth in favor of a pagan woman. Consequently, God was rejecting their offerings, tantamount to rejecting them. "You ask, 'Why?' It is because the Lord is acting as the witness between you and the wife of your youth, because you have broken faith with her, though she is your partner, the wife of your marriage covenant" (2:14).

242

7.5: HEBREW PROPHETS IN CONTEXT

Prophet	King of Judah	King of Israel
Nathan	David	
Gad	David	
Ahijah	Rehoboam	Solomon Jeroboam I
Iddo	Rehoboam	
Hanani	Asa	
Jehu, son of Hanani		Baasha
Elijah		Ahab and Ahaziah
Micaiah		Ahab
Elisha		Jehoram, Jehu, Jehoahaz, Jehoash
Jehaziel	Jehoshaphat	
Eliezer	Jehoshaphat	
Zechariah	Joash	
Jonah		Jeroboam II
Amos		Jeroboam II
Hosea		Zechariah
Isaiah	Hezekiah, Jotham	
Micah	Jotham, Ahaz, Hezekiah	
Nahum	Amon	
Zephaniah	Josiah	
Jeremiah	Josiah, Jehoahaz, Jehoiakim, Jehoiachin, Zedekiah	
Habakkuk	Jehoahaz, Jehoiakim	
Ezekiel	Jehoiakim, Exile	
Daniel	Exile	
Haggai	Postexilic	
Zechariah	Postexilic	
Malachi	Postexilic	

In spite of these and other sins, there is the possibility of vindication for those who turn to God. "I will spare them, just as in compassion a man spares his son who serves him. And you will again see the distinction between the righteous and the wicked, between those who serve God and those who do not" (3:17-18).

Summary

The Old Testament prophets were distinctive in their theological contribution in both doctrinal and moral content. Several convictions contributed to their outstanding ministry.

The primary conviction of all the prophets was the absolute sovereignty of God. While He was the God of Israel, He was not limited to that land like the gods of the other nations; He was Ruler of all the world. All human beings were under His control. Because of their deep conviction that the Lord was supreme, the prophets had no qualms about carrying His message not only to the common people, but to priests and kings as well.

Secondly, they had the deep conviction that God in His sovereignty had elected Israel as His special people. He had elected to love them as His own. His relationship—a relationship unique among all the peoples of the earth—with them was codified in the covenant He had made with them. He had promised to protect them and keep them secure in the land He had given them, and to prosper them if they were obedient to Him and kept His covenant.

But a special relationship implied a special responsibility. When Israel abdicated responsibility by reneging on the covenant, the prophets roundly denounced her for the sin and emphasized God's coming wrath. Sin for them was the breaking of the covenant—whether in apostasy, adultery, idolatry, or social injustice.

Fourthly, the prophets almost never warned Israel of coming divine wrath without also calling on them to repent and return to the Lord. No matter how grievous their sins, if they would humble themselves before the Lord, He would forgive them and accept them.

Lastly, the prophets were convinced that God's redemptive love for Israel could not be frustrated even by the destructive power of human sin. Almost all of the prophets insisted that, regardless of Israel's perversity, after He had judged His people, God would restore them to Himself.

Chapter Eight
The Writings on Sin

T he Writings—in the Hebrew *ketubhim*, and in the Greek *hagiographa*—form the third section of the Hebrew Scriptures. They do not follow the same sequence in all the extant manuscripts. Generally, Psalms, Proverbs, and Job begin this part, though not necessarily in that order. Gerhard von Rad has called the books of the Writings Israel's response to God's saving acts:

> Not only did she repeatedly take up her pen to recall these acts of Jahweh to her mind in historical documents, but she also addressed Jahweh in a wholly personal way. She offered praise to him, and asked him questions, and complained to him about her sufferings, for Jahweh had not chosen his people as a mere dumb object of his will in history, but for converse with him.[1]

There is much to learn from this third section of the Hebrew Scriptures. They give one an idea of how God's acts affected His people, and the nation's reaction in attempting to justify itself or in expressing its shame.[2] These books have much to say about the nature of sin.

Psalms

Psalms is the poetry of the Bible, its "hymnbook." It had its beginnings in the reign of David; almost half of the psalms are attributed to him. Others are ascribed to Solomon, the sons of Korah (a Levitical family and choir), Asaph (a Levite), Heman the Ezrahite and Ethan the Ezrahite (both choir leaders), and Moses.[3]

While they are primarily instruments of worship, the psalms contain a wealth of theological truth. Some of the themes that concern us include the covenant relation between God and humankind, sin, judgment, forgiveness, and salvation.

Psalms: The introduction

It is generally accepted that Psalm 1 is an introduction to the whole book. It begins by commenting on the road to happiness. Happiness belongs to the person "who does not walk in the counsel of the wicked or stand in the way of sinners or sit in the seat of mockers" (1:1). The words "counsel," "way," and "seat" refer to areas of thinking, behaving, and belonging by which one's essential commitment is determined and initiated. These three phases demonstrate three levels of turning away from God by depicting three degrees of conformity to the world: "accepting its advice, being party to its ways, and adopting the most fatal of its attitudes — for the *scoffers*, if not the most scandalous of sinners, are the farthest from repentance."[4]

The writer turns from the negative to the positive. The happy person not only does not heed the world, but delights and meditates in God's law. The psalmist is satisfied to focus on one thought, that whatever truly forms a person's thinking crafts one's very life.[5] The one who allows God's law to shape his or her existence is fruitful and prosperous (1:3). "Not so the wicked! They are like chaff that the wind blows away" (1:4).

The concluding verses present two completely divergent paths, based on what people have chosen to be. The wicked will go to judgment without any standing and having no place with the righteous; their path is the way to ruin. But the path of the upright is guarded by God.

The theme of this psalm is the theme of the whole book. It demonstrates the contentment of the person who commits himself to the Lord. And it addresses the folly of the wicked person who commits herself to the way of the world. Anderson notes that

since the godless have no regard for the Law of God, God cannot have a real regard for their way, because the Law is the God-given guide to his people, and consequently those who reject that guidance also repudiate God's concern for them, and thereby they cut the very ground from under their own feet.[6]

Psalm 2 is complementary, helping in the introduction to the Psalter. Verse 12, "lest . . . you be destroyed in your way," is reminiscent of 1:6, "but the way of the wicked will perish." Verse 12, "Blessed are all who take refuge in Him," may be seen as comparable to 1:1. Psalm 2 actually defines the wicked of Psalm 1 and how God deals with them. They are doomed to destruction under His wrath.

The God of righteous judgment

Righteousness is one of God's attributes. Over and over the Scriptures stress that He is a righteous and holy God. Because holiness means separation, God's holiness signifies that He is separate from sin and evil. Consequently, He must judge righteously, for an unfair decision would be sinful. A number of the psalms either extol or seek God's righteous judgment in the writer's situation.

Psalm 7 is one psalm which deals with this theme. Its superscription suggests a connection with an intense bitterness against David on the part of Benjamin, Saul's tribe.[7] If so, the king is appealing to God to vindicate him. In verses 3-5 he uses three "if" clauses to protest his blamelessness in respect to his enemies' slander.

O Lord my God, if I have done this and [if] there is guilt on my hands — if I have done this evil to him who is at peace with me or without cause have robbed my foe — then let my enemy pursue and overtake me; let him trample my life to the ground and make me sleep in the dust.

The psalmist wonders why God takes so long to respond to his pleas for justice (vv. 9-10). He comes to the conclusion that the Lord seems slow to act simply because He is giving the sinner a chance to repent. The desperate need for repentance is implied in three lines on retribution: God's anger (vv. 12ff), and the intrinsic futility (v. 14) and folly (vv. 15ff) of sin.[8]

Psalm 9 (also a psalm of David) celebrates the righteous judgment of God. In fact, the writer declares that God's throne has been established for the very purpose of judgment (v. 7). From there, "He will judge the world in righteousness; He will govern the peoples with justice" (v. 8). Justice for the psalmist means that "the Lord is a refuge for the oppressed, a stronghold in times of trouble" (v. 9), while at the same time judging the ungodly nations and striking fear into their hearts (v. 19). Kidner tells us that "a revealing nuance in the sentence pronounced on the wicked is that they will 'return' to Sheol (v. 17), not merely depart there. Death is their native element."[9]

The Psalmist Asaph also writes of a time when the Lord will judge uprightly. In Psalm 75 he depicts an earth being thrown off balance by the wicked, but God keeps its pillars steady (v. 3). In His justice the Lord "brings one down, [and] He exalts another" (v. 7). In another picture, Asaph likens God's wrath to "a cup full of foaming wine mixed with spices" (v. 8), which He pours out on the wicked, but the horns of the righteous will be lifted up (v. 10).

The nature of human sin

A study of the Psalms reveals extensive mention of sin. Some twenty-three different words for sin are used. The most frequent words include: *rāšā* (commit wickedness)—37:12, 14, 16; 106:6; *rā* (evil)—10:15; 73:8; *hattā't* (sin)—51:13; 59:3; *peša'* (transgression)—25:7; 51:1, 3; and 'āwôn (iniquity)—25:11; 103:9-10.[10]

Psalm 32 has much to say about sin. It begins with the nature of sin and moves to its forgiveness. The key to its theme is verse 5: "Then I acknowledged my sin to you and did not cover up my iniquity. I said, 'I will confess my transgressions to the Lord'— and you forgave the guilt of my sin." In this single verse three different Hebrew words are used to depict sin. The most outstanding is the term "transgression" *(peša'),* an idea which traces sin to its origin in the individual's will. Transgression "is not simply the thought of lawlessness, in the sense of defection from a prescribed law; it is rather a voluntary act of self-assertion in opposition to the will of a superior. It is a withdrawal from, or rebellion against, the Lawgiver."[11] The second word, "iniquity" *('āwôn)*, is synonymous with "offense" or "guilt." The third word, "sin" *(hattā't)*, is a more general term which means a failure to hit the mark or achieve the standard required.

Verses 3 and 4 show the function of the conscience in the sinner's life. Personal guilt was making the writer's life unbearable: "When I kept silent, my bones wasted away through my groaning all day long. For night and day your hand was heavy upon me; my strength was sapped as in the heat of summer." As a result of the torment of his conscience, the psalmist determined to confess his sin. He had decided that no factors could outweigh the salving of his oppressed soul. And in confessing his sin, he found forgiveness.

The writer stresses sensible cooperation with God in verses 8 and 9. He calls for a teachable spirit and an openness to God's counsel. And he warns against a spirit of intractability: "Do not be like the horse or the mule, which have no understanding but must be controlled by bit and bridle or they come not to you" (v. 9). His conclusions reflect the overarching theme of the whole book, namely, that the only true happiness is to be found in trusting the Lord (vv. 10ff).

Repentance and salvation

Throughout the Psalms there is an interweaving of experiences which include confession, repentance, and salvation from sin. Many of these verses emphasize strongly the willingness of God to forgive and redeem the repentant sinner.

Psalm 51 is exemplary of these spiritual experiences. It was written by David after the Prophet Nathan confronted him over his sin with Bathsheba (2 Sam. 11–12). Kidner says of this psalm: "It comes from David's blackest moment of self-knowledge, yet it explores not only the depths of his guilt but some of the farthest reaches of salvation."[12]

David's chief realization in this psalm is that his sin was against God alone (v. 4). This is not to say that he had not trespassed

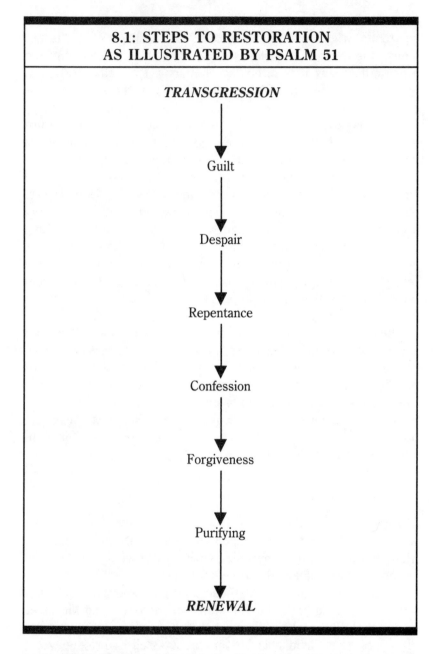

**8.1: STEPS TO RESTORATION
AS ILLUSTRATED BY PSALM 51**

TRANSGRESSION

Guilt

Despair

Repentance

Confession

Forgiveness

Purifying

RENEWAL

against both Uriah and Bathsheba, for he had. But he was aware that he had failed to observe the standard set by the Lord. We also have an acknowledgment in verse 4 that God's judgment upon him was completely just.

Verse 5 is particularly significant: "Surely I was sinful at birth, sinful from the time my mother conceived me." The psalmist recognizes that his sin was no freak occurrence; it was a part of the warp and woof of his very being, an expression of the flawed stock from which he originated. "David is, of course, not speaking against his mother in particular, nor against the process of conception. Nor is he excusing himself. It is the climax of the facts that he is facing: that his sins are his own . . . and inexcusable; worst of all, they are the very element he lives in."[13]

In the face of this horrific apprehension, David prays for a thorough cleansing of his sin through a spiritual washing: "Cleanse me with hyssop, and I will be clean; wash me, and I will be whiter than snow" (v. 7). Leupold tells us that

the verb for "wash" is more vigorous than the translation might suggest, for it includes pounding, stamping, and vigorous rubbing in order to loosen the dirt. But there again, if God does it, the effect will be adequate cleansing, in fact, he shall become "whiter than snow," a phrase that is reminiscent of Is. 1:18, which statement of the prophet could well be based on this passage.[14]

He further seeks a miracle of regenerating love in his life: "Create in me a pure heart, O God, and renew a steadfast spirit within me" (v. 10). He is well aware that ritual practices are insufficient to effect this transformation. The sacrifice of a burnt offering is not what God demands: "The sacrifices of God are a broken spirit; a broken and contrite heart, O God, you will not despise" (v. 17).

The Proverbs

The Book of Proverbs is of a much different genre from Psalms or any of the Old Testament writings we have thus far examined. It comes under that category known as "wisdom." Wisdom has been defined as "a practical knowledge of the laws of life and of the world, based on experience."[15] The book is a collection of capsules of wisdom ascribed to Solomon, anonymous wise men, Agur the son of Jakeh, and Lemuel king of Massa. They cover a wide range of subjects; on the negative side: pride, drunkenness, laziness, gossip, deceit, and adultery; on the positive side: hard work, fidelity, generosity, and sobriety.[16]

One of the major themes presented by Proverbs is that behavior which takes one to destruction. A synonym for such behavior is sin. Several different deviant behaviors receive comment.

The deviant is portrayed from the outset as a fool who ignores the instruction of Wisdom. Wisdom is depicted by the writer as a hypostasis, personified as an independent force emanating from God Himself.[17] In 1:20ff, she rebukes those who reject her: "How long will you simple ones love your simple ways? How long will mockers delight in mockery and fools hate knowledge?" (1:22) The simple one may be defined as one who is morally direction-less, but who tends toward evil. The end of such is sure: "the waywardness of the simple will kill them, and the complacency of fools will destroy them" (1:32). The following verse is antitheti-cal: "but whoever listens to me [Wisdom] will live in safety and be at ease, without fear of harm."

One of the chief sinners cited by the collection is the adulter-ess. "Her feet go down to death; her steps lead straight to the grave" (5:5), and the person who falls for her enticements has chosen death. Her potential customers are warned that the Lord is watching all they do (5:21). They are well to remember that "the evil deeds of a wicked man ensnare him; the cords of sin hold him fast. He will die for lack of discipline, led astray by his own great folly" (5:22-23).

Using a different approach, the writer pictures what he sees from his window, a young man being approached by a loose wom-an. He imagines the conversation that takes place between the two. She tells him: "My husband is not at home; he has gone on a long journey" (7:19). And with persuasive words she seduces him until he follows her "like an ox going to the slaughter . . . lit-tle knowing it will cost him his life" (7:22-23). The sage rein-forces his warning by pointing out to his readers that "her house is a highway to the grave, leading down to the chambers of death" (7:27).

Another vice is drunkenness. Certainly, strong drink height-ened life if used judiciously. But as with so many beneficial things, excessive use of spirits engendered a speedy destruc-tion.[18] The writer has little good to say about alcoholic beverages: "Wine is a mocker and beer a brawler; whoever is led astray by them is not wise" (20:1). Indeed, a fearful picture is painted of the person who has imbibed too much.

Who has woe? Who has sorrow? Who has complaints? Who has needless bruises? Who has bloodshot eyes? Those who linger over wine, who go to sample bowls of mixed wine. . . . In the end it bites like a snake and poisons like a viper. Your eyes will see strange sights and your mind imagine confusing things. You will be like one sleeping on the high seas, lying on top of the rigging. "They hit me," you will say, "but I'm not hurt! They beat me, but I don't feel it! When will I wake up so I can find another drink?" (23:29-30, 32-35)

Nor does the sage have anything but harsh words for the slug-gard. He employs many different figures of speech to heap his scorn on this laggard. In one instance he uses hyperbole, describing a person who is so lazy that when he sits down to a bowl of soup he cannot be bothered to raise it to his lips (19:24). In another, he sarcastically pictures a lazy person excusing his refusal to go outside by saying, "There is a lion outside!" or, "I will be murdered in the streets!" (22:13). And he describes the property of a sluggard.

I went past the field of the sluggard, past the vineyard of the man who lacks judgment; thorns had come up everywhere, the ground was covered with weeds, and the stone wall was in ruins. I applied my heart to what I observed and learned a lesson from what I saw: A little sleep, a little slumber, a little folding of the hands to rest — and poverty will come on you like a bandit and scarcity like an armed man (24:30-34).

Antisocial behavior of all kinds comes in for sharp censure. Seven of these sins are listed in 6:16-19. They include: "haughty eyes, a lying tongue, hands that shed innocent blood, a heart that devises wicked schemes, feet that are quick to rush into evil, a false witness who pours out lies, and a man who stirs up dissension among brothers." There is a common bond among these sins: they all have the tendency to fracture the bond of loyalty and respect between fellow human beings. William McKane observes that "what is described is a deep-seated corruption of motives which gives rise to a constant and dedicated malevolence tantamount to a total incapacity for neighborliness" which "wreaks havoc in a community."[19]

Conclusions

To avoid committing such deadly sins, the sage counsels complete reliance on the Lord and His wisdom: "Trust in the Lord with all your heart and lean not on your own understanding; in all your ways acknowledge Him, and He will make your paths straight. Do not be wise in your own eyes; fear the Lord and shun evil" (3:5-7).

Job

Job, which belongs to the wisdom genre, is a unique Israelite writing without equal in the ancient Near East. It concerns the righteousness of God in His relationship with humanity in particular and creation in general.[20] In it we are given some penetrating insights into Old Testament concepts both of sin and of Satan.

The prologue of the book introduces Job and his situation. At Satan's behest and with God's allowance, Job loses everything he has—family and goods—and sits on an ash heap in pain and sorrow. We are also introduced to Satan (in better parlance, *the* Satan). He intrudes upon an assembly of the sons of God (1:6-12). Francis Andersen observes:

> His insolence shows a mind already twisted away from God, but his hostility is not on a scale of a rival power. There is evil here, but not dualism. The Satan may be the chief mischief-maker of the universe, but . . . he is not God's minister of prosecution; it is the Lord, not the Satan, who brings up the case of Job.[21]

Satan's role in Job is not a major one. He serves essentially to introduce Job's suffering (of which the actual agent is God!). We see in this demonic angel only an embryo of his later depiction by Scripture as the tempter and accuser of God's people.

One of the ideas of sin in Job—common in many of the Old

Testament writings—is that sinfulness is born in the heart, regarded as the center of the will. We read, for example, that after his children enjoyed a round of merrymaking and feasting, Job would regularly make a sacrifice for them, worrying, "Perhaps my children have sinned and cursed God in their hearts" (1:5).[22]

Other types of sin mentioned in this book include blaspheming God (2:9), the lewd look at a girl (31:1), the adulterous desire for a married woman (31:9-10), the mistreatment of servants (31:13), and the oppression of the poor (31:16-21).[23] "To violate God's ethical laws, Job intimates, is to transgress seriously. Ethical wrongdoings are social sins because they threaten the welfare of society."[24]

When Job's "comforters" visit him, they intimate that sin brings suffering as a divine punishment. Job disputes such an idea: "Why do the wicked live on, growing old and increasing in power?" (21:7) It is the age-old question of why the wicked prosper and enjoy life. Job puzzles over this seeming paradox: "They spend their years in prosperity and go down to the grave in peace. Yet they say to God, 'Leave us alone! We have no desire to know your ways' " (21:13-14). Instead of receiving a wretched death without being mourned—as Job's friends have suggested—the wicked depart this life with pomp and circumstance, attended by throngs of people and with the highest honors. Such a perception is little consolation.[25]

In chapter 24, Job picks up on a similar theme, wondering why God does nothing to prevent the wicked from sinning. He describes the plight of the poor and needy at the hands of the evil ones who oppress them (v. 4). The height of Job's bewilderment at God's seeming indifference to sin comes in verse 12: "The groans of the dying rise from the city, and the souls of the wounded cry out for help. But God charges no one with wrongdoing." Beginning with verse 18, however, Job seems to do a "flip-flop" in his sentiments about the wicked, deciding that, after all, God will judge them, and life is not as rosy as it might seem for such perpetrators of wickedness: "He may let them rest in a feeling of security, but his eyes are on their ways. For a little while they are exalted, and then they are gone" (vv. 23-24). This section is a problem for many commentators. Some have attempted to explain it on the basis of a misplaced text (perhaps with Bildad speaking);[26] others take it as a quotation by Job of what his friends have told him and which he is rebutting.[27] But Job has been presented to us as a man in intense suffering; such people frequently make statements that go in one direction and then abruptly change their orientation as they seek reasons for their pain; it is entirely possible that Job is one such individual. Another possibility is that Job was not denying that while, eventually, death overtakes all humans including the wicked, it often seems as though they are prospering.[28]

Conclusions

Job sums up his conclusions on sin and righteousness in chapter 27. In a series of imprecations he steadfastly maintains before his friends and the Lord that he is innocent of any wrongdoing (vv. 1-6). Whatever the cause of his misery, it is not sin. As far as the wicked are concerned, he is convinced that God will ultimately deal with them. There is a future retribution coming, and his friends — for having wickedly suggested that he was to blame for his misfortune — will have a portion in it (v. 13). A list of adversities awaiting the wicked follow: The sword, starvation, and plague will destroy their progeny (vv. 14ff). Nor will their widows miss them! (v. 15) Their material possessions will be decimated (v. 19). And someday they will awaken to discover that they are dead (vv. 21-23).

Job obviously is not kindly disposed toward the wicked. Like many of his time, he saw them as fuel for the fires of destruction and everlasting loss. Forgiveness for them was not something he seemed to consider. They were seemingly beyond that point.

Ecclesiastes

Ecclesiastes is a book of wisdom of uncertain age (sometime prior to the third century b.c.) and authorship. It purports to be the work of a king of Israel, possibly Solomon, but its author is known simply as Qoheleth, which is a title generally translated as "the preacher." The book is an apologetic essay which defends commitment to God by depicting the grim alternative.[29] Qoheleth too has some observations on sin.

In 7:15-18, Qoheleth paints a picture of the superstitious pagan, who is aware of God, but is not committed to Him. This person's advice is to be neither too upright nor too sinful. "Moderation in all things"—including character—is the order of the day. Such a cynical attitude, however, is brought quickly down to earth with the confession of 7:20 that "there is not a righteous man on earth who does what is right and never sins." Here is an emphatic declaration of the universality of human sin.

The last section of chapter 7 is somewhat reminiscent of Proverbs. Qoheleth's failure to apprehend wisdom leads him to meditate on human sinfulness (vv. 25ff). Like the writer of Proverbs 7:6-27, he sets forth the tragedy of the adulterous woman: "I find more bitter than death the woman who is a snare, whose heart is a trap and whose hands are chains. The man who pleases God will escape her, but the sinner she will ensnare" (Ecc. 7:26). He then turns his attention to a more general evaluation of both men and women, finding both sexes lacking. Some may want to see a measure of male chauvinism in the writer; but when all is said and done, he finds men only one one-thousandth more upright than women, and so there is not much to choose between them. Other ancient Near-Eastern statements tend to much greater extremity on this subject![30] In spite of the fact that human beings were created with a disposition to righteousness, they have determinedly gone their own way into sin.

Like Job, Qoheleth wonders why the wicked are not more speedily punished for their evil ways (8:10-17). During their lifetime, many evil people pretend to be devout, attending religious services to the plaudits of the common people and being greatly honored at death (8:10). Delays in condemnation simply serve to increase their wicked deeds (8:11). Robert Davidson comments:

> Is Koheleth upset by this picture of the pseudo-pious wicked and their popularity, or does he simply note it as one of those facts of life which are there whether we like it or not? We do not know. He does, however, go on to ask the question as to why it is that people turn to crime to further their own ends. His answer is that they get away with it; crime pays because they are not swiftly punished. The greatest deterrent to crime, he is arguing, must be the certainty of being caught. But it does not happen that way. The chances of being caught and punished are not high. The forces of law and order seem to have had much the same problem in his day as in ours.[31]

In chapter 9, Qoheleth ruminates on death and what lies beyond. It is true, he confesses, that the destiny of the righteous and wise is in God's hands. But no one really can tell how God will react to them, whether with love or hate (v. 1). In fact, it would seem that the righteous and wicked share a common fate—Sheol (v. 2). Such an attitude confutes almost all of the sage's cultural and religious background, which held that there was a relationship between one's behavior and one's ultimate end. But Qoheleth asserts this distinctive concept as axiomatic.[32]

That the same end should overtake all human beings should not be surprising, however, for evil is universal. Qoheleth is blunt in his assessment of human beings: "The hearts of men, moreover, are full of evil and there is madness in their hearts while they live, and afterward they join the dead" (9:3).

Chapter 10 is a collection of proverbs on wisdom and folly. The sin of folly is so great that only a little is needed to outweigh much wisdom and honor (v. 1). A fool's folly is so obvious that all he has to do is go for a walk and everyone knows that there is a person parading his stupidity (v. 3). And should it not be expected that the fool "is condemned by his own lips. At the beginning his words are folly; at the end they are wicked madness" (10:12-13). Kidner asserts

> that end, in *wicked madness,* may look too lurid to be true; but its two elements, moral and mental, are the final fruits of refusing the will and truth of God. If there are innumerable unbelievers whose earthly end could hardly be described as either wickedness or madness, it is only because the logic of their belief has not been followed through, thanks to the restraining grace of God. But when a whole society goes secular, the process is far more evident and thoroughgoing.[33]

Conclusions

In spite of the seeming meaninglessness of life, Qoheleth arrives at some firm conclusions. The wise person will avoid sin and disobedience to God. Indeed, when all is said and done, "fear God and keep His commandments, for this is the whole duty of man. For God will bring every deed into judgment, including every hidden thing, whether it is good or evil" (12:13-14).

The Chronicler's History

Following 1 and 2 Kings we come to another history which covers much of the same material, except that it begins with a genealogy from Adam on and extends to the beginning of the Persian Empire. Known to the Hebrew Scriptures as a single volume called simply "the annals," 1 and 2 Chronicles has been considered for the last century and a half to be authored by the same person who wrote Ezra and Nehemiah (which act as a sequel to the former). Recent arguments by Hugh Williamson, however, have demonstrated the fallacy of such a view.[34]

When Chronicles was written is also a matter of some debate. Since 2 Chronicles refers to the kingdom of Persia coming to power (36:20), a date earlier than 539 B.C. is precluded. On the other hand, its existence was attested to prior to the mid-second century B.C. and so must have been written somewhat before that time. Williamson has suggested a date within the fourth century B.C.[35]

Who wrote Chronicles? Its author was probably an inhabitant of Jerusalem who fervently supported the temple and its services. Some scholars have mentioned Ezra as the author, but his dates would be too early for the time frame posited. One may point more probably to a teaching Levite, since the Chronicler's thought is similar to the form of preaching used by teaching Levites. Such a position would also explain the author's access to the various types of materials he used.[36]

Theological themes

While the Chronicler centers on a number of different emphases—such as the importance of all Israel as a unity, the importance of the Davidic dynasty, and the importance of the temple and its services—the most significant emphasis for our study is what is termed his doctrine of immediate retribution. Like the Deuteronomic historian he correlates blessing with faithfulness and condemnation with disobedience, but he stresses the immediacy of either within the same generation. For the most part, the king represents the whole nation; one who is faithful is blessed with economic, political, military, and personal success, while those who apostatize are punished with economic, military, political, and personal disaster.[37]

At the same time, judgment is never without warning. Nor must it be inevitable. Prior to God's condemnation a prophetic warning is issued to the offender(s), frequently in the form of a Levitical sermon (e.g., 2 Chron. 16:7-9). Should the offender repent, judgment might be averted.[38]

Gerhard von Rad observes:

The Chronicler is at pains to show that Jahweh's judgment or salvation still affected each generation individually. . . . each generation stands immediately before Jahweh, and stands or falls with its anointed. . . . the Chronicler is making his contribution to one of the hardest problems which cropped up in late Jahwism, namely, the question of the share of the individual in Jahweh.[39]

These themes become evident in the records of the kings of Judah.

David and Solomon

The Chronicler's history really begins in 1 Chronicles 9:35 with the genealogies and account of the removal of Saul from the kingship of Israel, "for Saul's death and the dispersal of his people are a type and model of the death and exile of Judah and its last kings."[40] Saul's death was also a fitting model for the Chronicler's theme of retribution for disobedience. He declares that "Saul died because he was unfaithful to the Lord. . . . So the Lord put him to death and turned the kingdom over to David son of Jesse" ((1 Chron. 10:13-14).

The account of David's reign is an account of the consolidation of Israel under his rule and of his preparation for the building of the temple by his son Solomon. No mention is made of his sin with Bathsheba, nor of his problems with Absalom. The only sin mentioned is that of numbering the people (1 Chron. 21:1ff). The Chronicler tells us that "Satan rose up against Israel and incited David" (21:1). Even though Joab remonstrated with him, David was insistent on the census. As a result the Lord punished Israel.

David was quick to confess his sin. The Lord gave him his choice of three punishments: to suffer three years of famine, three months of being bested by his enemies, or "three days of the sword of the Lord—days of plague in the land" (21:12). The king's response was immediate: "Let me fall into the hands of the Lord, for his mercy is very great" (21:13). In token of his repentance, David purchased the threshing floor of Arunah the Jebusite. It was this place that became the site of Solomon's temple.

In confiding to Solomon his ideas and plans for the temple, David gave him the following charge.

Acknowledge the God of your father, and serve Him with wholehearted devotion and a willing mind, for the Lord searches every heart and understands every motive behind the thoughts. If you seek Him, He will be found by you; but if you forsake Him, He will reject you forever. Consider now, for the Lord has chosen you to build a temple as a sanctuary. Be strong and do the work (1 Chron. 28:9-10).

Second Chronicles begins with Solomon's ascension to the throne of Israel and recounts the construction of the temple. In his prayer dedicating the new edifice, the king looked ahead to Israel's defeat by an enemy because of apostasy, and he asked God—when the people turned back to Him—to forgive their sin and reestablish them in the land (6:24ff). He also looked ahead to the Exile when Israel would be taken into Babylonian captivity because of their rebellion against the Lord, and asked that—when they repented and confessed their wickedness—"then from heaven, your dwelling place, hear their prayer and their pleas, and uphold their cause. And forgive your people, who have sinned against you" (6:39).

God's response to this prayer made clear His choice and acceptance of this new sanctuary. In the Chronicler's record here, however, are two verses which do not appear in the Deuteronomic history (1 Kings 9:2-9). Because they are so completely a part of the Chronicler's theology it may be supposed that they were added by him.[41]

When I shut up the heavens so that there is no rain, or command locusts to devour the land or send a plague among my people, if my people, who are called by my name, will humble themselves and pray and seek my face and turn from their wicked ways, then I will hear from heaven and will forgive their sin and will heal their land. Now my eyes will be open and my ears attentive to the prayers offered in this place (2 Chron. 7:13-15).

The Chronicler does not record any of the negative aspects of Solomon's life noted by the Deuteronomic historians. He is content to observe the splendor, wealth, and wisdom of the king. Anecdotes concerning Solomon's foreign wives, his construction of pagan worship centers for them, and his own apostasy would not be conducive to his theological intent.

The divided monarchy

With the division of the Hebrew monarchy into two kingdoms, the Chronicler focuses his attention on the Southern Kingdom, which remained under the house of David. Because, in his view, salvation is attained only through the twin institutions of the Davidic dynasty and the Jerusalem temple, he is interested in the Northern Kingdom only as it comes into contact with the South. The Northerners remain a part of Israel, albeit a part which has abandoned God and stands in need of repentance and restoration.[42]

The Chronicler places the blame for the loss of the bulk of the realm squarely on Rehoboam. It was his refusal to listen to the reasonable requests of the people which led to his realm's partition. At the same time, 2 Chronicles 11:4 makes it clear that God is really back of what has happened.

After the split, the priests and Levites left Jeroboam's realm for Judah, because of his increasing apostasy. "They strengthened the kingdom of Judah and supported Rehoboam son of Solomon three years, walking in the ways of David and Solomon during this time" (2 Chron. 11:17). But once Rehoboam had established himself in a strong position, "he and all Israel with him abandoned the law of the Lord. Because they had been unfaithful to the Lord, Shishak king of Egypt attacked Jerusalem in the fifth year of King Rehoboam" (12:1-2). When the Prophet Shemaiah brought this word to them, the king and his court humbled themselves before God. As a result, though Shishak plundered the city, he did not destroy it.

DeVries observes that the Chronicler

is harsher with Rehoboam than Kings is; he may have, after all, harbored resentment against him for letting the kingdom fall apart. 1 Kings 14:22-24 tells in detail of the abominations that prevailed in Judah during his reign, but . . . [the Chronicler] does not even mention these abominations. Rather, 12:14 seems like a mere slap on the wrist. . . . But at least [Rehoboam] followed [the Chronicler's] great cure-all remedy: repentance, humbling himself. He may have been foolish and proud, but he did respect the prophets, and when they said "humble yourself," he humbled himself.[43]

Abijah

War developed between Rehoboam's successor, Abijah, and Jeroboam. In this encounter, the former is presented in a much more favorable light by the Chronicler than by the Deuteronomist (in 1 Kings 15). Abijah appealed to the Northerners to end their rebellion and pledge their loyalty to their rightful ruler. Of course, the Northern army refused, whereupon God gave Judah the victory in battle because of its reliance on Him. "Jeroboam did not regain power during the reign of Abijah. And the Lord struck him down and he died. But Abijah gained in strength" (2 Chron. 13:20-21).

Asa

With Asa, Abijah's son and successor, the Chronicler again expands the comparable Deuteronomic account (1 Kings 15:9-24) and imposes upon it his familiar themes of reward for obedience and punishment for rebellion.[44] "Asa did what was good and right in the eyes of the Lord his God" (2 Chron. 14:2). He destroyed the worship places of the false gods and commanded his people to worship the Lord. As a result, "no one was at war with him during those years, for the Lord gave him rest" (14:6). When Zerah the Cushite attacked Judah, Asa called on God for help and crushed his enemy.

Unfortunately, in later life, Asa's devotion to God slackened. When threatened by Baasha of Israel, Asa struck an alliance with

Ben-Hadad of Syria, thus demonstrating a falling away from God. "At that time Hanani the seer came to Asa king of Judah and said to him: 'Because you have relied on the king of Aram and not on the Lord your God . . . from now on you will be at war' " (2 Chron. 16:7, 9). In anger, the king imprisoned the seer; he also brutalized some of his subjects (who no doubt protested his behavior). It comes, therefore, as no surprise to the reader to learn that Asa's last days were spent with a severe foot disease. "Though his disease was severe, even in his illness he did not seek help from the Lord, but only from the physicians" (16:12).

Jehoshaphat

The Chronicler has high praise for Jehoshaphat, Asa's son and successor as king of Judah. Not only did he seek the Lord as his father had done in his early years (2 Chron. 17:3-6), but he sent a team of officials, Levites, and priests throughout Judah to teach the people "the Book of the Law of the Lord" (17:7-9). As a result, the fear of the Lord fell on the surrounding nations and Judah enjoyed a time of peace. Because of his devotion to God, Jehoshaphat became increasingly powerful and wealthy.

But the Chronicler's admiration is diminished substantially as he records the king's alliance with Ahab of Israel. Against the advice of a prophet of God, Jehoshaphat entered a battle alongside Ahab and almost lost his life, "but Jehoshaphat cried out, and the Lord helped him" (18:31). When he returned home, however, he was upbraided by Jehu the seer for having helped Ahab who was God's enemy. "Because of this, the wrath of the Lord is upon you" (19:2). And yet, all was not lost, for the seer noted that "you have rid the land of the Asherah poles and have set your heart on seeking God" (19:3). Evidently the king took Jehu's prophecy to heart, for the remaining material shows how, because of Jehoshaphat's obedience to the will of God, Judah traveled a very different road from Israel, at least during his lifetime. And yet, the Chronicler sets the stage for a wrong turn by noting that "the people still had not set their hearts on the God of their fathers" (20:33), and that — before his death — the king made another alliance with Israel, this time with Ahaziah, "who was guilty of wickedness" (20:35).

Jehoram, a bad example

Jehoshaphat's son, Jehoram, is the first king of the Davidic dynasty about whom the Chronicler has nothing good to say.[45] The inference in 2 Chronicles 21:7 is that had the Lord not promised David that his house would be established forever, He would have destroyed Judah and terminated the royal line. As it was, retribution was exacted against Jehoram for his wickedness. Edom and Libnah revolted against Judah's rule. The Philistines and Arabs invaded and pillaged Judah. And the Lord afflicted Jehoram with an incurable bowel disease, from which he died in great pain.

Ahaziah, his father's son

When Jehoram died, he was sufficiently unpopular that he was accorded no burial honors. The people made his youngest son, Ahaziah, king. But he was no better than his father and "walked in the ways of the house of Ahab" (2 Chron. 22:3), for his mother Athaliah, a daughter of Ahab, encouraged him in wickedness. He associated with his cousin Joram of Israel in a number of endeavors and the two were both destroyed by Jehu in his revolt against the house of Omri (22:9).

A coup d'etat

Upon Ahaziah's death, his mother seized power in a coup d'etat. She consolidated her control by executing all of the royal family, excepting Joash, whose aunt (wife of the priest Jehoiada) spirited him away. After six years of Athaliah's rule, the people evidently had had enough and, in a counter-coup which had popular support, Jehoiada placed Joash on the throne and did away with the evil queen (2 Chron. 23:1-15).

Joash, good turned bad

Under Jehoiada's guidance, the temple of Baal was razed, the altars and idols were destroyed, and the priest of Baal was killed. Worship was reestablished in the temple of the Lord under the oversight of the priests and Levites.

Joash was seven years old when he ascended the throne of Judah. As long as Jehoiada was influencing him, he did what was right in God's sight. He even took steps to renovate the temple. But with Jehoiada's death, Joash listened to bad advice and turned his back on all the chief priest had taught him. He and his court abandoned the temple in favor of the Asherim. Nor would they listen to the prophets who were sent to reprove them. "Then the Spirit of God came upon Zechariah son of Jehoiada the priest. He stood before the people and said, 'This is what God says: Why do you disobey the Lord's commands? You will not prosper. Because you have forsaken the Lord, He has forsaken you'" (2 Chron. 24:20). Joash, however, ordered him stoned to death in the temple courtyard. "King Joash did not remember the kindness Zechariah's father Jehoiada had shown him, but killed his son, who said as he lay dying, 'May the Lord see this and call you to account'" (24:22).

But Joash was called to account for his crime. The Aramaeans invaded Judah and killed the Jewish leaders and plundered Jerusalem. They left Joash severely wounded. Some of his officials took advantage of the situation to assassinate the king for having caused Zechariah's death. De Vries observes that the Chronicler's

> rationale with regard to Joash's reign seems to be as follows: (1) Joash is a true "brand plucked from the fire," the symbol of the graciousness and persistence of the divine will; without initiative of his own, Joash is proof that the Davidic dynasty — and without it, the promise and the covenant — continues; (2) his thoroughgoing wickedness, once Jehoiada has passed from the scene, not only justifies his assassination but forebode the nation's ruin.[46]

Amaziah, his father's son

Joash was succeeded by his son Amaziah. As soon as he had secured his position, he had those who had assassinated his father executed. But he acted in accordance with the Mosaic law, and did not act against their sons.

The Chronicler's initial assessment of Amaziah is that "he did what was right in the eyes of the Lord, but not wholeheartedly"

266

(2 Chron. 25:2). When he hired Israelite mercenaries to help him in battle, a prophet reproved him; Amaziah listened and dismissed them. As a result, God gave him victory against his enemies.

Upon his return from victory over the Edomites Amaziah brought with him the idols of the conquered people. He made them his own gods and sacrificed to them. Consequently, "the anger of the Lord burned against Amaziah" (2 Chron. 25:15). Again, a prophet was dispatched to reprove him. But this time, instead of heeding the divine warning, the king warned him to be silent or die. His rejection of the prophet's (really, God's) injunction sealed his doom. He foolishly challenged Jehoash of Israel to battle. The latter captured him and plundered Jerusalem.

The Chronicler is demonstrating that sin brings God's judgment. But retribution because of sin does not have to take place. It is leveled only when the demand for repentance is repulsed. "When that appeal is heeded, however, the Chronicler is anxious to stress God's restoring forgiveness. Both possibilities are well illustrated in this chapter."[47]

Amaziah evidently did not return to God and, from the time he apostatized, some of his subjects began to conspire against him. The king ultimately learned of their plot and fled to Lachish, but they followed him and there they killed him. Thus, he shared in his father's inglorious demise. His sixteen-year-old son Uzziah was placed on the throne by the people.

Uzziah, spoiled by pride

The Chronicler sees Uzziah's story as an opportunity to demonstrate how an ideal reign may be spoiled by pride and impiety.[48] Uzziah "did what was right in the eyes of the Lord. . . . As long as he sought the Lord, God gave him success" (2 Chron. 26:4-5). He enjoyed great military triumph and extended the borders of his kingdom. "But after Uzziah became powerful, his pride led to his downfall" (26:16). He went to the temple to burn incense, a privilege reserved for the priests. When reproved by Azariah the chief priest and his associates, Uzziah became very angry at them. But he was then struck with leprosy, "so they hurried him out. Indeed, he himself was eager to leave, because the Lord had afflicted him" (26:20).

Uzziah was afflicted with leprosy for the rest of his life, and was forced to live in separate quarters. His son Jotham became regent and ruled for him. On his death, Jotham became king.

Jotham

Jotham was a king who did right in the Lord's sight (2 Chron. 27:2), even though the people of his realm did not follow his good example. His reward was that he became rich and powerful.

Ahaz

After a reign of sixteen years, he died, and was followed by his son Ahaz, who was everything his father was not. The Chronicler tells us that

> unlike David his father, he did not do what was right in the eyes of the Lord. He walked in the ways of the kings of Israel and also made cast idols for worshiping the Baals. He burned sacrifices in the Valley of Ben Hinnom and sacrificed his sons in the fire, following the detestable ways of the nations the Lord had driven out before the Israelites. He offered sacrifices and burned incense in the high places, on the hilltops and under every spreading tree (2 Chron. 28:1-4).

As punishment for his wickedness, God allowed him to be defeated by the Israelites under Pekah, who sacked Judah, taking back to Samaria women, children, and plunder (although, when confronted by Oded, a prophet of the Lord, they returned the captives to Judah). About the same time, he was raided by the Edomites and Philistines. When he sought the help of the Assyrians, they harassed Judah instead, and he was forced to buy them off with some of the treasures of the temple and the palace.

In spite of all his difficulties, Ahaz did not seek the Lord, but became more fixed in his apostasy. He began to worship the gods of Aram, closing the temple of the Lord, and setting up altars on the street corners of Jerusalem. "In every town in Judah he built high places to burn sacrifices to other gods and provoked the Lord, the God of his fathers, to anger" (2 Chron. 28:25).

Hezekiah, a devout ruler

The Chronicler devotes more space to his account of Ahaz's son and successor, Hezekiah, than to any ruler other than David or Solomon. He focuses substantially on the new king's reforms.

Hezekiah moved to undo the damage his father had caused. He reopened and reconsecrated the temple of God. When it had been rededicated, he sent couriers throughout Israel and Judah which called the people to

> return to the Lord the God of Abraham, Isaac and Israel, that he may return to you who are left, who have escaped from the hand of the kings of Assyria[49]. . . . Do not be stiff-necked, as your fathers were; submit to the Lord. Come to the sanctuary, which he has consecrated forever. . . . he will not turn his face from you if you return to him (2 Chron. 30:6, 8-9).

After the observance of the Passover and subsequent celebration, the people went throughout the land and "destroyed the high places and the altars throughout Judah and Benjamin and in Ephraim and Manasseh" (2 Chron. 31:1).

Undoubtedly, for the Chronicler the Babylonian captivity and the diaspora are very much in mind. His own generation needs this advice. If they are ever to be settled securely in their homeland, if Israel is to become a national entity once again, then they must not be "stiff-necked, as your fathers were," but must return to God. "So long as sin and unrepentance remain, the exile of God's people remains a threat."[50]

Because of Hezekiah's faithfulness, God richly blessed him. One example of blessing presented by the Chronicler is Hezekiah's deliverance from Assyria. When threatened by invasion, he urged the people not to be afraid of the Assyrian king, but to trust the Lord. Sennacherib and his officers spoke insultingly against Israel's God, asserting that He was no more capable of saving Judah from destruction than were the gods of those people presently captive.

> King Hezekiah and the prophet Isaiah son of Amoz cried out in prayer to heaven about this. And the Lord sent an angel, who annihilated all the fighting men and leaders and officers

in the camp of the Assyrian king. So he withdrew to his own land in disgrace. And when he went into the temple of his god, some of his sons cut him down with the sword (2 Chron. 32:20-21).

Thus, Hezekiah's confidence in God was vindicated, and he was blessed with peace and with high regard from the surrounding nations.

In spite of Hezekiah's depth of faith, he was not perfect. The Chronicler notes one fault, a problem with pride. Hezekiah was stricken ill and almost died, but God miraculously rescued him. "But Hezekiah's heart was proud and he did not respond to the kindness shown him; therefore the Lord's wrath was on him and on Judah and Jerusalem (2 Chron. 32:25). Even though the king repented, as did his people—and even though the Lord did not allow His wrath to come upon Judah during Hezekiah's lifetime—the Chronicler infers that God's wrath had been sufficiently aroused that a future generation would bear its brunt.[51]

Manasseh: an apostate restored

Hezekiah was succeeded by his twelve-year-old son Manasseh, who was to overwhelm Judah in his wickedness. He reversed all of his father's work, going even so far as to build pagan altars in the Lord's holy temple. "But Manasseh led Judah and the people of Jerusalem astray, so that they did more evil than the nations the Lord had destroyed before the Israelites" (2 Chron. 33:9). When confronted by God, Manasseh paid no attention.

Retribution for his sins was not long in coming. The Assyrians invaded Judah and deported Manasseh to Babylon. "In his distress he sought the favor of the Lord his God and humbled himself greatly before the God of his fathers" (2 Chron. 33:12). God heard his prayer and restored him to his throne. "Then Manasseh knew that the Lord is God" (33:13). Upon his return he tried to undo the evil he had caused, but his subjects continued to sacrifice in the pagan high places, although they now sacrificed to the Lord.

The Chronicler is demonstrating Manasseh's excessive wickedness as an omen of Judah's exile. Manasseh's sudden conversion under desperate circumstances is a reinforcement of the

Chronicler's contention that the repentant sinner—no matter how evil he has been—may be restored. It is intended, as well, as an encouragement for those returned exiles who, under foreign rule and impoverishment, might well feel that God's anger was still being poured out on them in full force.[52]

Amon

Manasseh's son, Amon, became king at age twenty-two. He evidently had not profited from his father's bitter lesson, for "Amon worshiped and offered sacrifices to all the idols Manasseh had made" (2 Chron. 33:22). In the end, his officials assassinated him.

Josiah: a brief national renewal

With popular support, Josiah, the eighteen-year-old son of Amon, was placed on the Jewish throne, and the assassins were executed. The Chronicler manifests considerable admiration for the new king: "He did what was right in the eyes of the Lord and walked in the ways of his father David, not turning aside to the right or left" (2 Chron. 34:2). As soon as he attained his majority, the young king began a series of reforms, tearing down pagan temples and altars, and smashing idols. His efforts to do away with idolatry extended into the far north of Israel.

When the Book of Law was found in the temple and Josiah learned its contents, he redoubled his efforts to purge his land of false gods and their worship centers. He also renovated the temple. In his work he was no doubt spurred on by the promises of the prophetess Huldah that God's anger would be poured out unmeasured on the land because of their sins, but because of the king's humility before God, "you will be buried in peace. Your eyes will not see all the disaster I am going to bring on this place and those who live here" (2 Chron. 34:28).

Josiah's death seems to have come somewhat prematurely when he opposed Neco of Egypt's promised peaceful march through his territory. The Chronicler has recorded a message sent from Neco to Josiah that "God has told me to hurry; so stop opposing God, who is with me, or he will destroy you" (2 Chron. 35:21). Sadly, the Jewish king would not listen, and in the ensuing battle he was fatally wounded.

271

The fall of Judah

The last chapter of 2 Chronicles (36) quite succinctly records the fall of Judah under its last four kings, the deportation of large numbers of Hebrews to Babylon, and infers ultimate restoration.[53] Jehoahaz succeeded Josiah, but had ruled only three months when he was deposed by Neco of Egypt, who exacted a tribute from Judah, and placed Jehoahaz's brother Eliakim on the throne, changing his name to Jehoiakim. This king "did evil in the eyes of the Lord his God" (36:5). As a consequence, he was attacked by Nebuchadnezzar of Babylon and exiled to that land in chains.

He was succeeded by his son Jehoiachin, who reigned only three months before he was deposed by Nebuchadnezzar. This,

8.2: THE CHRONICLER'S EVALUATION OF JUDAH'S KINGS	
Did right in the eyes of the Lord	*Did evil in the eyes of the Lord*
	Saul
David	
Solomon	
	Rehoboam*
Abijah	
	Asa*
Jehoshaphat	
	Jehoram
	Ahaziah
	Joash
	Amaziah
Uzziah*	
Jotham	
	Ahaz
Hezekiah	
	Manasseh*
	Amon
Josiah	
	Jehoahaz
	Jehoiakim
	Jehoiachin
	Zedekiah

*A mixture of good and evil, but basically belongs in this column.

for the Chronicler, was because "he did evil in the eyes of the Lord" (36:9). The Babylonian monarch appointed Zedekiah, Jehoiachin's uncle, king in his stead.

Zedekiah, was not only an evil king, but he foolishly rebelled against Nebuchadnezzar. The Chronicler interprets this move not only as folly, but as a sin against God, for Ezekiel 17:11ff makes it clear that the Jewish king had sworn by God's name a covenant with the king of Babylon. The Chronicler also shows that the people of Israel were no better, for they "became more and more unfaithful, following all the detestable practices of the nations and defiling the temple of the Lord, which He had consecrated in Jerusalem" (36:14).[54] When God reproved the people through the prophets, they mocked and scorned their words, "until the wrath of the Lord was aroused against His people and there was no remedy" (36:16). God's punishment was to hand them over to the Babylonians. Nebuchadnezzar killed many, and exiled the bulk of survivors, destroying Jerusalem (and the temple) in the process. The Exile, declares the Chronicler, lasted some seventy years — he sees it as a sabbath in the history of the Hebrew monarchy — until the supremacy of Persia. Chronicles closes with the promise, under Cyrus of Persia, to rebuild the temple in Jerusalem, a harbinger of future restoration.

Summary

The postexilic community of Israel has, in the Chronicles, interpreted itself and attempted to set up a faith orientation based on its previous theological history. While it is based on the Deuteronomic history, the historical context out of which it is crafted is very much different. The Deuteronomic history was written in a period of turmoil following a colossal disaster, whereas the Chronicler composed in a stable political climate in which the Hebrew community had been established for some time. Nor was the Deuteronomic history all he had at his disposal; he was able to use several other sources. These he shaped and formed according to his theological purposes.[55]

As has already been mentioned, one of the purposes he emphasizes is that of immediate blessing or retribution according to one's devotion to the Lord (or lack thereof). In this he differs from the Deuteronomic historian, whose focus is on recurring apostasy and its ultimate punishment versus obedience to the covenant and security in the land. Both, however, are intended to encourage discouraged Hebrews to place their hope and faith in the God of their fathers.

In setting out his theology of immediate blessing or punishment, the Chronicler gives substantial illustrations of both. The paragon of virtue and the standard of excellence against whom all others were compared was, of course, David. Those kings who are listed as having followed in his ways include Solomon, Jehoshaphat, Hezekiah, and Josiah. On the opposite side are Jehoram, Ahaz, Manasseh, Amon, and Zedekiah. The Chronicler is at pains to demonstrate how quickly God blesses the worthy and unleashes His anger on the wicked.

While retribution was immediate in the case of the kings, it seems that it was also cumulative. Toward the latter part of the monarchy God's wrath had built up sufficiently that not even a king of the high moral and spiritual caliber of Josiah could completely turn it back, although it was stayed during his lifetime. But under his successors it snowballed, until complete destruction and exile occurred.

And yet, the Chronicler holds out the hope that Israel can still be redeemed and restored. So the work ends on a somewhat optimistic note that repentance and humility on the part of the people would bring immediate blessing and reward.

Ezra-Nehemiah

The Masoretic compilers of the Old Testament Scriptures regarded Ezra and Nehemiah as a single unit written by Ezra. And so they stayed until about the third century A.D. At the same time, textual evidence (the second chapter of Ezra is repeated in Nehemiah 7:6-70) would indicate that initially they were two separate compositions.[56] They received their titles from the names of their respective chief characters, and they deal with life in post-exilic Israel, as those who return seek to rebuild their beloved Zion and its temple.

These books make the point that, if Israel is to survive as a nation, it must forego the attractions of pagan life in favor of obedience to God's commands. A theocratic system is necessary in which faithfulness to God and a godlike holiness are fostered.

Thus, the reorganization of life in postexilic Israel must be founded upon right cultic observance.

In preexilic Israel religious life was based on the temple at Jerusalem. One of its most important functions was to afford opportunity for the atonement of sins through the sacrificial system. With the devastation of Zion this entitlement was removed. Nothing was more catastrophic for the Jewish people than the destruction of the temple and the loss of their sacrificial system of atonement. What a joy it must have been for them to have the second temple constructed and the religious cult renewed! For the first time since the Exile the Hebrew people were able to atone properly for their sins. But, Charles Fensham points out in his commentary:

> As the prophets have shown, the continual atonement for sins could easily become mere custom and thus not a living reality. It was so easy to take a lamb to the altar as an offering yet live daily in disregard of all the religious principles implied in the religion of the Lord. The reforms of Ezra and Nehemiah, with their heavy emphasis on the law, are to be regarded as an attempt to counteract such a way of life.[57]

Hand in hand with cultic observance went a renewed emphasis on the covenant relationship between God and Israel. It contained instruction on relationships—both Jew to Jew and Jew to the Lord. Anything that interfered with these relationships as set forth in the covenant was not to be tolerated, but expunged.

Ezra and mixed marriages

It should come as no wonder that when Ezra discovers many of the Hebrew community married to foreign (pagan) women, in defiance of the covenant, he feels shame and disgrace in God's presence (Ezra 9:1-4). As a result, he confesses to God in an act of solidarity with them the shame and disgrace of the people who have committed such an outrageous evil (9:6ff).

A somewhat different view of sin is expressed in this prayer. It sees the sins of Israel as having been accumulating since their early history. During the times of the latter kings, however, their iniquity had sharply increased and had caused the Exile. Fensham

275

explains that "the burden of their guilt was heavy and was still increasing by the sin of intermarriage. They were punished for their sins, but the lesson was not taken to heart. They were still sinning."[58]

While Ezra is still praying to God, a large crowd of men and women and children assemble around him. They are deeply moved by his confession on their behalf (10:1). They resolve to make things right with God by reaffirming the covenant with God and divorcing themselves from pagan spouses and children. A solemn assembly of the Jewish people is called, and Ezra makes a proclamation.

> You have been unfaithful; you have married foreign women, adding to Israel's guilt. Now make confession to the Lord, the God of your fathers, and do His will. Separate yourselves from the peoples around you and from your foreign wives (10:10-11).

The people agree with him, and shortly thereafter his decree is carried out, restoring the people to the proper covenant relationship.

Nehemiah

One of the prominent sections of the Book of Nehemiah is the prayer of confession found in chapter 9. It details the history of Israel's relationship with God. In it we find a recurring cycle: God was good to Israel, but Israel broke the gracious covenant He had made with them; God was slow to anger, but Israel persisted in provoking Him to wrath; finally, He had to punish them. Now they confess:

> We are slaves today, slaves in the land you gave our forefathers so they could eat its fruit and the other good things it produces. Because of our sins, its abundant harvest goes to the kings you have placed over us. They rule over our bodies and our cattle as they please. We are in great distress (9:36-37).

This prayer does not complain of injustice; far from it, it is recognizing the legitimacy of what God has done. But, as Kidner says, it "is a sign of life and a vision that has not been tamely given up."[59]

The leaders of the people (probably the heads of the various clans of the tribes) get together and take a solemn oath to observe God's covenant fully (Neh. 10:1ff). Among some of the observances they agree to are to refrain from intermarriage with pagan peoples (10:30), to observe the Sabbath (10:31), to observe the holy days and their obligations (10:32-33), and to give to the Lord what is His due (10:34ff).

After twelve years in Jerusalem, Nehemiah returns to the court of Persia. After his departure, the people begin to deteriorate spiritually, breaking their covenant with the Lord by continuing commercial ventures on the Sabbath. In so doing, they are led by the bad example of their high priest, Eliashib, who has allowed his grandson to marry the daughter of Sanballat, a pagan. Nehemiah returns to Jerusalem to set things right, rebuking the people.

What is this wicked thing you are doing—desecrating the Sabbath day? Didn't your forefathers do the same things, so that our God brought all this calamity upon us and upon this city? Now you are stirring up more wrath against Israel by desecrating the Sabbath (Neh. 13:17-18).

In order to prevent trade occurring on the Sabbath, Nehemiah orders the gates of the city to be closed from the evening prior to it to the morning after, and to ensure obedience to his orders, he has his own retainers stationed at the gates (Neh. 13:19). Nonetheless, traders continue to gather just outside the city wall during the prohibited period, awaiting the opening of the gates (13:20). Nehemiah, determined to enforce his prohibitions, threatens these merchants with physical force (13:21) and, in keeping with his warnings, purifies some of the Levites to become a permanent team of guards for the city gates (13:22).

Nehemiah also faces many of the same difficulties regarding marriage that Ezra before him had to deal with. Jewish males have taken heathen wives, brides expressly forbidden by covenant law (Neh. 13:23): "Half of their children spoke the language of Ashdod or the language of one of the other peoples, and did

277

not know how to speak the language of Judah. I rebuked them and called curses down on them" (13:24-25). He does not resort to the drastic measures of Ezra, but he makes them swear not to negotiate mixed marriages for their children. John White notes here:

> Culture, religion, national identity — all depend on language. ... Children who speak only the language of their mothers are exposed predominantly to the culture, the values, the history, traditions and lifestyle of their mothers. At the very point in history at which a nation is being re-established, mixed marriages threaten to obliterate all that makes that nation distinctive. It could easily have become another nation entirely, beginning as a multiethnic group, a cultural mosaic, to merge into a new race with traditions blended of everything that God called Abram out from. And language was a key factor.[60]

Nehemiah concludes his work with a notation that his purposes have been to fulfill God's intentions for His people. His closing prayer asks God, "Remember me with favor, O my God" (13:31). All that he has done is for the Lord and, if the Lord will remember that, Nehemiah will be content.

Conclusions

Both Ezra and Nehemiah were particularly concerned with cultic sins, that is, offenses against the covenant God had concluded with the Jewish people. They were concerned that those who had returned from exile should maintain a linkage with the historic community which had preceded them, that the former see themselves as "the true Israel." To do so meant a clear separation from those around them who did not know God. Their loyalty to the Lord must not be diluted by the pagan nations who encircled them and, to some extent, had even infiltrated their ranks through commerce and intermarriage. Thus, not only the city walls and the temple needed rebuilding, but so did the forms of worship and the covenant regulations God had called on the historic community of Israel to obey. Old Testament scholar Derek Kidner reminds us that, in short, what we see in Ezra-Nehemiah is an Israel cut down almost to the roots, but drawing new vitality from its neglected source of nourishment in the Mosaic law and already showing signs, by its new concern for purity, of growing into the Judaism which we meet, both for better and worse, in the New Testament.[61]

Israel's sin had brought it to the brink of destruction. Now afforded another chance, Ezra and Nehemiah were determined that the nation should not be found wanting again, at least in regard to covenant and cultus.

A Summary of Old Testament Theology

The Old Testament presents a full-orbed theology of sin from original sin to forgiveness and redemption. Sin is seen early on as "a *conscious and responsible act,* by which Man rebelled against the unconditional authority of God in order to decide for himself what way he should take, and to make God's gifts serve his own ego."[62] Throughout the Hebrew Scriptures, then, we find decisively portrayed two wills in conflict, human against divine.

The Pentateuch

We find throughout the Pentateuch the origin of sin in the human race, and it tells us as well of its speedy and degenerative effect on human beings.

The Fall and its effects

While the serpent played an important role in the transgression of Adam and Eve, these two were guilty of a willful act of rebellion against God's command. The result of their sin was the breaking of fellowship and communion with God. Alienation became the order of the day from this moment on—alienation from God and from one's fellows.

Sin continued to increase, until human beings had become so evil and perverted that God destroyed all of them but the family of righteous Noah in the deluge. Yet even in this devout group sin persisted, and in their offspring sin began to exercise dominion once more, as we see evidenced in the building of the tower of Babel. Once again God acted decisively to frustrate their wicked designs by confusing their speech.

The Patriarchs

God had not given up on humanity. He selected one man, Abraham, and called him out to obey and serve Him. Because of his obedience, God made a covenant with Abraham, promising him that he would become a great nation and a blessing to all peoples. The covenant was reestablished with Isaac and Jacob.

The Mosaic era

When the covenant people, Israel, were enslaved in Egypt, God called Moses to lead them out of captivity. During this Exodus period many examples of sin were demonstrated, beginning with Pharaoh's hard-hearted refusal to obey God and release the Hebrews and continuing with Aaron's idolatrous behavior in constructing the golden calf and leading in its worship.

It was in this period that the law was incorporated into the covenantal system.

The Ten Commands (Exod. 20:2-17) may be seen not so much as prescriptions for individual morality as principles for communal life in which respect for individual human life as created in the image of God is upheld in the various critical areas of our life together (sanctity of life, integrity of the family, right to own property, obligation not to perjure on the witness stand, and obligation not to seek dishonest acquisition of another's property). At the same time, the law witnesses to our sinful dispositions. . . .[63]

The Prophets

The prophetic era of Israel has provided us with many illustrations of the epidemic of sin infecting all of God's people. During this period, the willful rebellion of God's people against His unconditional authority was measured in terms of lack of fidelity to the covenant.

The tribal confederacy

Under Moses' successor, Joshua, the Hebrews took possession of the Promised Land. There were dark moments—such as the disobedience of Achan— but, as a whole, the people were intent on being faithful to God. With Joshua's death, however, their good intentions began to evaporate, and soon sin held full sway in the lives of the Israelites. God's people who had displaced the Canaanites soon became more brutish and heathen in their life-style than their pagan predecessors.

With Samuel's accession as judge, the people were brought back to God and obedience. But their desire for a king like the surrounding nations was a sign of their rejection of God as their king. Saul began well, but soon fell from grace and was replaced by David, a man "after God's own heart," and whose throne He promised to establish forever.

The monarchy

While Israel enjoyed a period of great prosperity and growth under David, it was downhill following his death. There were a few kings who were faithful to God and led His people well, but most of them were wicked and apostate, and the nation (which split in two under David's grandson, Rehoboam) degenerated into a morass of social injustice and covenantal disregard.

To help combat the work of sin, God raised up prophets, people who were outspoken in their loyalty to Him. "The whole secret of their influence was that they had been gripped by a powerful divine will, which subjected the whole of life to its unconditional demand, and allowed no one to evade its call to decision."[64] They denounced sin wherever they found it and warned of the disastrous consequences of pursuing wickedness. But they were equally quick to promise God's forgiveness and restoration to those who would repent of their sins and turn to Him.

The prophets also focused the locus of sin in the human heart. "Before them rises *the enigma of an eradicable tendency to sin, which takes possession of men with compelling power and drives them along its own road.*"[65] Tragically, in spite of the fierce prophetic denunciation of sin, in spite of the warnings and temporary judgments undergone by the people, Israel continued its headlong rush toward destruction.

Indeed, the whole history of the nation showed how little the Law could prevent rebellion against God's will, but instead inevitably exposed the real depth of hostility to God. *The only course now left open was to turn one's eyes to the eschatological new creation of God's people,* which would be able to heal the irremediable rift between Man and God.[66]

Devastation and its consequences

Israel's apostasy led to the conquest and ultimate destruction of Jerusalem by the Babylonians, who carried into exile the bulk of the people. The postexilic prophets shifted their emphasis on sin to some degree, from a violation of the community relationship divinely engendered through the covenant, to a violation of God's holiness through willful opposition on a personal level to God's will. There was, however, the tendency to stress "the inner relationship with God as the really decisive element in cultic action, that which gives it its soul."[67] In all of this, nonetheless, there was the idea that only when the Messiah came from God would sin's ravages cease and peace be restored to humanity.

Chapter Nine
The New Testament Teaching on Sin

The starting point for New Testament theology and the basis for the Christian faith is Jesus Christ. The canon of the New Testament stresses the ministry of Jesus as summarized by Paul in 1 Corinthians 15:3-4, "that Christ died for our sins according to the Scriptures, that he was buried, that he was raised on the third day according to the Scriptures."[1] Christ—and particularly His resurrection victory over sin—was the proclamation of the New Testament writers and all of the apostolic church.

We shall examine the New Testament witness as it relates to the problem of sin. Though we shall begin with Jesus' own teachings as recorded by the synoptic writers, the strongest emphasis will be placed on the Pauline epistles. Paul was a theologian par excellence and his letter to the Romans more closely approaches a systematic theology than any other New Testament book. Of special importance to our development of a theology of sin will be an exegesis of Romans 5:12-21, which tells how both Adam's disobedience and Christ's perfect obedience have affected all of humankind. We shall also examine John's paradigm for sin and then close with the teachings of the remaining writers, followed by some conclusions.

Before looking at the New Testament teaching, however, we shall briefly study the basic New Testament words for sin. An understanding of their significance will help us to comprehend more fully the New Testament doctrine of the Fall and its ramifications.

A Word Study on Sin

The basic Greek word for sin is *hamartia* (αμαρτι'α). The word has as its root the verb *hamartanō* (αμαρτάνω) which in classical usage meant to miss, to miss the mark, or to be mistaken. The noun, *hamartia*, meant a mistake or failure to attain a goal (generally, a spiritual one). Other nouns include *hamartēma* (αμάρτημα), a failure or mistake (committed against someone), and *hamartōlos* (αμαρτωλός), a thing or person that fails.[2]

In the New Testament *hamartanō* and its derivative nouns came to signify everything that is opposed to God. *Hamartia* always denotes human sin aimed against God. *Hamartōlos*, an adjective, is synonymous with *ponēros* (πονηρνός), depraved or evil.[3]

A common, but more specialized, word is *adikeō* (αδικέω) and its cognates. The verb originally means to commit an injustice against, to injure, or to harm someone. The central noun, *adikia* (αδικία), meant those actions offending against morals or decency. In legal thinking, *adikia* was a synonym of *parabasis* (παράβασις), transgression, and as such referred to a long list of vices.[4]

In the New Testament literature, *adikia* and its related words stand in opposition to the justice and/or righteousness of God. It is also frequently used of the sins of the Gentiles who are under God's wrath.[5]

Parabasis, from the verb *parabainō* (παραβαίνω), classically signified a deviation, trespass, or transgression. In the New Testament it denotes a transgression of the law.[6]

Another word, *paraptōma* (παράπτωμα), is derived from the verb *parapiptō* (παραπίπτω) which originally meant to fall beside and, later, to miss the mark or make a mistake. The New Testament significance of *paraptōma* refers to a deliberate action by which a human being loses his standing with God.[7]

Anomia (ανομία) signifies lawlessness; not an ignorance of the

284

law, but a deliberate fracture of it. *Apistia* (απιστία) denotes lack of trust, infidelity, or even obstinate unbelief. *Asebeia* (ασέβεια) involves impiety in thought and/or act.[8]

9.1: A COMPARISON OF
OLD AND NEW TESTAMENT WORDS FOR SIN

Hebrew Word	English Meaning	Greek Equivalent	English Meaning
'āšaq	act unjustly	αδικέω *(adikeō)*	do wrong
šeqer	deceit, fraud	αδικος *(adikos)*	unjust
peŝa'	unlawful act	αδίκημα *(adikēma)*	unjust deed
'āwôn	offense, guilt	αδικία *(adikia)*	unrighteousness, wrongdoing
hatta't	lapse, sin	αμαρτία *(hamartia)*	sin
rāšā'	evildoer	αμαρτωλός *(hamartōlos)*	sinner
sûr *śātăh*	turn aside deviate	παραβαίνω *(parabainō)*	turn aside, transgress
mā'al	unfaithfulness	παράπτωμα *(paraptōma)*	trespass, false step

---

The Synoptic Teaching

The Synoptic Gospels record Jesus' concepts of sin. He began with the familiar societal ideas of sin and sinners as taught by the Pharisees. They believed that a sinner was someone who knew little about the law and cared less about keeping it. Noted particularly as sinners were tax collectors, harlots, and the Gentiles.[9]

Jesus accepted many of these ideas. In fact, He saw His mission on earth as that of rescuing these sinners. He met them in their own context, becoming known as "a friend of tax collectors and sinners" (Matt. 11:19; cf. Mark 2:14-15). Jesus' position was that "it is not the healthy who need a doctor, but the sick. I have not come to call the righteous, but sinners" (Mark 2:17). He further illustrated His mission in three parables about a lost sheep, a lost coin, and a lost son (Luke 15:1-32). Because He sought sinners out and befriended them rather than avoiding them (as did the Pharisees), Jesus redirected the attitudes of others toward sinners.[10]

But Jesus went beyond this teaching, extending the designation of sinner *(hamartōlos)* to all those — regardless of race or social position — whose actions, thoughts, and attitudes run contrary to God's will. Among these He included the politico-religious leadership of His day (Matt. 16:1-12; 23:1-38; cf. Luke 11:37-52). Indeed, everyone is a sinner who fails to obey God's perfect will.

> Not everyone who says to me, "Lord, Lord," will enter the kingdom of heaven, but only he who does the will of my Father who is in heaven. Many will say to me on that day, "Lord, Lord, did we not prophesy in your name, and in your name drive out demons and perform many miracles?" Then I will tell them plainly, "I never knew you. Away from me, you evildoers!" (Matt. 7:21-23)

While Jesus called attention to the sinfulness of groups (such as the hypocrisy of the Pharisees), He rarely condemned an individual. At the same time, He did warn His listeners that one could reach a point of no return. There was an unforgivable sin.

> And so I tell you, every sin and blasphemy will be forgiven men, but the blasphemy against the Spirit will not be forgiven. Anyone who speaks a word against the Son of Man will be forgiven, but anyone who speaks against the Holy Spirit will not be forgiven, either in this age or in the age to come (Matt. 12:31ff).

Here we have the sin of permitting oneself to fall into such a blind state that good is viewed as evil and vice versa. The human heart has become so hardened that the convicting power of the Holy Spirit cannot penetrate it. Consequently, forgiveness becomes impossible.[11]

Jesus also taught that sin was not only external but internal as well. The outward act was an extension of the inner root of sin. What defiles human beings is what comes out of their hearts.[12] For example, adultery was a sinful external act, but Jesus went beyond the action to those attitudes which caused it: "But I tell you that anyone who looks at a woman lustfully has already committed adultery with her in his heart" (Matt. 5:28).

Another feature emphasized by Jesus was the guilt attached to sin. McDonald observes that "the fact of sin's inwardness by an act of man's will carries with it the conclusion that man is responsible for what he is and is not."[13] The very fact that Jesus began His earthly ministry by calling on people to repent (Mark 1:15) is evidence of human accountability or guilt for sin.

Nor was Jesus' preaching limited to an indictment of the guilt of the individual. He was quick to recognize and condemn the social effects of sin. The influence of evil is not restricted to the perpetrator, but spills over onto others. No man is an island, and no one sins only to himself. Consequently, Jesus had harsh words for those who deliberately lead others into sin (Matt. 18:6ff). And He used equally strong language concerning those guilty of religious pride, who considered themselves more virtuous than others.[14]

So when you give to the needy, do not announce it with trumpets, as the hypocrites do in the synagogues and on the streets, to be honored by men. . . . And when you pray, do not be like the hypocrites, for they love to pray standing in the synagogues and on the street corners to be seen by men. I tell you the truth, they have received their reward in full (Matt. 6:2, 5).

Jesus hated the sin of hypocrisy, which led those guilty of spiritual pride to parade their supposed virtue in front of as many people as possible. Beneath that thin veneer of piety lurked the failure to demonstrate love and justice to the poor and afflicted. "They devour widows' houses and for a show make lengthy prayers. Such men will be punished most severely" (Mark 12:40).

Jesus furthermore exposed sin as rebellion. The Parable of the Lost Son (Luke 15:11-31) is an apt lesson of that. The crisis comes as the younger son realizes that he has sinned both against God and his father (vv. 18, 21). Guthrie comments that "sin is not a squandering of the family property, although this is not condoned. It is rather a refusal to act as a son, which in effect amounted to rebellion against the father."[15]

Because sin is rebellion, it is deserving of God's judgment. Jesus emphasized human accountability for every sin committed, whether in thought, word, or action. "But I tell you that men will have to give account on the day of judgment for every careless word they have spoken" (Matt. 12:36). At the same time, all punishments will not be of the same weight, but will be meted out according to the severity of the crime (Luke 12:48).[16]

In spite of Jesus' condemnation of sin, He nonetheless proclaimed the ready availability of forgiveness. Time and again Jesus offered people both healing and forgiveness (e.g., Matt. 9:2ff). Forgiveness, He promised, would be proffered to those who forgave others: "For if you forgive men when they sin against you, your heavenly Father will also forgive you. But if you do not forgive men their sins, your Father will not forgive your sins" (Matt. 6:14-15; cf. Luke 6:36ff).

The Pauline Epistles

As we have already noted, Paul was closer to being a systematic theologian than any of the other New Testament writers. And he is closer to a theology of sin than the others, as well. But many of the themes he espouses in his teaching are common to all the evangelists.

The Epistle to the Romans

The locus classicus is Paul's letter to the Romans. Here we discover Paul's most complete theology of sin. We shall examine it in some detail before moving on to a more cursory examination of his other epistles in regard to sin.

Romans 1–3

In this section, Paul begins by addressing the problem of sin as he sees it among the Gentiles of the empire. He asserts that God has revealed Himself to these people through His creation. They know that He is the eternal, all-powerful God. Therefore, they are without excuse, "for although they knew God, they neither glorified Him as God nor gave thanks to Him" (Rom. 1:21). Because they refused to acknowledge Him, God gave them over to a reprobate mind so that "they exchanged the truth of God for a lie, and worshiped and served created things rather than the Creator—who is forever praised" (1:25).

This deliberately chosen blindness led to a long catalog list of sins, beginning with both homosexuality and lesbianism (1:26ff); they were

> filled with every kind of wickedness, evil, greed, and depravity. They are full of envy, murder, strife, deceit, and malice. They are gossips, slanderers, murderers, God-haters, insolent, arrogant, and boastful; they invent ways of doing evil; they disobey their parents; they are senseless, faithless, heartless, ruthless. Although they know God's righteous decree that those who do such things deserve death, they not only continue to do these very things but also approve of those who practice them (Rom. 1:29-32).

Paul now turns from the Gentiles to examine the Jewish position. The Hebrews condemn the Gentiles for doing the things previously mentioned, but they then commit the same offenses themselves. Such behavior is inexcusable (2:1ff). Paul reminds his Jewish readers that God is no respecter of persons. "All who sin apart from the law will also perish apart from the law, and all who sin under the law will be judged by the law" (2:12). The apostle's conclusion as he looks at both groups is that "all have sinned and fall short of the glory of God" (3:23). Sin is universal. Gunther Bornkamm states that

> Paul means something more than, and different from, the bare truism that morally speaking all men are sinners and fail to measure up to ethical requirements. He does not absolutely deny in the case of either Gentiles or Jews that to some extent at any rate they do what the law commands. . . . Nevertheless, such zealous action fails to undo man's bondage to sin and sin's enthralling power; it does not make him "righteous."[17]

Romans 5:12-21

As we begin to exegete this passage, some general observations are appropriate. We have in these verses a series of parallels arranged in poetic stanzas. There appear to be three stanzas containing ten parallels which compare the evil caused by Adam with the blessing effected by Christ.[18] This use of parallelism means that we must proceed with extreme caution in our theological interpretation. Parallelism indicates a necessary balance; what one does to the one side of the parallel, one must also do to the other.

Romans 5:12-21 is generally accepted as a unity. Verse 12 is of crucial importance. Paul seeks to compare the first man, Adam, and the second — ultimate — man, Jesus Christ, who is also called the second Adam. Paul's argument seeks to explain how Christ's saving act affects humanity.[19]

Paul begins his first parallel between Christ and Adam in verse 12, but breaks off without stating its apodosis. Undoubtedly, he realizes that his readers might seriously misunderstand the comparison he is making. He therefore wants to underscore the great dissimilarity between Adam and Christ prior to completing it. He does not, in fact, complete his parallel until verse 18. Verses 13-14 explain the use of the verb "sin" in verse 12; verses 15-17 stress the dissimilarity between Adam and Christ; verse 18 is a repetition and completion of verse 12. Verse 19 explains verse 18; verses 20-21 explain the role of the law in God's plan.[20]

Verse 12 begins with "therefore": "Therefore, just as sin *[hamartia]* entered the world through one man, and death through sin, and in this way death came to all men, because all sinned." The usual sense means a referring back to previous material. One would naturally look to 5:1-11, which affirms that those who are made righteous by faith are people who have been transformed by God's love from a state of enmity with Him to one of reconciliation to Him. This reconciliation, Paul points out here, is the result of something Christ has done which is as universal in its results as was the sin of the first human being, Adam.[21]

In the phrase *"sin entered the world through one man, and death through sin,"* Paul personifies sin — *hamartia* — as an invading sovereign power. Adam's fall gave sin a beachhead of invasion into the human race. Death too is personified; it is depicted as arriving in sin's wake. The *Jerome Biblical Commentary* notes that " 'Death' is not the physical, bodily death of man . . . but denotes spiritual death as the definitive separation of man from God, the unique source of life."[22]

"And in this way death came to all men, because all sinned": this phrase has caused much controversy and confusion over the doctrine of original sin, largely because of Augustine's ineptness in translating this verse, and the refusal of many subsequent scholars to refute his error. Augustine was not a Greek scholar and so he relied on the Latin version. In Greek, the phrase is *eph' ho pantes hēmarton,* "because all have sinned." The Latin version, however, rendered *eph' ho* ("because") as *in quo,* "in whom." Augustine's whole doctrine of original sin and inherited guilt was founded upon this mistranslation. Interestingly, it is modern Roman Catholic scholars more than Protestants who have sought to correct this Augustinian error.[23]

Adam is the prototype of every human being. Just as he sinned, so does each one of us. What we find in this phrase is an existential picture of sin. Just as death came to Adam and Eve because they sinned, it comes to all human beings because each one has sinned. The text does *not* say that all have sinned collectively, nor does it say that all have sinned in Adam. Paul does note that because of Adam sin and death were able to enter the world, but death has spread to all humanity because each individual has sinned.[24]

Paul's second parallel comes in verse 13: "for before the law was given, sin *[hamartia]* was in the world. But sin *[hamartia]* is not taken into account when there is no law." Here we have the matter of sin in relation to the law, a matter raised by Paul in 3:20. "The counting of sin," Moody tells us, "is God's side of the human consciousness of sin. Unconscious tendencies towards transgression are inherited (physically, socially, psychologically), but — Paul stresses here — there is no guilt before consciousness."[25] This verse would seem to indicate that God does not impute to human beings a penalty for sin unless sin has been defined by the law. It is only in the context of the law's presence that the full gravity of sin is realized and the sinner is stripped of any excuse.

Verse 14 has the third parallel: "Nevertheless, death reigned from the time of Adam to the time of Moses, even over those who did not sin by breaking a command *[parabasis]* as did Adam, who was a pattern for the one to come." The verse makes apparent the difference between sin as a state and transgression as an act of consciousness. God gave Adam a concrete command which he disobeyed. Moses brought Israel the law clearly defined. In between, there was no law. Nevertheless, people died. Given the previous verse, why? Because, as Paul notes in 2:14ff, conscience functions as a natural law in all human beings when there is no formal law.

Of *"who is the type of the one coming,"* Nygren says that, "as Adam is head of the old aeon, so Christ is the head of the new. . . . Adam concerns Paul here only as 'a type of the one who was to come.' "[26] And Cranfield notes that "Adam in his universal effectiveness for ruin is the type which — in God's design — prefigures Christ in His universal effectiveness for salvation."[27]

Verses 15-17 present three more parallels.

[15]But the gift is not like the trespass *[paraptōma]*. For if the many died by the trespass *[paraptōma]* of the one man, how much more did God's grace and the gift that came by the grace of the one man, Jesus Christ, overflow to the many! [16]Again, the gift of God is not like the result of the one man's sin *[hamartia]:* The judgment followed one sin and brought condemnation, but the gift followed many trespasses *[paraptōma]* and brought justification. [17]For if, by the trespass *[paraptōma]* of the one man, death reigned through that one man, how much more will those who received God's abundant provision of grace and of the gift of righteousness reign in life through the one man Jesus Christ.

The majority of commentators note that these verses emphasize the dissimilarity between Adam's trespass and Christ's freely bestowed gift.[28]

In the first parallel (v. 15), Paul declares that whatever damage Adam did to the human race by his trespass *(paraptōma)*, Christ has by His grace greatly surpassed. The "many" should not be taken to signify a limited number; "many" here really means "all."[29] The actions of both Adam and Christ have universal significance.

Verse 16, the second parallel, reemphasizes the dissimilarity between Adam and Christ. If one individual's sin could do so much damage to the race, then by the same measure, another man's saving act — accompanied by the sovereign grace of God — can go beyond Adam's sin to repair the damage and bring life.[30]

The third parallel, in verse 17, complements the contrast between trespass and grace, condemnation and justification, death and life.[31] The Fall had catastrophic results, but the gift of grace and righteousness in Christ are much greater. We see too that in Adam's economy, death is sovereign and humanity is enslaved. But in Christ's economy, those who receive the gift will reign, for enslavement is a thing of the past.[32] We should also note that the Greek structure of this verse is what is called a condition of the first class, which means that it is no mere supposition, but absolute truth.

In verse 18, Paul completes the comparison begun in verse 12: "Consequently, just as the result of one trespass *[paraptōma]* was condemnation for all men, so also the result of one act of righteousness was justification that brings life for all men." As a consequence of the Fall, condemnation *(katakrima)* came to all human beings. The word is a judicial one, the execution of God's judgment.[33] But Christ's act of righteousness resulted in justification that brings life to all humanity. That "one act of righteousness" in Paul's thinking "means not just His atoning death, but the obedience of His life as a whole, His loving God with all His heart and soul and mind and strength, and His neighbor with complete sincerity, which is the righteous conduct which God's law requires."[34]

One of the most important words in this verse is "all men" (Gk. *pantas*). Does Paul really mean "all people" in both of these phrases? One must keep in mind the significance of the parallels. We will happily agree that "all" are condemned as a result of Adam's sin, but the "all" of the apodosis will undoubtedly bother many people. Cranfield eases the dilemma somewhat by noting

it will be wise to take it thoroughly seriously as really meaning "all," to understand the implication to be that what Christ has done He has really done for all men, that [justification and life] is truly offered to all, and all are summoned urgently to accept the proffered gift, but at the same time to allow that this clause does not foreclose the question whether in the end all will actually come to share it.[35]

Verse 19 both reiterates and explains the previous verse: "For just as through the disobedience of the one man the many became sinners *[hamartōlos]*, so also through the obedience of the one man the many will be made righteous." Barth tells us that Adam's action (i.e., his disobedience) defines all individuals – the many.[36] Adam's disobedience gave sin and death an entrée into human life. Now, all of humankind have been infected by the virus of sin, all "were made sinners."

Over against Adam's disobedience Paul posits Christ's obedience. Just as those who stand in Adam (i.e., who emulate him) receive condemnation and death, even so all those who stand in Christ (i.e., who emulate Him) receive righteousness and life.

The significance of the law in relation to sin is recounted in verses 20 and 21:

[20]The law was added so that the trespass *[paraptōma]* might increase. But where sin *[hamartia]* increased, grace increased all the more, [21]so that, just as sin reigned in death, so also grace might reign through righteousness to bring eternal life through Jesus Christ our Lord.

Nygren aptly notes that Adam and Christ represent two major opposites in human history, each at the forefront of his own aeon. How does the law fit into this? John (1:17) wrote, "The law was given through Moses, grace and truth came through Jesus Christ." To attempt, therefore, to posit three ages – ruled by Adam, Moses, and Christ – would be to misunderstand the part played by the law. Adam and Christ are the heads of the aeons of death and life; there is no room for a third. The law does not constitute an aeon, but has come in beside these two opposites.[37]

The intention of the law is to condemn sin and require righteousness. Its raison d'être is to restrict sin and advance righteousness. It does belong, nevertheless, to the old age and so it cannot bring forth true righteousness. Indeed, Paul tells us in Romans 3:20 that "no one will be declared righteous in his sight by observing the law."

In actual fact, Paul writes, the law which was given to heighten the recognition and visibility of sin for human beings, has had the effect instead of working hand in glove with sin. In 5:13, Paul tells us that sin was in the world prior to the advent of the law, "but sin is not taken into account when there is no law." The law raises sin to actual "transgression" *(parabasis)*. So, then, the real consequence of sin's advent was to make the Fall greater and sin abounded that much more. Sin has been shown in all its stark, tragic wickedness.

When one realizes the impotence of the law to best sin, then it may become an instrument of God's grace, for that person comes to recognize that only Christ can enable one to secure victory over sin and death. Nothing but God's grace in Christ is greater than sin.

The final parallel of this passage, verse 21, personifies sin and grace as two monarchs presiding over their representative ages. Paul contrasts the eternal reign of grace with the fading reign of sin. When he speaks of sin reigning in death, he does not mean that death is the instrumental handmaiden of sin. "For Paul, with Gen. 2.17 not far from his mind, death is the result of sin, willed not by sin but by God . . . death is the sign of God's authority, appointed by God as the inseparable, inescapable accompaniment of sin."[38] In the same way life is the inseparable and inescapable accompaniment of the righteousness of Christ which is appointed by the grace of God.

Although there is an obvious dissimilarity between Adam and Christ, there is a definite parallel between Adam-and-humanity and Christ-and-humanity. It is in this parallel structure that we see Adam as a "type" of Christ. As human beings identify with Adam in his sin, death is their lot. As they identify with Christ in His righteousness, they receive life. It comes down to solidarity with sin or solidarity with righteousness. Law does not help; it serves simply to highlight the only way to human salvation, God's grace in Christ Jesus.

Romans 5:13-14 is an important statement which sheds light on the whole matter of sin, for it is very clear in distinguishing sin from transgression.[39] In Romans 4:15 Paul declares that "where there is no law there is no transgression," and again in 7:8 that "apart from the law, sin is dead."

With the above in mind, let us proceed to a brief exegesis of Romans 7:7-12.

Romans 7:7-12

This is a very important passage of Paul's teaching on sin and the law which is often passed over by evangelical Christians. But it is one which needs to be examined carefully as a part of our developing theology of sin.

In immediately preceding material, Paul has been discussing the relationship of the law to sin. The close interaction of the two could give some of his readers the idea that the law is somehow evil. In this passage the apostle seeks to correct any such misconception by defending the law. It is not wicked, but good.

Are we to look at this passage as autobiographical? Scholars are divided on this issue. It may be considered, nonetheless, the norm for human beings, the way in which all people experience Adam's Fall as recorded in Genesis 3.[40]

In verses 7-8, Paul resorts to diatribe (not an unusual style for him) to stress that the law comes from God and is not evil in any way. "Indeed, I would not have known what sin *(hamartia)* was except through the law. For I would not have known what coveting really was if the law had not said, 'Do not covet.' " The law is the means by which sin is highlighted as sin.

At the same time, even though the law is not evil, sin has been able to manipulate it for its own wicked ends: "But sin *[hamartia]*, seizing the opportunity afforded by the commandment, produced in me every kind of covetous desire" (v. 8). The Greek says that sin used this commandment "as a bridgehead," or base of operations, to produce in the human all sorts of evil desires. The commandment not to covet or lust made him lust all the more. How does this happen? Cranfield tells us that "the merciful limitation imposed on man by the commandment and intended to preserve his true freedom and dignity can be misinterpreted and misrepresented as a taking away of his freedom and as an attack on his dignity"; as such it becomes an occasion for rebelling against God.[41] It is as when a person who is walking by a beautiful lawn sees a "keep off the grass" sign and is led to walk on the grass.

When Paul says that "apart from the law, sin *[hamartia]* is dead" (v. 8), he is not suggesting that it is nonexistent, but rather that it is dormant or inactive. He points out similarly in 1 Corinthians 15:56 that "the power of sin *[hamartia]* is the law." In Genesis 3, Satan was able to provoke Eve to sin only because God had given the commandment forbidding the eating of the fruit of the tree in the center of the garden.

Verses 9-10 have caused some scholarly discussion as to interpretation: "Once I was alive apart from the law; but when the commandment came, sin *[hamartia]* sprang to life and I died. I found that the very commandment that was intended to bring life actually brought death." Moody cites a historic view associated with the Hebrew *bar-mitzvah,* where a Jewish boy at the age of thirteen became a "son of the law," thus accepting personal responsibility for observing the Mosaic Law. There is much in educational psychology to sustain the traditional wisdom of *bar-mitzvah,* and there is sufficient autobiography in Paul to preserve this perspective. "In the age of innocence Paul was alive, but the commandment brought sin to life, and he died. This is the seesaw of sin in which a man is alive while sin is dead and man is dead when sin comes alive."[42]

Another, similar, view was taught by Tertullian in the third century. He held that a child is in a state of innocence until, at puberty, he is expelled from that garden into a world of guilt.[43]

Paul notes in verse 10 what he had hinted at in verse 8. The intention of the commandment was to preserve life by warning people not to break the commandment. Because, however, the law showed sin to be sin, it became an instrument of death, for its effort was to stimulate them to transgress.[44]

Verse 11 describes how the law became a source of death: "For sin *[hamartia]*, seizing the opportunity afforded by the commandment, deceived me, and through the commandment put me to death." Sin distorts the law to the human mind, making it seem repressive and unfair of God to have legislated it. Such was the case with Eve; the serpent led her to suspect that God was jealous of His position and afraid that she and her husband would attain His status. Sin led these first people to believe that their way was better than God's. The ultimate result was (spiritual) death.

Paul sums up the matter in verse 12: "So, then, the law is holy, and the commandment is holy, righteous, and good." This verse is Paul's ultimate response to the question of verse 7. Even though the law seems to bring death to humans, the fault lies not with it but with sin. God's law (in general) and His commandments (in particular) are divinely ordained and, therefore, are just and good.[45]

To sum up in a psychological sense what Paul is saying here: Children are born innocent, but as they approach adolescence they are increasingly able to handle abstract ideas, and ultimately, the realization of sin and guilt. It is the awareness of guilt that causes sin to kill spiritually. It is at this point that one senses one's true condition before God.

We find here the idea that sin becomes deadly in a human being when that person develops an awareness of the law and subsequent guilt for breaking the law. When we couple that awareness along with Romans 5:12ff, what do we find? Sin is not imputed against innocents. Until there is an awareness of guilt (i.e., of breaking the law), the penalty for sin—eternal death—is not imposed. It is evidently covered by Christ's atonement.

Other Pauline teachings

There are many other briefer or more general passages in the Pauline corpus which give us further insights into the nature of sin. First Corinthians 15:21ff reinforces what Paul says in Romans 5:12-21: "For since death came through a man, the resurrection of the dead comes also through a man. For as in Adam all die, so in Christ all will be made alive." Some interpreters have sought to use these verses to teach "that persons experience death not because of acts of their own, but by virtue of their participation in the sin of Adam."[46] But they have evidently failed to reckon with the parallelism here.

In the first parallel Paul compares how death came through Adam to the way the resurrection of the dead comes through Christ. If we accept the premise that because of Adam's sin all humans are condemned to death, then because of the parallel structure in use, we must also accept that all will be resurrected because of Christ's perfect obedience. Few evangelicals would be prepared to accept this second half of the parallel.

Looking at the second parallel, we should observe that Paul does not say that "in Adam all died," as many would suggest. The verb is a present tense; thus, each person dies as he becomes estranged from God by his own personal disobedience; in the same way, in the future tense all will be made alive in Christ as each one identifies with Him in an act of faith. If we accept the view of humanity's collective death in Adam, then we must accept Karl Barth's universalistic view that everyone will also be collectively redeemed in Christ.[47] We must agree with Frank Stagg who writes:

298

If 1 Corinthians 15:22 means that automatically all were lost in Adam, then it follows inescapably that all shall be made alive in Christ. Of course, Paul is saying neither of these things. He is saying that one is saved in Christ in the manner *(hosper . . . houtos)* that he is lost in Adam—by commitment to the one or the other. Paul is not teaching that being lost or saved is arbitrary.[48]

One of Paul's more commonly used terms is *sarx* (σάρξ), translated as "the flesh" and, by the NIV as "the sinful nature." For Paul, *sarx* denotes the whole fallen nature of humankind. It is alienation from God, from one's fellows, from oneself, marked by transitoriness and sin.[49] It stands over against the Holy Spirit. Hans Conzelmann tells us that

> flesh and spirit are both active powers. I stand under the one or the other; but the standing here or there is on different levels, and not on the same formal, ontological plane. Under the σάρξ I am alienated from myself; in the πνευμα [spirit] I fulfill what I am. Both powers are transubjective. But the πνεῦμα is not alien to me in the sense that it falsifies and annihilates my being. . . . In the spirit I am not only driven, but I can lead my life freely, actively in the face of the σάρξ (Gal. 5:16-18).[50]

In Galatians 5:16ff, Paul gives us a catalog of sinful deeds as an illustration of the outworkings of the sinful nature, followed by a list of the fruit of the Spirit. The former include sexual immorality, impurity, debauchery, idolatry, witchcraft, hatred, discord, jealousy, rage, selfish ambition, division, factions, envy, drunkenness, and orgies. Paul warns his readers that "those who live like this will not inherit the kingdom of God" (5:21). By contrast, the fruit of the Spirit is love, joy, peace, patience, kindness, goodness, faithfulness, gentleness, and self-control. "Against such things there is no law" (5:23). The person who walks in the flesh is a slave to sin (and Satan), but the person who walks in the Spirit is controlled by God. In fact, "those who belong to Christ Jesus have crucified the sinful nature with its passions and desires" (5:24).

Because all persons have broken the laws of God and so have

given themselves over to the power of Satan (2 Tim. 2:26), they fall under the wrath of God: "Let no one deceive you with empty words, for because of such things God's wrath comes on those who are disobedient" (Eph. 5:6). The ultimate punishment will be eschatological.

> This will happen when the Lord Jesus is revealed from heaven in blazing fire with his powerful angels. He will punish those who do not know God and do not obey the gospel of our Lord Jesus. They will be punished with everlasting destruction and shut out from the presence of the Lord and from the majesty of his power (2 Thes. 1:7-9).

Ladd observes that "in Paul, the wrath of God is not an emotion telling how God feels; it tells us rather how he acts toward sin – and sinners."[51]

With Paul's emphasis on the relationship between sin and the law, it is not surprising that he should see sin as *anomia* or lawlessness. In 2 Corinthians 6:14 he contrasts *anomia* and righteousness: "Do not be yoked together with unbelievers. For what do righteousness and wickedness have in common? Or what fellowship can light have with darkness?" All that detracts from or opposes God's rights is *anomia*.[52]

Conclusions

While Paul recognizes Adam as the first sinner and that original sin has in some way affected the whole human race, he emphasizes individual responsibility for personal sin. No one is under divine condemnation because of what Adam has done (other than Adam!). At the same time, sin is universal, for "all have sinned and fall short of the glory of God" (Rom. 3:23). Sin is rebellion against God, a deviation from God's law. Those who sin are in bondage to wickedness. Those who are guilty of sin are under God's wrath and are subject to spiritual death. But through a commitment to Jesus Christ one may be restored to life.

Johannine Writings

Christian teaching on sin tends to be based more fully on Pauline theology than on the remainder of the New Testament teaching, which is unfortunate, for the Johannine literature is a rich and ample source of teaching on sin, especially in regard to sin's end in spiritual death.

John's Gospel

The theological emphasis of the fourth Gospel is markedly different from that of the Synoptic Gospels. Whereas the Synoptic writers stress a horizontal dualism—the contrast between this age and the age to come—John's focus is on a vertical dualism—the contrast between the world above and the world below: "You are from below; I am from above. You are of this world; I am not of this world. . . . if you do not believe that I am the one I claim to be, you will indeed die in your sins" (8:23-24). The world below, generally referred to as "this world," is evil and is under the sovereignty of Satan (16:11). Jesus was sent from the world above to be the light of the world (11:9).[53]

Darkness and light

The world above is the realm of light, whereas this world is the realm of darkness. As mentioned above, Jesus came to be the light of the world. John depicts the light and darkness as conflicting principles, but Christ is victorious over the darkness (1:5). As human beings receive Christ they will become children of light: "Put your trust in the light while you have it, so that you may become sons of light" (12:36). Rudolf Bultmann takes this to mean that "Jesus promises freedom; he *alone* can bestow it, and *only that* is genuine freedom."[54] Despite the coming of the light into this world, humanity preferred the darkness because their deeds were evil (3:19). In John, then, the consummate evil is enmity with the light, namely, unbelief in Jesus.[55]

Belief and unbelief

Sin is slavery to falsehoods fostered by Satan. It issues in alienation from God through refusing to trust Him. The end of refusal is eternal judgment: "whoever believes in Him shall not perish but have eternal life. . . . Whoever believes in Him is not condemned, but whoever does not believe stands condemned already because he has not believed in the name of God's one and only Son" (3:16, 18). Jesus warned the Pharisees that because of their unbelief they would die in their sins (8:12ff).

Flesh and Spirit

The flesh is a part of this world, while the Spirit belongs to the world above. Unlike Paul, John does not depict the flesh as sinful; it is synonymous with humankind. Because of the impotence of the flesh, a person must be born from above (3:3) by the agency of the Spirit.[56]

Death and life

The Apostle John assumes the existence of death as part of the human situation. Without the new birth which leads to life, the human lot is death. Life — or, more often, eternal life — is in John's parlance what the Synoptic writers call the kingdom of God.[57] Unless one seeks the life of Jesus Christ, one will die in one's sins (8:24).

Satan and Christ

Like the Synopticists, John sees the world under the sway of an evil supernatural being known as the devil (8:44; 13:2), alias Satan (13:27). His title is "the prince of this world"(12:31; 14:30; 16:11). Jesus taught that "he was a murderer from the beginning . . . a liar and the father of lies" (8:44). His purpose in the world is to short-circuit God's plans for humanity. In trying to achieve his ends, Satan attempted to conquer Jesus (14:30), but was powerless to do so. In His death and resurrection, Christ won a complete victory over the devil (12:31-33).

The Johannine Epistles

John retains the dualism of his Gospel in his epistles, but his focus is more concentrated because of his purpose in writing. Because of the brevity of the last two epistles, we shall deal essentially with the first. As a polemic against false teachers, the first letter has much to say about sin.

1 John 1:5–2:2

John addresses the problem of sin here in the context of the light-darkness motif. His statement in 1:5 that "God is light; in Him is no darkness at all," is his way of saying, "God is good, and evil can have no place beside Him."[58] Anyone who walks in darkness cannot have fellowship with God, regardless of what he may say (1:7). One of the ramifications of these new relationships is that "the blood of Jesus Christ, his Son, purifies us from every sin" (1:7). I. Howard Marshall declares, "To say that the blood of Jesus purifies us is to say that our sin is removed and forgiven; its defiling effects no longer condemn us in the sight of God."[59]

Sin is a universal human condition, and so anyone who claims to be without sin is guilty of lying and self-deception (1:8). How can one be forgiven who denies being a sinner? What we must do is to go before God in humility and honesty, admitting that we have sinned, asking forgiveness. If we do so, "he is faithful and just and will forgive us our sins and purify us from all unrighteousness" (1:9). Those who would stubbornly maintain that they are free from personal sin make Christ out to be a liar, for He has declared that sin is a universal human failing (1:10).

In 2:1 John reiterates to his Christian readers one of his purposes in penning this missive, "that you will not sin." He wishes that his readers would recognize the all-pervasive character of sin—and yet live without sinning.[60] But then, by way of consolation should any of them have fallen to sin, he reminds them that "if anyone does sin, we have one who speaks to the Father in our defense—Jesus Christ the Righteous One." The thought here is of a single act of sin into which a believer may slip, as over against habitual sin.[61] Why can Jesus intercede for the sinner? Because He is the "atoning sacrifice" (or, expiation) for our sins (2:2), namely, in His death on the cross.

1 John 2:15-17

John is writing to warn his readers of the potential dangers which lie in lingering associations with the world. It is possible for Christians who have confessed their sins before God and have been forgiven to be overcome by the lure of the world's attractions. We need to keep in mind that the world is humankind influenced by Satan to reject God. Marshall says that "John is thinking of the attractions of a life lived in opposition to the commandments of God, one in which God's laws for the use of the world and the things in it are disobeyed."[62] Christians must be aware that if they love the world they will lose the love of God (2:17).

In verse 16, John gives grounds for his warning in the previous verse: "For everything in the world—the cravings of sinful man, the lust of his eyes and his pride in possessions—comes not from the Father but from the world." What John seems to have in mind is a context of the pagan society of his day, one dedicated to pursuing gross sensual pleasure ("the cravings of sinful man"), to a materialistic concept of existence ("the lust of his eyes"), and to self-aggrandizement ("pride in possessions").[63] Such desires do not come from God; they are entirely worldly.

Verse 17 is the high point of John's teaching in this passage: "The world and its desires pass away, but the man who does the will of God lives forever." A desire for the things offered by the world is folly because it is all transitory. The world, ruled by Satan, will not last.[64] Only the one who is dedicated to God's purposes will possess that which is durable.

1 John 3:4-10

We find another contrast here, this time between the children of God and the children of the devil. In this context John follows a previous warning, reinforcing the necessity for believers to refrain from sin.

John defines sin in verse 4: "Everyone who sins breaks the law; in fact, sin is lawlessness." Sin is not to be taken lightly. It is rebellion against God.

Verse 5 is actually parallel to the preceding one, stressing why believers should not be involved in sin. Jesus had to come to this world and die in order to deal with sin. Sin cost God's Son His life; how terrible, then, it must be! Further evidence of the horrific nature of sin is found in Jesus' life which was and is sinless. Marshall says that the thought here "is not of [Jesus'] fitness to take away sin, but rather of His total opposition to sin, a character which should be shared by believers."[65]

The sixth verse has engendered considerable controversy: "No one who lives in Him keeps on sinning. No one who continues to sin has either seen Him or known Him." Is John saying that the Christian is sinless? Other passages (1 John 1:8; 2:1; 5:16) would suggest differently. Indeed, why would John warn believers against sinning if they are sinless? We know from our own spiritual experience that Christians do sin. No explanations given by commentaries have been entirely satisfactory.[66] Perhaps a straightforward acceptance of the NIV rendering (above) is as good as any interpretation.

In 3:7-10 John focuses on the contrast between the children of the devil and the children of God. The person who lives a righteous life is of the same nature as Christ (v. 7). The person who lives a sinful life is of the same nature as the devil (v. 8). It follows, then, that the righteous person is of the seed of God, that is, God's child (v. 9), just as the unrighteous one is of the seed of Satan.[67] "This is how we know who the children of God are and who the children of the devil are: Anyone who does not do what is right is not a child of God: neither is anyone who does not love his brother" (v. 10). John reminds his readers that righteous living involves horizontal relationships as well as vertical.

1 John 5:16-19

Here John is approaching the end of his letter and begins to summarize by restating his purposes in writing. The immediate context has to do with the believer's assurance that God hears his or her prayer. John's preoccupation with the potential dangers of sin to his Christian audience leads him to advocate the power of prayer to help a fellow believer who is overtaken by sin.

> If anyone sees his brother commit a sin that does not lead to death, he should pray and God will give him life. I refer to those whose sin does not lead to death. I am not saying that he should pray about that. All wrongdoing is sin, and there is sin that does not lead to death (5:16-17).

John does not enlighten us as to which sins lead to death and which do not. We must presume that his readers knew.

What does John mean here by death? That has been the source of some scholarly debate. Is it physical or spiritual death? Moody provides an answer which seems reasonable.

The climax to sin as defilement and disobedience is spiritual death. 1 John is very emphatic . . . about the possibility that a brother may pass again into spiritual death (1 John 5:16). There are those who argue that the passage from life to death in 1 John 5:16 refers to physical death, but 1 John 5:11-17 when read as a whole does not support this view.[68]

Verses 18 and 19 are a reiteration and strengthening of 3:6. John declares that "we know that anyone born of God does not continue to sin" (v. 18). Stagg notes that "evil lives refuted the false claims of those who boasted that they were above sin. No epistle more forcefully refutes proud claims to sinless perfection than 1 John does."[69]

Again, John reminds his readers that believers know with certainty "that we are children of God, and that the whole world is under the control of the evil one" (v. 19). Once again we are taken back to the fourth Gospel where John quotes Jesus' labeling of Satan as prince of this world. The Greek of verse 19 literally depicts the whole world lying in the presence of this evil one, helpless and passive.

Other New Testament Teachings

Of the remaining books of the New Testament, Acts, Hebrews, James, and Peter all have some important things to teach us about sin. The most common term in use is *hamartia,* sometimes in the singular as a general state, and sometimes in the plural as particular acts of sin.

Acts

Early Christian preaching, fragments of which are recorded in the Book of Acts, reveal certain aspects of sin and its cure. On the Day of Pentecost Peter, in his sermon to the audience of Diaspora and local Jews, accused many among them of the terrible sin of causing Jesus' death.

Jesus of Nazareth was a man accredited by God to you by miracles, wonders and signs, which God did among you through him, as you yourselves know. This man was handed

306

over to you by God's set purpose and foreknowledge; and you, with the help of wicked men, put him to death by nailing him to the cross (2:22-23).

After the healing of the lame man at the gate called Beautiful, Peter again charged his contemporaries with the responsibility for their Messiah's murder. "You disowned the Holy and Righteous One. . . . You killed the author of life" (3:14-15).

The proper response to such an atrocious sin? "Repent, then, and turn to God, so that your sins may be wiped out" (3:19). Repentance requires the abandonment of our false notions about God along with their resultant lifestyle and the simultaneous acceptance of truth as mediated by the Gospel. Even when our sinful rejection of the grace mediated to us in Christ is the consequence of ignorance, repentance is still demanded.[70]

Peter advised his listeners that, in spite of their evil behavior, God's intention was to bless them. In fact, "when God raised up his servant, he sent him first to you to bless you by turning each of you from your wicked ways" (3:26).

Hebrews

The writer of this epistle uses the Hebrew sacrificial system as a paradigm for the work of Christ, demonstrating His superiority as High Priest in removing the sins of humanity. Thus, the Old Testament concept of sin is recognized and accepted.

Christ's purpose in coming to earth, says the author, was to provide "purification for sin" (1:3). He died so that "he might destroy him who holds the power of death—that is, the devil—and free those who all their lives were held in slavery" (2:14; cf. 9:26). Christ's sacrifice of Himself on the cross was a one-time event by which He took away "the sins of many people" (9:28). Here the term "many" has the same significance as in the Pauline epistles (i.e., all). When Christ comes again, it will be "not to bear sin, but to bring salvation to those who are waiting for him" (9:28).

The author is under no illusions about the nature of sin. He cautions people (in this context, Christians) against being "hardened by sin's deceitfulness" (3:13). Sin's pleasures are short-lived (11:25), but it clings to a person (12:1) and is a constant hindrance to one's progress.

Sin as rebellion

One of the chief themes of Hebrews is sin as rebellion, particularly the rebellion of Christians which leads to the outright rejection of God. What is in view is what we term "apostasy." Throughout the epistle warnings are given to believers "that we do not drift away" (2:1). Time and again they are reminded, "How shall we escape if we ignore such a great salvation?" (2:3) When a believer allows oneself to drift away, there is a hardening of his or her heart which will lead one away from God (3:7-12).

Hebrews 6:4-6 is a passage whose meaning is greatly disputed. When one interprets it in its context by the *sensus literalis,* however, its message is blunt and direct: It is impossible for one who has accepted Christ as personal Savior and Lord who then falls away to be brought back to salvation. Christ cannot be crucified for sins a second time. A.T. Robertson asserts, "It is a terrible picture and cannot be toned down."[71] These warnings on apostasy are repeated in 10:19-39 and in 12:1-29.

James

James makes the source of evil very clear. In 1:12-15 he declares that no one should ever accuse God of being the author of temptation, "for God cannot be tempted by evil, nor does he tempt anyone" (v. 13). Temptation gains access to human beings through their own evil desire (v. 14). "Then, after desire has conceived, it gives birth to sin; and sin, when it is full-grown, gives birth to death" (v. 15). Thus, for James, sin is conceived from some evil within its human host; then it acts as a parasite, feeding upon its host until—full-grown—it destroys a person.

Nor is sin just a matter of committing wrong acts. The failure to do what is right is equally sin. "Anyone, then, who knows the good he ought to do and doesn't do it, sins" (4:17).

James concludes his letter with a passionate appeal to believers to engage in preventive measures with regard to sin. If a Christian wanders from the truth and one of his fellows brings him back, he should know that "whoever turns a sinner from the error of his way will save him from death and cover a multitude of sins" (5:20). Just how this occurs, James does not say. He is more concerned that sin should be prevented than in theologizing.[72]

The Petrine Epistles

In the context of encouraging persecuted believers, Peter reminds Christians that they have assurance that Christ has won the ultimate victory over evil, and they share that victory through their baptism (that is, through their participation in His death): "For Christ died for sins once for all, the righteous for the unrighteous, to bring you to God. He was put to death in the body but made alive by the Spirit . . . [baptism] saves you by the resurrection of Jesus Christ" (1 Peter 3:18, 22).

Majority opinion among scholars suggests that this passage has been composed out of existing liturgical or catechetical material.[73] This may help to explain its similarity in thought to 1 Corinthians 15:3, Galatians 1:4, and Hebrews 10:12; and the emphatic use of "once for all" in Romans 6:10 and several places in Hebrews (7:27; 9:12, 26; 10:10).[74] The focus of the passage is Christ's victorious death to vanquish sin and bring us to God.

The following chapter (4:1ff) continues Peter's argument on the significance of his readers' baptism. Verses 1-6 vigorously contrast the new life in Christ and their former, shameful past. There is a substantial catalog of sins given in verse 3: "debauchery, lust, drunkenness, orgies, carousing, and detestable idolatry." The author emphasizes in verse 5 that those who continue in such a lifestyle "will have to give account to Him who is ready to judge the living and the dead."

Like James, Peter urges the practice of "body life" in the church. Believers must be supportive of each other: "Above all, love each other deeply, because love covers a multitude of sins" (4:8). Does the author mean that love on the part of one believer will mitigate the sins of another? Kelly does not think so, declaring that it is more likely that the former will in the coming judgment receive mercy for his own sins; at the final judgment love or lack of love will be the determinative factor.[75]

In the context of a denunciation of false teachers who seek to undermine the faith of the church, 2 Peter 2 provides a remarkable record of the possible ways sin shows itself in human life. It is illustrative of what happens when people "never stop sinning" (2:14).[76] He refers to these perpetrators as "brute beasts . . . and like beasts they too will perish" (2:12). Their fate will be "blackest darkness" (2:17), for even though they once knew

Christ as Savior, they allowed themselves to be again entangled by sin and so turned their backs on the way of righteousness (2:20ff).

Conclusions

We may make a number of observations about sin from our study of the New Testament. We find from the teachings of both Jesus and Paul that sin is universal. Jesus declares all to be sinners whose actions and attitudes are contrary to God's purposes. James broadens the definition to include the failure to do what is right.

Even though sin affects all human beings, that does not mean that they are worthless. They have great value to God, for He sent Jesus to earth to rescue them. Just as sin is universal, so is the need for salvation.

Paul is particularly emphatic on the universality of sin and death, as well as the universal accessibility of salvation and life. All who imitate Adam's disobedience experience death; all who imitate Christ's obedience experience life. Though the picture of humans as rebellious lawbreakers is presented in many of the New Testament books, it is strongest in Paul.

Paul, Peter, and the writer to the Hebrews all present extensive lists of sins. They also declare that the end of those who engage in such behavior is God's condemnation. Of all sins the most heinous is apostasy, for which there is no forgiveness. A willful rejection of Christ after a salvific experience of Him can bring only divine wrath.

Guthrie sums up the New Testament teaching thusly:

[Sin] merits punishment. . . . the condemnation of sin by a righteous God is an integral assumption behind the New Testament teaching on salvation and must be borne in mind if the mission of Jesus is to be rightly understood. Indeed, many of the particular facets in which sin is presented in the New Testament contribute to the different interpretations of the work of Christ. If sin is enslavement, Christ brings deliverance. If it is falsehood, Christ presents truth. If disobedience, Christ shows the way of obedience. If deviance from the will of God, Christ sets the perfect example of righteousness.[77]

Section Three
A Systematic Theology of Sin

Chapter Ten
The Nature and Universality of Sin

An understanding of the nature of sin is crucial for all human beings. After all, sin is a vicious and destructive power, the most deadly enemy any human being will ever have, a foe that threatens our very existence. The Bible recognizes the menace posed by sin, for it calls upon the Christian to resist sin "to the point of shedding your blood" (Heb. 12:4). The more one can discover about one's enemy the more likely one is to be able to conquer it. The more we can discern about the nature and extent of sin—what it is and how it manifests itself among humans—the more apt we are to discover the means to subdue or overcome it.

Our studies have shown us that sin seriously affects our relationship with God,[1] for it is everything that stands in opposition to Him. At the same time, it manifests itself in flawed interpersonal relationships; it is evidenced in our treatment of and attitudes toward our fellow human beings.

In studying the biblical information on the nature of sin, we may place it under two broad categories: sin as ungodliness and sin as unrighteousness.[2] The first category essentially concerns our relationship with God and the second, our relationships with each other.

313

Sin as Ungodliness

The Greek word for ungodliness is *asebeia.* It is formed by affixing the negative *alpha* privative prefix to the word for godliness. *Sebeia* means godliness, humility, reverence, or piety. *Asebeia* indicates just the opposite: arrogance or self-glorification. It signifies life apart from the acknowledgment and worship of God. Ungodliness has many aspects, the more prominent of which we shall explore, but its essence is a willful ignorance of God.

Rebellion

One of the oldest theories of the nature of sin posits a dualism of eternal evil versus eternal good. The Gnostics and Manicheans, for example, believed that these two perpetually antagonistic principles are intermingled in the human constitution—the pure spirit striving against the impure material body. Charles Hodge succinctly summarizes this dualistic concept: "Sin is thus a physical evil; the defilement of the spirit by its union with a material body; and is to be overcome by physical means, i.e., by means adapted to destroy the influence of the body on the soul. Hence the efficacy of abstinence and austerities."[3] In this economy evil is that material part of humankind which has failed to be brought under the control of the spirit.

But sin is not coeternal with good. As Emil Brunner declares, it "is not the primary phenomenon, it is not the beginning, but it is a turning-away from the beginning, the abandonment of the origin, the break with that which God had given and established."[4] From almost the point of their creation human beings have willfully rejected God's standards for their own. Adam and Eve decided that the serpent's interpretation of the results of eating the fruit from the tree in the center of the garden was more reliable than God's (Gen. 3:1ff), and so—in defiance of His prohibition—they ate of the fruit.

The history of Israel was one of persistent rebellion against God. There were a number of episodes in their journey from Egypt to Canaan where they griped about the hardships they faced or refused to accept God's leading in certain directions (e.g., Ex. 17:1-7; 32:1ff; Num. 11:1-3; 14:1-10). In fact, the Deuteronomist's conclusion was that "from the day you [Israel] left

Egypt until you arrived here [Canaan], you have been rebellious against the Lord" (Deut. 9:7). As an established nation in Palestine, Israel fared little better. The prophets continually berated them for their disobedience to God.

Isaiah called upon them to repent of their evil and return to the Lord, "but if you resist and rebel, you will be devoured by the sword" (Isa. 1:20). Jeremiah pronounced God's judgment upon His rebellious people because "each pursues his own course like a horse charging into battle" (Jer. 8:6). And Ezekiel (chap. 20) recounted the entire history of Israel from its outset as one of constant rebellion right to his own day. Their typical attitude was, "We want to be like the nations, like the peoples of the world, who serve wood and stone" (Ezek. 20:32).

The New Testament also comments on the nature of sin as rebellion. John the Baptist, termed by many "the last of the Old Testament prophets," saw his role as one of calling God's "disobedient [people] to the wisdom of the righteous — to make ready a people prepared for the Lord" (Luke 1:17). In Romans 1 Paul declares that human beings have known about God since creation, but "they neither glorified him as God nor gave thanks to him, but their thinking became futile and their foolish hearts became darkened" (Rom. 1:21). In Ephesians 5:6 the apostle warns that "God's wrath comes on those who are disobedient" to His law by indulging in immorality, impurity, and greed. The Apostle Peter notes that even back in Noah's time people were disobedient (1 Peter 3:20) and fell under God's wrath in the Flood.

Rebellion is also described as enmity with God. Paul writes that "the sinful mind is hostile to God" (Rom. 8:7). To be the enemy of God is to be dead in one's transgressions and sins, following "the ways of this world and of the ruler of the kingdom of the air, the spirit who is now at work in those who are disobedient" (Eph. 2:2).

Ralph Venning asserts that

here then is the desperately wicked nature of sin, that it is not only *crimen laesae Majestatis,* high treason against the Majesty of God, but it scorns to confess its crime. It is obstinate and will not that he reign over it. It is not only not subject, but it will not be subject, nor be reconciled to God; such is its enmity![5]

We may say, as well, that another facet of rebellion is the failure to love God. The first commandment (in the sense of being the most important), according to Jesus, is to "love the Lord your God with all your heart and with all your soul and with all your mind" (Matt. 22:37). The sinner is one who has displaced God as the primary Object of his affection.

Conclusions

Scripture declares that the knowledge of God is universal. Not only does nature reveal the glory of God (Ps. 19:1-4; Rom. 1:18-20), but even those who have not received a special revelation (viz., the Bible) "show that the requirements of the law are written on their hearts" (Rom. 2:15). No one, therefore, can rightly claim ignorance of God. Failure to act upon the knowledge one has – no matter how scant it may be – and so give God His rightful place in the human economy, constitutes rebellion.

Sin as covenant unfaithfulness

God deals with His people through covenant. A covenant is much like a modern contract. It may be concluded between a ruler and his people or between two equal parties. Or it may be concluded between God and His people. In the Old Testament, the term "covenant" is used to signify the meaning of the Hebrew *berît,* which probably meant "fetter" or "obligation." In all cases, each party is bound to do certain things in return for obligations performed by the other. A normal aspect of the Old Testament *berît* is its unchangeable and permanently binding nature. A broken covenant would incur divine wrath upon the one responsible for its fracture.[6] The type of covenant which we have in view here is that effected by a monarch (unilaterally) with his people; he would promise them protection and security in return for their loyalty and support. God has unilaterally established His covenant with His people.

The Old Testament records God's covenant dealings with the Hebrew people. The basis for this covenant goes back to Genesis 12:1ff when God made a covenant with Abram that He would make of him a great nation. The covenant was confirmed several times with the patriarch (Gen. 15:1-21; 17:1-14; 22:15-18), with his son Isaac (Gen. 26:24), and again with Isaac's son Jacob (Gen. 28:13-15; 35:9-12). This covenant was reaffirmed with Israel through Moses (Ex. 6:2-8) and through Joshua (Josh. 24:1-27). And Joshua warned the Hebrews that if they broke it, "he will turn and bring disaster on you and make an end of you, after he has been good to you" (Josh. 24:20).

Sadly, the Israelites were not faithful to the covenant throughout their history, and covenant-breaking became a paradigm for sin in the Old Testament. God gave them opportunity after opportunity to repent and renew the covenant with Him. He punished them, rescued them from that punishment, and exhorted them through His prophets. But to no avail. They were utterly ungrateful and this ingratitude was the hallmark of their covenant unfaithfulness.[7]

Apostasy

In Jesus Christ God has concluded a New Covenant with all humankind: "For God so loved the world that he gave his one and only Son, that whoever believes in him [Jesus] shall not perish but have eternal life" (John 3:16). The covenant was confirmed in Christ's blood (Luke 22:20).

One might expect that believers would have no problem remaining faithful to Christ, but there are those who — after having professed faith in Him and having begun a faith relationship with Him — turn away from Him and immerse themselves in their sins once more, just as Old Testament Israel turned away from God.

The idea of apostasy for a Christian is a contentious one with reputable scholars on both sides of the issue.[8] But it is hard to ignore that the majority of New Testament books warn against the dangers of falling away from the living God to the point of no return.

Jesus refers to this danger in His Parable of the Sower (Luke 8:9-15). While some receive and immediately reject the Word (the rocky ground), others receive it and believe for a time until in temptation they fall away (the ground with thorns and weeds). The latter are obviously sincere and made a genuine beginning on their Christian pilgrimage.[9]

Paul devotes an entire book to the danger of apostasy, his letter to the Galatians. He protests, "I am astonished that you are so quickly deserting the one who called you by the grace of

Christ and are turning to a different gospel—which is really no gospel at all" (1:6-7). Nor is this the only warning. All of Paul's epistles except Philemon warn against apostatizing.

The Letter to the Hebrews contains five warnings against apostatizing: 2:1-4; 3:7–4:13; 6:1-20; 10:19-39; and 12:1-29. Moody says that three things may be gleaned from its teaching: (1) a believer can press forward to Christian maturity and whole-hearted assurance; (2) believers who do not press forward to maturity are in danger of apostatizing; and (3) the sin of apostasy cannot be undone.[10]

The Apostle John is equally adamant. In John 15:1-11 Jesus refers to Himself as the Vine and His disciples as the branches. He warns, "If anyone does not remain in me, he is like a branch that is thrown away and withers; such branches are picked up, thrown into the fire and burned" (John 15:6). His epistles and Revelation also have these warnings (e.g., 1 John 5:16ff; 2 John 8; Rev. 3:15ff).

Apostasy is a form of rebellion on the part of those who have responded to and stand under the covenant of Christ's blood. It begins with the failure to mature in the faith, is confirmed in backsliding or turning away from the faith, and is crystallized in a willful rejection of God in Christ.

Sin as idolatry

In the Old Testament economy, idolatry was seen as a sin "with a high hand." That is, it was a sin not remediable under covenant legislation. Those guilty of idolatry were condemned to death (although such a penalty was not often enforced), for it was held to be the gravest of sins against God.[11] Israel was guilty of following after false gods from the time of the Exodus (Ex. 32:1ff; Num. 25:1-5). Various kings—such as Asa (2 Chron. 15:8-18), Hezekiah (2 Kings 18:1-4), and Josiah (2 Kings 23:4ff)—attempted to stem the tide, but were unable to eradicate completely the worship of foreign gods. Ultimately, the Northern Kingdom of Israel fell to Assyria, never to rise again, and Judah was conquered by Babylon and was not reconstituted as a nation for some seventy years.

In the New Testament, Paul has more to say about idolatry than any of the other writers. In his classic statement on ungodliness he writes:

> For although they [human beings] knew God, they neither
> glorified him as God nor gave thanks to him, but . . . [they]
> exchanged the glory of the immortal God for images made
> to look like mortal men and birds and animals and reptiles.
> . . . They exchanged the truth of God for a lie, and wor-
> shiped and served created things rather than the Creator
> (Rom. 1:21-23, 25).

The apostle declares emphatically that humans have deliberately
and willfully rejected God in preference for gods of their own
making—gods of wood, stone, and metal, fashioned in the image
of creatures.

Many Christian theologians hold idolatry to be the basis for sin.
Reinhold Niebuhr states that "the sin of man is that he seeks to
make himself God."[12] Erickson insists that "idolatry in any
form . . . is the essence of sin."[13] John Macquarrie declares that
"the claim that idolatry is the basic sin is confirmed when we
consider the various manners in which the idolatrous self is distorted or inhibited from growth."[14]

Idolatry is that form of rejection of God which seeks to replace
Him with an object of one's own choosing. Whatever has priority
in one's life—if not the God of heaven—is an idol. In biblical
times idols were items of wood, stone, and metal. In our day they
are more sophisticated, taking the form of political and social
idealogies, wealth, fame, and even other human beings (to name
only a few possibilities). But in that they are the most important
object in one's life, they are idols.

Sin as unbelief

Sin as unbelief is essentially a New Testament theme. John in his
Gospel is a major proponent of this idea as he presents Jesus'
atonement as the supreme evidence of God's love for the world,
"that whoever believes in him shall not perish but have eternal
life" (3:16). John emphasizes that "whoever believes in him is
not condemned, but whoever does not believe is condemned already because he has not believed in the name of God's one and
only Son" (3:18). Jesus' determination of unbelief was that it is
willful blindness (9:39-41). That unbelief is sin is clear from 16:9:
"because men do not believe in me."

319

John equates unbelief with disobedience: "There is a judge for the one who rejects me and does not accept my words; that very word which I spoke will condemn him at the last day" (12:48). Unbelief leads to a rejection of both Jesus and His commands. This refusal to heed His will leads to condemnation. G.C. Berkouwer asserts that here "is the sin in all sin, not in a general moral sense or in the sense of a formal transgression of the law, but rather in the sense of the lawless reality of sin which is both defined and made known in this relation to Jesus."[15]

The intensive form of unbelief in the New Testament teaching is blasphemy against the Holy Spirit. The sin against the Spirit is a persistent and intentional rejection of His conviction to believe in Christ as Savior and Lord. Garrett notes that unbelief is not a matter of rejecting theological statements about Jesus' being God's only Son, but a rejection "of Jesus Himself as God's Son and Word, the Revealer and Redeemer. It implies an exposure to the light and truth of God in Jesus Christ, and it involves a deliberate rejection of that light and truth."[16]

Conclusions

While some theologians have characterized sin as natural defect, error, or sickness, our study shows that sin goes far beyond such problems. Erickson has correctly diagnosed the predicament as "simply failure to let God be God."[17] It is essentially the determination of humans to ignore God and do their "own thing." This state of ignoring may negatively manifest itself in open rebellion—purposeful resolve that God's will will not be sovereign—or in deliberate unfaithfulness to the covenant (and its New Testament equivalent, apostasy), or in obstinate unbelief—the willful rejection of Jesus Christ as God's redeeming Word to humankind, the only way to salvation.

And yet, humanity is intrinsically and incurably religious, which leads to the positive aspect of ungodliness, namely, idolatry. Idolatry is the enthronement of some finite object, regardless of what it may be, in the supreme place which belongs to God.[18] It is a perverted commitment of faith. Generally, it is a proclamation of faith in oneself. Macquarrie says that the "temptation for man to idolize himself and become his own god has reached overwhelming proportions in the current theological age."[19] When one becomes his or her own god, a person moves farther and farther away from the real God until, as Paul says, God gives one over to the sinful desires of his or her heart (Rom. 1:24).

Ungodliness, whether expressed negatively or positively, is deserving of God's wrath. To persist in ungodliness is to place oneself in the way of God's condemnation and to invite destruction.

Sin as Unrighteousness

Ungodliness manifests itself in unrighteousness, broken relationships with other human beings. In New Testament parlance, unrighteousness translates the Greek word *adikia*. Like *asebeia*, it is formed by adding the negative *alpha* privative to the Greek *dikia*, straight, right, just, or true. Thus, unrighteousness means "crooked, untrue, or unjust." It is derived from ungodliness, for if one is ungodly, then all other relationships will be perverted or twisted.

Sensuousness

Schleiermacher held that the essence of sin is sensuousness. He believed that the flesh dominates the soul and that the body is a conduit for all temptations.[20] Muller followed suit, contending that "it is the undeniable teaching of history that the obliterating [of] the distinction between spirit and nature always ends in naturalizing spirit, and never in spiritualizing nature."[21] Some later theologians followed Schleiermacher's views, but attributed the dominance of the flesh to human evolution from lower life forms. Borden Bowne attributed it to "a relic of the animal not yet outgrown, a resultant of the mechanism of appetite . . . for which the proper inhibitions are not yet developed."[22]

While one cannot, on the basis of Scripture, accept the latter view, Schleiermacher's identification of the flesh with sensuousness has a biblical basis provided one does not associate the flesh only with the material aspect of humanity (*sarx*, the Greek word for flesh in the New Testament, has a spiritual dimension). That unrighteousness may be manifested in the search for physical pleasure is undeniable. Paul writes about those who are separated from the life of God: "Having lost all sensitivity, they have

321

given themselves over to sensuality so as to indulge in every kind of impurity, with a continual lust for more" (Eph. 4:19). The apostle's catalog of sins in Galatians 5:19-21 includes sexual immorality, debauchery, drunkenness, orgies, and so on. And, of course, he also comes down hard on homosexuality in Romans 1:26-27.

> Because of this [their rejection of God], God gave them over to shameful lusts. Even their women exchanged natural relations for unnatural ones. In the same way the men also abandoned natural relations with women and were inflamed with lust for one another. Men committed indecent acts with other men, and received in themselves the due penalty for their perversion.

Sexual perversion both heterosexual and homosexual has become the normal order of our day. Among heterosexuals adultery, fornication, "swapping," and other types of debauchery are accepted by many without condemnation as legitimate forms of "recreational" sex. Among homosexuals "outing" (a public declaration of one's sexual preference) has become popular as the "gay movement" lobbies to become accepted as another "minority" which needs protection from discrimination. That movement is now attempting to demonstrate scientifically that homosexuality is a matter of birth (i.e., genetic) and not choice. And some theologians have suggested that "anti-homosexual passages" (such as Rom. 1:26-27 above) are cultic in orientation and have nothing to say about long-term monogamous homosexual relationships.

Nor are indecent sexual acts the only form of sensuousness. While the Bible has little — if anything — to say about drugs, the underlying principle is the same as that which condemns drunkenness. It should not be surprising that cocaine and alcohol are drugs of choice for "respectable" people.

Selfishness

According to Strong, the essential principle of sin is selfishness. He defines selfishness as "that choice of self as the supreme end which constitutes the antithesis of supreme love to God."[23] Selfishness, or self-love as we may term it, is closely related to idolatry since it displaces God as primary in one's life.

Self-love is also a rejection of Christ's command to self-denial. In his soliloquy on love, Paul notes that genuine love "is not self-seeking" (1 Cor. 13:5). Selfishness not only militates against God but also against one's fellow human beings. Strong declares that

> selfish desire takes the forms respectively of avarice, ambition, vanity, pride, according as it is set upon property, power, esteem, independence. Selfish affection is falsehood or malice, according as it hopes to make others its voluntary servants, or regards them as standing in its way. . . .[24]

We have already demonstrated that the sinner has failed to obey the first and greatest commandment to love God with his entire being (Matt. 22:37). Self-love fractures the second commandment cited by Christ: "And the second is like it [the first]: Love your neighbor as yourself" (Matt. 22:39). Sin, then, is lovelessness. Berkouwer tells us that "no other description can possibly do better than saying that 'sin is lovelessness.' "[25]

We are to love our neighbor. Jesus' Parable of the Good Samaritan (Luke 10:29ff) teaches us that our neighbor is whoever is "nigh" us. In our modern global village, that is all the world. And as we survey our "neighborhood," and become aware of the squalor and misery in which so many people live, we realize the near universality of the failure to observe this commandment to love our neighbor.

Because of selfishness human beings abuse and exploit other human beings. White slavers, slumlords, and drug pushers hurt other people for self-aggrandizement. Women working in sweat shops, migrant workers toiling long hours for low wages, and abused wives and children are all victims of the sin of selfishness. But these are extreme examples. Selfishness great and small abounds in all humanity.

Nor is the breaking of this commandment limited only to individuals. As Rauschenbusch and Reinhold Niebuhr have shown us, "the community is the frustration as well as the realization of individual life."[26] Societies and institutions are as selfish as individuals, or perhaps more so. Much of the misery of the Third-World poor, for example, is the result of the oppressive actions not only of their own governments, but of the governments and corporations of First-World nations who exploit them for greater profits and wealth. And one does not have to go across the ocean to find examples of collective injustice. They abound in our own society. All—whether individual or corporate—are the product of selfishness and the result of human failure to love one's neighbor as oneself.

A violation of God's law

Transgression has been said to be "the leading idea and the most profound word for human wrong."[27] In the New Testament the word is rendered by the Greek *parabasis,* a term which denotes a deliberate violation of God's law. It describes a fracturing of the standard or norm by which one's life is regulated.[28] A related term in the New Testament is *anomia,* lawlessness. It is a more general term than *parabasis,* but it refers to antisocial and unlawful actions.[29]

There are three biblical types of law: (1) the legal code, which would include the penal code, as we think of it; (2) the ceremonial or traditional law; and (3) the ethical law, which governs societal life, proper relations with one's fellow human beings (including right internal attitudes).[30] People violate all these laws.

The Old Testament prophets frequently condemned the Israelites for breaking God's laws. Amos struck out at the injustice of people: "They sell the righteous for silver, and the needy for a pair of sandals. They trample on the heads of the poor as upon the dust of the ground, and deny justice to the oppressed" (Amos 2:6-7). Micah was of like opinion: "They covet fields and seize them, and houses, and take them. They defraud a man of his home, a fellowman of his inheritance" (Micah 2:2). Habakkuk was also concerned with this uncaring lawlessness: "Woe to him who piles up stolen goods and makes himself wealthy by extortion!" (Hab. 2:6)

Paul speaks about lawlessness in 2 Thessalonians, referring to events prior to Christ's return. He mentions the appearance of the "man of lawlessness" (2:1ff). In this connection, he notes that "the secret power of lawlessness is already at work" (2:7). And the Apostle John is very definite that "everyone who sins breaks the law; in fact, sin is lawlessness" (1 John 3:4). Because all law is rooted in the will of God, violating the law is tantamount to violating God's will, and is therefore sin.

Conclusions

The way one relates to God necessarily shapes one's relationships to one's fellow human beings. A perverted relation to God means a perverted relation to other people. The latter is the essence of unrighteousness.

Contrary to some twentieth-century theologians, unrighteous-

10.1: A SUMMARY OF THE NATURE OF SIN

Sin as Ungodliness

Rebellion—the willful rejection of and resistance to God's standards.

Covenant Unfaithfulness—the fracture of the covenant effected between God and human beings.

Apostasy—a form of rebellion on the part of those who have accepted by covenant to become the people of God.

Idolatry—the replacing of God with an object of one's own choosing as the supreme recipient of one's adoration.

Unbelief—willful blindness to the truth and love of God as revealed in Christ Jesus.

✠

Sin as Unrighteousness

Sensuousness—the placing of the search for physical pleasure above all else in one's life.

Selfishness—the choice of self as the supreme end in one's life (a form of idolatry).

Transgression—a violation of the (biblical) standards or norms by which life is regulated.

---

ness is not "man's inheritance from a brute ancestry,"[31] but his inheritance from a rejection of God. Whether it is in the form of sensuousness, self-love, or a willful violation of the law of God, unrighteousness is the result of a wrong attitude toward God which leads to the exploitation and abuse of one's neighbor — whether across the street or across the world.

Some observations

Theologians, through the ages, have attempted to identify the essence of sin. Some have pointed to idolatry, some to sensuousness, and some to selfishness. None of these, however, is entirely satisfactory by itself. As we have seen from our investigation of the nature of sin, its character transcends these categories to a larger one. All of these have as their causative component the desire to rob God of His rightful place as God. We must come to the conclusion, then, that the root or essence of sin is the rejection of God as God.

The Universality of Sin

The idea of the universality of sin raises some interesting concerns. What underlies its pervasiveness? Who is responsible? Is sin a culpable matter? Or (because it is universal) are we to suppose that there is some natural cause which renders innocent all those infected? After all, if sin is quite literally omnipresent and cannot be avoided, how can an individual be blamed for doing what cannot be helped? Much hangs, it would seem, on whether sin is or is not truly universal.

Evidence for the universality of sin

The Bible emphatically declares the universality of sin as a fact. The Apostle Paul has gone to the Old Testament to compose a hymn on the empirical evidence that all have sinned in thought, word, and deed.[32] We find it in Romans 3:10-18. He stresses that "there is no one righteous, not even one . . . no one who seeks God . . . there is no one who does good, not even one. . . . There is no fear of God before their eyes." Paul's intent here is to demonstrate that all the Jewish people — God's chosen — are guilty before Him, and so *a fortiori* are all humankind.[33] In Romans 5:12, the apostle reiterates that "death came to all men, because all sinned."

Nor is Paul the only inspired writer who insists that no one escapes the destructiveness of sin. The Psalmist David observes that "all have turned aside, they have together become corrupt; there is no one who does good, not even one" (Ps. 14:3). Berkouwer tells us that this verse may be considered "a compendium of the whole witness of Scripture on the universal character of sin. In that witness there is no room for any exception."[34] Solomon, in his prayer of dedication, confesses to God that "there is no one who does not sin" (1 Kings 8:46). Isaiah asserts that "we all, like sheep, have gone astray, each of us has turned to his own way" (53:6). And our Lord Jesus Himself has noted that "no one is good — except God alone" (Mark 10:18).

Doctrinal presuppositions

That sin is universal is also a presupposition of many of the essential Christian doctrines. The doctrine of condemnation, for example, determines that "there will be trouble and distress for every human being who does evil" (Rom. 2:9), and that "all have sinned and fall short of the glory of God" (Rom. 3:23). The doctrine of spiritual rebirth (or, regeneration) tells us that, "no one can see the kingdom of God unless he is born again [or, born from above]" (John 3:3). The doctrine of repentance emphasizes that God "commands all people everywhere to repent" (Acts 17:30). All of these doctrines — and a number of others — depend for their validity on the fact of universal human sin.

The testimony of other religions

That all human beings are guilty of sin is presented in non-Christian religious systems, as well. The Buddhists seek nirvana, a state of nonbeing; all human beings need to achieve this state to be freed from wicked passions, false views, and general ignorance.[35] Hindus see evil as ignorance — a lot common to all — and encourage the self to transcend it.[36] Taoists and Confucians find evil to be alienation from the ultimate; all people suffer from a sense of estrangement. Only the monotheistic faiths — Islam, Judaism, and Christianity—depict sin as a transgression of the will of a personal God. Christianity alone moves beyond disobedience to divine law into the realm of belief or unbelief.[37]

Collective sin: A kingdom of evil

Far worse than the universality of individual sin is its collective nature. Individual evils combine to form what Ritschl referred to as a "kingdom of evil."[38] Emil Brunner advises us to remain always cognizant of how wickedness spreads to institutions, infecting them and giving birth to more wickedness which, in turn, reimpacts the lives of individual human beings. "Further, it is evident that the evil which becomes a mass phenomenon, waxes great and assumes demonic forms, which, as a rule, are not found in any individual evil."[39]

The Bible has much to say about the collective and demonic nature of human sin. John refers to the collective concept of sin as "the world." The world and its demonic prince, Satan, stand under God's judgment for their wickedness (John 12:31). At the same time, Jesus did not come to judge the world, but to save it (John 12:47). Nonetheless, the world hates Christ and those who belong to Him (John 15:18ff).

Paul tells us that those who follow the ways of the world and of its ruler who is at work in disobedient humans are dead through their sins and trespasses (Eph. 2:1ff). He uses similar thought in Galatians when he speaks of "the sinful nature" (5:16ff).

John Macquarrie comments on this corporate dimension of sin.

When we think of sin as . . . a massive disorientation and perversion of human society as a whole, we begin to perceive the really terrifying character of sin. For the "world," or κόσμος, the collective mass of mankind in its solidarity, is answerable to no one, and has a hardness and irresponsibility that one rarely finds in individuals.[40]

Collective sin—demonic though it may be—should never be allowed to become a "smokescreen" whereby the responsibility for individual guilt is watered down. Scripture places culpability firmly and squarely upon the individual. Ezekiel made this clear when he reprimanded Israel for blaming their misfortunes on the sins of their ancestors: "The fathers eat sour grapes and the children's teeth are set on edge" (18:2). On the contrary, declared the prophet, "The soul who sins is the one who will die" (18:4).

Explanations for sin's universality

The evidence for the universality of sin among humankind is abundant. But why is sin universal? As we examine its pervasiveness, what explanations for it can be uncovered?

Many Christian theologians hold that human nature has been disturbed by the disobedience of the first two human beings, our original parents. Other explanations have also been advanced, however, and we shall examine them.

The essential wickedness of human nature

One explanation for the omnipresence of sin posits that in some way sin is necessary. While there are various forms of this concept, the most common version ascribes sin to the bodily nature of humankind, stressing the sensuous nature at the expense of the rational and spiritual aspects.

Such a theory may go in two different directions: It may verge into dualism, such as we find in Zoroastrianism and Manicheanism. Or it may be found in a metaphysical speculation—as dictated by Spinoza and Hegel—that sin is the necessary result of the limitation of finite being as an unavoidable portion of human development.[41]

At first glance, there may seem to be considerable biblical support for this sensuous theory. There are passages which appear to present human nature—at least, in part—as intrinsically sinful. They speak of the flesh as the root of sin; those who are carnal *(sarkikoi)* or fleshly *(en sarki)* or after the flesh *(kata sarka)* are placed over against the spiritual *(pneumatikoi)*, who are possessed by the Spirit.

This contrast has been understood by many to be simply that between the body and soul, the animal and rational parts of human nature; and hence it has been inferred that the New Testament writers, especially Paul, who presents

329

this contrast most frequently, traced sin ultimately to the animal or sensuous element in man, as its cause.[42]

The Greek *sarx* originally meant simply the body (2 Cor. 12:7; Gal. 4:13ff). In 1 Corinthians 15:39 it signifies the essence of one's nature, and in Romans 11:14 and Ephesians 5:29 it expresses a psychic unity created by marriage. Thus, "flesh" has to do with observable, outward matters. Grayston tells us that

> in this sense there is often an implication of inferiority (Rom. 2:28) which arises from the standard contrast between mankind and God (cf. 1 Cor. 15:50, Gal. 1:16, Eph. 6:12). Flesh is therefore the sphere of imperfection. . . ; in 1 Cor. 3:1, 3 "carnal" means defective in spiritual apprehension because of strife, etc. Because of this weakness, sarx is the sphere of sinfulness. . . .[43]

Unfortunately, this latter meaning was taken to extremes by Protestant theologians in the sixteenth and seventeenth centuries. This interpretation of *sarx* was applied to situations where the former meanings should have been used. But to assert that sarx always signifies the creaturely or sensuous nature — and that Paul held this as the underlying basis of sin — is extremely problematic, as can be easily demonstrated. Much of the apostle's teaching on sin has nothing to do with a theory of sensuousness — matters such as hatred, discord, selfish ambition, dissension, factionalism (Gal. 5:19ff), legalistic righteousness and spiritual pride (Phil. 3:4-6). Another major impediment to the acceptance of such a theory is Paul's stress on the sacredness of the body along with its natural drives and needs (as in 1 Cor. 6–7). And when one adds to that mix his determination in Romans 5:12ff that sin entered the world as the result of Adam's transgression, any theory of sin's being caused by the sensuous or animal nature of human beings is thoroughly debunked.[44]

Another great defect of the sensuous theory is that it supports a theological dualism. "For if the body be essentially evil it cannot have been created by the perfect holy God, but must either be the creation of an evil being, like the Ahriman of the Parsee system, or consist of matter independent of and eternally coexisting with God."[45] Such explanations contradict the biblical teaching of one eternal God by whom all things were created.

Sin as a necessary aspect of evolution

Those theologians who hold to an evolution of humankind from lower life forms posit a theory of universal sin closely linked to the aforementioned one, namely, that sin is a necessary aspect of the evolutionary transition from brute being to civilized human.

Such was the theory of Georg Hegel, whose idea of the evolution of *Geist* (mind or spirit) actually predated Darwin. What distinguishes animals from humans is that, while the former are premoral or innocent, civilized human beings possess moral consciousness. As people move upward from brute to civilized, they cannot develop moral consciousness without acquiring a sense of guilt. But guilt is acquired only through sin. Therefore, sin is a necessary concomitant to the upward movement to the attainment of civilization and moral consciousness.[46] F.R. Tennant held similar opinions, believing sin to be found in the acquisition of moral consciousness as human beings emerged from an animal existence through the evolutionary process.[47] In modern people, sin is universal because of the desire of all—a natural impulse—for self-preservation.[48]

This evolutionary theory of sin comes to grief, however, when one examines the history of human character. Regardless of how far back one may go in time, good and evil are found to coexist. Nor are they always so far apart from one another. Homer's *Iliad*, for example, shows little variance between the characters of Achilles and Paris, or Andromache and Helen. But as time goes on, those contrasts increase until, in the Renaissance era, we find a Savonarola coexisting with the Borgias and Medici; and in the eighteenth century, the Wesleys are in about the same time frame as Robespierre. In our own time, we find an ever-widening gap as we consider people like Mother Teresa over against Adolf Hitler and Josef Stalin. We may say, then, that the evolutionary theory of character's progress has gone seemingly in reverse, if in any direction at all.

And when one looks at individual human progress, the theory also breaks down. The sins of children and the young are not nearly as atrocious as are those of a more mature age.[49] Such a hypothesis is clearly unacceptable.

More cogent reasons

The two basic explanations we have examined have been discounted. As we look to biblical and systematic theology, what reasons can be found for the universality of sin?

Temptation a universal experience

Behind all sin lies temptation. And the Bible reveals to us that the original source of temptation is none other than "that ancient serpent, who is the devil, or Satan" (Rev. 12:9).

James Buswell II tells us that "no human being has ever been confronted with a temptation to sin without the agency of a personal being or beings who had previously sinned."[50] Thus, temptation may come to human beings through the agency of Satan alone, or through a sinful world, or from other individual fallen humans, or some combination thereof.[51]

John Owen has defined temptation as "any thing, state, way or condition that . . . hath a force or efficacy to seduce, to draw the mind and heart of a man from its obedience, which God requires of him, into any sin, in any degree of it whatever."[52]

Temptation works by either bringing evil into the human heart or by drawing out the evil already resident in the human heart. It seeks to divert human beings from the universal obedience God requires of them.[53] All human beings are tempted, and all human beings at some point give in to that temptation. It is universal, without exception.

The universal preconditions of sin

Reinhold Niebuhr has aptly described three preconditions of sin which are universally experienced and which are strongly linked to temptation. These are: finite freedom, anxiety, and inordinate self-love.

Evil originated with Satan's rebellion against God, with his attempt to exceed the limits which had been placed on his existence. Thus, Satan fell prior to the human Fall, and so it follows that the Fall is not the result of deliberate perversity. "The situation of finiteness and freedom in which man stands becomes a source of temptation only when it is falsely interpreted. . . . It is suggested to man by a force of evil which precedes his own sin."[54] This situation which causes the temptation (that is, the precondition to sin) is "that man is a finite spirit, lacking identity with the whole, but yet a spirit capable in some sense of envisaging the whole, so that he easily commits the error of imagining himself the whole which he envisages."[55] Humans are tempted to deny their finiteness and think of themselves as possessing unlimited freedom. When they act upon this belief, going their own way rather than God's—as they invariably do—they sin.

The sense of being both limited and limitless, of finiteness and freedom, causes anxiety in human beings. Niebuhr refers to it as "the inevitable concomitant of the paradox of freedom and finiteness in which man is involved. . . . the internal precondition of sin."[56] In and of itself it is not sin. Anxiety is to be differentiated from sin, for it is sin's precondition and because it is also the underlying cause of human creativity. "The same action may reveal a creative effort to transcend natural limitations, and a sinful effort to give an unconditioned value to contingent and limited factors in human existence."[57] And it is impossible to separate the two aspects.

The third universal precondition of sin is inordinate self-love. Self-love is the product of the self's excessive devotion to certain aspects within it. This preference for the self leads to a rejection of God and His purposes for the self.[58]

The universality of Adam's sin

Adam may be seen in a threefold light: as an historical individual who was the first male human; as a corporate being who embodies the whole human race; and generically as male and female, representing each and every individual human being.

Adam is unquestionably held responsible by the Bible for the origin of human sin. Paul declares that "sin came into the world through one man" (Rom. 5:12). If sin is universal—and it is—then the process of universalization was initiated by the historical Adam.

Adam is also symbolic of the solidarity of human sin. Emil Brunner is correct in his determination that "in Jesus Christ we stand *before* God as one 'Adam,' as a humanity which is totally infected with an indissoluble identical burden of guilt."[59] In regard to sin and guilt, the whole human race—like Adam—stands condemned before God.

Adam as male and female is the prototype of each and every human being. Paul says that sin entered the world through one man and death through sin "inasmuch as all men have sinned" (Rom. 5:12, NEB). John Whale puts it, "Everyman is his own 'Adam.' "[60] Every man and woman has done just exactly what Adam did—disobey God's law.

Conclusions

There is ample evidence for the universality of sin among human beings. That "all have sinned" is attested to not only by the Bible, but by religion in general. Only Christianity, however, sees sin in terms of both disobedience and unbelief. The idea of all having sinned extends beyond individuals to groups, institutions, and societies. Sinners banded together may incorporate into a "kingdom of evil" which is demonic in scope.

While many ideas have been advanced in an effort to explain the universality of sin, only one may be deemed fully acceptable. Adam transgressed and allowed sin to come into the world of human beings. How that has occurred (i.e., the transmitting of sin from Adam to his progeny) will be examined in the following chapter.

Chapter Eleven
The Origin of Sin and Original Sin

T he matter of how sin entered the world (the origin of sin) and the resulting effects on human beings of sin's entry into the world (original sin) is undoubtedly one of the more problematic aspects of Christian theology. As we have seen in our study of historical theology (section 1), a great many responses have been given — many of them at odds with others — most of which have purported to be biblical. There is evidently considerable confusion here. And yet, as we look at the world in which we live, and see the sordid and tragic results of evil, the need to understand the origin of sin and original sin becomes all the more vital.

It has been said that "the origin of evil is second only to the origin of being as the greatest enigma in man's life," and that "it is certainly the hardest cross for man's understanding to bear."[1] Some have attempted to place the cause of evil in the doctrine of the absolute sovereignty of God, referring to it as "the dark side of God" or "the club foot of God." After all, if God is fully sovereign, then He must be in some way responsible for evil. But the Bible declares that "God cannot be tempted by evil, nor does he tempt anyone" (James 1:13). It also tells us that "God is light; in him there is no darkness at all" (1 John 1:5). It insists, further,

335

that God does not delight in wickedness, but hates evildoers (Ps. 5:4-5). Berkouwer calls this witness "the biblical *a priori,*" namely, "that God is not the Source, or the Cause, or the Author of man's sin."[2]

God's Image: The Original State

That God cannot be held culpable for the entry of sin into the human race may be seen in His creation of humankind. The original state in which humans were created is clear evidence that His intent was utterly benign. The key Bible passage describing this original condition is Genesis 1:26-27.

> Then God said, "Let us make man in our image, in our likeness, and let them rule over the fish of the sea and the birds of the air, over the livestock, over all the earth, and over all the creatures that move along the ground." So God created man in his own image, in the image of God he created him; male and female he created them.

There are essentially three interpretations of the significance of the image. The first sees it as substantive; the image is an integral aspect of the human makeup. The second views it as relational; the image is the relationship of the person to God and to one another. The third sees the image as functional; it consists in the human exercising dominion, or stewardship, over the rest of the created order. Of the varying arguments as to the meaning of the image, the most likely is advanced by Millard Erickson, that it is substantive or structural, something one is.[3] That human beings experience relationships and exercise stewardship over creation are not the image but arise out of it. Erickson notes that

> these relationships and this function presuppose something else. Man is most fully man when he is active in these relationships and performs this function, for he is then fulfilling his *telos,* God's purpose for him. But ... the image itself is ... those qualities of God which, reflected in man, make worship, personal instruction, and work possible. If we think of God as a being with qualities, we will have no

11.1: INTERPRETATIONS OF THE IMAGE OF GOD AND THEIR CHIEF PROPONENTS

Substantive

The image is something structural or inherent in the human being. Many have seen "image" as being synonymous with reason or intellect; others as an innate holiness.

Proponents

Irenaeus of Lyons
Gregory of Nyssa
Augustine of Hippo
Thomas Aquinas
Martin Luther
John Calvin
Charles Ryder Smith
Millard Erickson

Relational

The image is the perfect and proper way the human relates to his or her Creator and to fellow human beings.

Proponents

Karl Barth
Dietrich Bonhoeffer
Emil Brunner
William W. Stevens

Functional

The image is the way the human functions in regard to the rest of creation, namely, in exercising stewardship or dominion over it.

Proponents

Sigmund Mowinckel
F.R. Tennant
C.F.D. Moule
Frank Stagg
Dale Moody
Gerhard von Rad
D.J.A. Clines
Henri Blocher

problem accepting the fact that man has such qualities as well.[4]

Out of these qualities theologians throughout the church's history have gleaned ideas concerning humanity's original state.

Early Catholicism

Augustine of Hippo, foremost theologian of the first Christian millennium, held that Adam — had he continued in obedience to God — would ultimately have achieved immortality. As it was, our first parents possessed excellent health and a mind unbothered by passion. Intellectually, they had an ability far surpassing any of their progeny.[5] All they had to do was to continue to eat of the tree of life and obey God's commands, and their lives in the Garden would continue in bliss and harmony. In their Garden state they possessed the ability not to sin *(posse non peccare)*.[6]

Augustine's great opponent, Pelagius, believed that humans are innately good; they have the power to choose good at all times. Sin is something environmental, not inherent. The first couple did not have any special quality later called by theologians "original righteousness." They were mortal, not immortal, and death was a natural expectation, not a penalty.[7]

Tridentine Catholicism

The Council of Trent, which formulated official dogma held by the Roman Church until Vatican II, posited a concept of the original state of humankind which went beyond natural endowments. Following their creation, our first parents received four "preternatural gifts": freedom from death, freedom from pain, divinely infused knowledge, and a total lack of concupiscence.[8]

Reformation theology

The Protestant Reformers (Luther, Zwingli, and Calvin) refuted the idea of preternatural gifts, but retained the idea of "original righteousness" held by Rome, although they filled it with a somewhat different content. The latter connoted both freedom from sin and rightness with God and the created order.[9]

Some biblical observations

It is evident from the Bible that Adam and Eve were moral beings. They were holy in their character. Because of their love for God and for one another they sought to serve each other and Him. They were filled with an innate humility which gave preference to self last. We see, as well, that they were relational beings. Genesis 3:8 tells us that they enjoyed a daily intimate fellowship with God. Gordon Lewis and Bruce Demarest observe that "the first pair enjoyed also faithful loving relationships with each other. No evidence of suspicion, envy, jealousy, or hatred occurred before the Fall."[10]

Genesis 2:24, which is a commentary on marriage arising out of the creation narratives, teaches us that our first parents were "one flesh." This *henosis* (union) was more than simply physical or sexual. It was a oneness of spirit, emotion, and purpose.

Thus, the original fabric of human life was one of *shalom* (peace). The word signifies fidelity, tranquillity, and security. Indeed, "the original shalom covered human well-being in the evident sense of the word."[11]

The Fall of Humanity

Our study of biblical theology, both Old and New Testaments, must lead us to the conclusion that the agent of human sin was human. Paul settles the matter in Romans 5:12 when he says that "sin entered the world through one man, and death through sin." Genesis 3 identifies that man as Adam.

The historicity of the account

Since humanity's descent into sin and alienation from God are events which took place well before recorded history (and some of which occurred outside of human experience), one must question how it has come into our possession. And, for the same reason, we must ask whether the account is indeed historical narrative or if it is of a different literary genre.

For some seventeen centuries overwhelming theological opinion held the opening chapters of Genesis to be simple factual history.[12] But with the advent of the Enlightenment, the facticity of the accounts was called into question by many and were

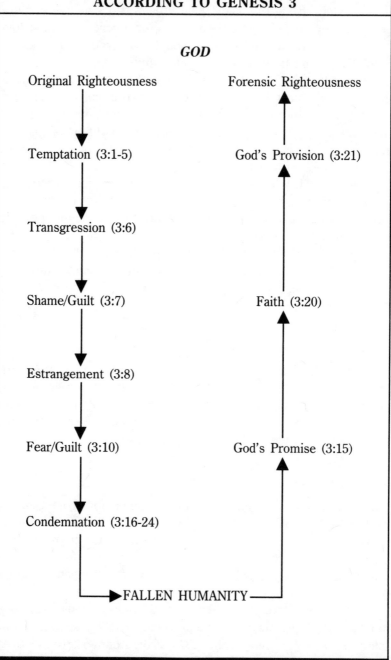

11.2: THE PATTERN OF SIN AND SALVATION ACCORDING TO GENESIS 3

GOD

Original Righteousness   Forensic Righteousness

Temptation (3:1-5)   God's Provision (3:21)

Transgression (3:6)

Shame/Guilt (3:7)   Faith (3:20)

Estrangement (3:8)

Fear/Guilt (3:10)   God's Promise (3:15)

Condemnation (3:16-24)

FALLEN HUMANITY

viewed by some in much the same light as the legends of the Norse, Greek, and Roman gods.

One of the early scholars to reject the biblical account was Baruch Spinoza (1632–1677). Spinoza was a philosopher who anticipated Freud's thought in many ways. He posited a human being who follows an experiential pilgrimage from childhood sensory experiences to a final level of happiness, which he saw as the intellectual love of God. But the impulse toward happiness leads from bewilderment to clearly defined ideas. The person beset by bewilderment will find trouble.[13]

Jean-Jacques Rousseau (1712–1778), a philosopher of the early Romantic period, is generally acknowledged as the first to attempt to formulate a secular explanation of the Fall. Though influenced somewhat by Catholicism and Protestantism alike, he rejected Christian notions of Adam's sin. He saw sin as the forces of a capitalistic society which corrupt human beings. He firmly believed that primitive peoples were happy (i.e., free of sin).[14]

Georg Hegel (1770–1831), a German philosopher, introduced into scholarship an extensive scheme of the evolution of mind or spirit moving upward from innocence to mature social awareness. At one point in time humans were premoral (lacking moral conscience). In order to move from one point up to the other, one must possess a sense of guilt, possible only through sin. Thus, it was both necessary and good for Adam to eat the forbidden fruit.[15]

As the twentieth century dawned, liberal theologians followed Darwinian evolution, holding that it had rendered incredible not only the Genesis account of creation but also the idea of a literal, historical Fall. Theologian F.R. Tennant may be viewed as typical of liberal thinkers. He criticized the idea of an historical Fall on the ground that modern science had shown it to be false. Human beings could not develop conscience at such an early point in their evolution, and only after such a development could they sin. He considered sin to be the residue of human flaws from humankind's animal past.[16]

Attempting to combat the liberal view, but remain true to science, many neo-orthodox and even some conservatives held the accounts of the Fall to be myth. Representative of the former was John S. Whale who declared that "Eden is on no map, and Adam's fall fits no historical calendar."[17] James Orr, a conservative, questioned whether the account was mythical or historical, stating: "I do not enter into the question of how we are to interpret the third chapter of Genesis—whether as history or allegory or myth, or, most probably of all, as old tradition clothed in oriental dress."[18]

Many contemporary evangelicals have sought to reconcile an historical Fall and present-day science, but do not feel that they can accept all the baggage connected with the idea of myth. Bruce Waltke points to "obvious incongruities in the text" arranged by the author for theological purposes, and suggests that "Moses did not intend to write a straightforward history, but an artistic literary account in anthropomorphic language (so that God's people might imitate him)."[19] Clark Pinnock argues for a symbolic view of the initial chapters of Genesis but without denying the historicity of the Fall, noting that

> this is a story with the following features: a talking snake, symbolic trees, Eve's origin through divine surgery, cherubim, a flaming sword, God walking in the garden, God modeling Adam from the clay and breathing into his nose, a perfect garden, the world rivers, the parade of animals. It is a story in which God is described very anthropomorphically as potter, as surgeon, and as gardener.[20]

His conclusion is that we have no business imposing our "imperialistic agendas" onto the Bible; it must be allowed to speak for itself.[21]

Bernard Ramm posits divinely inspired reconstruction of these texts. Such reconstruction is theology by narration; that is, theological concepts expressed in story form.[22] Although history is the vehicle of the theological story, it cannot be taken literally because one cannot take anthropomorphisms literally. It must be seen as generic history.

> Gen. 2–3 concerns the generic relationship of the Creator to the human race, the generic relationship of the creature to the creation, and generic temptation. Adam is a generic man, Eve is the generic woman, and the sin is a generic sin.[23]

Some observations

Are we to take these opening chapters of Genesis—including chapter 3 on the Fall—as legends, myths, symbols, or history?

To hold the account of humanity's Fall from grace as legend on par with those of other ancient peoples would be to reject our primary — and absolutely necessary — presupposition that the Bible is God's truth. This we cannot do. On the same basis we cannot accept the evolutionary hypothesis of sin, whether Hegelian or Darwinian.

The evangelical attempts to reconcile science and theology — or, at least, not to alienate the two from each other — are admirable and entirely plausible. They stress the Fall and its consequences for Adam and Eve and for all of humanity.

Gordon Lewis and Bruce Demarest seek to debunk Ramm's thesis of theology by narration, declaring that New Testament attestations of Adam, the serpent, and the Fall as historical realities should cause us to view Genesis 3 as historical reality.[24] But they are reading into the New Testament their own presuppositions of history in a twentieth-century sense. While the New Testament writers certainly took the stories as true, there is nothing to suggest that they did so according to the expectations of modern epistemology.

Conclusions

In order for human beings to be held responsible for their sins, they must have committed them. A meta-historical Fall would be unjust. The origin of sin in the human race must be a space and time historical event. At the same time, one must concur with Karl Barth that the reason for believing Genesis 3 is not because it is history (generic or literal), but because it is in the Bible which is the Word of God.[25] While there is no strong reason to suppose that the Genesis account is not a valid report of the sin of the first two created beings (albeit dressed in some highly figurative and anthropomorphic language), there is nothing in Ramm's concept of theology by narration, or in Pinnock's symbolic approach, or in Waltke's literary approach which would militate against the orthodox doctrine of Scripture as God's absolute truth.

The temptation and the sin

In our discussion above it was noted that — in order for humankind to be held accountable for sin — humankind must have committed sin in a literal, space and time episode. Whether one wishes to see Genesis 3 as literal history or as "generic history" makes no difference because it speaks to both interpretations, telling us how sin came to the human race.

On the tempter

Sin was a part of the created order prior to the creation of humankind. It was not something inherent in the first human couple, but was introduced from the outside. The Genesis 3 account demonstrates (as we have seen) that Adam and Eve were created as God's image and that everything "was very good." But, as James O. Buswell II points out, "man was tempted to sin by a personal being of another kind or order, who had previously sinned against God. This fact indicates that the record of the original sin of man is not intended as an account of the absolute origin of sin in the universe."[26]

The Genesis writer depicts this external agent as an intelligent, malevolent personal being. Buswell suggests that "the Serpent" should be considered a proper name; nowhere in Scripture is it ever said to be a wild animal, but rather *"more crafty* than any of the wild animals the Lord God had made" (3:1).[27] John's Revelation clearly establishes his identity when it describes "that ancient serpent, who is the devil, or Satan" (Rev. 20:2). Our Lord Himself gives us further information, that the devil "was a murderer from the beginning, not holding to the truth, for there is no truth in him" (John 8:44). And John adds that "the devil has been sinning from the beginning" (1 John 3:8).

The temptation

The Lateranum IV declares that *homo vero diaboli suggestione pecccavit* ("man sinned by the suggestion of the devil").[28] The Genesis account tends to bear that out. The tempter used a combination of exaggeration, lie, and half-truth to convince Eve to eat from the tree of the knowledge of good and evil.

Genesis 3:6 describes the nature of the temptation: "When the woman saw that the fruit of the tree was good for food and pleasing to the eye, and also desirable for gaining wisdom, she took some and ate it. She also gave some to her husband, who was with her, and he ate it." We see in this passage a threefold temptation analogous to the threefold lusting described by John (1 John 2:16). There is the excessive desire for sensual gratification ("the cravings of sinful man"). There is the inordinate desire for possessions ("the lust of his eyes"). And there is the inordinate desire to achieve ("the boasting of what he has and does"). None of these desires, when normal, are wrong, but when they are escalated to where they must be satisfied regardless of cost, then they become sin.[29]

The sin

Despite the record we have of the tempter and the temptation, we do not really possess an explanation of human sin. As Berkouwer points out, "Nowhere does Scripture give the slightest explanation for making this transition from God's originally good creation to man's exploitation a matter that is psychologically 'explicable.' "[30]

When all is said and done, sin is ultimately a human decision. To speak of Satan's unbounded power which is irresistible is pure rationalization on the part of a guilty human being.[31] James puts it very bluntly when he writes that "each one is tempted when, by his own evil desire, he is dragged away and enticed. Then, after desire has conceived, it gives birth to sin; and sin, when it is full-grown, gives birth to death" (1:14-15).

Sin is the human attempt to achieve freedom; it is an attempt, as well, to be free of dependence on God. Adam and Eve believed that eating the fruit of the tree at the middle of the Garden would elevate them to the status of God and so they would attain absolute independence. That effort involved their whole being. Sin, then, by its very nature affects the totality of a person, because it seeks to effect the freedom of the whole person. Emil Brunner maintains that

it is as a whole that the person commits sin; this is not due to some part of the personality. I am a sinner, not this or that aspect of my nature. . . . The whole is before the parts. The whole man rebels against God, *ego totus,* and in this rebellion all the individual powers of his mind-body economy are mobilized.[32]

345

The Results of the Fall

Adam and Eve disobeyed God's command not to eat of the tree of the knowledge of good and evil. Their sin had disastrous consequences both immediate and long-term. Human beings still transgress God's laws in a variety of ways and human sin—both individual and collective—still has frightful results.

Alienation

The Fall effected an immediate change in the relationship Adam and Eve had enjoyed with God and the relationship they had enjoyed with each other. Their transgression caused a separation between each of them and the object of their relation, the formal term for which is "alienation."

Alienation portrays "a pathological situation, in which one part of the psyche is out of touch with another part."[33] Garrett uses it as synonymous with "enmity,"[34] and Paul Tillich makes it interchangeable with "estrangement."[35]

John Macquarrie describes alienation as an imbalance within one's existence. It is actually an alienation from oneself which, in turn, results in an estrangement from other existents. Worst of all, it is an awareness of "lostness," of being separated both from one's own being and the being of others, to the degree that one has no "place" in the scheme of life. Such lostness is the result of separation from God.[36]

Alienation from God

Shortly after their sin, Adam and Eve "heard the sound of the Lord God as He was walking in the garden in the cool of the day" (Gen. 3:8). It was evidently His daily custom to meet them. But they sought to avoid Him, hiding from Him in fear—fear resulting from their disobedience.

Sin brought a sense of estrangement or alienation between our first parents and God. He had warned them of the catastrophic consequences should they eat of the forbidden fruit. But they chose willfully to disobey, thereby incurring His wrath and their expulsion from the Garden (Gen. 3:23).

Sin always incurs God's wrath, for it denotes a state of hostility toward Him on the part of the sinner. Paul asserts that "the sinful mind is hostile to God. It does not submit to God's law, nor can it do so" (Rom. 8:7). Brunner contends that alienation from God—from the human point of view—is irreparable; nevertheless,

> man's sin does not shut God out of human existence. The man who has "distorted" his relation with God finds God's presence in a different way. To the sinful man God is present as the Holy God, who allows the disobedient man to feel His resistance. The Bible calls this "resistance" the Wrath of God. . . . As sinner—and this is his "theological existence"—man stands under the Wrath of God.[37]

Alienation from one another

The very first thing that happened after Adam and Eve ate the forbidden fruit was that "the eyes of both of them were opened, and they realized they were naked; so they sewed fig leaves together and made coverings for themselves" (Gen. 3:7). The realization of their nakedness caused them embarrassment and created a separation of the *henosis* they had previously enjoyed.

Further estrangement between the two may be seen in Adam's attempt to blame Eve when God confronted them: "The woman you put here with me—she gave me some fruit from the tree, and I ate it" (Gen. 3:12). Nor would this mutual alienation be only temporary, for God told Eve that "your desire will be for your husband and he will rule over you" (3:16). The union of the two was ruptured for all time.

Since that time, alienation has plagued the whole of the human race. It made itself evident in the children of Adam and Eve. Hatred and jealousy caused Cain to kill his brother Abel (Gen. 4:8). Dale Moody has translated John's reference to Cain's antisocial behavior as follows.

> Everyone who does not do righteousness is not of God, and anyone who does not continue to love his brother, because this is the message which you have heard from the beginning, that we should continue to love one another; and do not be like Cain who was of the evil one and cut the throat of his brother (1 John 3:10-12).[38]

347

While not all human beings since Cain have been criminals, all have been guilty of being estranged from their fellow human beings. Parents are alienated from their offspring, and vice versa; husbands are estranged from their wives, and vice versa; citizens are alienated from their political leaders; workers are alienated from their bosses; and so forth.[39]

Alienation from the created order

When Adam and Eve fell from grace, creation was drastically affected. Paul describes it as being in "bondage to decay" (Rom. 8:21). As a result of sin, humankind and creation became alienated. God told Adam, "Cursed is the ground because of you; through painful toil you will eat of it all the days of your life. It will produce thorns and thistles for you, and you will eat the plants of the field" (Gen. 3:17-18).

This estrangement of humanity from creation may be seen in the human abuse of our ecosystem. Humans have polluted the atmosphere to the point where there is no pure air to be found anywhere in the world. The oceans have become sewers. The land in many areas has been burnt out by chemical fertilizers. Many species of fish and animals have been hunted into extinction. And this is only a small portion of the catalog of evils perpetrated on the created order by people.

Guilt

Our first parents' transgression resulted in guilt. When we talk of guilt here we mean not guilt feelings (which one may experience whether one has committed an offense or not), but rather "the objective state of having violated God's intention for man and thus being liable to punishment."[40] Adam and Eve violated God's command that they should not eat of the tree of the knowledge of good and evil, and they were punished in a variety of ways, including being banished from the Garden of Eden. Cain violated God's intention for him to master sin; he killed his brother Abel and so was placed "under a curse and driven from the ground" (Gen. 4:11).

Guilt arising from sin disrupts the relationship between humankind and God. God made human beings in His image, holy and innocent, and appointed them to be the stewards of His creation. In return, He demanded human fidelity and worship. But they were disobedient. They were unfaithful and rejected God's claims on them by willfully and insolently going their own way. Paul explains it this way: "For although they knew God, they neither glorified him as God nor gave thanks to him, but their thinking became futile and their foolish hearts were darkened" (Rom. 1:21).[41]

Since all humans "have sinned and fall short of the glory of God" (Rom. 3:23), all are guilty. Each one is accountable for his own personal sin. All are liable to God's condemnation and punishment.

Punishment

Closely connected to guilt, as we have seen, is punishment. We know from the Old Testament that, early in their history, human beings became so sinful that God sent a flood in which — with the exception of righteous Noah and his family — "everything on dry land that had the breath of life in its nostrils died" (Gen. 7:22). The history of God's chosen people was a series of sinful behaviors which were punished with retributive acts such as drought, famine, and political oppression. And because the Hebrews would not turn from their sins, God sent the Babylonians to destroy their land and carry them off into exile.

God's wrath

Isaiah summed up God's attitude to the fracture of His laws: "they rebelled and grieved his Holy Spirit. So he turned and became their enemy and he himself fought against them" (Isa. 63:10). Paul Ricoeur defines wrath as the countenance of God's holiness for sinful human beings.[42] It is, he declares, "the sadness of love."[43] God loves human beings with an overwhelming and undeserved love. When they callously rupture that bond of love, His fury is aroused because of the offense to His holiness.

As we have seen, above, God's wrath may be manifested in many forms. Punishment, the outpouring of His wrath, may be physical, natural, or spiritual. It spans a range from privation to physical death to spiritual death.

Death

God warned Adam and Eve against eating the forbidden fruit, telling them that "when you eat of it you will surely die" (Gen. 2:17). Paul makes an observation regarding all sinners, "For the wages of sin is death" (Rom. 6:23). Moody argues that the death in view in both references is not physical but spiritual.

> The physical termination of life does indeed belong to the natural cycle of life, as argued by naturalism. There are limits to physical life, whether the limit be 70, 120 or a thousand years. Therefore, the result of sin in Genesis 2:17 was spiritual death. Man cut himself off from the tree of life (Gen. 3:22-24) on the very day he disobeyed.[44]

Suggestions that Genesis 2:17 can mean "in that day you will surely *begin* to die" do not suit the context very well and misinform later biblical interpretation.[45]

Spiritual death is separation from God. Sin causes such separation at once, and its duration—apart from a divine remedy—is eternal. Its end is the "lake of fire" or "second death" (Rev. 20:14).

The purpose of punishment

Punishment for sin has varying purposes. The first of these is retribution. This is evident in Genesis 9:6: "Whoever sheds the blood of man, by man shall his blood be shed, for in the image of God has God made man." Because of the sacrilege of destroying God's image, the death penalty—not rehabilitation, obviously, but clearly retributive—was exacted. Psalm 94:1 speaks of God as "the God who avenges," vengeance being the synonym for retribution. The Old Testament records several instances of divine retribution against sinners (Isa. 1:24; 61:2; Jer. 46:10; Ezek. 25:14).[46] James Orr contends:

> One thing certain is that the presence and working of a retributive justice in men's lives and in the history of the world have ever had a place among the deepest and most solemn convictions of the noblest portions of our race. The Bible need not be appealed to: its testimony is beyond

dispute. . . . retribution, nevertheless, stern and terrible, there is, interweaving itself with every strain of sinful existence. . . .[47]

Orr demonstrates convincingly that retribution is an underlying universal factor in religious thought, whether it be Hinduism, Buddhism, or ancient Greek polytheism.[48]

Punishment is also disciplinary in nature. God punishes people in an effort to motivate them to change. The Bible tells us that the Lord disciplines those whom He loves (Prov. 3:11-12). We have seen such disciplinary punishment in the life of the Israelites. The Psalmist Asaph notes about the Hebrew people:

> God's anger rose against them; He put to death the sturdiest among them, cutting down the young men of Israel. In spite of all this, they kept on sinning; in spite of His wonders, they did not believe. So He ended their days in futility and their years in terror. Whenever God slew them, they would seek Him; they eagerly turned to Him again. They remembered that God was their Rock, that God Most High was their Redeemer (Ps. 78:31-35).

Punishment should be seen as a favor to the offender, as a help to a proper appreciation of the malignity of what he has done.[49] Once again, this concept of severely punishing a wrongdoer, without attempting to be vindictive, is a universal principle.

Unfreedom

Because of sin, Adam and Eve lost their original freedom to achieve the destiny God had intended them to have. They "sold out" to Satan and, as a consequence, became the possession of evil.

Since sin is universal in its scope (see the following chapter), for all have sinned, the human state is one — as Augustine has put it — of *non posse non peccare* ("not able not to sin"). Humans accordingly are unable to accept the consequences of being God's image, namely, of relating lovingly toward both God and their fellow creatures.[50]

None of what has been said should be seen in a deterministic sense. Even as sinners, human beings remain responsible persons. They are still the image of God, despite having abdicated most of their responsibilities as such. Brunner argues

> sin itself is a sign and an expression of the fact of our humanity; the more we understand man as a sinner, the more we understand him as a responsible being. The depth of human sin does not diminish man's responsibility; on the contrary, the greater the sin, the more responsible and therefore the more guilty does man become. Thus we would be minimizing the gravity of sin, were we to deny that man possesses the *Imago Dei* in this sense, or even were we to minimize its reality.[51]

Because of the image and in spite of sin, humans retain a potential for cultural and innovative freedom. Consequently, they may be painters, sculptors, musicians, poets, scientists, politicians, and so forth. Yet all of these endeavors are tinged to some degree with sin (as is every human concern). But not all endeavors have been corrupted by sin to the same extent. As one moves farther and farther away from the relationship between human and human, and especially between human and God, the less obvious the taint of sin may become.[52]

When we discuss human freedom, we are really discussing a particular kind of relationship. To live a truly free life is to live in a relationship of *(agapē)* love with one's fellows and with one's God. E. Cherbonnier asserts that the difference between a false god and the true One is that "a false god can be detected by the fact that, having once become the repository of a man's allegiance, it straightway proceeds to destroy his freedom. Conversely, the true God preserves and enhances it."[53] When one is oriented toward the true God, one's relationships are transformed. No longer is fulfillment sought by enslaving one's neighbor, becoming apathetic toward him, or becoming her psychological slave. Sin may be seen in an opposite light: it does not free human beings but places them in bondage.[54]

Conclusions

So, then, while sinners do have freedoms of some sorts, they do not possess freedom to be righteous or holy, the freedom to relate properly to their fellow humans and their God. The sinner "possesses freedom in the sense of a *libertas civilis* — not only freedom from compulsion, but creative and moral freedom, in so far as we eliminate from this freedom the element of true goodness, in the sense of real love to God and man."[55]

Egocentricity

Gustaf Aulén describes sin as "negatively unbelief and positively egocentricity."[56] Reinhold Niebuhr attributes it to "pride and self-love to the observable behavior of men."[57] And Augustus Strong determines it to be the "choice of self as . . . the antithesis of supreme love to God."[58]

This choice of self over God may manifest itself in various forms, the chief of which is that pride which replaces the glory of God by the glory of humankind. Paul has summed it up well in Romans 1:23. Millard Erickson defines this consequence of sin as

preferring one's own ideas to God's truth. It is preferring the satisfaction of one's own will to doing God's will. It is loving oneself more than God. The dethronement of God from his rightful place as Lord of one's life requires the enthronement of something else, and this is understood to be the enthronement of oneself.[59]

Egocentricity may be seen in a wide spectrum of sin — indeed, in all sin. Kierkegaard hit the nail on the head when he argued that disobedience to God and His commands is self-assertion (or, egocentricity). Such disobedience may yield itself in the well-known kinds of sin such as vice and willfulness or in the lesser-noticed types such as legal righteousness and resulting despair.[60] But all are examples of the rebellion of the ego or self against God.

Self-deceit

Concomitant to egocentricity is human self-deceit. Because human beings have chosen to exalt self in the place of God, their opinion of themselves tends to be somewhat lavish. Reinhold Niebuhr avows that an element of deceit is involved in this self-glorification. . . . Since [humanity's] determinate existence does not deserve the devotion lavished upon it, it is obviously necessary to practice some deception in order to justify such expressive devotion. While such deception is constantly directed against competing wills, seeking to secure their acceptance and validation of the self's too generous opinion of itself, its primary purpose is to deceive, not others, but the self.[61]

The Bible is replete with allusions to sin's use of deception. Paul, in particular, accuses humans of self-delusion because of the effects of sin on their lives: "For although they knew God, they neither glorified him as God nor gave thanks to him, but their thinking became futile and their foolish hearts were darkened" (Rom. 1:21). He also notes how sin works to affect humans: "For sin, seizing the opportunity afforded by the commandment, deceived me, and through the commandment put me to death" (Rom. 7:11). The writer to the Hebrews exhorts his readers toward daily mutual encouragement, "so that none of you may be hardened by sin's deceitfulness" (3:13). And John calls Satan that ancient serpent "who leads the whole world astray" (Rev. 12:9).

The self-deception which follows sin is neither complete ignorance nor yet complete dishonesty. Rather, it is a combination of some of each. The sinner is ignorant (in the true sense of the word), thinking self to be the very center of existence, not realizing that its ability for self-transcendence is by no means complete and that it is not the ultimate judge. The Babylonians are representative of such ignorance; Isaiah describes their mind-set: "Your wisdom and knowledge mislead you when you say to yourself, 'I am, and there is none besides me' " (Isa. 47:10). In spite of such a mind-set, deep down the individual is aware of his or her finiteness. Thus, his or her pretensions can be maintained only by voluntary ignorance. "In moments of crisis the true situation may be vividly revealed to the self. . . . "[62]

Since the self can never fully obscure the truth of its sin and finiteness, it must resort to these less than fully convincing deceptions in an effort to persuade itself of the truth of a lie. Thus, it is particularly important to deceive others into believing what it cannot fully believe; then it has acquired allies in the effort to deceive itself.[63]

Shame

In their original state, Adam and Eve "were both naked, and they felt no shame" (Gen. 2:25). But then they sinned, breaking God's law and betraying the trust that had existed between them and their Creator and between them and each other. "Then the eyes of both of them were opened, and they realized they were naked . . . and made coverings for themselves" (Gen. 3:7). Their transgression introduced the need for self-protection from all others—the Lord included—because of a sense of shame. As Adam put it, "I was afraid because I was naked, so I hid" (Gen. 3:10).

We see from the Genesis account that transgressing God's command has relational consequences, not just between God and a human being, but between persons. Fracturing God's law issues in shame before a fellow human being. Claus Westermann evidences considerable concern that, in our day and age, we are losing that sense of shame's purpose. Its significance, he anguishes, "both with regard to human life and with regard to the nature of human community, is something of which we are scarcely aware anymore."[64] He blames the possibility of human existence without shame on a tendency to restrict the meaning of the word to sexual interaction. Shame, however, has to do with the whole human being. Indeed, "it is bound up even more intimately and unqualifiedly with human existence than is the act of sinning, or sins, or guilt."[65] While one may hypothesize sinless human existence, because of Christ, it is impossible to sever shame from human existence. To talk about one being shameless is very well in regard to a child, for whom it signifies innocence, but in an adult it refers to absolute degradation to a subhuman level. "This riddle of man who was made by God and yet in his own existence invariably exemplifies a telltale defect is most crassly presented in the phenomenon of being ashamed."[66]

Shame, one writer has remarked,

brings terrifying self-doubt. Eve and Adam are no longer sure they are worthy as they are, unadorned and naked. Hiding from each other and from God is a way of hiding from themselves, guarding their nakedness from another who might speak honestly about what he or she sees. And notice how quickly man and woman, now doubting their own worth, try to direct attention away from themselves by pointing the finger at someone else.[67]

Shame has been defined as the failure to live up to a socio-parental goal or ideal. Shame frequently is the result of situations of incongruity which jeopardize "who a person is."[68] In this instance, the socio-parental ideal is the standard of perfect obedience and righteousness set by the Father of creation, God.

Because all human beings are sinners, all are subject to the experience of shame. Shame makes one feel vulnerable. Hiding and covering that vulnerability serves only to multiply it. Unable to deal constructively with their shame, people seek power in an effort to make themselves more secure. And often, shame is the very weapon they use to hurt and destroy others as they seek to isolate themselves from its effects. "Shame relies predominantly on external or group pressure and is reinforced by the internal pressure of fear of being shamed."[69]

Conclusions

Originally human beings were created as God's image, righteous and holy, capable of fulfilling His purposes for them as relational beings and stewards of creation. The sin of the first human couple shattered the serenity of this original state. While they did not lose God's image, sin led to their abdicating many of its obligations. Relationally—to God and one another—their capacities were seriously flawed. Instead of being stewards of God's creation, they became its abusers.

This Fall was a time and space event perpetrated by a literal pair of human beings, the first originally created by God. It is no myth. That the story is recounted in highly figurative language does not remove it from the realm of actual historical occurrence.

That our first parents were tempted by an external sinful agent does not remove them from the sphere of accountability. Satan's power is not—nor has it ever been—irresistible. The reason for this original sin was a conscious, active decision on the part of those who committed it.

The sin of Adam and Eve had calamitous results both for them and for all human beings since. Sin brings to human beings alienation from God, one another, and all of creation. It engenders guilt within the transgressor and makes one liable to God's condemnation and punishment. God's wrath, poured out upon these human rebels, leads to spiritual death.

Sin also brings bondage. Adam and Eve lost their original freedom with all of its privileges. Nor are present-day sinners able to live a life of genuine freedom, regardless of how much liberty they may seem to enjoy in certain areas of their existence. They are still slaves to sin. Egocentricity, the choice of self above God, is a sign of one's sin. It comes about through self-deceit, a choice deliberately made by the sinner to foster certain delusions of grandeur and transcendence which simply are not true. Above all, sin brings feelings of shame, as offenders seek to hide their vulnerability under varying cloaks physically, emotionally, intellectually, and spiritually.

One may counter by admitting that, while the above is true with regard to Adam and Eve, it was *their* sin and no one else's. In view of the Old Testament teaching that no one is held liable for another's sin, how can it be said that the sin of the first human couple had calamitous results for all humankind? Such an argument would seem to become especially implauisble given the rejection of Genesis as a symbol of the universal sin of all humanity. These problems will be dealt with in the following chapter on the transmission of sin.

Chapter Twelve
The Transmission
of Sin

W
e have demonstrated that sin is universal; all human beings, with the exception of Jesus Christ, are transgressors. We have further established that sin entered the world through an historical person—Adam. Beyond this point, however, things become somewhat murky. Scholars can agree that Adam's transgression has some bearing on the universality of sin. But there is very little agreement on exactly what the link is, or on how sin is communicated from one person to another.

The Difficulty: Augustine of Hippo

Much of the problem in establishing a reasonable doctrine of the transmission of sin may be laid at the doorstep of the premier theologian of the church, Augustine of Hippo. He believed that, because of Adam's transgression, he (Adam) and all of his posterity were infected with depravity, so much so that even infants who perished unwashed by the waters of baptism would be shut out of heaven. Because he did not feel that these little ones deserved hell, he created limbo (a place neither of suffering nor of bliss) as their ultimate destiny.

The reason for such a supposition, as we noted earlier, was

Augustine's use of a Latin mistranslation of Romans 5:12. He changed the statement "because all sinned" to "in whom all sinned," thereby creating the idea of a guilt universally inherited from Adam.

> Nothing remains but to conclude that in the first man all are understood to have sinned, because all were in him when he sinned; whereby sin is brought in with birth and not removed save by the new birth. . . . It is manifest that in Adam all sin, so to speak, en masse. Hence, by that sin we become a corrupt mass — *massa perditionis*.[1]

The church by and large — and especially the Reformers — have perpetuated this error of interpretation. Calvin revived the Augustinian view, defining original sin as "a hereditary depravity and corruption of our nature, diffused into all parts of the soul, which first makes us liable to God's wrath" and "since we through his transgression have become entangled in the curse, he is said to have made us guilty."[2] Henri Rondet's *Original Sin*[3] tracks the history of the interpretation of this misinterpretation from Augustine to modern times, but accepts its idea of inherited guilt because it is Catholic tradition. G.C. Berkouwer, the Dutch Calvinist, in his classic work, *Sin*, notes Augustine's mistranslation of the Greek of Romans 5:12 and then asks, "Is an essential difference implied when we change the translation from *in whom* to *because?* Or is there no difference at all?"[4] But he appeals to various theologians and doctrinal statements rather than Scripture to support the Augustinian theory. Dale Moody's conclusion to all of this is that, "if ever there was a triumph of erroneous tradition over the teaching of Scripture, here is exhibit A."[5] This perpetuation of Augustine's error has made getting at the truth a slow and tempestuous process.

Some Treatments of Sin's Transmission

If the doctrine of sin were a peripheral concern for the church, the confusion surrounding how sin is transmitted might be understandable and permissible. But an understanding of sin is vital to the Christian faith. And over the years, theologians have attempted to advance various theories of sin's transmission.

Realism

The theory of realism teaches that all human nature existed in Adam prior to his transgression. When he sinned, therefore, the common human nature that was in him fell too. Thus, Adam's act of disobedience was quite literally the disobedience of all humanity. Consequently, every human being who enters this world — being an individualization of the common nature fallen in Adam — is guilty of, and punishable for, Adam's sin.[6] That sin, someone has said, "is ours not because it is imputed to us; but it is imputed to us, because it is truly and properly ours."[7]

Charles Hodge suggests that the above statement is true and yet not true. Adam's sin is not our sin in the same way as it was his. His transgression was the result of his own willful action; but our will and conscience were not employed in his act. "The sense in which many assert that the act of Adam was our act, is, that the same numerical nature or substance, the same reason and will which existed and acted in Adam, belong to us; so that we were truly and properly the agents of his act of apostasy."[8]

Jonathan Edwards: a Platonic variation

Edwards taught a variation on the realistic theory. His view was that, while humans are not one and the same in numerical identity of substance, they are nonetheless one because God wills to regard them as such. All of creation, including the human soul, he contended, is one "as a series of new effects produced in every successive moment by the renewed efficiency of God."[9]

Such a view of sin makes God purely arbitrary in His determination, declaring that those who are in fact separate identities are one. A declaration of common guilt, therefore, is also an arbitrary act. While this variation on the realistic theory fits in extremely well with a hyper-Calvinistic theory of double predestination (a position held by Edwards) — for it clearly predestines to condemnation all who have not been elected to salvation — it militates against the biblical teaching of the character of God as perfect love and justice.

North American realism

Realism was popularized in North America by W.G.T. Shedd. He declared that human nature existed en masse in Adam; when he fell, all human nature fell with him, and so every living person enters this world having participated in and guilty of Adam's transgression.[10] Augustus Strong also emphasized realism, holding that all people "existed, not individually, but seminally" in Adam.[11] More recently, Millard Erickson has espoused this position (with minor modifications), asserting that "we were all involved in Adam's sin, and thus receive both the corrupted nature that was his after the fall, and the guilt and condemnation that attach to his sin."[12]

Conclusions

The realistic theory of sin falls far short in its endeavor to explain original sin, or to help us to determine how sin is transmitted. Rather than making an attempt to formulate a biblical theology of sin, it seeks merely to uphold and explain the Augustinian error of hereditary guilt, suggesting that we all committed Adam's sin, and that we voluntarily rebelled against God while still in our first parents' loins. Even worse, it makes God appear to be vindictive and arbitrary. If we who are sinful human beings would not punish anyone who committed a wrongful act but who was incapable of responsibility, God who is perfect in His character and justice would not condemn His creatures for an act they supposedly perpetrated before they were even born, much less before attaining to an age of reason and moral responsibility.

Federalism

The federal or covenantal theory posits that God selected Adam to represent all of humanity in a supposed "covenant of works" He had made with all human beings. This covenant—an informal and unstructured arrangement—is set out in Genesis 1:28ff. That God commanded Adam and Eve to "be fruitful and multiply" is an indication of the involvement of all of Adam's posterity. A further aspect of this covenant is found in Genesis 2:15-17. While God's commands here do not explicitly mention any descendants of Adam and Eve, Eve understood them in such a light, for she quotes (in Gen. 3:3) the prohibition given Adam in 2:17. If Adam obeyed God, humans would gain eternal life; but if he disobeyed, all humans would suffer corruption and death. All the sad results of the sin of Adam and Eve which are described in Genesis 3:14-19 are a divinely inspired catalog of the effects of original sin. Buswell argues:

> Certainly, if these things are, as the Scripture declares, the consequence upon all mankind of the sin of Adam, we must understand a covenant relationship between God and Adam for all his posterity as the logical basis for what has taken place.[13]

Because of Adam's transgression, the guilt of his sin has been imputed to all human beings. As a consequence, all are born subject to a depraved human nature. This depravity is the consequence of the imputation and not its cause. "Thus, like realism, the federal theory is a theory of immediate imputation of Adamic guilt to all human beings."[14]

One of the earliest proponents of federalism was John Cocceius. Charles Hodge and James P. Boyce popularized the theory in North America. Hodge (1797-1878), longtime professor at Princeton Theological Seminary, defended federalism as the correct theory of the imputation of guilt because Adam was both the natural (i.e., realistic) as well as the federal head of his progeny: "This is plain . . . from the narrative given in Genesis. Everything there said to Adam was said to him in his representative capacity."[15] Boyce felt that federalism was necessary for "conferring the privileges of success where the evils of failure would not be increased, and preparing the way for future grace in the representation in Christ."[16]

Conclusions

Federalism has two great weaknesses. There are no passages of Scripture which explicitly set forth a covenant as suggested by the theory's promoters. And the idea of God *imputing* guilt to Adam's posterity seems to make God capricious in His judgment. As Berkouwer points out, "Therefore we stand before an entirely different conception of original sin than we find in the doctrine of realism. . . . here the sin of Adam is imputed and assigned to all his progeny."[17]

Example

The theory of a bad example, as we have seen (in section 1), was initially proposed by the Pelagian school (A.D. 409). It reacted against the Latin (Catholic) idea as typified by Augustine that all humans have inherited guilt—and hence condemnation—for Adam's transgression. Pelagius held to a creationist theory of the soul's origin, namely, that every soul is individually and immediately created by God. It must therefore be created innocent and free from any taint of sin. Thus, each newborn person comes into the world as able to be obedient to God's law as were Adam and Eve at their creation.

The Pelagians, then, denied that a person could be held responsible for something over which he had no control. Their doctrine was constructed upon an Eastern Orthodox foundation of freedom of the will. Apart from the inability to choose freely between good and evil, one cannot be held morally responsible.

Pelagius denied both original sin and the transmission of guilt from one person to another by biological means. Adam's sin affected Adam and no one else. His sin was imputed only to himself and to no one else. Indeed, insisted Pelagians, the idea of innately sinful nature would make God the author of sin because He is the Creator of that nature.

Arminianism

Arminius held to a concept of the Adamic unity of humankind as taught by John Calvin, but he reinterpreted it in the direction of Semi-Pelagianism. He maintained that all human beings have, because of Adam's sin, lost original grace, and therefore they are totally incapable apart from divine assistance of obeying God and so attaining eternal reward. Because God is perfectly just, He grants to every human from birth a special empowering of His Holy Spirit which overcomes the pejorative effects of inherited corruption and permits perfect obedience to the divine will, if that individual is willing to cooperate with the Holy Spirit.[18]

While corruption is inherited from Adam, God does not—because of His justice—impute guilt and condemnation to Adam's posterity because of it. Adam's corrupt nature and its consequent guilt accrue to each human being only at the point of his or her own voluntary transgression (which is avoidable because of prevenient grace).[19]

Contemporary views

In more recent times, the Socinians and the Unitarians have carried on the Pelagian teachings on sin. Adam in sinning hurt only himself and no one else. But while his sin and guilt were not imputed to his posterity and had no debilitating effect on human nature, it did set a terrible example for every human being who came after him. That there is any causal relationship, however, between the sin of the first human couple and the sins of their descendants is absurd. Adam was not a legal representative of humanity and no person is condemned to death or loss because of him. Each person sins by his or her own light, and God judges human beings only for those sins they have personally committed.[20]

Conclusions

Pelagianism, not surprisingly, was condemned as a heresy. Socinianism and Unitarianism has been regarded in a similar vein. While one may sympathize with the desire of these groups to obviate original sin in the sense of inherited moral guilt and condemnation, the idea of Adam's sin having only an exemplary effect produces results which run counter to biblical truth. If all humans are born in a state of innocence or original righteousness, and have essentially the same freedom of will that was possessed by Adam and Eve, then some may possibly be living in a sinless state. Such a condition would refute the biblical teaching that "all have sinned and fall short of the glory of God" (Rom. 3:23). Because of universal sin, we must conclude that Adam's sin had some substantial universal effect beyond that of being simply a negative example.

Social and biological transmission

Walter Rauschenbusch argued for the social aspect of sin while retaining its character as rebellion against God. As an evolutionist, he relegated the Genesis account of Adam to mythology. Rauschenbusch believed that moral evil—and he held as examples such as retardation, neuroses, and perverse desires—was passed on biologically.

Science, to some extent, corroborates the doctrine of original sin. Evil does flow down the generations through the channels of biological coherence. Idiocy and feeble-mindedness, neurotic disturbances, weakness of inhibition, perverse desires, stubbornness and anti-social impulses in children must have had their adequate biological causes somewhere back on the line, even if we lack the records.[21]

At the same time, he considered the "old theology" in regard to original sin and its transmission overworked. It failed to recognize freedom of the human will and made the effect of hereditary sin so overwhelming that personal sin was trivialized and made virtually irrelevant.

Much more important was the social transmission of evil. "Only the lack of social information and orientation in the past can explain the fact that theology has made so little of this."[22] Here, he followed Ritschl in depicting a "Kingdom of Evil" to blame for social sins. The profligacy of adulthood is not conveyed by heredity, but is achieved through socialization. Vices such as alcoholism, narcotics usage, and sexual perversity all are "hereditary social evils . . . forced on the individual embedded in the womb of society."[23] While some theologians put such evils down to bad example, it goes far beyond such simplistic interpretations. One must consider the spiritual authority society exerts upon its constituents. "In the main the individual takes over his moral judgments and valuations from his social class, profession, neighbourhood, and nation, making only slight personal modifications in the group standards."[24]

Because Rauschenbusch rejected the historicity of the Adam account, he also denied any traditional theories of the imputation of guilt, limiting it to actual sins, whether individual or corporate.[25]

Voluntarily appropriated depravity

The theory of voluntarily appropriated depravity asserts that, because of Adam's disobedience, human beings do not possess original righteousness. As a consequence, unless God intervenes supernaturally to help them, they cannot obey Him. Such inability is physical and mental, but excludes the will. If the will is willing to cooperate with God's Holy Spirit, He will help it to be obedient. Human depravity is imputed only when the individual actively and consciously transgresses. Like the early Eastern Church, the holders of this theory believe that physical and spiritual death do not result from Adam's transgression but rather are the result of the sin of each human.[26]

Original Sin but Not Original Guilt

Augustine's formulation of inherited guilt because of original sin was made in the context of the Pelagian controversy. Pelagius, building on the Orthodox concept of sin, held that all human beings are born with the freedom to choose good or evil. Nor are they under any compulsion toward depraved behavior. As far as he was concerned, original sin and original guilt beyond Adam and Eve themselves are nonexistent.

Pelagius did not argue against the universality of sin. But he responded to it by positing that it is the result of imitation. Like many others who argue against original sin, he was concerned about individual personal accountability. He wanted to stress that transgression is the result of one's own will; it cannot be blamed on someone else.

Pelagius' theology was condemned in 418 by the Council of Carthage — and rightly so. Scripture is clear on the fact of original sin. Heredity tends toward sin; human consciousness is scarcely moral from its outset; all human beings enter a sinful environment.[27] Because of Adam's transgression, all of his progeny suffer a predisposition toward sin.

Original — or inherited — guilt is another matter. Augustine's doctrine that all human beings are made guilty (and the similar doctrine of others since) because of Adam's sin is simply unbiblical. Ezekiel disposes of such a concept.

> What do you people mean by quoting this proverb about the land of Israel: "The fathers eat sour grapes and the children's teeth are set on edge?" As surely as I live, declares the Sovereign Lord, you will no longer quote this proverb in Israel. For every living soul belongs to me, the father as well as the son — both alike belong to me. The soul who sins is the one who will die (18:2-4).

12.1: A SUMMARY OF THE THEORIES OF THE TRANSMISSION OF SIN

Realism

Jonathan Edwards   *W.G.T. Shedd*
Augustus Strong   *Millard Erickson*

All human nature resided in Adam; when he fell, all human nature fell with him. All, therefore, are guilty of Adam's sin.

Federalism

John Cocceius   *Charles Hodge*
James P. Boyce   *J.O. Buswell II*

God established with Adam (who represented all his posterity) a covenant. By breaking this covenant, Adam implicated all his progeny. Guilt as covenant-breakers is therefore imputed to all humanity.

Example

Pelagius   *Socinians*
Unitarians

All human beings are born into the world in the same innocent pre-Fall state as Adam and Eve. Sin is not transmitted, except by example.

Social Transmission

Albrecht Ritschl   *Walter Rauschenbusch*
Reinhold Niebuhr

Sinful behavior, both individual and corporate, is achieved through socialization, not by heredity.

Biological Transmission

Augustine of Hippo   *John Calvin*
E.Y. Mullins

There are two different views here: (1) (Original) sin and guilt are biologically transmitted from Adam to all his kin.

(2) Only the tendency to sin (and not condemnation) is transmitted from Adam to his posterity.

The prophet gives an illustration of a righteous man who faithfully keeps God's laws (18:5ff). "That man is righteous; he will surely live, declares the Sovereign Lord" (18:9). That man has a son who is violent and perverse (18:10ff). "Will such a man live? He will not! Because he has done all these detestable things, he will surely be put to death and his blood will be on his own head" (18:13). If that wicked man has a son who witnesses his father's evil deeds but does not follow in his footsteps (18:14), "he will not die for his father's sin; he will surely live. But his father will die for his own sin" (18:17-18). Ezekiel reiterates that

> the soul who sins is the one who will die. The son will not share the guilt of the father, nor will the father share the guilt of the son. The righteousness of the righteous man will be credited to him, and the wickedness of the wicked will be charged against him (18:20).

Ezekiel makes it very clear, then, that the guilt of the fathers is not charged against their children. Thus, we may be sure that Adam's guilt has not been passed on to us. The idea of inherited guilt contradicts the biblical teaching here.

A Proposal on Sin's Transmission

We have established that human beings have been affected by Adam's sin. At the same time, the Bible teaches that the father's sin will not be charged against his children; we may conclude, then, that God does not impute the sin of Adam against his posterity. Consequently, we may rule out the concept of inherited guilt.

How does one become guilty before God? The Bible declares that every soul is guilty before God because of that individual's personal sin. Thus, divine condemnation occurs not for hereditary sin, but only for actual, personal sin.[28]

What part does Adam's sin play in the lives of his posterity? It gave sin the opportunity to establish a beachhead or staging area within humankind. All human beings have been infected by the "virus" of sin. As Moody argues, "There is no denial of inherited sin when inherited sin is interpreted as a state of sin in which there are tendencies that later lead to actual transgression."[29]

In speculating on how this "original sin" or tendency which leads to actual transgression is transmitted from Adam to his progeny, Augustine may have been right in his premise that it is biologically passed on from parent to child (though not necessarily by the father alone!), even though he was in error in regard to the transmission of guilt. Studies have shown that varying aspects of personality such as shyness are genetically transmitted; we know that tendencies toward alcoholism and depression may be transmitted biologically;[30] why not the tendency toward sin? We may assume, then, that each infant born into the world possesses that gene, as it were, that predisposes toward sin.[31]

Sin, however, does not move into actual transgression apart from the law. Paul asserts that "where there is no law there is no transgression" (Rom. 4:15). He notes that "before the law was given, sin was in the world. But sin is not taken into account [i.e., imputed] when there is no law" (Rom. 5:13). Furthermore, "apart from the law, sin is dead" (Rom. 7:8). Until one becomes aware of the law, sin is dormant in that individual's life. That is why Paul says, "Once I was alive apart from the law; but when the commandment came, sin sprang to life and I died" (Rom. 7:9).

Sin may be compared to the HIV virus. It lurks seemingly dormant within its human host; but at some point it suddenly explodes into AIDS, and its destructive power becomes evident to all. Ultimately, it causes death. Sin is seemingly inactive in one ignorant of the law (as in a child), but when knowledge of the law dawns, guilt over transgression occurs and sin kills spiritually as one becomes cognizant of one's real condition before God. As we have already demonstrated (in section 2), until there is an awareness of guilt (that is, of having transgressed the law), the penalty of eternal death is not imputed. It is mitigated by the Savior's atonement.

We see that guilt is charged against the sinner only on account of his or her own personal transgression, not because of Adam's. Because all transgress, all are guilty. In this way there is a solidarity of all human beings with Adam.

Because penalty for sin is charged against a person only upon awareness of the law, we realize that fears for the salvation of infants or for those who are born and grow up mentally incapacitated (to the point where they cannot deal with abstract principles such as guilt) are unnecessary. Because these people cannot repent, believe, or realize that they have committed any sin, guilt is not imputed to them and, should they die in that state, they will go to be with Christ. As Mullins says, "We do not know how the grace of God operates in them. But we are fully assured that Christ provided for them, and that they are created anew in him and saved."[32]

Some Conclusions

The Bible, while emphasizing that Adam's transgression exacted a toll from his posterity, does not set out in specific details exactly what that toll is or the way in which it occurs. The result has been that systematicians, in trying to formulate a theology of sin — especially in regard to its effects and transmission — have faced some real stumbling blocks. Accordingly, we have seen a variety of explanations, some closer to the biblical faith than others.

But the Bible does give us strong hints in some places, and in others advises, as to what effects Adam's sin has not incurred. On these bases, therefore, we may proceed to recognize those doctrinal positions which are (at least) more correct biblically than others. We know from Ezekiel 18 that the guilt of the parents is not imputed to their children; accordingly, we may conclude that the guilt of Adam and Eve, our first parents, has not been imputed to us. We know that God is not the author of sin and so any doctrine that would make Him such is specious. We know from Romans 5 that Adam's sin had much more of an impact on the human race than simply that of a bad example; when combined with the knowledge that sin is universal, we may discard any theories of example. Adam's sin had much more impact than that alone. Some theories, such as biological and social transmission, and some forms of voluntarily appropriated depravity are all right as far as they go, but tend to be incomplete, or they miss the mark by failing to consider all of the biblical evidence.

Even though most theories fall short, we must not give up trying to make sense of how sin infects us and of the ramifications of that disease. We would propose, therefore, that human beings have indeed been affected on a universal scale by what transpired in that first sin in Eden. But we do not share in the actual guilt of Adam and Eve, and so would rule out inherited guilt and its resultant condemnation. The Bible teaches that we are guilty before God because of our own sins (Rom. 5:12).

Adam's sin does nonetheless play a major role in our lives, for because of it, sin established a beachhead in human life. Adam's sin created a "virus," so to speak, tending toward sin, which infects every human being coming into the world, being passed from parent to child in biological transmission. The guilt for sin, however, is not imputed to an individual until he recognizes that he is a sinner by apprehending his or her guilt under the law. When that awareness of accountability as a lawbreaker occurs, the virus of sin becomes full-blown and guilt for transgression is then imputed and spiritual death occurs. Thus, those who do not reach a point of awareness and accountability are in a state of imputed innocence in which their sins are covered by the finished work of Christ on Calvary. They are one with the saints in belonging to Christ.

All human beings, however, both saved and unsaved alike, are never free from sin and its effects in this life. Not only do we strive with the sin nature within ourselves, but always, waiting for an opportunity to push us over the edge into transgression, are those superhuman beings known as Satan and his demonic forces.

Chapter Thirteen
The Power and Dominion of Sin

O ur studies have shown that the author of sin—and the first sinful being—was an angelic creature called the devil. He is depicted in Genesis as the beguiling serpent in the Garden of Eden and in Revelation as the dragon whose end is in the lake of fire. Throughout Scripture he is shown hard at work causing havoc, misery, and loss for human beings.

Some theologians (e.g., Rudolf Bultmann) would have us believe that Satan is only a myth, and that he should be accepted as such so that we can move into the modern age theologically as well as technologically. Not all theologians are of that same opinion. Emil Brunner, for instance, cites the wars and despotism of our age, observing that, "on the contrary, it is just because our generation has expressed such diabolical wickedness that many people have abandoned their former 'enlightened' objection to the existence of a 'power of darkness' and are now prepared to believe in Satan as represented in the Bible."[1]

The Devil

The ultimate determination for Christians of the devil's existence as a personal being of evil is simply that Jesus has affirmed his reality. Our Lord had more to say about the devil than anyone else in Scripture. As Michael Green states, "One would have thought that the teaching and behaviour of Jesus on this important subject was sufficient to settle the matter for Christians."[2]

Satan's origin

If God created all that exists out of nothing, where did Satan come from? There is only one possible answer: he is a creature of God. What is more, since God created all things good (Gen. 1:31), Satan must be one of God's good creatures who went bad.

We do not receive much information from the Bible on the origin of Satan. Some have cited Ezekiel 28:11ff—the dirge on the prince of Tyre—as a symbolic account of the devil's origin and fall.[3] But the context seems to go against such a view. And even if one discounts the context, the passage is symbolic of the expulsion of Adam and Eve from the Garden, and not the ejection of Satan from Paradise.

The Old Testament does give us a hint, however, in Job. Here, we find the devil among the sons of God or angels (1:6). We may assume, then, that he is an angel who fell from grace.

The New Testament gives us more information. Revelation 12:7-9 fills in some of the gaps in our knowledge.

And there was war in heaven. Michael and his angels fought against the dragon, and the dragon and his angels fought back. But he was not strong enough, and they lost their place in heaven. The great dragon was hurled down—that ancient serpent called the devil or Satan, who leads the whole world astray. He was hurled to the earth and his angels with him.

We discover here that Satan was an habitué of heaven, an angel who rebelled against God. Michael, to whom Jude refers as an archangel (v. 9), evidently the captain of the heavenly host, swept the offender and his minions out of heaven. They now inhabit the earth. From the Jude account we must surmise that Satan was of a higher order than even Michael, for the latter "when he was disputing with the devil about the body of Moses, did not dare to bring a slanderous accusation against him, but said, 'The Lord rebuke you!' " (v. 9)

Rebuking suggests official superiority. Had the archangel been of an order superior to the devil, he would have rebuked him and not have felt it necessary to appeal to the Lord to do so.[4]

The devil's aliases

The archenemy does not go only under the title of "devil." We find from Scripture that he operates under a variety of aliases, many of which are descriptive of his character or work.

Satan

The devil's most popular pseudonym comes from the Hebrew *Sātān*, which means "adversary." In the Old Testament, surprisingly to some, Satan occurs only four times, both as a title ("the" Satan)—twice in Job and once in Zechariah—and as a proper name (in 1 Chronicles). In Job, he is seen as the accusing angel who seeks to test Job's devotion to God (1:6-12; 2:1-7). In Zechariah 3:1ff, Satan accuses Joshua the high priest and is rebuked by God. In 1 Chronicles 21:1, he incites David to number Israel, a sinful act which earns God's punishment for the Israelite king.

While Satan is not clearly viewed by the Old Testament as a wicked being, but more as an accusing angel, he is fully unmasked in the New as the devil (Gk. *diabolos*). The antipathy between God and Satan is indicated by the latter's attempts to coerce Jesus into worshiping him (Matt. 4:1ff). Our Lord identifies him as the head of the kingdom of evil (Matt. 12:26). Satan's end is forecast in Revelation 20:10 as the lake of fire where "he will be tormented day and night for ever and ever."

The serpent

We first run across the devil in the Old Testament in the guise of a serpent. Although the Genesis writer calls him only "serpent," other inspired writers (e.g., Rev. 12:9) identify him as Satan, the devil. That the creature described in Genesis 3 could not have been a mere reptile is obvious, for no reptile could talk, let alone argue or reason. Paul tells us that Satan will disguise himself as an angel of light (2 Cor. 11:14) and some interpreters have suggested that the devil appeared to Adam and Eve as a being of splendor and light.[5] Certainly, it would be much easier to picture Eve being deceived by a creature of beauteous light than by a slithering snake!

In the literature of Bible times, the identification of the devil with the serpent is quite common. For example, in the Apocrypha we find such references in Wisdom (2:24) and in the Psalms of Solomon (4:9); in the New Testament, in Romans (16:20) and Revelation (12:9; 20:2).

Son of God

In Job, Satan appears to be numbered among the "sons of God" (1:6, Heb.). This term generally applies to the *kedoshim*, the court of angels presided over by the Lord God Himself. We find the term *bene elohim* (sons of God) in Genesis 6:3, Deuteronomy 32:8, Job, and Psalm 89:6. Some groups—such as the Church of the Process, the Mormons, and the Branhamites—have taken these passages to suggest that Satan is a brother to Jesus. But such an interpretation is fallacious; Satan "was originally God's creation, and he remains God's devil, subject to God's ultimate control."[6]

The evil one

Jesus frequently referred to the devil as "the evil one" (Gk. *ho ponēros).* He taught His disciples to pray, "And lead us not into temptation, but deliver us from the evil one" (Matt. 6:13). Humans must seek to be freed from the evil one, for when the Gospel of the kingdom of God is proclaimed, "the evil one comes and snatches [it] away" (Matt. 13:19). Paul advises Christians to protect themselves by taking up "the shield of faith, with which you can extinguish all the flaming arrows of the evil one" (Eph. 6:16). Trevor Ling observes that, for Paul, "all kinds of dangers, persecutions, afflictions, or beguilement are simply regarded as the work of ὁ πονηρός, the evil one."[7]

Beliar and Beelzebul

A little used name for Satan in the New Testament is Beliar, which is probably a mutation of the Hebrew *Belial,* an abstract noun in the Old Testament (e.g., Deut. 13:13; 1 Sam. 1:16) meaning "worthlessness." Paul warns believers against entering into partnership with unbelievers, for "what harmony is there between Christ and Belial [Gk. *Beliar*]?" (2 Cor. 6:15) In the apocryphal Testament of the Twelve Patriarchs, the term gains a new prominence; there it becomes the personification of evil, diametrically opposed to God.[9]

Beelzebul or Beelzebub is used more often (Matt. 10:25; 12:27; Luke 11:15). There is some question as to its meaning. It has been variously interpreted as "Lord of the flies" or "Lord of filth" or — most likely — "Lord of the dwelling." Green notes that, "on any showing it refers to the devil — Beelzebub is specifically called 'prince of the demons,' and the name draws attention to the grip that Satan gets on a life once entry is effected. He becomes Lord of the dwelling, however much men may ridicule him as Lord of the flies or hate him as Lord of filth."[10]

The prince of this world

In speaking of His approaching death, Jesus referred to the judgment of the world and the defeat of "the prince of this world" (John 12:31; 14:30; 16:11). Paul uses a closely related title, calling Satan "the god of this age" (2 Cor. 4:4). Since Paul elsewhere declares that there is no God but the Lord (1 Cor. 8:4), we realize that Satan is a false god, set up in the Lord's place through his deception of apostate humanity, but his tenure is limited by the cross. Ray Summers has aptly observed that "at the cross of Jesus, 'the ruler of this world' was judged (John 16:11). Jesus was not the defeated one in that struggle with the power of evil, the forces of darkness. He was the victor. The one who was defeated was Satan. The cross was God's judgment on sin and Satan."[11] The title "prince of this world" is similar; Satan is the ruler of this world by default, powerful because human beings have willfully cooperated with him in sin.

The ruler of the power of the air

In his letter to the Ephesians, Paul reminds his readers of their condition before their salvation: "As for you, you were dead in your transgressions and sins, in which you used to live when you followed the ways of this world and of the ruler of the kingdom of the air" (2:1-2). The people of New Testament times believed the air (or, atmosphere) to be the realm of the evil one. "The symbolism," declares Green, "indicates Satan's 'in between' position, a rebel banished from the throne of God but all the same a mighty force to be reckoned with, far more powerful than man."[12]

Apollyon

The destructive nature of Satan's character is brought out by John in Revelation 9:11, where the king of the demonic hosts is known as Apollyon or, in the Hebrew, Abaddon. In the Greek, the word literally means "the Destroying One." In the Hebrew it is an epithet of Sheol or Hades, and is literally rendered as "destruction."[13] We are reminded of Genesis 3 and the entry of sin and death into the world and its resultant destruction of relationship because of the Fall, brought on by the machinations of the tempter.

Conclusions

The Revelation passages emphasize Satan's power; he leads the whole world astray. He is very adept at blinding the minds of human beings, especially of the unsaved. And yet, we are also reminded that "his power is a power that is 'thrown down' before the dynamic salvation and kingship of God and His Anointed One. His power is subject to God's own dynamis [power] and exousia [glory]."[14]

Demons

Along with the rise in interest in the Holy Spirit engendered by the charismatic movement came an interest in demons and the demonic. Multitudes of books were written for popular consumption and scores of exorcists promoted their ability to cast demons out of "possessed" people. Such a near obsession on the part of many with the spirit world requires a fresh examination of the demonic: Do demons exist? Where did they come from? What are they like? What is their intent? These and other issues we shall examine in the light of biblical theology.

13.1: A SUMMARY AND COMPARISON OF THE SUPERNATURAL HOSTS AS MENTIONED IN THE SCRIPTURES	
Benevolent Beings	*Malicious Beings*
GOD	**THE DEVIL** *a.k.a.* Satan The Serpent A son of God The Evil One Beliar (Belial) Beelzebul Prince of this World Prince of the Power of the Air Apollyon (Abaddon)*
Archangel(s)	*Some would place Apollyon in this ranking as chief (under Satan) of the demonic hosts. In 1 Enoch, this position is occupied by Azazel (the scapegoat).
Angels	Angels
Cherubim Seraphim	Demons: Shedhim Seirim Elilim Lilith Rulers of this Age

The origin of demons

The origin of demons is not specifically stated in the Bible, but we may conclude that they are fallen angels who along with their leader Satan rebelled against God and were expelled from heaven (Rev. 12:4). Support for such a view is compelling. Demons have a similar relation to the devil as do his angels. Several biblical expressions may be regarded as parallel: "the devil and his angels" (Matt. 25:41), "the dragon and his angels" (Rev. 12:7), and "Beelzebub, prince of demons" (Matt. 12:24). The demon-locusts released from the pit in the end time are ruled over by Apollyon, or Satan (Rev. 9:11). Demons and angels are seen to have the same essence. Angels are called "spirits" (Ps. 104:4; Heb. 1:14), as are demons (Matt. 8:16; Luke 10:17, 20). Both seek to dominate human beings (Matt. 17:14-18; John 13:27), and both war against God and humanity (Rev. 12:7-17; Mark 9:17-26; Rev. 9:13-15).[15]

According to the New Testament, those fallen angels are in two categories: confined and free. Those who are free live in the heavenly realms and make war on humans (Eph. 6:12). Other demons are not free, but are imprisoned in the Abyss (Rev. 9:1ff), on earth (Rev. 9:14), and in Tartarus (2 Peter 2:4), waiting for the final judgment.[16]

Varieties of demons

Like angels, demons are not all alike. They may be divided into a variety of positions or roles. Both the Old Testament and the New make these divisions.

The Old Testament

The Greek words for "demon" (*daimon* and *daimonion*) translate several different Old Testament Hebrew words, each of which gives us some insight into the demonic economy. The first of these is *shedhim,* which occurs in Deuteronomy 32:17 and Psalm 106:37, and is rendered in English as "demons." The latter passage tells us about those apostate Israelites who "sacrificed their sons and their daughters to demons." The following verse (38) is explanatory: "They shed innocent blood, the blood of their sons and daughters, whom they sacrificed to the idols of Canaan." The *shedhim* were not just the pagan idols, but the demonic spirits behind them who inspired the perverted worship of those who were disobedient to God.[17]

A second word is *seirim,* "he-goats" (in the NIV, "goat idols"). The Book of Leviticus (17:1ff) forbade the Hebrews to go into the desert to "offer any of their sacrifices to the goat idols to whom they prostitute themselves" (17:7). The cult of the he-goats was viewed as apostasy from the Lord God; those who were devotees of this cult would be executed (17:4). This demonic cult was evidently practiced for centuries among the Israelites, for we find it in the Northern Kingdom during the reign of Jereboam I, who rejected the Levites and the worship of the Lord, "and appointed priests from all sorts of people . . . sacrificing to the calves he had made" (1 Kings 12:31-32). These pagan deities were regarded as demons in the form of satyrs (goat-like creatures).[18]

A third Hebrew word is *'elilim,* translated as "idols." Psalm 96:5 declares, "For all the gods of the nations are idols, but the Lord made the heavens." This passage makes a clear connection between idols and demons. The Hebrew word is the plural for "empty" or "vain." The passage suggests that while the idols of the nations are empty or nothing, the demonic spirits back of them are very real.[19]

Other evil spirits mentioned in the Old Testament include Azazel, the scapegoat (Lev. 16:8-26); Azazel is depicted in the apocalyptic book, 1 Enoch (6:7; 9:16; 10:4-6) as the leader of the fallen angels. There is also Lilith, the night demon (Isa. 34:14; Ps. 91:5).[20]

The New Testament

There are a variety of names given to demonic spirits, many of which are suggestive of function. Others indicate orders or classes of fallen angels. In the Synoptic Gospels, the term "angel" is used both positively and negatively. In his discussion of the sheep and the goats, Jesus says that the "goats" will be sent off "into the eternal fire prepared for the devil and his angels" (Matt. 25:41). In the pejorative sense, the term is used of those who used to be good angels and became corrupt through their insurrection against God.[21]

The Pauline Epistles concur with the Old Testament perspective on demons that connects them with pagan deities. Heathen sacrifices are devoted to demons, not to the Lord; thus, those who take part in such sacrifices worship those demons and not God in Christ (1 Cor. 10:20ff).[22]

The Pauline teaching on demons is the most fully developed in the New Testament. The apostle refers to demons as "the rulers of this age," demonic spirits controlling those who "crucified the Lord of glory" (1 Cor. 2:8). They are the "basic principles of the world" to whom humans are enslaved prior to their liberation by Christ (Gal. 4:3); that these are evil spirits is made clear by Paul in Galatians 4:8: "Formerly, when you did not know God, you were slaves to those who by nature are not gods." They are especially those who are members of the invisible created order who are obvious in visible rulers who are wicked in their demeanor:[23] "For our struggle is not against flesh and blood, but against the rulers, against the authorities, against the powers of this dark world and against the spiritual forces of evil in the heavenly realms" (Eph. 6:12).

The demonic nature

Since demons are fallen angels, what is true of angels is undoubtedly true of their fallen counterparts. A quick overview of their attributes will give us insight into their infernal natures.

Personality

Demons, like angels, are persons with the various attributes of personality. Christ used personal pronouns in referring to them, and the demons themselves used personal pronouns of themselves (Luke 8:27-30). They spoke intelligently (Luke 4:33-35, 41; 8:28-30). They recognized who Jesus was (Mark 1:23-24) and acknowledged the spiritual authority of Paul (Acts 16:16ff). We are also told that they are capable of demonstrating emotion, trembling in terror at the thought of their coming judgment (Luke 8:28; James 2:19).[24]

Spirit

Demons are spirit beings. Paul tells us that "our struggle is not against flesh and blood, but . . . against the spiritual forces of evil in the heavenly realms" (Eph. 6:12). There are those who would seek to deny the existence of these spiritual beings, trying to "demythologize" them into earthly structures, such as the class struggle, oppressive corporations, and government evil. "This has the double attraction of divesting ourselves of belief in so unfashionable a concept as a hierarchy of angels . . . it also enables us to find a good deal more in the New Testament about our modern preoccupation with social structures."[25] But the Bible portrays demons as very real spiritual creatures; invisible beings, though they may assume visible forms at times, including appearing as angels of light (2 Cor. 11:14) and as gruesome and horrendous creatures (Rev. 9:7-10, 17; 16:13-16).[26]

Power

That demons possess tremendous power is evidenced by their names (which also define them): "dominion," "authority," "power," "principality," and "might." They control some human beings. Mark records the story of the Gerasene demoniac, under the power of a legion of wicked spirits; "no one could bind him any more, not even with a chain. For he had often been chained hand and foot, but he tore the chains apart and broke the irons on his feet. No one was strong enough to subdue him" (5:3-4). Another aspect of demonic power is their ability to perform miracles. There are "all kinds of counterfeit miracles, signs and wonders . . . every sort of evil that deceives those who are perishing" (2 Thes. 2:9-10).[27]

Immoral

The New Testament frequently proclaims the utter depravity of these demonic powers. They are referred to as "evil" or, literally in Greek, "unclean" (Matt. 10:1; Mark 1:27; 3:11; Luke 4:36; Acts 8:7; Rev. 16:13). They induce human beings to become "instruments of wickedness" (Rom. 6:13), to formulate "things taught by demons" as the result of consciences "seared as with a hot iron" (1 Tim. 4:1ff), and to the inculcation of "destructive heresies" (2 Peter 2:1). They lead mortals into immoral conduct.

> The actions of the demonized seem to indicate that the unclean spirit takes possession in some instances for the purpose of sensual gratification, and uses every type of uncleanness. This may explain the desire of the possessed to live in a state of nudity, to have licentious thoughts (Luke 8:27), and to frequent such impure places as tombs.[28]

Their purpose

The untiring purpose of the demonic hosts is the support of their satanic master's promotion of evil throughout the created order. Because Satan is a creature, he is limited by space and time; and so he must multiply his power and extend his influence via his demonic minions.

Opposition to God

Satan's whole program is geared to rebellion against the Lord. His philosophy is to displace God with self. Human beings fell from grace because of that lie: "You will be like God" (Gen. 3:5).

These fallen angels seek to dethrone God by seducing human beings to idol worship. Among the Hebrews they enjoyed a measure of success: "They [the Jews] yoked themselves to the Baal of Peor and ate sacrifices offered to lifeless idols; they provoked the Lord to anger by their wicked deeds" (Ps. 106:28-29).

In opposing God, wicked spirits promote false world religions and a maze of cults of Christendom. Whether it be in animistic religions where superstition, magic, and the worship of spirits bring men into bondage, or whether it be in attractive philosophical systems seemingly promoting good, the dynamic is the same—demons distracting from the only true and living God and from His unique Son, the only Savior for the whole world.[29]

Oppression of humans

Evil spirits manifest a destructive attitude toward human beings. Their desire is to do whatever they can to hinder human physical, mental, emotional, and spiritual well-being.

Probably the principal method by which demons seek to damage human welfare is by seducing people into sin. Since Satan is known as the tempter, it is reasonable to suppose that the power of temptation belongs to his support network, as well. Fallen angels "may be thought of as conjointly, perpetually, and indefatigably engaged in a vast program of suggestion and solicitation for evil."[30]

Demons also seek to distract human beings from spiritual truth as revealed by God in Christ. In order to accomplish their wicked ends they will sometimes propound what seems to be high and lofty in religion, psychology, the sciences, and the arts. Paul reminds us of our past life which was subject to "the ruler of the kingdom of the air, the spirit who is now at work in those who are disobedient. All of us also lived among them at one time, gratifying the cravings of our sinful nature and following its desires and thoughts" (Eph. 2:2-3). A preoccupation with material things and worldly pleasures and luxuries is the result of a world view engendered demonically.[31] Good things are demonic if they entice us away from Christ.

The Bible also records illnesses and injuries as the result of demonic activity within human beings. Matthew chronicles Jesus' encounter with "a man who was demon-possessed and could not talk." But when Jesus had exorcised the demon, "the man who had been mute spoke" (9:33). In another case, Jesus was brought "a demon-possessed man who was blind and mute, and Jesus healed him, so that he could both talk and see" (Matt. 12:22). Luke records an episode involving a woman "who had been crippled by a spirit for eighteen years. She was bent over and could not straighten up" (13:11). Jesus restored her to new health and strength. Contrary to what some have said, Scripture does not see all illnesses as the work of evil spirits, but dichotomizes between natural maladies and demonic disorders (Matt. 4:24; Mark 1:32, 34; Luke 7:21; 9:1).[32]

Opposition to believers

Because they are opposed to God, demons also stand against those who belong to Him. Dickason asserts that

> demons would divide and defeat genuine unity in the church, locally or universally. They use doctrinal divisions through false teachers or faddists (1 Tim. 4:1-3). They question the genuine deity, genuine humanity, or the very historicity of Christ (1 John 4:1-4; 2 Tim. 3:5; 2 Peter 1:16). They use practical divisions through jealousy, selfish ambition, arrogance, and personality cults (James 3:14-16; 1 Cor. 3:1-4). They create harshness and lack of forgiveness (2 Cor. 2:5; Ephes. 4:26-27).[33]

We sense from the Book of Revelation that the persecution of believers is demonic (2:8-10), a persecution often derived from other religious sources (2:9).

Conclusions

Though demons wreak tremendous havoc in human lives, their power is limited by God. In fact, God can turn demonic activity to His own purposes and to the ultimate triumph of His kingdom in this world.

The Lord may use the demonic to bring fallen believers to repentance and new faith. Both 1 Timothy 1:19-20 and 1 Corinthians 5:1-5 mention handing people over to Satan for correction. Further, through the ordeal of oppression by the demonic, Christians may mature in the faith and come to rely more fully on God (2 Cor. 12:7-10).[34]

Demonization

As noted earlier, the recent increase in interest in the Holy Spirit has raised equal interest in the contemporary activities of demons in our society. While many people have gone overboard and find demons under every bush and behind every blade of grass, it would be a grave mistake to suppose that demonic activity is something which may have happened during more primitive times but is no longer relevant. Evil is still very much alive and active in our present-day society.

A definition

The term "demonization" comes from the Greek present participle *daimonizomenos,* which signifies the continuing state of being oppressed by a demon. "This indicates a control other than that of the person who is demonized; he is regarded as the recipient of the demon's action. In other words, demonization pictures a demon controlling a somewhat passive human."[35]

To think of demonization as "demon possession" is inaccurate because it implies absolute ownership of an individual by demonic forces. But Scripture sees these fallen spirits as purloiners of realms which do not rightfully belong to them. Thus, the term "demonization," the state of being oppressed or controlled by one or more demons, is more suitable.[36]

Who may be demonized?

The question is often asked whether Christian believers may be the victims of demonization. The proper biblical response is that, while all human beings may suffer the depredations of demons, no believer can be invaded and controlled by them.

The Bible teaches that, upon conversion to Christ, an individual is indwelt by the Holy Spirit of God, who baptizes him into the body of Christ (1 Cor. 12:13). Paul reminds believers, "Do you not know that your body is a temple of the Holy Spirit, who is in you, whom you have received from God?" (1 Cor. 6:19) The Holy Spirit will not share His glory with an evil spirit. We may be sure, then, that a demon cannot enter a Christian believer. Any persecution of believers must be limited to external actions.

Unbelievers are a different matter. Paul tells us that the demonic is "at work in those who are disobedient" (Eph. 2:2). One who is not "in Christ" seems to be fair game for invasion and control by demons. "And there is no apparent reason why he may not . . . suffer demonic invasion of his personality to the partial or total eclipse of his individuality and thus manifest all the symptoms of the possessed."[37] Thus, the unbeliever may be affected and/or controlled by evil either internally or externally.

Deliverance

The work of Satan and his lackeys is completely contrary to the intentions and will of God. Accordingly, the Bible emphasizes the need for human deliverance and protection from the demons.[38]

The remedy for demonization is simple. We find it in 1 John 1:7: "the blood of Jesus, his [God's] Son, purifies us from all sin." Jesus Christ, by His death and resurrection, has overcome the power of Satan.

Just as the power of the Holy Spirit filled Jesus, enabling Him to cast out demons, so that same Spirit fills those who are fully surrendered to Jesus, empowering them to do the same. When Jesus sent out the seventy to proclaim the kingdom of God, they returned in great excitement, exclaiming, "Lord, even the demons submit to us in your name" (Luke 10:17). That same power is given to followers of Christ today through the Great Commission (Matt. 28:18-20).

Conclusions

As we have pointed out, Calvary marks the turning point of the war between God and Satan. As the "second Adam," Jesus demonstrated perfect obedience to God, something the first Adam had failed to accomplish. "And being found in appearance as a man, he humbled himself and became obedient to death—even death on a cross! Therefore God has exalted him to the highest place" (Phil. 2:8-9).

He also took upon Himself the sins of the whole world. "God made him who had no sin to be sin for us, so that in him we might become the righteousness of God" (2 Cor. 5:21). By so doing, Christ has "put them in the right, justified them, by taking responsibility for all the sin and failure. And thus the devil is robbed of his power as 'Satan' or 'Accuser.' For 'there is now no condemnation for those who are in Christ Jesus' (Rom. 8:1)."[39]

Ultimately, Satan will meet his just fate in the lake of fire (Rev. 19:20; 20:10). The hosts of evil will be eliminated from God's economy; "God will be all in all and the redeemed will be for ever satisfied with their Lord, who has turned Paradise lost into Paradise regained."[40]

Powerful as he may seem, Satan is *not* divine, nor is he all-powerful. His defeat is assured by the Lamb of God who is both eternal and omniscient.

Chapter Fourteen
The Conquest
of Sin

We have seen the gargantuan impact of sin on the created order. Its effects are universal. All human beings are enmeshed in the tentacles of the evil one, slaves to sin's leading. They cannot possibly help themselves. And without some form of superhuman assistance these sinful people—every one of us—are doomed to death, both physical and eternal.

When people look to the church for aid, they may be told that they should be like Jesus, that they should imitate His lifestyle, or that they should seek through meditation to achieve Christ's consciousness. But no sinner weighed down with guilt could possibly imitate Jesus. Nor could the sinner ever attain the consciousness of Christ. "No gospel which begins with any basal fact save that of man's actual unworthiness and his sense of ill-desert can meet the needs of man. In a word, the gospel of God's grace is necessary to meet the fact and the consciousness of sin."[1]

Steps to Overcoming Sin

In his classic systematic theology, E.Y. Mullins lists five elements which are involved in extricating us from the domination of sin.[2] We shall consider each one in turn.

God's revelation

There is considerable controversy among contemporary theologians in regard to revelation, with those on the far right insisting that revelation is contained in a set of formal propositions divinely given (the Bible) and those on the left asserting that it is the self-giving of Being which inexpressibly grasps the whole being of a person. But there is no reason to suppose that revelation must be such an *either/or* affair. It is better seen as *both/and*. Theologian John Macquarrie has expressed this tension well when he argues that "in the absence of articulate communication, there could hardly be a sharing of the revelation; and without a sharing, there could be no community of faith founded upon the revelation; and thus in turn there could be no transmission and no appropriation of the revelation."[3] Revelation is certainly God's unveiling of Himself through His inspired and authoritative Word, the Scriptures, but it goes far beyond the simple human vessel of language. The supreme self-disclosure of God to humanity is Jesus Christ: "But when the time had fully come, God sent His Son, born of a woman" (Gal. 4:4). Macquarrie keenly observes that

> this, for Christianity, is the classic, or primordial, revelation on which the community of faith is founded and which determines its way of understanding Being (God) and of comporting itself toward Being. The earliest historical revelations of the Old Testament, taken over by the Christian community as part of its heritage, are regarded as summed up and brought to their completion in the new, decisive historical revelation in Christ, who is "sent forth" in the "fullness" of the time.[4]

God's revelation in Christ Jesus clearly is evidence of His love for the sinner. "But God demonstrates his own love for us in this: While we were still sinners, Christ died for us" (Rom. 5:8). This principle is well-illustrated in the account of Jesus' calling of Matthew. When the Pharisees questioned the Lord's eating with tax collectors and sinners, Jesus replied, "It is not the healthy who need a doctor, but the sick. But go and learn what this means: 'I desire mercy, not sacrifice.' For I have not come to call the righteous, but sinners" (Matt. 9:12-13). God in His mercy had sent His only Son to search out and befriend these sinners and bring them into His kingdom.[5] In His encounter with Zaccheus Jesus observed, "For the Son of Man came to seek and to save what was lost" (Luke 19:10).

Jesus Christ believed that His purpose in coming to planet earth was to rescue lost sinners. He became known as the "friend of tax collectors and sinners." He portrayed His concerns in His Parables on the Lost Sheep, the Lost Coin, and the Lost (Prodigal) Son (Luke 15:1-32). No one can read the New Testament witness without sensing the depth of divine love for fallen humanity.

The atonement of Christ

That the Bible reiterates God's love for human beings time and time again should not astonish anyone, for it unequivocally states that "God is love" (1 John 4:8). What is the feeling of the God who is love toward sin? One preacher has responded thusly: "God feels it and has always felt it. Absalom has broken his father's heart; and we are Absalom. The grand old king goes up over Olivet weeping, with his head covered and his feet bare; and that king is God."[6] God's anguish over sin is eternal, and so He has made eternal provision for the atonement of sin in Jesus Christ, the lamb slain "from the creation of the world" (Rev. 13:8).

It is in Christ's atonement that the sinner comprehends how mercy, forgiveness, and reconciliation are possible, in spite of his or her lack of merit. Paul presents what Christ has done in concise terms: "There is no difference, for all have sinned and fall short of the glory of God, and are justified freely by his grace through the redemption that came by Christ Jesus. God presented him as a sacrifice of atonement, through faith in his blood" (Rom. 3:22-25). Charles Cranfield, in commenting on this passage, notes that

> God, because in his mercy he willed to forgive sinful men, and, being truly merciful, willed to forgive them righteously, that is, without in any way condoning their sin, purposed to direct against his very own self in the person of his Son the full weight of that righteous wrath which they deserved.[7]

Forgiveness

God has always been more ready to forgive than to condemn. Forgiveness, for example, is an important theme of Isaiah: " 'Come now, let us reason together,' says the Lord. 'Though your sins are like scarlet, they shall be as white as snow; though they are red like crimson, they shall be like wool' " (1:18). Forgiveness is a God-given prospect, but it necessitates the sinner's recognition of what he or she has done or failed to do, and turn away from those sins to God's way of life. Isaiah declares that there is the possibility of forgiveness and life with God under a new covenant.[8] And God still has the same message for wayward humans today that He had for the Hebrews in Hosea's time: "Return, O Israel, to the Lord your God. Your sins have been your downfall. Take words with you and return to the Lord. Say to him, 'Forgive all our sins and receive us graciously' " (14:1-2). Derek Kidner interprets this as, "The runaway must return, the sinner plead, the formalist use his mind and lips, to come back into fellowship with God."[9] John makes God's purposes in Jesus' coming to earth crystal clear: "For God did not send his Son into the world to condemn the world, but to save the world through him" (3:17).

The most poignant depiction of divine forgiveness is made in Jesus' Parable of the Prodigal Son. Here we see the eagerness of the father as he waits for the first indication of his wayward son's repentance; and then the joyous reunion, hastened by the father's seeing the son's approach from afar and running out to meet him; finally, there is the revelry as the son's return home is celebrated — this is the biblical picture of God's desire to be reunited with sinful humanity.

> It is plain . . . that God forgives as a Father. Jesus speaks almost uniformly of forgiveness in connection with his teaching about God's fatherhood and man's true sonship to him. . . . And when Jesus wishes to illustrate at once the nature of sin and of recovery from it, he pictures an unfilial life from which the wandering son is restored by paternal love to his normal relations in the home of his father.[10]

God calls upon sinners to repent, that is, to turn away from sin by turning to Him. If they will do so, He will forgive their sins.

14.1: THE CONDITIONS FOR FORGIVENESS

One frequently hears televangelists and other preachers tell their listeners that obtaining forgiveness for their sins and a new standing with God is relatively easy: "All you have to do is believe in Jesus." Such a statement is, at the same time, both false and true.

It is quite true that God has provided for human redemption through Christ Jesus. It is also true that trusting Christ for one's salvation is the key to forgiveness of one's sin and reconciliation to God. What needs to be stressed, however, is that much more is involved in "believing" than might ordinarily meet the eye.

"Believing" in Jesus means much more than a simple intellectual assent to the events of Jesus' death and resurrection. James 2:19 tells us that the demons believe in the one true God, but they nonetheless shudder in their lostness! Their belief will not save them.

Many people think of salvation in forensic (legal) terms. When one makes a profession of faith in Christ, the heavenly court declares that that individual is now declared "not guilty" by virtue of his declaration. While such an idea is true—as far as it goes—it does not go far enough.

Salvation is more than a forensic transaction; it is a life-long relational process. The Gospels clearly delineate this relationship. In John 17:3, His prayer on behalf of His followers, Jesus says: "Now this is eternal life: that they may know you, the only true God, and Jesus Christ, whom you have sent." Apart from knowing Jesus Christ, salvation is impossible. To know someone requires the establishment of a relationship. A declaration of faith begins the relationship; but it is every bit as important that the relationship continue and develop. Someone has asked whether it is more important to get married or to stay married. How can one answer such a question? What is the point of one without the other! And there is no point to making a profession of belief in Jesus Christ as Savior and Lord without the establishment of an ongoing relationship with Him.

"Believe" in our day is a rather nebulous term. It can mean a great many things. We are probably better to go to one of the other—equally valid—meanings of the Greek word *(pisteuo)*, such as "rely on": "Rely on the Lord Jesus, and you will be saved" (Acts 16:31). It is impossible truly to rely on someone (at least on an ongoing basis) whom you do not know, and with whom you have established no relationship whatever!

Nor should we be surprised at such news. The original sin involved the breaking of the God-human relationship. It had to do with the rejection of trust in God. And sin today is no different. Most theologians would agree that sin goes far beyond unacceptable ethical behavior; it is the violation and loss of relationship with God. Sin is separation from God.

John 6:53-54 is a further indication of the need for relationship if our sins are to be forgiven: "Jesus said to them, 'I tell you the truth, unless you eat the flesh of the Son of Man and drink his blood, you have no life in you. Whoever eats my flesh and drinks my blood has eternal life.' " Jesus declares that He is the source of life and, unless He is made an integral part of a person's existence (such as when we eat a steak, it becomes an integral part of us quite literally), that person does not have eternal life (or the forgiveness of his sins).

In this regard, it is necessary to realize that—though important—one's actions are not the basis for our relationship with God. The basis of relationship (as in marriage) is loving fellowship (i.e., spending time together). God will always love us (just as a proper father always loves his children, no matter what), but relationship with Him depends on our communicating with Him (as well as vice versa). If we do nothing to maintain the relationship, if we stop relating to God, then the relationship will end. The technical term for such a permanent state is apostasy.

While there are endless arguments over the concept of apostasy, one thing is sure. If you stay close to Jesus Christ on a continuing basis, you will never have to question whether or not you are eternally secure! You will have the ongoing assurance of His presence with you and of your eternal salvation from sin and its disastrous consequences.

Forgiveness removes the barrier of sin and allows the dispensing of restoration and reconciliation to occur.[11] Forgiveness brings release from the bondage of sin.

393

Reconciliation

With forgiveness comes the possibility of reconciliation. Because of Calvary, God reconciles forgiven humans to Himself. "All this is from God, who reconciled us to himself through Christ and gave us the ministry of reconciliation: that God was reconciling the world to himself in Christ, not counting men's sins against them" (2 Cor. 5:18-19).

Reconciliation is the antithesis of estrangement or alienation. Sinners are unfulfilled and disorientated, unable to grasp their identity or their freedom in the way God had created them to do so. Reconciliation restores the original human relationship with God. It is the circumstance by which God and people, heretofore separated from each other, are made "at one" once more.[12]

The atonement, then, allows the sinner to realize that—contrary to being hated and condemned—God loves him or her and has made provision for salvation. The sinner is invited to accept divine forgiveness and be reconciled to God.

A deepening sense of sin

One might suppose that, upon receiving the good news of God's salvation, a sinner would immediately and gratefully turn to Him. Generally, however, that does not happen immediately. Instead, the sinner's sense of guilt and shame are deepened, not removed, and he is doubly aware of his unbelief. In John 16:8-11, Jesus refers to the work of the Holy Spirit in this regard:

> When he comes, he will convict the world of guilt in regard to sin and righteousness and judgment: in regard to sin, because men do not believe in me; in regard to righteousness, because I am going to the Father, where you can see me no longer; and in regard to judgment, because the prince of this world now stands condemned.

This conviction, however, is not conviction to despair. It is, rather, conviction to hope, because it demonstrates the necessity and opportunity for trust in Christ as the only way to liberation from sin. If the Holy Spirit were to be active in the human heart, revealing the horror of sin and the terror of God's wrath against sin, but offering no hope for the sinner, the result would indeed be overwhelming despair. But the Spirit's convicting action is intended to produce faith in the Lord Jesus who destroys the power of sin.[13]

Faith in Christ

The sinner who is convicted of his or her sin and need for salvation realizes that God's good news of Christ is the divine response to the individual's needs. The sinner recognizes that God would have one repent of one's sinful ways and receive forgiveness and reconciliation with Him. Such realization leads to an act of will, namely, trust in Christ as personal Savior and Lord. An act of trust which commits oneself to Christ in obedient submission is an exercise of saving faith.[14]

Saving faith: offer and demand

It is important to recognize that faith in Christ is not a mere assent to a series of fundamental religious propositions. Jesus was quite blunt in proclaiming that the act of saving faith implies a demand as well as an offer. "He never lowered his standards or modified his conditions to make his call more readily acceptable. He asked his first disciples, and he has asked every disciple since, to give him their thoughtful and total commitment. Nothing less than this will do."[15] Thus, prior to making such a faith commitment it well behooves a person to count its cost.

> The Christian landscape is strewn with the wreckage of derelict, half-built towers—the ruins of those who began to build and were unable to finish. For thousands of people still ignore Christ's warning and undertake to follow him without first pausing to reflect on the cost of doing so. The result is the great scandal of Christendom today, so-called "nominal Christianity."[16]

Nominal Christians are no Christians at all, but simply people who have duped themselves into believing that they are saved when they are still, in fact, dead in sins and trespasses.

What is the cost of following Christ? It is best stated in Luke 9:23-25 by our Lord Himself: "If anyone would come after me, he must deny himself and take up his cross daily and follow me. For whoever wants to save his life will lose it, but whoever loses his life for me will save it. What good is it for a man to gain the whole world, and yet lose or forfeit his very self?"

There must be a willingness to abandon whatever prevents the person from wholeheartedly following Christ. This, of course, includes a renunciation of sin (what we call repentance). There must also be a renunciation of self. "To follow Christ," advises John Stott, "is to surrender to him the rights over our own lives. It is to abdicate the throne of our heart and do homage to him as our King."[17] It is to give up all self-interest in deference to the interests of Christ.

Christ also demands that His followers take up the cross daily. It is not until we are prepared to deny self that we are even capable of taking up the cross. The cross signifies suffering; in this case, it is particularly the suffering which comes about because of our full allegiance to Christ's purposes for our lives. Dietrich Bonhoeffer has given a striking interpretation of this aspect of the Christian faith.

> When Christ calls a man [or woman], he bids him come and die. It may be a death like that of the first disciples who had to leave home and work to follow him, or it may be a death like Luther's, who had to leave the monastery and go out into the world. But it is the same death every time — death in Jesus Christ. . . . The call to discipleship, the baptism in the name of Jesus Christ means both death and life. . . . [It] sets the Christian in the middle of the daily arena against sin and the devil. Every day he encounters new temptations, and every day he must suffer anew for Jesus Christ's sake.[18]

Since Christ came into the world to combat sin through self-denial in favor of His Father's will, and through enduring the suffering and death of the cross, why should His followers count it strange to imitate this aspect of His ministry in their own daily lives?

It is a natural part of the imitation of Christ as a disciple. The act of saving faith unites the trusting sinner to God as He is revealed in Christ. Union with God begins in the converted sinner a process of sanctification by which he begins to be conformed to the will and image of Christ.

The formation of a new consciousness

Sanctification has been defined as the remaking of the soul (or, self) in a more virtuous shape, namely, after the perfection that is Jesus Christ.[19] This perfection is mirrored by the Scriptures, and believers are to pattern themselves after this revelation. While there are many books about Jesus and many teachers who are happy to guide us in the imitation of Christ, the most reliable guide to sanctification is the life of Christ as presented by the Gospels. "If, however, the Gospels are to have their due effect, and one is to see in their pages the very face of Jesus, he must come without prejudice and without preconceptions—in fact, as St. Paul would say, 'with unveiled face.' "[20]

The Christian is well to remember that sanctification in the Christian life is progressive. It does not happen overnight. John Watson describes the process fittingly.

What occurs to the plain person who . . . is only possessed with an overwhelming idea of the excellence of Christ, is that sanctification will advance on a series of levels, one rising above the other. Each level, as we look at it from below and toil to reach it, will seem perfection, because it is the complete face of Christ as we have seen it from our standpoint. When we have completed a fresh ascent, our vision will have grown; we shall then discover fresh imperfection in ourselves and unsuspected beauty in Christ. Again we shall be inspired with adoration, again we shall be smitten with dissatisfaction—adoration of the new glory, dissatisfaction with our own defects.[21]

And so it will continue throughout life. Sanctification in the sense of moral and spiritual growth, at least, is a never-ending process.

The process of sanctification results in a new God-consciousness. It contains an awareness of the ability to make moral progress. Instead of a perception of moral failure and loneliness, there is the realization of victory over sin and of the abiding presence of the Holy Spirit. Paul reflects this victory and presence of the Helper when he cries, "What a wretched man I am! Who will rescue me from this body of death? Thanks be to God— through Jesus Christ our Lord!" (Rom. 7:24-25). The transformed sinner has moved from despair to triumph.[22]

Conclusions: The breaking of sin's power

Because of Adam's transgression, the law of sin and (eternal) death has become operative in the human economy. All human beings become subject to that law. If they are to be liberated from the power of sin and death, that law must be annulled. Paul held such a view, which he expresses in Romans 8:2: "through Christ Jesus the law of the Spirit of life set me free from the law of sin and death." He continues in the verse following, "For what the law was powerless to do in that it was weakened by the sinful nature, God did by sending his own Son in the likeness of sinful man to be a sin offering. And so he condemned sin in sinful man."

Paul's idea is that "this death principle, operative in humanity, must be overcome and destroyed by the obedience-life principle operative in Christ."[23] Christ became one with human beings, even to the point of death, so that His righteousness might become a salvific power to them. "The law of the Spirit of life in him overcame thus the law of sin and death in them."[24]

The final conquest of sin

Although the death and resurrection of Christ serve to set the sinner free from the law of sin and death by placing him or her under the law of the Spirit of life, we still "groan" for deliverance from "this body of death," because—like it or not—we are aware that we still stumble and fall spiritually. Even though Paul declares that, "if anyone is in Christ, he is a new creation; the old has gone, the new has come" (2 Cor. 5:17), we are often too much aware of the presence of the old nature acting out within us.

There is an obvious tension here. How can we reconcile Paul's statement that "we know that our old self was crucified with him so that the body of sin might be done away with" (Rom. 6:6) with the reality of our experience? When Paul talks about being "dead to sin" (Rom. 6:11), he is writing under inspiration, and we must therefore accept his words as absolute truth. But the need remains to reconcile our continuing sin with biblical truth.

Progressive victory

Part of the answer to the problem of continuing sin in the life of the Christian is to be found in the nature of salvation. The process of regeneration does not destroy the original sinful human nature, but creates a new nature dominated by the indwelling Holy Spirit, which moves in alongside of the old. "For the sinful nature desires what is contrary to the Spirit, and the Spirit what is contrary to the sinful nature. They are in conflict with each other, so that you do not do what you want" (Gal. 5:17).

As we grow spiritually, the flesh is more and more controlled. Both flesh and Spirit coexist, nonetheless, and the strife between the two can be bitter and unrelenting. John Stott teaches that "we do not deny that there is such a thing as moral conflict in non-Christian people, but we assert that it is fiercer in Christians because they possess two natures — flesh and Spirit — in irreconcilable antagonism."[25]

The secret to progressive victory over sin is given in Galatians 5:24-25 where Paul exhorts believers, "Those who belong to Christ Jesus have crucified the sinful nature, its passions and desires. Since we live by the Spirit, let us keep in step with the Spirit." We are to yield ourselves to the control of the Holy Spirit. But we are also to "keep in step with the Spirit" by setting ourselves to live the way God expects. "We turn from what is evil in order to occupy ourselves with what is good."[26] As we become progressively adept at remaining yielded to the Spirit, we become progressively free of sin. To the degree that we do so, we win the victory over sin in our lives. This is actually an aspect of progressive sanctification.

The forensic conquest of sin

In a forensic sense, we are declared dead to sin from the moment of our regeneration. Our baptism is a sign and symbol of what has already taken place in our lives. Paul carefully explains this change in his letter to the Romans.

> We died to sin; how can we live in it any longer? Or don't
> you know that all of us who were baptized into Christ Jesus
> were baptized into his death? We were therefore buried
> with him through baptism into death in order that, just as
> Christ was raised from the dead through the glory of the
> Father, we too may live a new life (6:2-4).

In verses 6-7, the apostle clarifies his meaning: "For we know
that our old self was crucified with him so that the body of sin
might be done away with, that we should no longer be slaves to
sin — because anyone who has died has been freed from sin." In
the same act that God reckons us to be justified, He also reckons
us to be dead to sin. This is a declarative (or, forensic) act of God;
the believer is not made free from sin in practice. Because he has
been declared dead to sin, however, he has received the opportunity to begin the pilgrimage toward complete victory over sin
through the power of the Holy Spirit.

Berkouwer refers to this differentiation between the reckoning
of death to sin and the progressive movement toward victory as a
"struggle of faith." He asserts that "here we are not suggesting
an evolutionary process of sanctification which man has in his
own hands. The victory is already promised but is only realized in
the struggle of faith and prayer for the power of the Holy
Spirit."[27]

The ultimate victory

The ultimate defeat of sin will occur at the Parousia of our Lord.
"Christ was sacrificed once to take away the sins of many people;
and He will appear a second time, not to bear sin, but to bring
salvation to those who are waiting for him" (Heb. 9:29). In His
first advent, Christ came to deal with our sins by dying on Calvary. In His second coming (or, Parousia), Christ is coming to save
us fully and completely for eternity. Berkouwer explains that

> Christ's second coming stands in the light of his first.
> Therefore it is a gracious and unfathomable manifestation of
> the end of sin in the visio Christi. . . . Here we find a com-

fort which manifests itself in every niche and cranny of our earthly living. It manifests itself till one day we experience a *new and full estrangement from the power of our sin.* To that end Jesus Christ once died, broken and alone, outside the gates of Jerusalem.[28]

On that great day when Christ appears, a chain of events will be set into motion which will completely destroy not only the power of sin, but sin itself. Satan and his cronies will be cast into the lake of burning sulphur where "they will be tormented day and night for ever and ever" (Rev. 20:10). Last of all, "death and Hades were thrown into the lake of fire. The lake of fire is the second death" (Rev. 20:14). With Satan, his demons, and death disposed of, human beings will never again be disturbed by temptation or sin. They will be, in Augustine's language, *non posse peccare* — not able to sin.

Conclusion
A Practical
Theology of Sin

As we have seen in the previous sections of our study of the theology of sin, one of the major effects of the Fall was to damage the relationship enjoyed by human beings with their Creator and God. Because of sin, estrangement took the place of intimacy. A second, but closely related, effect was the creation of a gap between what God intended humans to be and what they have become. These results of sin are particularly tragic because our worth and identity as human beings are completely bound up in our relationship to our Maker. As one church leader has put it:

> It is my conviction that whenever a person's true identity is tied to something or someone other than God through Christ, he/she is in fact not a child of God and is doomed to ultimate despair (eternal death) as well as eventual misery in this life. It is also my conviction that whenever believers do not appropriate and live out their new-found true identity as sons and daughters in God's family, they are not doomed to ultimate despair (they will not necessarily lose their salvation), but neither will their present lives be lived with joy and zest or with power for furthering the Kingdom.[1]

402

We shall examine ways and means by which sin may be overcome and the right relationship between God and the human being may be restored, by which humans may be realigned with what God originally intended them to be.

The Value of Human Beings

The innate value of human beings is inextricably connected to their creation as the image of God. Men and women, as the apogee of God's creative activity, both separately and together reflect God's Person. "That we are created in/as the image of God does not mean that people either perfectly or completely physically reflect the spiritual reality of YHWH, but it does mean that whatever aspects of the infinite God people do represent, they are represented accurately."[2]

Theologians have hotly debated what the image of God entails. A few have considered it to be the physical form of humans; others see it as some psychological or spiritual aspect of human nature. Some regard the image as the relational character of people; still others consider it to be functional, the exercise of human stewardship over the rest of creation.[3] But attempts to demonstrate just exactly what constitutes the image are somewhat nebulous at best; each interpretation has its own difficulties. Nor does it really matter. What is vital to understand is that "the image refers to elements in the makeup of man which enable the fulfillment of his destiny. . . . the powers of personality which make man, like God, a being capable of interacting with other persons, of thinking and reflecting, and of willing freely."[4]

While the Fall destroyed the personal relationship which existed between God and humankind, it did not in any way affect the ontological relationship which exists. We see this borne out in Genesis 9:6: "Whoever sheds the blood of man, by man shall his blood be shed; for in the image of God has God made man." Human beings remain as God's image. Nor is there any suggestion to be found anywhere in Scripture that the image has been either destroyed or lost because of the Fall.

It is this ontological correspondence to God (i.e., the image) which gives to every human being dignity and immense value. To suggest that the image has been destroyed or flawed is to imply that unsaved sinners have no value or dignity. If, indeed, it has been damaged, then ontologically we are less now than we used to be, and so we possess less value or dignity.

> But just as importantly, the implication of an image tainted by sin is that we should be able to infer the degree of taintedness from the degree of sin. It then follows that because some people . . . are more overtly sinful than others, their "image" has been more drastically marred . . . some people must therefore have more worth than others in the eyes of God.[5]

Such denigrating views must be rejected. We are all of inestimable value to our Creator Lord.

Love the Sinner, Hate the Sin

Because human beings remain the image of God in spite of their sins and regardless of how depraved they may become, they possess innate worth. And as far as we know, every sinful human being is a candidate for salvation. After all, the Bible does say that God is not willing that any should perish (2 Peter 3:9). It also tells us that Christ did not come to this earth to condemn, but to save the world (John 3:17).

Moreover, we have Jesus' own example. He was a friend to tax collectors and sinners (Matt. 11:19). His Parable of the Good Samaritan demonstrated the need for us to "love our neighbor as ourself," without regard to who or what the neighbor is (Luke 10:25-37). He went even further, exhorting His followers, "But love your enemies, do good to them, and lend to them without expecting to get anything back. Then your reward will be great, and you will be sons of the Most High, because He is kind to the ungrateful and wicked. Be merciful, just as your Father is merciful" (Luke 6:35-36).

At the same time, Jesus neither approved of nor countenanced sin, in the pericope of the woman taken in adultery,[6] Jesus refused to condemn this adulteress, but He nonetheless warned her, "Go now and leave your life of sin" (John 8:11).

We would do well to imitate Jesus' pattern in dealing with sinners. That means freely associating with them, practically demonstrating the *(agape)* love of God toward them, and yet refraining from participating in, or giving tacit approval to, their sins.

Abhor evil

If we are going to love the sinner while avoiding any attitude or behavior which would approve sin in any way, then we must see sin in the same light as does God, we must abhor, or hate, it. To do so is not always easy, for we are immersed in a sinful society and have become so saturated with depravity that we do not always recognize evil when we come across it.

God is well aware that all of the created order has been tainted by sin's corruption. But He equally recognizes what atrocious damage sin has done and is doing to His creation. God realizes, more than any human being, how sin holds a person captive in the morass of his own personal guilt, how addictive it becomes. He knows the misery and pain that invades the human psyche as sinful act piles upon sinful act until the person staggers beneath its load.

We must understand, further, that God's wrath is directed against all sin. He does not distinguish between "little" sins and "big" ones. We see this inclusiveness in Proverbs 6:16-19: "There are six things the Lord hates, seven that are detestable to him: haughty eyes, a lying tongue, hands that shed innocent blood, a heart that devises wicked schemes, feet that are quick to rush into evil, a false witness who pours out lies and a man who stirs up dissension among brothers." We might feel that murder is worse than "haughty eyes," but the sage places them all in the same grouping as things hated by God. Paul says much the same thing in Galatians: "The acts of the sinful nature are obvious: sexual immorality, impurity and debauchery; idolatry and witchcraft; hatred, discord, jealousy, fits of rage, selfish ambition, dissensions, factions and envy; drunkenness, orgies, and the like. I warn you, as I did before, that those who live like this will not inherit the kingdom of God" (5:19-21). We would consider jealousy to be much less sinful than sexual immorality or orgies, but all of these are regarded by God as sufficient grounds for exclusion from His kingdom.

Unlike humans, God does not rationalize sin by calling it something less pernicious. He does not, like us, refer to fornication as

"a love affair," or cheating someone as "good business dealing."
He does not glorify theft, covetousness, and licentiousness in
stories, films, and television. He sees all sins in all of their
vileness.

As Christians, we must pray with the psalmist, "Search me,
O God, and know my heart; test me and know my anxious
thoughts. See if there is any offensive way in me, and lead me in
the way everlasting" (139:23-24). We must also agree with Him
that "because I consider all your precepts right, I hate every
wrong path" (119:128). Gordon Lewis and Bruce Demarest summarize aptly: "Until sin is the stench in our nostrils that it is in
God's, we will not grasp the seriousness with which he takes it.
Hatred of sin is necessary if one is to have the determination to
overcome it."[7]

Battle Temptation

It is important to realize that there is a major difference between
temptation and sin. Temptation is the attempt to seduce to sin, or
to entice to sin, but it is not sin in and of itself. At the same time,
to entertain temptation passively, or to solicit it actively, borders
on sin. Sin is a deviation from a perfect alignment with the will of
God, and to allow oneself deliberately or willfully to ponder the
possibility of such a deviation is to teeter on the brink of the
abyss of evil.

The story is told of a young woman visiting a coal mine. She
was dressed in a very expensive white dress and when told that
it was possible to go down into the shaft and visit the mine
works, she asked the superintendent of operations, "Is it all right
if I go down into the mine with this white dress on?" He replied,
"You may, but you don't have to!" So it is with temptation; the
person may court temptation, but doesn't have to. And if one
does dally with it, he or she should not be surprised if a fall into
sin occurs.

Jesus warned in no uncertain terms about the danger of giving
in to temptation. It is to be avoided at all costs.

> If your hand or foot causes you to sin, cut it off and throw it
> away. It is better for you to enter life maimed or crippled
> than to have two hands or two feet and be thrown into

eternal fire. And if your eye causes you to sin, gouge it out and throw it away. It is better for you to enter life with one eye than to have two eyes and be thrown into the fire of hell (Matt. 18:8-9).

Our Lord had much the same warning in regard to sexual temptation (Matt. 5:29-31), and noted that sin can be more than an action; the temptation to lust, for example, may easily become the lustful thought, which is sin: "You have heard that it was said, 'Do not commit adultery.' But I tell you that anyone who looks at a woman lustfully has already committed adultery with her in his heart" (Matt. 5:27-28). The temptation to sexual sin received similar attention from the Apostle Paul. In his pastoral advice to believers at Corinth, he warned against prolonged sexual abstinence by husband or wife: "Do not deprive each other except by mutual consent and for a time, so that you may devote yourselves to prayer. Then come together again so that Satan will not tempt you because of your lack of self-control" (1 Cor. 7:5).

We do well to overcome temptation by following as our model Christ's method of battling it. Jesus, when He was tempted by Satan following His baptism, fought back by quoting from God's Word (Luke 4:1-13). The words "it is written" were constantly on His lips. Like Him, we must be so saturated with the Scriptures that when temptation strikes God's Word comes instantly to mind. There is no better way to avoid falling into sin.

We must also remember that the excuse that a temptation was so powerful it could not be overcome is a false one. In warning believers against giving in to temptation, the Apostle Paul clearly declared,

so, if you think you are standing firm, be careful that you don't fall! No temptation has seized you except what is common to man. And God is faithful; He will not let you be tempted beyond what you can bear. But when you are tempted, He will also provide a way out so that you can stand up under it (1 Cor. 10:12-13).

God always provides a way out of temptation. Frequently, that way out is simply by saying "no."

Recognizing Human Depravity

There are three things that we must always keep in the forefront of our minds in regard to sin: (1) all of the created order has been tainted by sin; (2) every human being has inherited the tendency or desire to sin; and (3) human beings are incapable of doing anything on their own to overcome their sinfulness.

Reformed theologians often use the term "total depravity" when discussing the pervasive character of sin, although when properly understood it is a doctrine essential to all evangelicals. When we talk about "total depravity," we do not mean that human beings are absolutely corrupt, but rather that every aspect of human existence has been infected by sin.[8] This means that everything humans do is tinged with sin, including our best institutions and highest endeavors. Our music, our drama, our charitable concerns, our legal and political systems—even our churches—are all diseased to some degree.

Furthermore, when we speak of "human depravity," we mean that a person will inevitably sin "on account of his moral weakness and inherent tendency toward evil."[9] Human depravity begins very early in life, even though sin is not imputed until the age of accountability. Thus, we see even in children an inclination to do wrong, and we must expect it to be so. Consequently, we should anticipate that our children will get into trouble, that siblings will fight, and that our families will from time to time disappoint us. In our dealings with other people, we must not be surprised when we are not treated honestly or above board; we may well anticipate that others may attempt to exploit or manipulate us. Our finest institutions may well disappoint us. Because of sin, for example, churches have fights and schisms, and the Christian world is sadly divided. Even the best-intentioned people (perhaps ourselves included!) go wrong, and our greatest spiritual heroes frequently turn out to have feet of clay. Sin is universal and so touches all and everything.

Because of human inability to remedy the effects of sin, we must avoid seeking human-fashioned solutions to the problem of sin, for they are bound to fail. Many church leaders of the late nineteenth and early twentieth centuries were convinced that education and the advance of modern technology would help people to transcend their sinful inheritance. Such expectations were soon crushed by a world war followed by worldwide financial depression. Unfortunately, the mistakes of history are bound to be repeated, and educators and governmental officials in our day seem increasingly to feel that psychology and educational methodology can bring healthy living for almost all human beings. Others—such as New Age sects—believe that sin may be overcome by the absorption of the self into cosmic consciousness. Still others hold that a return to holism and nature are the proper recourse. But we know that all of these ventures are doomed to failure.

Recognize Personal Accountability

The Augustinian concept of original guilt asserts that humankind is condemned from before birth to eternal perdition. Is it any wonder in the light of such a burden that many people feel that they are not responsible for their actions? After all, if we are doomed to hell—and therefore worthless—from conception, and if we are going to be punished for someone else's sins, what chance do we have and how can we really be blamed for the way we are?

But we have shown that Adam's sin is not imputed to his posterity. The only sins for which we shall be judged are our own. Each individual, therefore, stands personally and morally accountable before God.

Because we are responsible and self-determining, we must refrain from rationalizing our sins or from attempting—like Adam—to place culpability elsewhere than where it belongs, on ourselves. And we must remind others of their responsibility for themselves. It is easier to put blame elsewhere than to face the fact that one's sin is one's own fault. It makes a person feel better (for a while, perhaps!) to pretend that one's environment, heredity, or family have forced one to do what he has done or to be what she has become. But we can no more evade our personal culpability than Adam could evade his. We must do all that we can to help people accept personal and moral accountability for their actions.

Be Prophetic about Sin

We must take sin seriously. An "I'm okay—you're okay" attitude will help no one. Christians must be quick to promote the biblical dictum on sin, identifying it for what it really is—a loathsome and defiant rebellion against God, an attempt to dethrone Him and place ourselves in charge of our own destiny.

We have already mentioned that human-crafted remedies for the disease of sin simply will not effect a cure. Educate a sinner and all one has is a more intelligent doer of evil. Get rid of a tyrannical political system and institute democracy in its place, and one has less oppressed sinners. In all cases, though, no real solution to the problem of sin has been achieved.

The only solution to the quandary of sin in the world is to transform the sinner. Jeremiah put the problem well: "The heart is deceitful above all things and beyond cure. Who can understand it?" (17:9) But he also received the answer to his question from the Lord: "I will give them a heart to know me, that I am the Lord. They will be my people, and I will be their God, for they will return to me with all their heart" (24:7). Lewis and Demarest express the matter eloquently.

> Until the inner self is born anew all the education, culture, and environmental improvements, like aspirin, may remove symptoms, but they do not address our most radical need. Until a provision is made for reconciliation to the transcendent, personal God, all other spiritual disciplines will serve only like band-aids. . . . Humans universally are depraved, alienated, and condemned. Only those with the gospel of Christ have the resources to address these radical needs.[10]

We need to have a revival of preaching against sin. The church seems to have lost its concern that those who persist in their sinful condition will go to hell and experience eternal loss. Many seem to follow the path of Karl Barth who believed that in Christ *all* human beings would avoid perdition.[11] Such neglect goes against the tenor of the New Testament church as represented by the Apostle Paul, "Since, then, we know what it is to fear the Lord [in regard to judgment], we try to persuade men" (2 Cor. 5:11). One reason for the decline of the church in our society is a lessening of evangelistic fervor. Unless and until we can restore a practical concern for the redemption of the lost, decline will continue and people will continue to flock into hell.

One means of restoring this lost fervor is to recall our own condition before our salvation. We were guilty and alienated from God until He reached out in His grace and mercy to reconcile us to Himself, until He alleviated our guilt through the crucified and risen Christ. It will also help, perhaps, to remember that we are still sinners, albeit redeemed. As someone has said, evangelism is one beggar telling another beggar where to find bread (in this case, the Bread of Life!).

Christian believers must be (or, become) prophetic in proclaiming the bad news of sin and the good news of salvation. In regard to the former, a major difficulty is a lack of a valid perception of God on the part of most of our contemporaries. Even many churchgoers operate under misconceptions of His nature. The most common seems to be that, because God is loving and merciful, He would never punish sin. Presbyterian pastor D. James Kennedy asserts that

> in a time when this heresy is so prevalent, we need to stress the true nature of God—that he is not only loving and kind and merciful, but that he is also holy and cannot condone sin. He is also righteous and has promised to punish sin and visit our iniquity with stripes. It is the nature of God that makes the whole concept of Christ's person and work meaningful.[12]

One aspect of God's holiness, mentioned earlier, is His wrath. John tells us that the perennial sinner "will not see life, for God's wrath remains on him" (John 3:36). Add to that God's righteousness which demands justice: "But the Lord Almighty will be exalted by his justice, and the holy God will show himself holy by his righteousness" (Isa. 5:16).

In confronting sin, some standard of righteousness must be used. The Decalogue is such a standard of measure (Ex. 20:1ff). The first four commandments involve human responsibilities toward God; the remaining six, with inter-human relationships. The Decalogue is summed up in Jesus' two greatest commandments, to love God with one's whole being and to love one's neighbor as oneself (Mark 12:29-31). Any honest person, when confronted, will confess that he or she has neither loved God wholeheartedly nor one's neighbor as oneself. Such an honest admission is a good beginning point.

Institutional sin

In being prophetic about sin, one must not confine oneself to individuals. An indictment must be returned against corporate sin. We have shown that all human entities have been touched by evil, institutions and societies included. Because they are constituted by sinful people, they too are sinful.

When institutions — whether political, economic, religious, or educational — oppress, exploit, or manipulate people, Christians must speak out against them. We should remember God's punishment of the Hebrew people in Old Testament times because they allowed social injustice and failed to take any steps against the situation.

> You trample on the poor and force him to give you grain. . . . You oppress the righteous and take bribes and you deprive the poor of justice in the courts. . . . Therefore, this is what the Lord, the Lord God Almighty, says, "There will be wailing in all the streets and cries of anguish in every public square. . . . for I will pass through your midst," says the Lord (Amos 5:11-12, 16-17).

God has not been lenient in regard to corporate sin, and we need to follow the prophets of the eighth and seventh century (B.C.) period in condemning such transgression.

Proclaim the Possibility of Forgiveness

There is no point in warning people against sin without also exhorting them to repentance and forgiveness. The willingness and desire of God to forgive sinners is a theme of both the Old Testament and the New. Hosea proclaimed God's promise to Israel that if they would turn to Him and seek His pardon, then "I will heal their waywardness and love them freely" (14:4). And the Chronicler records a similar promise: "If my people, who are called by my name, will humble themselves and pray and seek my face and turn from their wicked ways, then I will hear from heaven and will forgive their sin and will heal their land" (2 Chron. 7:14). A corresponding willingness is expressed by Peter on the Day of Pentecost when he tells the people to repent and be baptized in Jesus' name for the forgiveness of their sins, for "the promise is for you and your children and for all who are far off" (Acts 2:39). And God told Paul that He was sending him to the Gentiles "to open their eyes and turn them from darkness to light, and from the power of Satan to God, so that they may receive forgiveness of sins and a place among those who are sanctified by faith in me" (Acts 26:18).

God is still ready, willing, and able to forgive sinful people today. The very fact that Scripture tells us that He does not desire that any should perish (2 Peter 3:9), but that all should come to Him in the reestablishment of personal relationship (reconciliation) is an indicator that all human beings—all images of God—whether repentant or unrepentant, are of innate ontological value to Him. Such a realization is a good place to begin in reaching out to people; "the hopeless, unloved, and despairing people to whom we minister can be shown that there is hope, love, and joy available to them in spite of any circumstances solely because they are created in God's image."[13] Indeed, they are so valuable in the sight of God that Jesus "made himself nothing . . . humbled himself and became obedient to death—even death on a cross" (Phil. 2:7-8). As individuals realize their present innate worth as well as their desperate need for redemption from sin's bondage, they become able to accept what Christ has done for them on Calvary. When one accepts Christ's forgiveness, that person has reestablished the essence of personal fellowship with God enjoyed in pre-Fall Eden.[14] He becomes a new creation (2 Cor. 5:17), a child of God. She moves, as it were, from membership in Adam's sinful humanity to membership in Christ's righteous humanity.

The Christian's task, after leading a sinner to a salvific experience in Christ, is to affirm that person in his or her new identity in Christ. "Jesus knew perfectly well who he was. He had no identity crisis in his life, and . . . it is in part because Jesus knew precisely who he was . . . that he was able perfectly to fulfill the Father's will."[15] As the new believer grows in Christ, that person will become increasingly conformed to the Savior, who is the perfect image of the Father (Col. 1:15), and he or she will be increasingly removed from the old Adamic humanity enslaved by sin.

NOTES

Introduction
1. Karl Menninger, *Whatever Became of Sin?* (New York: Hawthorne, 1973), 242.
2. Ibid., 14.
3. James Leo Garrett, *Systematic Theology* (Grand Rapids: Eerdmans, 1990), 1:452.

Chapter 1
1. David Christie-Murray, *A History of Heresy* (Oxford, Great Britain: Oxford Univ. Press, 1989), 23.
2. Hans Jonas, *The Gnostic Religion*, 2nd ed. (Boston: Beacon, 1963), 193–94.
3. Frederik Wisse, trans., Introduction to "The Apocryphon of John," *The Nag Hammadi Library in English*, ed. James M. Robinson (San Francisco: Harper and Row, 1977), 98.
4. See also Elaine Pagels, *Adam, Eve, and the Serpent* (New York: Random House, 1988), 57–77 on Gnostic interpretations of humankind and sin.
5. J.N.D. Kelly, *Early Christian Doctrines*, rev. ed. (San Francisco: Harper and Row, 1978), 166.
6. Edward Yarnold, *The Theology of Sin* (Notre Dame: Fides Publishers, 1971), 58.
7. F.R. Tennant, *The Sources of the Doctrine of the Fall and Original Sin* (New York: Shocken, 1968), 276.
8. R.P.C. Hanson, ed. and trans., *Selections from Justin Martyr's Dialogue with Trypho, A Jew* (London: Lutterworth, 1963), 50.
9. Kelly, *Early Christian Doctrines*, 167.
10. Hanson, *Selections*, 100.
11. Justin Martyr, *First Apology*, in *The Ante-Nicene Fathers: Translations of the Fathers Down to A.D. 325*, ed. Alexander Roberts and James Donaldson (Grand Rapids: Eerdmans, 1953), 1.183.
12. Yarnold, *Theology of Sin*, 52.
13. Henri Rondet, *Original Sin: The Patristic and Theological Background*, trans. Cajetan Finnegan (Shannon, Ireland: Ecclesia, 1972), 69.
14. Clement, "The Epistle of S. Clement to the Corinthians," *The Apostolic Fathers*, vol. 3, ed. J.B. Lightfoot and J.R. Harmer (Grand Rapids: Baker, 1988), 58.
15. Ibid., 60.
16. Tatian, *Address of Tatian to the Greeks, The Ante-Nicene Fathers*, 2.70.
17. Ibid., 2.71.
18. Theophilus, *Theophilus to Autolycus, The Ante-Nicene Fathers*, 2.104.
19. Kelly, *Early Christian Doctrines*, 168.
20. Ibid., 101.
21. John Meyendorff, *The Byzantine Legacy in the Orthodox Church* (Crestwood, N.Y.: St. Vladimir's Seminary Press, 1982), 27.
22. Kelly, *Early Christian Doctrines*, 178–79.
23. N.P. Williams, *The Ideas of the Fall and of Original Sin* (London: Longmans, Green, 1927), 191.

24. Irenaeus, *Against Heresies, The Ante-Nicene Fathers,* 1.543.
25. Ibid., 1.454.
26. Ibid., 1.455.
27. Ibid.
28. Ibid., 1.544.
29. Tennant, *Sources of the Doctrine,* 292.
30. Justo L. Gonzalez, *Christian Thought Revisited* (Nashville: Abingdon, 1989), 44.
31. Justo L. Gonzalez, *From the Beginning to the Council of Chalcedon in* A.D. *451,* vol. 1 of *A History of Christian Thought* (Nashville: Abingdon, 1970), 208.
32. Clement, *Stromata* 2.2, *The Ante-Nicene Fathers,* 2.348.
33. Tennant, *Sources of the Doctrine,* 295.
34. Johannes Quasten, *The Ante-Nicene Literature After Irenaeus,* vol. 2 of *Patrology* (Westminster, Md.: Christian Classics, 1990), 36.
35. Clement, *Stromata* 3.16, *The Ante-Nicene Fathers,* 2.427.
36. Tennant, *Sources of the Doctrine,* 296.
37. Origen, *De Principiis* 2.8.3, trans. G.W. Butterworth, *Origen on First Principles* (London: S.P.C.K., 1936), in *The Early and Medieval Church,* vol. 1 of *A History of Christianity,* ed. Ray C. Petry (Grand Rapids: Baker, 1962), 99.
38. Kelly, *Early Christian Doctrines,* 180–81.
39. Tennant, *Sources of the Doctrine,* 311. See also Athanasius, *On the Incarnation of the Logos* 3.3–4, *A Select Library of the Nicene and Post-Nicene Fathers of the Christian Church,* 2nd ser. (Grand Rapids: Eerdmans, 1961), 4.37–38.
40. Athanasius, *On the Incarnation of the Logos,* 4.37–38.
41. Ibid.
42. Athanasius, *Orations Against the Arians,* 1.51, *The Nicene and Post-Nicene Fathers,* 4.336.
43. Ibid.
44. Kelly, *Early Christian Doctrines,* 347–48.
45. Athanasius, *Against the Heathen* 5, *The Nicene and Post-Nicene Fathers,* 4.42.
46. Athanasius, *On the Incarnation of the Logos,* 11.4, 7, *The Nicene and Post-Nicene Fathers,* 4.42.
47. Rondet, *Original Sin,* 88.
48. George Park Fisher, *History of Christian Doctrine* (Edinburgh, Scotland: T & T Clark, 1986), 165.
49. Tennant, *Sources of the Doctrine,* 317.
50. Ibid., 323.
51. Gregory of Nyssa, *Catechetical Orations* 8, *The Nicene and Post-Nicene Fathers,* 5.482–83.
52. Kelly, *Early Christian Doctrines,* 351.
53. Gregory of Nyssa, *On Infants' Early Deaths,* vol. 5 of *The Nicene and Post-Nicene Fathers,* 5.479.
54. Gregory of Nyssa, *Catechetical Orations,* vol. 5 of *The Nicene and Post-Nicene Fathers,* 5.479.
55. Ibid., 5.497.
56. Ibid., 5.482.
57. Gregory of Nyssa, *The Life of Moses,* trans. Abraham J. Malherbe and Everett Ferguson (Toronto: Paulist, 1978), 32.
58. Gregory Nazianzus, *Orations* 40.23, in *The Later Christian Fathers,* ed. and trans. Henry Bettenson (New York: Oxford Univ. Press, 1970), 1030.
59. John Chrysostom, *Homilies in Genesis* 13.4 and 15.4, *The Nicene and Post-Nicene Fathers,* 11.382.

60. Chrysostom, *Epistle to the Romans,* Homily 10, *The Nicene and Post-Nicene Fathers,* 11.401.
61. Yarnold, *Theology of Sin,* 63.
62. Chrysostom, *Epistle to the Romans,* Homily 10, *The Nicene and Post-Nicene Fathers,* 11.402.
63. Ibid.
64. Rondet, *Original Sin,* 107.
65. Tennant, *Sources of the Doctrine,* 326.
66. Kelly, *Early Christian Doctrines,* 351.
67. Chrysostom, *Epistle to the Romans,* Homily 13, *The Nicene and Post-Nicene Fathers,* 11.433.
68. Ibid., Homily 10, v. 19, 11.403–4.
69. Ibid.
70. Chrysostom, *On Infants, The Later Christian Fathers,* 169.
71. Chrysostom, *Epistle to the Romans,* Homily 16, *The Nicene and Post-Nicene Fathers,* 11.465.
72. Tennant, *Sources of the Doctrine,* 327.
73. Johannes Quasten, *The Golden Age of Greek Patristic Literature from the Council of Nicaea to the Council of Chalcedon,* vol. 3 of *Patrology* (Utrecht, Netherlands: Spectrum, 1960), 419.
74. Kelly, *Early Christian Doctrines,* 373.
75. Jaroslav Pelikan, *The Emergence of the Catholic Tradition* (100–600), vol. 1 of *The Christian Tradition: A History of the Development of Doctrine* (Chicago: Univ. of Chicago Press, 1971), 286.
76. A.H. Armstrong and R.A. Markus, *Christian Faith and Greek Philosophy* (New York: Sheed and Ward, 1960), 43.
77. Tertullian, *A Treatise on the Soul* 28, *The Ante-Nicene Fathers,* 3.209.
78. Ibid.
79. Ibid., 220.
80. Tertullian, *Against Marcion* 22, *The Ante-Nicene Fathers,* 3.287.
81. Tennant, *Sources of the Doctrine,* 328.
82. Tertullian, *On Exhortation to Chastity* 2, *The Ante-Nicene Fathers,* 4.51.
83. Tertullian, *A Treatise on the Soul* 41, *Early Christian Fathers,* 118.
84. Ibid., 116–17.
85. Tertullian, *Against Marcion* 2.15, *The Ante-Nicene Fathers,* 3.309.
86. Tertullian, *On Baptism* 18, *The Ante-Nicene Fathers,* 3.678.
87. Ibid.
88. William Shedd, *A History of Christian Doctrine* (New York: Charles Scribner's Sons, 1909), 2.29.
89. Cyprian, *Letters* 59, *The Ante-Nicene Fathers,* 5.354.
90. Louis Berkof, *The History of Christian Doctrines* (Grand Rapids: Eerdmans, 1959), 134.
91. Adolf Harnack, *Outline of the History of Dogma,* trans. Edwin Knox Mitchell (London: Hodder and Stoughton, 1933), 331.
92. Tennant, *Sources of the Doctrine,* 343.
93. Ibid., 340.
94. Ambrose, *Apolo Dav.* 2.12, *The Later Christian Fathers,* 177.
95. Ambrose, *On Sacraments* 3.7, *The Later Christian Fathers,* 178.
96. Kelly, *Early Christian Doctrines,* 355.
97. Ambrose, *Apolo Dav.* 1.76, *The Later Christian Fathers,* 178.
98. Rondet, *Original Sin,* 122.
99. Gerald Bonner, *God's Decree and Man's Destiny: Studies on the Thought of*

Augustine of Hippo (London: Variorum Reprints, 1987), 35.

100. Williams, *The Ideas of the Fall and Original Sin*, 380–82.

101. Pagels, *Adam, Eve, and the Serpent*, 99.

102. Roy W. Bettanhouse, ed. *A Companion to the Study of St. Augustine* (Grand Rapids: Baker, 1979), 49.

103. Williams, *The Ideas of the Fall and Original Sin*, 398.

104. Rondet, *Original Sin*, 118.

105. Ibid., 137.

106. Kelly, *Early Christian Doctrines*, 362.

107. Augustine, *City of God* 13.14, trans. Gerald G. Walsh, Demetrius B. Zema, Grace Monaham, and Daniel J. Honan (Garden City, N.Y.: Image, 1958), 279.

108. Kelly, *Early Christian Doctrines*, 363.

109. Augustine, *Confessions* 8.10 in *Augustine of Hippo: Selected Writings*, trans. Mary T. Clarke, *The Classics of Western Spirituality*, ed. John Farina (New York: Paulist, 1984), 94.

110. Ibid., 8.5.

111. Harnack, *Outlines of the History of Dogma*, 374–75.

112. Augustine, *Augustine: Earlier Writings* (Philadelphia: Westminster, 1953), 381.

113. Augustine, *On Forgiveness of Sins and Baptism* 1.20, in *The Nicene and Post-Nicene Fathers*, 5.22.

114. Ibid., 2.4.

115. Harnack, *Outlines of Christian Dogma*, 375.

116. Augustine, *Retractations* 1.1.3, *The Later Christian Fathers*, 202.

117. Arthur C. McGiffert, *The West from Tertullian to Erasmus*, vol. 2 of *A History of Christian Thought* (New York: Charles Scribner's Sons, 1954), 91.

118. Augustine, *On the Gospel of John* 11, *The Nicene and Post-Nicene Fathers*, 7.73.

119. Augustine, *On Forgiveness of Sins and Baptism* 1.9, *The Nicene and Post-Nicene Fathers*, 5.18.

120. Augustine, *On Forgiveness of Sins and Baptism* 3.15, *The Nicene and Post-Nicene Fathers*, 5.74.

121. Augustine, *On Original Sin* 2.11, *The Later Christian Fathers*, 198.

122. Augustine, *Epistles* 143.6, *The Nicene and Post-Nicene Fathers*, 1.492.

123. Rondet, *Original Sin*, 122–25.

124. Pagels, *Adam, Eve, and the Serpent*, 112. Emphasis hers.

125. Augustine, *City of God* 14.18, 316–17.

126. Augustine, *City of God* 17, 294.

127. Albert Henry Newman, *A Manual of Church History* (Philadelphia: American Baptist Publication Society, 1900), 1.367.

128. Augustine, *De correp. et gratia* 23, 29, as quoted in Petry, *A History of Christianity*, 111.

129. Ibid.

130. Newman, *Manual of Church History*, 1.367.

131. Pagels, *Adam, Eve, and the Serpent*, 99.

132. Bradley L. Nassif, "Towards a 'Catholic' Understanding of St. Augustine's View of Original Sin," *Union Seminary Quarterly Review* 39 (1984): 289.

133. Augustine, *On the Proceedings of Pelagius* 23, *The Nicene and Post-Nicene Fathers*, 5.193.

134. Kelly, *Early Christian Doctrines*, 357.

135. Ibid., 359.

136. Augustine, *On the Proceedings of Pelagius* 23, *The Nicene and Post-*

Nicene Fathers, 194. Since this account of Pelagius' doctrine comes from the pen of his greatest enemy, Augustine, one must question how accurate a rendering it actually is!
137. Pagels, *Adam, Eve, and the Serpent,* 132.
138. Ibid., 136.
139. Augustine, *Epistles,* 166.16.
140. Augustine, *Contra Julianum Pelagianum* 1.2.9, *The Nicene and Post-Nicene Fathers,* 3.838.
141. Ibid.
142. Kelly, *Early Christian Doctrines,* 361.
143. David Weaver, "The Exegesis of Romans 5:12 Among the Greek Fathers and Its Implications for the Doctrine of Original Sin: The 5th–12th Centuries, Part 3," *St. Vladimir's Theological Quarterly* 29 (1985): 251.
144. Meyendorff, *The Byzantine Legacy,* 294.
145. Kelly, *Early Christian Doctrines,* 372.
146. Weaver, "The Exegesis of Romans 5:12," Part 2, 146–47.
147. Kelly, *Early Christian Doctrines,* 378.
148. Yarnold, *Theology of Sin,* 66.
149. Fisher, *History of Christian Doctrine,* 195.
150. Ibid., 197.
151. Williams, *The Ideas of the Fall,* 397.
152. Kelly, *Early Christian Doctrines,* 371–72.

Chapter 2
1. Gregory I, *Moralia,* 25.9.22 as cited by G.R. Evans, *The Thought of Gregory the Great* (Cambridge, Great Britain: Cambridge Univ. Press, 1986), 100.
2. Gregory I, *Moralia,* 18.52.84 as cited by Reinhold Seeberg, *History of Doctrines in the Middle Ages and Early Modern Ages,* vol. 2 of *Textbook of the History of Doctrines,* trans. Charles E. Hay (Grand Rapids: Baker, 1954), 21–22.
3. Ibid., 33.21.39.
4. Seeberg, *History of Doctrines,* 2.22–23.
5. Ibid., 2.30–31.
6. William C. Placher, *A History of Christian Theology* (Louisville: Westminster, 1983), 126.
7. Gottschalk, *Migne,* PH 121, 368A, as quoted by Bengt Higglund, *History of Theology,* 3rd ed., trans. Gene J. Lund (St. Louis: Concordia, 1968), 153.
8. Gottschalk, quoted in Florus of Lyons, *On the Three Epistles,* 21 cited by Jaroslav Pelikan, *The Growth of Medieval Theology* (600–1300), vol. 3 of *The Christian Tradition,* 83.
9. Placher, *Christian Theology,* 127.
10. Fisher, *History of Christian Doctrine,* 206.
11. Seeberg, *History of Doctrines,* 2.32.
12. Philip Schaff, *The Middle Ages,* vol. 5 of *History of the Christian Church* (Grand Rapids: Eerdmans, 1907), 750.
13. N.P. Williams, *The Ideas of the Fall and of Original Sin* (London: Longmans, Green, 1927), 418.
14. John McIntyre, *St. Anselm and His Critics* (Edinburgh: Oliver and Boyd, 1954), 68.
15. Ibid., 69.
16. Ibid., 70.
17. Anselm, *Cur Deus Homo,* 1.12 cited by Seeberg, *History of Doctrines,* 2.67.

18. Seeberg, *History of Doctrines,* 2.67.
19. Eugene R. Fairweather, ed. and trans., *A Scholastic Miscellany: Anselm to Ockham,* vol. 10 of *Library of Christian Classics,* ed. John Baillie, John T. McNeill, and Henry P. Van Dusen (Philadelphia: Westminster, 1956), 58.
20. Geoffrey W. Bromiley, *Historical Theology: An Introduction* (Grand Rapids: Eerdmans, 1978), 150.
21. William T. Shedd, *A History of Christian Doctrine* (New York: Charles Scribner's Sons, 1909), 2.121.
22. Rondet, *Original Sin,* 149.
23. Anselm, *Why God Became Man and the Virgin Conception and Original Sin,* trans. Joseph M. Colleran (New York: Magi, 1969), 208.
24. Ibid., 210.
25. McGiffert, *The West from Tertullian to Erasmus,* 205–6.
26. Fisher, *History of Christian Doctrine,* 222.
27. Schaff, *History of the Christian Church,* 5.626.
28. McGiffert, *The West from Tertullian to Erasmus,* 216–17.
29. Seeberg, *History of Doctrines,* 2.81–82.
30. Rondet, *Original Sin,* 144.
31. Thomas Aquinas, *Summa Theologica,* trans. Fathers of the English Dominican Province (New York: Benziger Brothers, 1947), 956.
32. Thomas Aquinas, *Compendium of Theology,* trans. Cyril Vollert (St. Louis: B. Herder, 1947), 205.
33. Aquinas, *Summa,* 959.
34. Ibid., 953.
35. Ibid., 952.
36. Ibid., 958.
37. Aquinas, *Compendium,* 209.
38. Aquinas, *Summa,* 976.
39. Ibid.
40. Schaff, *A History of the Christian Church,* 5.670.
41. Aquinas, *Summa,* 907.
42. Ibid., 897.
43. Ibid., 911.
44. Philip J. Neudorf, "Thomas Aquinas and His View of Sin" (Paper presented to History of the Church to the Reformation class, Providence Theological Seminary, April 1992), 9.
45. Aquinas, *Summa,* 2404.
46. Neudorf, "Thomas Aquinas," 10.
47. Aquinas, *Summa,* 945.
48. Ibid., 945.
49. Ibid., 949.
50. Ibid.
51. Ibid., 968.
52. Neudorf, "Thomas Aquinas," 14.
53. Seeberg, *History of Doctrines,* 2.148.
54. Williams, *The Ideas of the Fall,* 418.
55. John Duns Scotus, *God and Creatures, The Quadlibetal Questions,* trans. Felix Alluntis and Allan B. Wolter (Princeton: Princeton Univ. Press, 1975), 375.
56. Seeberg, *History of Doctrines,* 2.154.
57. Ibid., 2.157.
58. Ibid., 161.

59. McGiffert, *The West from Tertullian to Erasmus*, 2.304–05.

60. John P. Dolan, *The Essential Erasmus* (New York: Mentor-Omega, 1964), 17–20.

61. Erasmus, *Enchiridion Militis Christiani*, 1.1 in Dolan, *The Essential Erasmus*, 29.

62. Ibid.

63. Ibid., 30.

64. Ibid., 32.

65. Ibid., 35.

66. Ibid., 1.6, 49.

67. Ibid., 50.

68. Ibid.

69. Ibid., 2.5, 65.

70. Ibid., 66.

71. Erasmus, *Concerning the Immense Mercy of God*, in Dolan, *The Essential Erasmus*, 253.

72. Harnack, *History of Dogma*, 496.

Chapter 3

1. Jaroslav Pelikan, *Reformation of Church and Dogma* (1300–1700), vol. 4 of *The Christian Tradition: A History of the Development of Doctrine* (Chicago: Univ. of Chicago Press, 1984), 129.

2. Reinhold Seeberg, *History of Doctrines in the Middle and Early Modern Ages*, vol. 2 of *The History of Doctrines*, trans. Charles E. Hay (Grand Rapids: Baker, 1954), 236.

3. Martin Luther, *Luther's Works*, 35.369 as cited by Paul Althaus, *The Theology of Martin Luther*, trans. Robert C. Schultz (Philadelphia: Westminster, 1966), 145.

4. Martin Luther, *Works of Martin Luther*, 2.364 as quoted by Althaus, 145.

5. Bengt Hägglund, *History of Theology*, 3rd ed., trans. Gene J. Lund (St. Louis: Concordia, 1968), 229.

6. Martin Luther, *Lectures on Genesis*, 1.26 as quoted by Pelikan, *The Christian Tradition*, 4.143.

7. Hägglund, *History of Theology*, 230.

8. Seeberg, *History of Doctrines*, 2.242.

9. Althaus, *Theology of Martin Luther*, 157–58.

10. Ibid., 158.

11. Luther, *Luther's Works*, 25.376 as quoted by Geoffrey W. Bromiley, *Historical Theology: An Introduction* (Grand Rapids: Eerdmans, 1978), 344–45.

12. Luther, *Luther's Works*, 16.143 as quoted by Althaus, *Theology of Martin Luther*, 159.

13. Martin Luther, "Preface to the Old Testament," in *Word and Sacrament I*, vol. 35 of *Luther's Works*, trans. Theodore Bachmann (Philadelphia: Westminster, 1960), 242.

14. Altman F. Swihart, *Luther and the Lutheran Church (1483–1900)* (New York: Philosophical Library, 1960), 72.

15. Seeberg, *History of Doctrines*, 2.240–41.

16. Ibid., 245.

17. Martin Luther, "The Holy and Blessed Sacrament of Baptism," *Luther's Works*, 35.30.

18. Swihart, *Luther*, 105–6.

19. Luther, "Baptism," 30.
20. Ibid., 37.
21. Samuel M. Jackson, *Huldreich Zwingli, The Reformer of German Switzerland 1484–1531,* 2nd ed. rev. (New York: G.P. Putnam's Sons, 1900), 376–77.
22. Seeberg, *History of Doctrines,* 2.309.
23. Jackson, *Huldreich Zwingli,* 377.
24. Ibid.
25. Ibid., 377–78.
26. G.R. Patten, *Zwingli* (Cambridge, Great Britain: Cambridge Univ. Press, 1976), 336.
27. Robert C. Walton, *Zwingli's Theocracy* (Toronto: Univ. of Toronto Press, 1967), 171–72.
28. Seeberg, *History of Doctrines,* 2.309–10.
29. Philip Melancthon, "Loci Communes Theologici," in *Melancthon and Bucer,* ed. William Pauck, trans. Lowell J. Satre, vol. 19 of *The Library of Christian Classics* (Philadelphia: Westminster, 1969), 30–31.
30. Ibid., 31.
31. Ibid.
32. Ibid., 33.
33. Ibid., 36–37.
34. Ibid., 45.
35. John Calvin, *Institutes of the Christian Religion,* trans. Ford L. Battles, ed. John T. McNeill, vols. 20–21 of *The Library of Christian Classics* (Philadelphia: Westminster, 1977), 232.
36. Ibid., 245.
37. Ibid., 338.
38. Ibid.
39. Ibid.
40. Ibid., 249.
41. Ibid., 250.
42. Ibid., 251.
43. Ibid., 246.
44. Ibid., 251.
45. John Calvin, *Psalms,* trans. James Anderson, vol. 5 of *Calvin's Commentary* (Grand Rapids: Baker, 1979), 290.
46. John Calvin, *Romans,* trans. John Owen, vol. 19 of *Calvin's Commentary,* 200.
47. G.C. Berkouwer, *Sin: Studies in Dogmatics* (Grand Rapids: Eerdmans, 1980), 484.
48. Calvin, *Institutes,* 250.
49. Ibid., 251.
50. Ibid., 423.
51. Ibid., 355.
52. Ibid., 294.
53. W.N. Dean Murphy, "Calvin on the Fall, Sin, and Man's Will" (Theology Colloquium paper, Providence Theological Seminary, 1989), 9–10.
54. Calvin, *Institutes,* 267.
55. Ibid., 328.
56. Ibid., 309.
57. Ibid., 288.
58. Ibid., 296.
59. Ibid.

60. Ibid., 294.
61. Ibid., 295.
62. Ibid., 295–96.
63. Ibid., 300.
64. Ibid., 926.
65. Ibid., 956.
66. John Calvin, *Corpus Reformatorum*, 29:836 as quoted by Pelikan, *The Christian Tradition*, 4.222.
67. R.T. Jones, "Schwenkfeld, Caspar (1489–1561)," in *New Dictionary of Theology*, ed. Sinclair B. Ferguson, David F. Wright, and J.I. Packer (Downers Grove, Ill.: InterVarsity, 1988), 624.
68. Fisher, *History of Christian Doctrine*, 318.
69. Ibid., 320–21.
70. Hugglund, *History of Theology*, 323.
71. Ibid., 268.
72. W.R. Bagnall, Preface to *The Writings of James Arminius*, trans. James Nichols, ed. W.R. Bagnall (Grand Rapids: Baker, 1956), 1.iii.
73. James Arminius, "Declaration of Sentiments," in *The Writings of James Arminius*, 1.221–22.
74. Ibid., 1.227.
75. Ibid., 1.229.
76. Ibid., 1.248.
77. Arminius, "Apology," in *The Writings of James Arminius*, 1.318.
78. Ibid., 1.319.
79. Arminius, "Public Disputations," in *The Writings of James Arminius*, 1.484–85.
80. Ibid., 1.486.
81. Ibid., 1.489–90.
82. Ibid., 1.490.
83. Ibid., 1.491.
84. Pelikan, *The Christian Tradition*, 4.248.
85. Fisher, *History of Christian Doctrine*, 326–27.
86. Ibid., 327.
87. Seeberg, *History of Doctrines*, 2.432.
88. Ibid.
89. Ibid., 2.432–33.
90. Ibid., 2.437–38.
91. Fisher, *History of Christian Doctrine*, 334.
92. Seeberg, *History of Doctrines*, 2.453.

Chapter 4
1. Gerald R. Cragg, "Introduction to John Wesley," in *The Appeals to Men of Reason and Religion and Certain Related Open Letters*, vol. 2 of *The Works of John Wesley*, ed. Gerald R. Cragg (Oxford, Great Britain: Clarendon, 1975), 14–15.
2. John Wesley, "The Doctrine of Original Sin," in *The Works of John Wesley*, 3rd ed. (1872; reprint, Grand Rapids: Baker, 1979), 9.415–16.
3. Ibid., 9.416.
4. Ibid., 9.417.
5. Ibid., 9.418.
6. John Wesley, "Letter to Dr. Robertson," in *The Letters of the Rev. John*

Wesley, A.M., 3.107 in Philip S. Watson, comp., *The Message of the Wesleys* (Grand Rapids: Francis Asbury, 1984), 82.

7. Wesley, "Original Sin," *Works*, 9.196–238.

8. Ibid., 9.429.

9. John Wesley, "Sermon 44.2.7" as cited by William R. Cannon, *The Theology of John Wesley* (New York: Abingdon, 1946), 193.

10. Watson, *Message of the Wesleys*, 82.

11. Cannon, *Theology of John Wesley*, 195.

12. John Wesley, "Thoughts on Salvation by Faith," in *Works*, 11.405.

13. Geoffrey W. Bromiley, *Historical Theology: An Introduction* (Grand Rapids: Eerdmans, 1978), 336.

14. Ibid., 334.

15. Wesley, "On Sin in Believers," in *Works*, 5.152.

16. Ibid., 155.

17. Ibid., 156.

18. Wesley, "Plain Account of Christian Perfection," in *Works*, 11.374–75.

19. Ibid., 11.378.

20. Ibid., 11.394.

21. Ibid., 11.395.

22. Justo L. Gonzalez, *A History of Christian Thought* (Nashville: Abingdon, 1975), 3.120.

23. Friedrich Schleiermacher, *The Christian Faith*, 2nd ed., ed. H.R. Mackintosh and J.S. Stewart (Edinburgh, Scotland: T & T Clark, 1928), 12.

24. Ibid., 18.

25. Ibid., 19.

26. Ibid., 23.

27. Ibid., 20.

28. Gonzalez, *History of Christian Thought*, 3.324.

29. Schleiermacher, *Christian Faith*, 238.

30. Ibid., 240.

31. Gonzalez, *History of Christian Thought*, 3.325.

32. Schleiermacher, *Christian Faith*, 244.

33. Gonzalez, *History of Christian Thought*, 3.325.

34. Schleiermacher, *The Christian Faith*, 270.

35. Ibid., 272.

36. Ibid., 273.

37. Ibid., 279.

38. Ibid., 281.

39. Ibid.

40. Ibid., 282.

41. Ibid., 306.

42. Bernard Ramm, *Offense to Reason: The Theology of Sin* (San Francisco: Harper and Row, 1985), 130.

43. Gonzalez, *History of Christian Thought*, 3.326.

44. Schleiermacher, *Christian Faith*, 355–56.

45. Gonzalez, *History of Christian Thought*, 3.328.

46. James Orr, *The Ritschlian Theology and the Evangelical Faith* (London: Hodder and Stoughton, 1897), 42.

47. Gonzalez, *History of Christian Thought*, 3.342–43.

48. David L. Mueller, *An Introduction to the Theology of Albrecht Ritschl* (Philadelphia: Westminster, 1969), 70.

49. Ibid., 70–71.

50. Orr, *Ritschlian Theology*, 145.
51. Albrecht Ritschl, *The Christian Doctrine of Justification and Reconciliation: The Positive Development of the Doctrine*, 3rd ed., trans. H.R. Mackintosh and A.B. Macaulay (Edinburgh, Scotland: T & T Clark, 1902), 335 as quoted by Mueller, *An Introduction*, 72.
52. Albrecht Ritschl, *Instruction in the Christian Religion* in Albert Swing, *The Theology of Albrecht Ritschl* (Longmans, Green, 1901), 204 as quoted by Mueller, *An Introduction*, 73.
53. Gonzalez, *History of Christian Thought*, 3.343.
54. Ibid., 3.343–44.
55. Walter Rauschenbusch, *A Theology for the Social Gospel* (Nashville: Abingdon, 1945), 5.
56. Ibid., 24.
57. Ibid., 40–41.
58. Ibid., 42.
59. Ibid., 43.
60. Ibid., 44.
61. Ibid., 47.
62. Ibid., 48.
63. Ibid., 50.
64. Ibid., 53.
65. Ibid., 58.
66. Ibid., 59.
67. Ibid., 61.
68. Ibid., 85.
69. Ibid.
70. Ibid., 92–93.
71. Ibid., 117.
72. Anthony C. Thiselton, "An Age of Anxiety," in *Eerdmans' Handbook to the History of Christianity*, ed. Tim Dowley (Grand Rapids: Eerdmans, 1977), 600.
73. George E. Arbaugh and George B. Arbaugh, *Kierkegaard's Authorship* (London: George Allen and Unwin, 1968), 20–21.
74. Ramm, *Offense to Reason*, 54.
75. Arbaugh, *Kierkegaard's Authorship*, 163.
76. Ibid., 167.
77. Ibid., 168.
78. Gonzalez, *History of Christian Thought*, 3.339.
79. Alexander J. McKelway, *The Systematic Theology of Paul Tillich, A Review and Analysis* (Richmond, Va.: John Knox, 1964), 17–18.
80. David L. Smith, *A Handbook of Contemporary Theology* (Wheaton, Ill.: BridgePoint/Victor Books, 1992), 79.
81. McKelway, *Systematic Theology of Paul Tillich*, 26–27.
82. Paul Tillich, *Systematic Theology* (Chicago: Univ. of Chicago Press, 1967), 1.211.
83. Paul Tillich, as quoted by John Hick, *Philosophy of Religion* (Englewood Cliffs, N.J.: Prentice-Hall, 1963), 67.
84. Tillich, *Systematic Theology*, 2.44.
85. Ibid., 2.45.
86. Ibid.
87. Ibid., 2.46.
88. Ibid., 2.29.
89. Ibid., 2.56.

90. Ibid., 2.61.
91. Ibid., 3.41.
92. Ibid.
93. Ibid., 2.43–44.
94. Ibid., 1.49.
95. Ibid., 2.166.
96. Smith, *Contemporary Theology*, 27.
97. Karl Barth, *The Doctrine of Reconciliation*, vol. 4/1 of *Church Dogmatics*, trans. G.W. Bromiley (Edinburgh, Scotland: T & T Clark, 1956), 508.
98. Ibid.
99. Ibid., 509.
100. Ibid., 511.
101. Ibid., 512.
102. Ibid., 516.
103. Bengt Hägglund, *History of Theology*, 3rd ed., trans. Gene J. Lund (St. Louis: Concordia, 1968), 402.
104. Smith, *Contemporary Theology*, 30–31.
105. Ibid., 31.
106. Emil Brunner, *The Christian Doctrine of Creation and Redemption*, vol. 2 of *Dogmatics*, trans. Olive Wyon (Philadelphia: Westminster, 1952), 48.
107. Ibid., 52.
108. Ibid., 89.
109. Ibid., 91.
110. Ibid., 92.
111. Ibid., 95.
112. Ibid., 96.
113. Ibid., 97.
114. Ibid., 97–98.
115. Ibid., 103–5.
116. Ibid., 106.
117. Ibid., 107.
118. Ibid., 125.
119. Ibid., 130.
120. Ibid., 133.
121. Ibid., 136.
122. Ibid., 138.
123. Ibid., 141.
124. Smith, *Contemporary Theology*, 33.
125. Reinhold Niebuhr, *The Nature and Destiny of Man* (New York: Charles Scribner's Sons, 1964), 1.179–80.
126. Ibid., 180.
127. Ibid., 180–81.
128. Ibid., 183.
129. Ibid., 188.
130. Ibid., 192.
131. Ibid., 194–95.
132. Ibid., 196.
133. Ibid., 200.
134. Ibid., 201.
135. Ibid., 208.
136. Ibid., 222.
137. Ibid., 226.

138. Ibid., 242–43.
139. Ibid., 250.
140. Ibid., 251.
141. Ibid.
142. Reinhold Niebuhr, *The Self and the Dramas of History*, 237 as quoted by Gordon Harland, *The Thought of Reinhold Niebuhr* (New York: Oxford Univ. Press, 1960), 82.
143. Ibid.

Chapter 5
1. Jürgen Moltmann, *Theology of Hope*, trans. James W. Leitch (London: SCM, 1967), 22.
2. Ibid.
3. Ibid., 23.
4. Ibid., 32.
5. Ibid.
6. Jürgen Moltmann, *Man: Christian Anthropology in Conflicts of the Present*, trans. John Sturdy (Philadelphia: Fortress, 1974), 19–20.
7. Ibid., 116–17.
8. E. Frank Tupper, *The Theology of Wolfhart Pannenberg* (Philadelphia: Westminster, 1973), 21–24.
9. Smith, *Contemporary Theology*, 140, 147.
10. Wolfhart Pannenberg, *Anthropology in Theological Perspective*, trans. Matthew J. O'Connell (Philadelphia: Westminster, 1985), 89.
11. Ibid., 87–88.
12. Ibid., 91.
13. Ibid., 92.
14. Ibid., 99.
15. Ibid., 107.
16. Ibid., 108.
17. Ibid., 109.
18. Ibid., 110.
19. Ibid., 119.
20. Ibid.
21. Ibid., 119–20.
22. Ibid., 122.
23. Ibid., 123.
24. Ibid., 124.
25. Ibid., 125–27.
26. Ibid., 129–30.
27. Ibid., 133.
28. Ibid., 134.
29. Ibid., 138.
30. Daniel Day Williams, "God and Man," in *Process Theology: Basic Writings*, ed. Ewart H. Cousins (New York: Newman, 1971), 175.
31. Ibid., 178.
32. Ibid., 179.
33. Ibid.
34. Ibid., 185–86.
35. Norman Pittenger, *Loving Says It All* (New York: Pilgrim, 1978), 17.
36. Ibid., 25.

37. Ibid., 36.
38. Ibid., 74.
39. Ibid., 77.
40. Ibid., 57.
41. Norman Pittenger, "Process Thought: A Contemporary Trend in Theology," in Cousins, *Process Theology*, 33.
42. Smith, *Contemporary Theology*, 203.
43. Gustavo Gutiérrez, *The Truth Shall Make You Free: Confrontations*, trans. Matthew J. O'Connell (Maryknoll, N.Y.: Orbis, 1990), 136.
44. Gustavo Gutiérrez, *A Theology of Liberation*, trans. and ed. Sister Caridad Inda and John Eagleson (Maryknoll, N.Y.: Orbis, 1973), 35.
45. Gutiérrez, *Confrontations*, 137.
46. Ibid., 138.
47. Ibid.
48. Gutiérrez, *A Theology of Liberation*, 177.
49. James H. Cone, *Black Theology and Black Power* (New York: Seabury, 1969), 1.
50. Ibid., 31.
51. James H. Cone, "Black Theology and the Black Church: Where Do We Go From Here?" in *Liberation Theologies*, No. 4 of Mission Trends, ed. Gerald H. Anderson and Thomas F. Stransky (New York: Paulist, 1979), 134–35.
52. Cone, *Black Theology and Black Power*, 9–10.
53. James H. Cone, *God of the Oppressed* (New York: Seabury, 1975), 146.
54. James H. Cone, *The Spirituals and the Blues* (Maryknoll, N.Y.: Orbis, 1991).
55. Ibid., 74–75.
56. Ibid., 76.
57. Ibid., 76–77.
58. Cone, *God of the Oppressed*, 147.
59. James H. Cone, *A Black Theology of Liberation* (Philadelphia: Lippincott, 1970), 160.
60. Cone, *God of the Oppressed*, 148.
61. Ibid., 149–50.
62. C.S. Song, *Theology from the Womb of Asia* (Maryknoll, N.Y.: Orbis, 1986), 132.
63. Ibid., 189.
64. Ibid., 190.
65. Ibid., 191.
66. Ibid.
67. Ibid., 192.
68. Gutiérrez, *Confrontations*, 31.
69. Smith, *Contemporary Theology*, 224.
70. Ibid., 292–93.
71. Matthew Fox, *Creation Spirituality* (San Francisco: Harper/Collins, 1991), 7.
72. Ibid., 9.
73. Ibid., 11.
74. Ibid., 17–18.
75. Matthew Fox, *Original Blessing* (Santa Fe: Bear and Company, 1983), 119.
76. Ibid.
77. Ibid., 121.
78. Ibid., 160.
79. Ibid., 161.
80. Ibid., 163.

81. Ibid., 232.
82. Ibid.
83. Ibid., 235.
84. Ibid., 295.
85. Ibid.
86. Ibid., 296.
87. Ibid., 297.
88. Ibid., 50.
89. Smith, *Contemporary Theology*, 300.
90. Matthew Fox, *Whee!, We, Wee All the Way Home* (Santa Fe: Bear and Company, 1981), 102.
91. Ibid., 90.
92. Karl Rahner, *Foundations of the Christian Faith*, trans. William V. Dyck (New York: Seabury, 1978), 90.
93. Ibid., 91.
94. Ibid., 92–93.
95. Ibid., 100.
96. Ibid., 103.
97. Ibid.
98. Ibid.
99. Ibid., 111.
100. Ibid., 113–14.
101. Ibid., 115.
102. See Piet Schoonenberg, *Man and Sin: A Theological View*, trans. Joseph Donceel (Notre Dame, Ind.: Univ. of Notre Dame Press, 1965), 98ff.
103. Roger Haight, "Sin and Grace," in *Systematic Theology: Roman Catholic Perspectives*, ed. Francis S. Fiorenza and John P. Galvin (Minneapolis: Fortress, 1991), 87–88.
104. D. Parker, "Original Sin: A Study in Evangelical Theory," *The Evangelical Quarterly*, 61 (1989): 64.
105. Donald G. Bloesch, *Essentials of Evangelical Theology*, vol. 1 (San Francisco: Harper and Row, 1978), 104.
106. Ibid.
107. Ibid., 105.
108. Ibid., 106.
109. Ibid., 107.
110. Bloesch, *Essentials of Evangelical Theology*, vol. 2, 133.
111. Parker, "Original Sin," 65.
112. Millard J. Erickson, *Christian Theology* (Grand Rapids: Baker, 1983–85), 638.
113. Ibid., 639.
114. Ibid.

Chapter 6
1. Henri Blocher, *In the Beginning*, trans. David G. Preston (Downers Grove, Ill.: InterVarsity, 1984), 15.
2. Francis A. Schaeffer, *Genesis in Space and Time* (Downers Grove, Ill.: InterVarsity, 1972), 9.
3. Claus Westermann, *Genesis 1–11: A Commentary*, trans. John J. Scullion (Minneapolis: Augsburg, 1984), 275.
4. Blocher, *Beginning*, 135.

5. Westermann, *Genesis 1–11*, 275–76.
6. See Blocher, *Beginning*, 135.
7. Gerhard von Rad, *Genesis*, rev. ed., *Old Testament Library* (Philadelphia: Westminster, 1972), 81.
8. Schaeffer, *Genesis in Space and Time*, 71.
9. Von Rad, *Genesis*, 87.
10. See Westermann, *Genesis 1–11*, 239 and Von Rad, *Genesis*, 88.
11. C.F. Keil, *Commentary on the Old Testament* (1878; reprint, Grand Rapids: Eerdmans, 1975), 1.86.
12. Westermann, *Genesis 1–11*, 243.
13. Von Rad, *Genesis*, 89.
14. Blocher, *Beginning*, 126–27.
15. Ray C. Stedman, *Understanding Man* (Waco: Word, 1975), 75.
16. Claus Westermann, *The Genesis Accounts of Creation*, trans. Norman E. Wagner (Philadelphia: Fortress, 1964), 31.
17. Westermann, *Genesis 1–11*, 254.
18. Von Rad, *Genesis*, 91.
19. Westermann, *Genesis 1–11*, 256.
20. Blocher, *Beginning*, 179.
21. See Susan T. Foh, "What Is the Woman's Desire?" *Westminster Theological Journal* 37 (Spring 1975): 376–83.
22. Blocher, *Beginning*, 179. Emphasis his.
23. Von Rad, *Genesis*, 97.
24. The argument may also be made that being banned from the tree of life is in sequence with the claim to deity that "the man has become as one of us." The claim to autonomy made them in some sense like God, but they did not have the ability to be as God, for they did not have within themselves the power of life. They were not like God in that sense. They had "become as one of us" only in their acting autonomously. But in actual fact, they were subordinate to Him and must now die because they had cut themselves off from the source of life in severing themselves from God.
25. Von Rad, *Genesis*, 297.
26. Blocher, *Beginning*, 207.
27. Westermann, *Genesis 1–11*, 302.
28. Von Rad, *Genesis*, 106.
29. Ibid.
30. Ibid., 107.
31. Blocher, *Beginning*, 200.
32. See Westermann, *Genesis 1–11*, 369–79 and Von Rad, *Genesis*, 113–16.
33. See Schaeffer, *Genesis in Space and Time*, 125–27.
34. Blocher, *Beginning*, 206.
35. E.A. Speiser, as quoted by Westermann, *Genesis 1–11*, 548.
36. Ibid., 548–49.
37. Schaeffer, *Genesis in Space and Time*, 153.
38. See Von Rad, *Genesis*, 226ff who sees Genesis 12:1ff as a Yahwistic composition while Genesis 20:1ff is from the hand of the Elohistic redactor. But cf. Clyde T. Francisco, "Genesis," in *The Broadman Bible Commentary*, rev. ed. (Nashville: Broadman, 1969), 1.180 who says that it is perfectly conceivable that Abraham tried this manuever a second time.
39. Von Rad, *Genesis*, 224.
40. Ibid., 267.
41. Chester K. Lehman, *Biblical Theology* (Scottdale, Pa.: Herald, 1971).

42. Von Rad, *Genesis,* 291.
43. B.T. Dahlberg, "On Recognizing the Unity of Genesis," *Theology Digest,* 24 (1977): 361 as cited by David J.A. Clines, *The Theme of the Pentateuch,* vol. 10 of *Journal for the Study of the Old Testament,* Supplemental Series (Sheffield, Great Britain: JSOT, 1978), 84.
44. Ibid.
45. Clines, *Theme of the Pentateuch,* 85.
46. A. Noordtzij, *Leviticus,* trans. Raymond Togtman, *Bible Student's Commentary* (Grand Rapids: Zondervan, 1982), 1.
47. Philip Budd, "The Sacrificial System," in *Eerdmans' Handbook to the Bible* (Grand Rapids: Eerdmans, 1973), 174.
48. Noordtzij, *Leviticus,* 63.
49. Ibid., 68.
50. Gerhard von Rad, *Old Testament Theology,* trans. D.M.G. Stalker (New York: Harper and Row, 1962), 1.259.
51. Noordtzij, *Leviticus,* 69.
52. J.C. Rylaarsdam, "Atonement, Day of," in *The Interpreter's Dictionary of the Bible* (Nashville: Abingdon Press, 1962), 1.313.
53. Ibid., 1.315.
54. Noordtzij, *Leviticus,* 168–69.
55. Rylaarsdam, "Atonement," 1.316.
56. Donald L. Williams, "Deuteronomy in Modern Study," *Review and Expositor,* 61 (Fall 1964): 270.
57. For a discussion of various dates and reasons therefore, see J.A. Thompson, *Deuteronomy, Tyndale Old Testament Commentaries* (Downers Grove, Ill.: InterVarsity, 1974), 47–68.
58. Ibid., 68.
59. Marvin E. Tate, "The Deuteronomic Philosophy of History," *Review and Expositor* 61 (Fall 1964): 311.
60. Ibid., 314.
61. John D.W. Watts, "The Deuteronomic Theology," *Review and Expositor* 74 (Summer 1977): 321.
62. Martin Noth, *The Deuteronomistic History* (Sheffield, England: JSOT, 1981), 5.
63. Watts, "Deuteronomic Theology," 322.
64. Thompson, *Deuteronomy,* 14–15. Other views of the book's structure are noted in pp. 15–21.
65. Ibid., 102.
66. Ibid., 114.
67. Gerhard von Rad, *Deuteronomy, The Old Testament Library* (Philadelphia: Westminster, 1966), 59.
68. A.D.H. Mayes, *Deuteronomy, New Century Bible Commentary* (London: Marshall, Morgan and Scott, 1979), 176.
69. Tate, "The Deuteronomic Philosophy of History," 314–15.
70. Thompson, *Deuteronomy,* 142.
71. Mayes, *Deuteronomy,* 219–20.
72. Von Rad, *Deuteronomy,* 173.
73. See von Rad, *Deuteronomy,* 173–74 and Mayes, *Deuteronomy,* 349–50.
74. Thompson, *Deuteronomy,* 279.
75. Ibid.
76. Mayes, *Deuteronomy,* 365–66.
77. Von Rad, *Deuteronomy,* 183ff. holds to a later date for Deuteronomy and so

presumes that the Exile has already taken place at the time of writing and that the people have become repentant.

78. David J.A. Clines, "Images of God in the Pentateuch," *Studies in Old Testament Theology,* ed. Robert L. Hubbard, Robert K. Johnston, and Robert P. Meye (Waco, Texas: Word, 1992), 81.

79. Von Rad, *Old Testament Theology,* 1.155.

Chapter 7

1. Gnana Robinson, *Let Us Be Like the Nations: A Commentary on the Books of 1 and 2 Samuel* (Grand Rapids: Eerdmans, 1993), 2.

2. Walter E. Rast, *Joshua, Judges, Samuel, Kings, Proclamation Commentaries* (Philadelphia: Fortress, 1978), 16.

3. John D.W. Watts, "The Deuteronomic Theology," *Review and Expositor* 74 (Summer 1977): 332.

4. Ibid.

5. Marten H. Woudstra, *The Book of Joshua, The New International Commentary on the Old Testament* (Grand Rapids: Eerdmans, 1981), 4.

6. See Woudstra, *Joshua,* 33.

7. Ibid.

8. Trent C. Butler, *Joshua, The Word Biblical Commentary* (Waco: Word, 1983), 71.

9. Ibid., 83.

10. Woudstra, *Joshua,* 129.

11. Butler, *Joshua,* 93.

12. Ibid., 236.

13. Woudstra, *Joshua,* 337.

14. Ibid., 353–54.

15. Arthur E. Cundall, *Judges,* in Arthur E. Cundall and Leon Morris, *Judges and Ruth, The Tyndale Old Testament Commentaries* (Downers Grove, Ill.: InterVarsity, 1968), 15.

16. While there is not unanimity among scholars as to the dating of this period, Cundall, *Judges,* 28–33 places it from about 1230–1020 B.C.

17. Ibid., 35.

18. Interview with August Konkel, Professor of Old Testament Studies, Providence Theological Seminary, 20 May 1993.

19. Rast, *Joshua, Judges, Samuel, Kings,* 27.

20. Daniel I. Block, "Echo Narrative Technique in Hebrew Literature: A Study in Judges 19," *Westminster Theological Journal* 52 (1990): 326.

21. Ibid., 336–37.

22. Joyce G. Baldwin, *1 and 2 Samuel, Tyndale Old Testament Commentaries* (Downers Grove, Ill.: InterVarsity, 1988), 84–85.

23. Ibid., 115.

24. Otto J. Baab, *The Theology of the Old Testament* (New York: Abingdon, 1949), 168.

25. Baldwin, *1 and 2 Samuel,* 235.

26. Ibid., 239.

27. Rast, *Joshua, Judges, Samuel, Kings,* 37.

28. Richard Nelson, *First and Second Kings, Interpretation: A Bible Commentary for Teaching and Preaching* (Atlanta: John Knox, 1987), 120.

29. Ibid., 156.

30. William Sanford LaSor, "The Prophets During the Monarchy: Turning

Points in Israel's Decline," in *Israel's Apostasy and Restoration: Essays in Honor of Roland K. Harrison*, ed. Avraham Gilead (Grand Rapids: Baker, 1988), 64.

31. Nelson, *First and Second Kings*, 103.
32. Ibid., 154.
33. John Gray, *1 and 2 Kings*, The Old Testament Library (Philadelphia: Westminster, 1963), 511.
34. Ibid., 523.
35. Nelson, *1 and 2 Kings*, 221.
36. Ibid., 227.
37. Gray, *1 and 2 Kings*, 641.
38. Nelson, *First and Second Kings*, 260.
39. Von Rad, *Old Testament Theology*, 1.336.
40. Ibid.
41. Ibid., 339.
42. Watts, "Deuteronomic Theology," 335.
43. Ibid.
44. James M. Ward, *Thus Says the Lord, The Message of the Prophets* (Nashville: Abingdon, 1991), 22.
45. Emil G. Kraeling, *The Prophets* (Chicago: Rand McNally, 1969), 25–26.
46. James D. Newsome, Jr., *The Hebrew Prophets* (Atlanta: John Knox, 1984), 24.
47. Eric C. Rust, *Covenant and Hope* (Waco: Word, 1972), 50.
48. Ibid., 51.
49. Kraeling, *Prophets*, 48–49.
50. Newsome, *Hebrew Prophets*, 37.
51. Ibid., 38.
52. Ibid., 39.
53. Ward, *Thus Says the Lord*, 34.
54. Ibid., 39.
55. Rust, *Covenant and Hope*, 78.
56. Ibid., 79.
57. Ibid.
58. James Leo Green, *God Reigns: Expository Studies in the Prophecy of Isaiah* (Nashville: Broadman, 1968), 64.
59. Patrick D. Miller, Jr., *Sin and Judgment in the Prophets* (Chico, Calif.: Scholar's, 1982), 42.
60. Green, *God Reigns*, 132.
61. Ibid., 133.
62. Newsome, *Hebrew Prophets*, 42.
63. Ibid., 46–47.
64. Ward, *Thus Says the Lord*, 233.
65. Kraeling, *Prophets*, 123.
66. Ward, *Thus Says the Lord*, 258.
67. Newsome, *Hebrew Prophets*, 85.
68. Ward, *Thus Says the Lord*, 129.
69. Rust, *Covenant and Hope*, 112.
70. Ibid., 113–14.
71. Ibid., 114.
72. Lehman, *Biblical Theology*, 1.347.
73. B.J. Oosterhoff, "The Prophets," in *The World of the Old Testament*, ed. A.S. van der Woude (Grand Rapids: Eerdmans, 1989), 254.
74. Ibid.

75. Willem A. VanGemeren, *Interpreting the Prophetic Word* (Grand Rapids: Zondervan/Academie, 1990), 144.
76. Ibid., 146.
77. Ibid., 147.
78. Ibid., 149.
79. Ward, *Thus Says the Lord,* 172.
80. Newsome, *Hebrew Prophets,* 133.
81. Ibid., 134.
82. Rust, *Covenant and Hope,* 136.
83. Ibid., 137.
84. Ward, *Thus Says the Lord,* 181.
85. Ibid.
86. Oosterhoff, "Prophets," 250.
87. VanGemeren, *Interpreting the Prophetic Word,* 126.
88. Newsome, *Hebrew Prophets,* 162.
89. VanGemeren, *Interpreting the Prophetic Word,* 200.

Chapter 8
1. Von Rad, *Old Testament Theology,* 1.355.
2. Ibid., 1.356.
3. Derek Kidner, *Psalms 1–72* (Downers Grove, Ill.: InterVarsity, 1973), 35–36.
4. Ibid., 47–48.
5. Ibid., 48.
6. A.A. Anderson, *Psalms (1–72), The New Century Bible Commentary* (Grand Rapids: Eerdmans, 1972), 63.
7. Kidner, *Psalms 1–72,* 63.
8. Ibid., 65.
9. Ibid., 70.
10. Chester K. Lehman, *Biblical Theology* (Scottdale, Pa.: Herald, 1971), 1.435.
11. John Adams, *The Lenten Psalms* (New York: Charles Scribner's Sons, 1912), 22.
12. Kidner, *Psalms 1–72,* 189.
13. Ibid., 191.
14. H.C. Leupold, *Exposition of the Psalms* (Grand Rapids: Baker, 1959), 404.
15. Von Rad, *Old Testament Theology,* 1.418.
16. James L. Crenshaw, *Old Testament Wisdom, An Introduction* (Atlanta: John Knox, 1981), 74.
17. Walther Eichrodt, *Theology of the Old Testament,* vol. 2, *The Old Testament Library,* trans. J.A. Baker (Philadelphia: Westminster, 1967), 2.86.
18. Ibid., 88.
19. William McKane, *Proverbs, A New Approach, The Old Testament Library* (Philadelphia: Westminster, 1970), 326.
20. H.A. Brongers, "The Literature of the Old Testament," in *The World of the Old Testament,* ed. A.S. Van der Woude, trans. Sierd Woudstra (Grand Rapids: Eerdmans, 1989), 158.
21. Francis I. Andersen, *Job, Tyndale Old Testament Commentaries* (Downers Grove, Ill.: InterVarsity, 1976), 83.
22. Israel J. Gerber, *Job on Trial: A Book for Our Time* (Gastonia, N.C.: E.P. Press, 1982), 91.
23. Ibid., 92.

24. Ibid.
25. Andersen, *Job*, 201.
26. See Dianne Bergant, "The Wisdom Books," in *The Catholic Study Bible (New American Bible)* (New York: Oxford, 1990), RG234.
27. As in the RSV which begins 24:18 with "you say. . . ."
28. See Andersen, *Job*, 213.
29. Michael A. Eaton, *Ecclesiastes, Tyndale Old Testament Commentaries* (Downers Grove, Ill.: InterVarsity, 1983), 44.
30. Ibid., 116.
31. Robert Davidson, *Ecclesiastes and the Song of Solomon, The Daily Study Bible* (Edinburgh, Scotland: Saint Andrew, 1986), 60.
32. James L. Crenshaw, *Ecclesiastes, A Commentary, The Old Testament Library* (Philadelphia: Westminster, 1987), 160.
33. Derek Kidner, *A Time to Mourn and a Time to Dance: The Message of Ecclesiastes* (Downers Grove, Ill.: InterVarsity, 1976), 92.
34. Hugh G.M. Williamson, *1 and 2 Chronicles, The New Century Bible Commentary* (London: Marshall, Morgan and Scott, 1982), 5–11.
35. Ibid., 16.
36. Ibid., 16–17.
37. Ibid., 31.
38. Ibid., 32.
39. Von Rad, *Old Testament Theology*, 1.349.
40. Simon J. DeVries, *1 and 2 Chronicles*, vol. 11 of *The Forms of the Old Testament Literature* (Grand Rapids: Eerdmans, 1989), 98.
41. Williamson, *1 and 2 Chronicles*, 225.
42. Ibid., 237.
43. De Vries, *1 and 2 Chronicles*, 287.
44. Williamson, *1 and 2 Chronicles*, 255.
45. Ibid., 303.
46. DeVries, *1 and 2 Chronicles*, 347.
47. Williamson, *1 and 2 Chronicles*, 327.
48. DeVries, *1 and 2 Chronicles*, 357.
49. The Chronicler presupposes the reader's knowledge that the Northern Kingdom has fallen and numbers of people have been exiled by the Assyrian conquerors.
50. DeVries, *1 and 2 Chronicles*, 387.
51. Ibid., 395.
52. Ibid., 400.
53. Williamson, *1 and 2 Chronicles*, 412.
54. Ibid., 416.
55. Von Rad, *Old Testament Theology*, 1.344–45.
56. Roland K. Harrison, *Introduction to the Old Testament* (Grand Rapids: Eerdmans, 1969), 1135–36.
57. F. Charles Fensham, *The Books of Ezra and Nehemiah, The New International Commentary on the Old Testament* (Grand Rapids: Eerdmans, 1982), 17.
58. Ibid., 128.
59. Derek Kidner, *Ezra and Nehemiah, Tyndale Old Testament Commentaries* (Leicester, England: Inter-Varsity, 1979), 113.
60. John White, *Excellence in Leadership* (Downers Grove, Ill.: InterVarsity, 1986), 129.
61. Kidner, *Ezra and Nehemiah*, 23.
62. Eichrodt, *Old Testament Theology*, 2.383.

63. Alan F. Johnson and Robert E. Webber, *What Christians Believe: A Biblical and Historical Summary* (Grand Rapids: Zondervan/Academie, 1989), 195–96.
64. Eichrodt, *Old Testament Theology*, 2.386.
65. Ibid., 2.389.
66. Ibid., 2.390.
67. Ibid., 2.391.

Chapter 9
1. Leonhard Goppelt, *Theology of the New Testament*, trans. John L. Alsup, ed. Jurgen Roloff (Grand Rapids: Eerdmans, 1981), 123–24.
2. W. Gunther, "ἁμαρτία," *New International Dictionary of New Testament Theology*, ed. Colin Brown (Grand Rapids: Zondervan, 1978), 3:577.
3. Ibid., 579.
4. Gunther, "αδικία," *New International Dictionary*, 3:573–74.
5. Ibid., 575–76.
6. Gunther, "παράβασις," *New International Dictionary*, 3:583–84.
7. W. Bauder, "παράπτωμα," *New International Dictionary of New Testament Theology*, ed. Colin Brown (Grand Rapids: Zondervan, 1978), 3:585–86.
8. Frank Stagg, *New Testament Theology* (Nashville: Broadman, 1962), 15–16.
9. Goppelt, *Theology of the New Testament*, 1.127–28.
10. Ibid.
11. H.D. McDonald, *Living Doctrines of the New Testament* (Grand Rapids: Zondervan, 1972), 72–73.
12. Donald Guthrie, *New Testament Theology* (London: Inter-Varsity, 1981), 191–92.
13. McDonald, *Living Doctrines*, 73.
14. Ibid.
15. Guthrie, *New Testament Theology*, 192.
16. Ibid.
17. Günther Bornkamm, *Paul*, trans. D.M.G. Stalker (London: Hodder & Stoughton, 1971), 123.
18. Dale Moody, "Romans," in *The Broadman Bible Commentary*, ed. Clifton Allen (Nashville: Broadman, 1970), 10:195.
19. C.C. Cargoulis, "Romans 5:15-16 in the Context of 5:12-21: Contrast or Comparison?" *New Testament Studies* 31 (1985): 143.
20. C.E.B. Cranfield, *Commentary on Romans*, International Critical Commentary (Edinburgh, Scotland: T & T Clark, 1975), 1.269–70.
21. Ibid. But cf. Anders Nygren, *Commentary on Romans*, trans. Carl C. Rasmussen (Philadelphia: Muhlenberg, 1949), 209–10 for an opposing view.
22. Joseph A. Fitzmeyer, "The Letter to the Romans," *Jerome Biblical Commentary* (Englewood Cliffs, N.J.: Prentice-Hall, 1968), 2.307.
23. Moody, "Romans," 196.
24. Werner Georg Kümmel, *The Theology of the New Testament*, trans. John E. Steely (Nashville: Abingdon, 1973), 179.
25. Ibid.
26. Nygren, *Commentary on Romans*, 217.
27. Cranfield, *Commentary on Romans*, 283.
28. See Cranfield, *Commentary on Romans*, 284; Moody, "Romans," 196; and Karl Barth, *Epistle to the Romans*, 6th ed., trans. E.C. Hoskyns (Oxford, Great Britain: Oxford Univ. Press, 1933), 176–77. But cf. Cargoulis, "Romans 5:15-16," 142–48 who presents an opposing viewpoint.

29. Gerald R. Cragg, "The Epistle to the Romans," in *The Interpreter's Bible*, ed. George A. Buttrick (Nashville: Abingdon-Cokesbury, 1953), 464.

30. Cargoulis, "Romans 5:15-16," 145.

31. Moody, "Romans," 197.

32. Nygren, *Commentary on Romans*, 221.

33. Gordon R. Lewis and Bruce A. Demarest, *Integrative Theology* (Grand Rapids: Zondervan/Academie, 1990), 202.

34. Cranfield, *Commentary on Romans*, 288.

35. Ibid., 290.

36. Barth, *Epistle to the Romans*, 181.

37. Nygren, *Commentary on Romans*, 224–25. Cf. Barth, *Epistle to the Romans*, 182–83.

38. Cranfield, *Commentary on Romans*, 294.

39. Dale Moody, *The Word of Truth* (Grand Rapids: Eerdmans, 1981), 290.

40. Douglas Moo, "Israel and Paul in Romans 7:7-12," *New Testament Studies* 32 (January 1986): 122–35 believes that this passage is reflective of Israel's encounter with the law, but also holds that it "strongly implies some degree of autobiographical reference as well." Cranfield, *Commentary on Romans*, 342ff. declares that Paul is speaking in the name of Adam or of human beings in general. Moody, "Romans," 207 takes it to be autobiographical and typical of all humans.

41. Cranfield, *Commentary on Romans*, 350.

42. Moody, "Romans," 208.

43. Ibid. Cf. Moody, *The Word of Truth*, 290.

44. George E. Ladd, *A Theology of the New Testament* (Grand Rapids: Eerdmans, 1974), 508.

45. Krister Stendahl, *Paul Among the Jews and Gentiles* (Philadelphia: Fortress, 1976), 92 observes that "Paul here is involved in an argument about the Law; he is not primarily concerned about man's or his own cloven ego or predicament."

46. See Lewis and Demarest, *Integrative Theology*, 2:202.

47. Moody, *Word of Truth*, 286.

48. Stagg, *New Testament Theology*, 334-35.

49. Hans Conzelmann, *An Outline of the Theology of the New Testament*, trans. John Bowden (London: SCM, 1968), 179.

50. Ibid., 277.

51. Ladd, *Theology of the New Testament*, 407.

52. Guthrie, *New Testament Theology*, 202.

53. Ladd, *Theology of the New Testament*, 223.

54. Rudolf Bultmann, *The Gospel of John: A Commentary*, trans. G.R. Beasley-Murray (Oxford: Basil Blackwell, 1971), 440.

55. Ibid., 224.

56. Ibid.

57. Goppelt, *Theology of the New Testament*, 15.

58. I. Howard Marshall, *The Epistles of John, The New International Commentary on the New Testament* (Grand Rapids: Eerdmans, 1978), 109.

59. Ibid., 112.

60. Ibid., 116.

61. John R.W. Stott, *The Epistles of John, Tyndale New Testament Commentaries* (Grand Rapids: Eerdmans, 1964), 80.

62. Marshall, *The Epistles of John*, 143.

63. Ladd, *Theology of the New Testament*, 612.

64. Kümmel, *Theology of the New Testament,* 289.
65. Marshall, *The Epistles of John,* 177–78n.
66. Ibid., 178–82. Marshall lists and interacts with various possible interpretations.
67. For helpful interaction on a more detailed analysis of the meaning of "the seed of God" and "the seed of the devil," see Dale Moody, *The Letters of John,* (Waco: Word, 1970), 65ff.
68. Moody, *Word of Truth,* 284. Cf. Moody, *The Letters of John,* 111ff.
69. Stagg, *New Testament Theology,* 109.
70. Johnson and Webber, *What Christians Believe,* 203.
71. A.T. Robertson, *Word Pictures in the New Testament* (Nashville: Sunday School Board of the Southern Baptist Convention, 1930), 5.375.
72. Guthrie, *New Testament Theology,* 215–16.
73. See J.N.D. Kelly, *The Epistles of Peter and of Jude* (London: Adam and Charles Black, 1969), 146.
74. Ibid., 148.
75. Ibid., 178.
76. Guthrie, *New Testament Theology,* 216.
77. Ibid., 217–18.

Chapter 10

1. Garrett, *Systematic Theology,* 1:452. Cf. Brunner, *Christian Doctrine of Creation and Redemption,* 89.
2. See Moody, *Word of Truth,* 276–78.
3. Charles Hodge, *Systematic Theology* (Grand Rapids: Eerdmans, 1977), 2.132.
4. Brunner, *Christian Doctrine of Creation and Redemption,* 91.
5. Ralph Venning, *The Plague of Plagues* (1669 reprint; London: Banner of Truth Trust, 1965), 32.
6. G.L. Archer, Jr., "Covenant," in *Evangelical Dictionary of Theology,* ed. Walter A. Elwell (Grand Rapids: Baker, 1984), 277.
7. Walther Eichrodt, *Theology of the Old Testament,* vol. 1, trans. J.A. Baker (Philadelphia: Westminster, 1961), 1:59.
8. Representative of those holding to the possibility of apostasy by a believer is Robert Shank, *Elect in the Son* (Springfield, Mo.: Westcott, 1970) and of those opposed, G.C. Berkouwer, *Divine Election* (Grand Rapids: Eerdmans, 1960).
9. Robertson, *Word Pictures in the New Testament,* 2:113.
10. Moody, *Word of Truth,* 355.
11. Edgar Y. Mullins, *The Christian Religion in Its Doctrinal Expression* (Philadelphia: Judson, 1917), 289.
12. Reinhold Niebuhr, *The Nature and Destiny of Man* (New York: Scribners, 1941), 1:150.
13. Millard J. Erickson, *Christian Theology* (Grand Rapids: Baker, 1985), 580.
14. John Macquarrie, *Principles of Christian Theology,* 2nd ed. (New York: Scribners, 1977), 260.
15. C. Berkouwer, *Sin,* trans. Philip C. Holtrop (Grand Rapids: Eerdmans, 1971), 224.
16. Garrett, *Systematic Theology,* 1:460.
17. Erickson, *Christian Theology,* 580.
18. Ibid.
19. Macquarrie, *Christian Theology,* 260.
20. Friedrich Schleiermacher, *The Christian Faith* (New York: Harper and Row,

1963), 1:272ff. But cf. Augustus H. Strong, *Systematic Theology: A Compendium* (Valley Forge, Pa.: Judson, 1907), 559–63 for a rebuttal of this view.

21. Cited by Hodge, *Systematic Theology*, 2.140–41.

22. Borden P. Bowne, cited by Strong, *Systematic Theology*, 559.

23. Strong, *Systematic Theology*, 567.

24. Ibid., 568.

25. Berkouwer, *Sin*, 254.

26. Niebuhr, *Nature and Destiny of Man*, 2.320.

27. Moody, *Word of Truth*, 275.

28. W. Gunter, "παράβασις," *The New International Dictionary of New Testament Theology*, ed. Colin Brown (Grand Rapids: Eerdmans, 1978), 3:583.

29. Ibid., 3.584.

30. Brunner, *Christian Doctrine of Creation and Redemption*, 214.

31. Strong, *Systematic Theology*, 559.

32. Moody, *Word of Truth*, 280.

33. C.K. Barrett, *The Epistle to the Romans, Black's New Testament Commentaries* (London: Adam and Charles Black, 1957), 70.

34. Berkouwer, *Sin*, 485.

35. Chan Wing-Tsit, "Buddhist Terminology," in *An Encyclopedia of Religion*, ed. Vergilius Ferm (New York: Philosophical Library, 1945), 105–6.

36. Charles S. Braden, "Hinduism," in Ferm, ed., *An Encyclopedia of Religion*, 337–38.

37. Moody, *Word of Truth*, 281–82.

38. Ritschl, *Christian Doctrine of Justification and Reconciliation*, 336.

39. Brunner, *Christian Doctrine of Creation and Redemption*, 96.

40. Macquarrie, *Christian Theology*, 262.

41. James S. Candlish, *The Biblical Doctrine of Sin* (Edinburgh, Scotland: T & T Clark, 1893), 69.

42. Ibid., 70.

43. Kenneth Grayston, "Flesh, Fleshly, Carnal," in *A Theological Word Book of the Bible*, ed. Alan Richardson (New York: Macmillan, 1950), 84.

44. Candlish, *Biblical Doctrine of Sin*, 70–71.

45. Ibid., 72.

46. Ramm, *Offense to Reason*, 16–17.

47. Frederick R. Tennant, *The Origin and Propagation of Sin* (Cambridge: Cambridge Univ. Press, 1902), 27.

48. Ibid., 109.

49. Candlish, *Biblical Doctrine of Sin*, 74.

50. James O. Buswell, Jr., *A Systematic Theology of the Christian Religion* (Grand Rapids: Zondervan, 1962), 1.280.

51. John Owen, *Temptation and Sin* (Evansville, Ind.: The Sovereign Grace Book Club, 1958), 95.

52. Ibid., 96.

53. Ibid.

54. Niebuhr, *Nature and Destiny of Man*, 1.18–81.

55. Ibid., 1.181.

56. Ibid., 1.182.

57. Ibid., 1.184.

58. Ibid., 1.232.

59. Brunner, *Christian Doctrine of Creation and Redemption*, 104.

60. John S. Whale, *Christian Doctrine* (New York: Macmillan, 1941), 52.

Chapter 11

1. Herman Bavinck, *Gereformeerde Dogmatik*, 3.29 as cited by G.C. Berkouwer, *Sin*, trans. Philip C. Holtrop (Grand Rapids: Eerdmans, 1971), 13.
2. Ibid., 26–27.
3. Millard J. Erickson, *Christian Theology* (Grand Rapids: Baker, 1983–85), 513.
4. Ibid., 514.
5. Garrett, *Systematic Theology*, 1.474.
6. Johnson and Webber, *What Christians Believe*, 217.
7. Garrett, *Systematic Theology*, 1.474–75.
8. Ibid., 1.475.
9. Ibid., 1.476.
10. Lewis and Demarest, *Integrative Theology*, 2.206.
11. Ibid.
12. An exception to this view was Tertullian who saw the account of the Fall, according to *De Anima*, 38 and *De Baptismo*, 18:4, to be allegorical of human development from the innocence of childhood into the guilt of adolescence.
13. Bernard Ramm, *Offense to Reason: A Theology of Sin* (San Francisco: Harper and Row, 1985), 11–12.
14. Ibid., 13–14.
15. Ibid., 16–17.
16. Garrett, *Systematic Theology*, 1.468–69.
17. Whale, *Christian Doctrine*, 52.
18. James Orr, *The Christian View of God and the World as Centering in the Incarnation* (1893; reprint, Grand Rapids: Eerdmans, 1948), 185.
19. Bruce Waltke, "The First Seven Days," *Christianity Today*, 12 August 1988, 46.
20. Clark H. Pinnock, "Climbing Out of a Swamp," *Interpretation* 43 (April 1989): 152.
21. Ibid., 155.
22. Ramm, *Offense to Reason*, 68–70.
23. Ibid., 71.
24. Lewis and Demarest, *Integrative Theology*, 206–7.
25. Karl Barth, *Church Dogmatics III/1*, 23 as cited by Ramm, *Offense to Reason*, 73–74.
26. Buswell, *A Systematic Theology*, 264.
27. Ibid.
28. Berkouwer, *Sin*, 111n.
29. Erickson, *Christian Theology*, 597.
30. Berkouwer, *Sin*, 111.
31. Ibid., 112.
32. Brunner, *Christian Doctrine of Creation and Redemption*, 94–95.
33. Ramm, *Offense to Reason*, 126.
34. Garrett, *Systematic Theology*, 1.310–11.
35. Tillich, *Systematic Theology*, 2.44ff.
36. Macquarrie, *Christian Theology*, 71–72.
37. Brunner, *Christian Doctrine of Creation and Redemption*, 118–19.
38. Moody, *Word of Truth*, 273.
39. Ramm, *Offense to Reason*, 127.
40. Erickson, *Christian Theology*, 605.
41. Ibid., 607.
42. Paul Ricoeur, *The Symbolism of Evil*, trans. Emerson Buchanan (Boston:

Beacon, 1967), 63.
43. Ibid., 67.
44. Moody, *Word of Truth,* 295.
45. Ibid.
46. Erickson, *Christian Theology,* 608–9.
47. James Orr, *Sin as a Problem of Today* (London: Hodder and Stoughton, 1910), 268–69.
48. Ibid., 269–70.
49. William DeWitt Hyde, *Sin and Its Forgiveness* (Boston: Houghton Mifflin, 1909), 80.
50. Brunner, *Christian Doctrine of Creation and Redemption,* 122.
51. Ibid., 123.
52. Ibid., 124.
53. E. LaB. Cherbonnier, *Hardness of Heart: A Contemporary Interpretation of the Doctrine of Sin* (Garden City, N.Y.: Doubleday, 1955), 45.
54. Ibid., 57.
55. Brunner, *Christian Doctrine of Creation and Redemption,* 124.
56. Gustaf Aulén, *The Faith of the Christian Church,* trans. Eric H. Wahlstrom (Philadelphia: Muhlenburg, 1960), 260.
57. Niebuhr, *Nature and Destiny of Man,* 1.188.
58. Strong, *Systematic Theology,* 567.
59. Erickson, *Christian Theology,* 579.
60. Søren Kierkegaard, *The Sickness Unto Death,* trans. Walter Lowrie (Princeton: Princeton Univ. Press, 1941), 131–32.
61. Niebuhr, *Nature and Destiny of Man,* 1.203.
62. Ibid., 204–5.
63. Ibid., 206–7.
64. Westermann, *Genesis Accounts of Creation,* 31.
65. Ibid.
66. Ibid.
67. Rodney Clapp, "Shame Crucified," *Christianity Today,* 11 March 1991, 27.
68. Lyn M. Bechtel, "Shame as a Sanction of Social Control in Biblical Israel: Judicial, Political, and Social Shaming," *Journal for the Study of the Old Testament* 49 (1991): 49.
69. Ibid., 51.

Chapter 12
1. Augustine, as quoted by D. Parker, "Original Sin: A Study in Evangelical Theory," *Evangelical Quarterly* 61 (1989): 53.
2. Calvin, *The Institutes,* vol. 20, 2.1.8 (251).
3. Henri Rondet, *Original Sin,* trans. Cajetan Finnegan (Shannon, Ireland: Ecclesia, 1972).
4. Berkouwer, *Sin,* 492.
5. Moody, *Word of Truth,* 290.
6. Garrett, *Systematic Theology,* 1.486–87.
7. Charles Hodge, *Systematic Theology* (Grand Rapids: Eerdmans, 1977), 2.216.
8. Ibid., 2.216–17.
9. Ibid., 2.218.
10. William G.T. Shedd, *Dogmatic Theology* (New York: Charles Scribner's Sons, 1888–94), 2.29–32, 41–44, 181–92.
11. Cited by Garrett, *Systematic Theology,* 1.487.

12. Erickson, *Christian Theology*, 639.
13. Buswell, *Systematic Theology*, 1.310.
14. Garrett, *Systematic Theology*, 1.488.
15. Hodge, *Systematic Theology*, 2.197.
16. James P. Boyce, *Abstract of Systematic Theology* (Pompano Beach, Fla.: North Pompano Baptist Church, 1887), 253.
17. Berkouwer, *Sin*, 451.
18. Augustus H. Strong, *Systematic Theology*, (Valley Forge, Pa.: Judson, 1907) 601.
19. Ibid.
20. Garrett, *Systematic Theology*, 1.489.
21. Walter Rauschenbusch, *A Theology for the Social Gospel* (Nashville: Abingdon, 1945), 58.
22. Ibid., 60.
23. Ibid., 60.
24. Ibid., 61.
25. Garrett, *Systematic Theology*, 1.489–90.
26. Ibid., 1.490.
27. Edgar Y. Mullins, *The Christian Religion in Its Doctrinal Expression* (Philadelphia: Judson, 1917), 301.
28. Mullins, *The Christian Religion*, 301.
29. Moody, *Word of Truth*, 290.
30. Janice Keller Phelps and Alan E. Nourse, *The Hidden Addiction and How to Get Free* (Boston: Little, Brown, and Co., 1986), 87. Cf. John White, *Masks of Melancholy* (Downers Grove, Ill.: InterVarsity, 1982), 135–36.
31. This is, in actual fact, a restatement of Tertullian's theory of traducianism, namely, that the soul as well as the body is procreated by one's parents.
32. Mullins, *The Christian Religion*, 302.

Chapter 13
1. Brunner, *Christian Doctrine of Creation and Redemption*, 135.
2. Michael Green, *I Believe in Satan's Downfall* (London: Hodder and Stoughton, 1981), 27.
3. See Green, *I Believe*, 36–39 and Lewis Sperry Chafer, *Satan*, rev. ed. (Chicago: Bible Institute Colportage Ass'n, 1927), 3–7.
4. Frederick C. Jennings, *Satan and His Person, Work, Place and Destiny* (New York: Publication Office "Our Hope," n.d.), 21.
5. See Stedman, *Understanding Man*, 57.
6. Green, *I Believe*, 42.
7. Trevor Ling, *The Significance of Satan* (London: SPCK, 1961), 46.
8. H.H. Rowley, *The Relevance of Apocalyptic*, 62 as cited by Ling, *Significance of Satan*, 46.
9. Ling, *Significance of Satan*, 46–47.
10. Green, *I Believe*, 46.
11. Ray Summers, *Behold the Lamb* (Nashville: Broadman, 1979), 204.
12. Green, *I Believe*, 46.
13. Gleason L. Archer, Jr., "Abaddon," in *Evangelical Dictionary of Theology*, ed. Walter A. Elwell (Grand Rapids: Baker, 1984), 1.
14. Berkouwer, *Sin*, 116.
15. C. Fred Dickason, *Demon Possession and the Christian, A New Perspective* (Chicago: Moody, 1987), 24–25.

16. Ibid., 24.
17. Merrill F. Unger, *Biblical Demonology* (Chicago: Scripture Press, 1952), 59–60.
18. Ibid., 60.
19. Ibid., 60–61.
20. Moody, *Word of Truth*, 305.
21. Ling, *Significance of Satan*, 67.
22. Moody, *Word of Truth*, 306.
23. Ibid.
24. Dickason, *Demon Possession*, 25.
25. Green, *I Believe*, 84.
26. Dickason, *Demon Possession*, 26.
27. Ibid.
28. Unger, *Biblical Demonology*, 67.
29. Dickason, *Demon Possession*, 28.
30. Unger, *Biblical Demonology*, 69.
31. C. Fred Dickason, *Angels, Elect and Evil* (Chicago: Moody, 1975), 174.
32. Ibid., 174–75.
33. Dickason, *Demon Possession*, 30.
34. Ibid.
35. Ibid., 37.
36. Ibid., 38. Cf. Merrill F. Unger, *What Demons Can Do to Saints* (Chicago: Moody, 1977), 86–87.
37. Unger, *Biblical Demonology*, 100.
38. Ibid., 215.
39. Green, *I Believe*, 210.
40. Ibid., 217.

Chapter 14

1. Mullins, *The Christian Religion*, 299.
2. Ibid., 299–300.
3. Macquarrie, *Christian Theology*, 104–5.
4. Ibid., 270.
5. As R.V.G. Tasker, *The Gospel According to St. Matthew, Tyndale New Testament Commentaries* (Grand Rapids: Eerdmans, 1973), 97–98 points out, Jesus' comment here goes beyond a simple demonstration of love for sinners. He is using satire to stress that all human beings are sinners.
6. Roswell D. Hitchcock, "Eternal Atonement," a sermon cited by George Barker Stevens, *The Christian Doctrine of Salvation* (Edinburgh, Scotland: T & T Clark, 1909), 437.
7. Cranfield, *Romans*, 1.217.
8. William Henry Crouch, "A Father's Heart," in *Interpreting Isaiah for Teaching and Preaching*, ed. Cecil P. Staton, Jr. (Greenville, S.C.: Smyth and Helwys, 1991), 33–34.
9. Derek Kidner, *The Message of Hosea, The Bible Speaks Today* (Downers Grove, Ill.: InterVarsity, 1981), 122.
10. Stevens, *Christian Doctrine of Salvation*, 344.
11. Vincent Taylor, *Forgiveness and Reconciliation* (London: MacMillan, 1941), 25–26.
12. John R.W. Stott, *The Cross of Christ* (Downers Grove, Ill.: InterVarsity, 1986), 193.

13. Mullins, *The Christian Religion*, 367.
14. Ibid., 372.
15. John R.W. Stott, *Basic Christianity*, 2nd ed. (Downers Grove, Ill.: InterVarsity, 1971), 108.
16. Ibid.
17. Ibid., 111.
18. Dietrich Bonhoeffer, *The Cost of Discipleship*, rev. ed., trans. R.H. Fuller (New York: Macmillan, 1959), 79.
19. John Watson, *The Doctrines of Grace* (London: Hodder and Stoughton, 1900), 188.
20. Ibid., 196.
21. Ibid., 202.
22. Ibid., 300.
23. Mullins, *The Christian Religion*, 319.
24. Ibid.
25. John R.W. Stott, *Only One Way — The Message of Galatians* (Downers Grove, Ill.: InterVarsity, 1968), 146.
26. Ibid., 153.
27. Berkouwer, *Sin*, 563.
28. Ibid., 567.

Conclusion

1. W. Kelly Bokovay, "The Search for Identity: Pastoral Caregiving and the 'Who Am I?' Question" (Pastoral Theology research paper, Providence Theological Seminary, March 1992), 3–4.
2. Ibid., 4.
3. For a competent summary of these varying views, see Erickson, *Christian Theology*, 498ff.
4. Ibid., 513.
5. Bokovay, "Search for Identity," 5.
6. While it is freely acknowledged that this passage is not found in the earliest and best manuscripts, and so is probably not a part of the inspired text, it is certainly accurate of the behavior and attitude of Christ.
7. Lewis and Demarest, *Integrative Theology*, 2.238.
8. Bloesch, *Essentials of Evangelical Theology*, vol. 1, 90; cf. L. Berkhof, *Systematic Theology* (Grand Rapids: Eerdmans, 1939), 246–47.
9. Walter T. Cooner, *The Gospel of Redemption* (Nashville: Broadman, 1945), 22.
10. Lewis and Demarest, *Integrative Theology*, 2.242.
11. See Brunner's criticism of Barth's position in Emil Brunner, *The Christian Doctrine of God*, vol. 1 of *Dogmatics*, trans. Olive Wyon (Philadelphia: Westminster Press, 1949), 346–53.
12. D. James Kennedy, *Evangelism Explosion*, 3rd ed. (Wheaton: Tyndale House, 1983), 63.
13. Bokovay, "Search for Identity," 6.
14. Ibid.
15. Ibid.

SUBJECT INDEX

A

Abaddon 377–78
Abyss 112, 379
Adultery 223–24, 238, 252, 255,
  287, 404, 407
Alexandrians 23–26
Alienation — See Estrangement
Angels 46, 85, 118, 147, 170–71,
  238, 254, 372–73, 375, 378–81,
  383
Anxiety 110, 120, 122–23, 127,
  146, 332–33
Apollyon 377–78
Apologists 18–21
Apostasy 187, 192, 194, 202–3,
  206, 211, 219–21, 224, 233,
  261–62, 267–68, 281–82, 308,
  317–18, 320, 325
Archangel 373, 378
Atonement 177, 179, 275, 298,
  303, 369, 379, 389, 394
  Day of 179–80, 228–29
Azazel 378, 380

B

Babel 167–68, 280
Baptism 24, 27–32, 35, 37, 40–41,
  43–45, 50, 56–57, 61, 67, 69, 70,
  87, 309, 358, 399–400, 412
Beelzebul 375–76, 378–79
Being Itself 112
Beliar 375–76, 378
Branhamites 375

C

Cappadocians 26–27
Carthage, Council of 42, 45
Chiersey, Council of 48
Chiersey, Synod of 48

Concern, Ultimate 111

Concupiscence 37, 42, 51, 87,
  101, 128, 130, 133, 338
Confirmation 57
Consciousness 96–100, 336, 388,
  397
Correlation, Method of 111
Council, Fourth Lateran 64, 344
Covenant 172, 184–86, 188,
  192–96, 204, 208, 215, 221, 223,
  225–26, 233, 242, 244, 273,
  275–78, 280–82, 316–18, 320,
  325, 361–62, 367
Creationism 37
Culpability 37, 42, 44, 57, 328,
  336

D

Death 19, 21–22, 24, 28, 30, 40,
  44, 49, 62, 69, 74, 83, 91, 116,
  136, 148, 162, 169, 181–82, 239,
  247, 248, 255–56, 258, 260, 264,
  281, 289–91, 294, 297–98, 300,
  302–3, 305, 307–9, 318, 349–51,
  362, 368–69, 376, 386–87, 396,
  398–401, 410, 402, 213
Decalogue 183–84, 193, 280, 411
Demonic, Demons 21, 46, 60, 83,
  105, 116, 118, 131, 147, 151,
  254, 328, 334, 371, 377–85, 392,
  401
Demonization 385–87
Dependence 96, 99
Depravity 25, 65, 73, 75, 77, 148,
  166, 171, 188, 284, 289, 358–59,
  365–66, 370, 404–5, 408–9
Despair 126, 128, 353, 402, 413
Deuteronomic,
  Deuteronomist 181–82,
  190–220, 262–63, 273, 314
Devil 46, 58, 147, 302, 304–5,

445

PERSON INDEX

A

Aaron 174–75, 180, 280
Abel 164, 173, 347–48
Abelard, Peter 51, 53–54
Abijah 210, 217, 263, 272
Abimelech 169–70
Abraham 168–71, 194, 269, 278
Absalom 202–3, 260
Achan 192–93, 281
Adam 18–19, 21–23, 25–28,
 31–32, 38, 40, 42–45, 47, 49,
 56–57, 66, 69, 72, 74, 77, 83, 86,
 89, 91, 101, 105, 110, 112–16,
 120, 129–30, 145, 147–48,
 156–63, 188, 223, 259, 290–92,
 294, 296, 298, 300, 310, 314,
 330, 333–34, 338–39, 341–44,
 346–47, 351, 355, 357–58,
 360–62, 364–65, 367–71, 373,
 375, 409
Agur 251
Ahab 206–7, 209, 211, 215, 219,
 223, 235, 243, 264–65
Ahaz 213–14, 217, 229, 268–69,
 272, 274
Ahaziah (of Israel) 206–7, 209,
 211, 264
Ahaziah (of Judah) 212, 217, 265,
 272
Alexander III 88
Amaziah 212, 217, 219
Ambrose of Milan 31ff, 34, 44
Amittai 236
Amnon 202
Amon 214–15, 217, 243, 271–72,
 274
Amos 221–22, 236, 243
Amoz 224, 269
Andersen, Francis 254
Anselm of Canterbury 49–50, 52,
 54, 59, 62

Aquinas, Thomas 12, 46, 49, 53,
 55–59, 62, 337
Arminius, Jacob 82, 89
Arunah 261
Asa 210–11, 217, 219, 243,
 263–64, 272
Asaph 246, 248, 351
Athaliah 212, 217, 265
Athanasius 24–26, 34
Augustine of Hippo 32–42, 44,
 46–47, 61, 88, 117, 128, 144,
 337–38, 351, 358–59, 363,
 366–67, 401
Aulén, Gustaf 353
Autolycus 21
Azariah 213, 217, 219, 221, 225,
 243, 267–68

B

Baasha 205, 209, 243, 263
Baldwin, Joyce 202
Barth, Karl 108, 114–16, 123,
 128, 298, 337, 343, 410
Basil of Caesarea 26, 34
Bathsheba 202, 249–50
Benhadad 264
Berechiah 241
Berkouwer, G.C. 320, 323, 327,
 336, 345, 359, 362, 400–401
Beza, Theodore 82
Bildad 255
Blocher, Henri 155–56, 166, 337
Bloesch, Donald 146–47, 150–51
Blount, William 60
Boesak, Alan 149
Boff, Leonardo 149
Bonhoeffer, Dietrich 337, 396
Bornkamm, Gunther 289
Bowne, Borden 321
Boyce, James P. 362, 367
Brunner, Emil 108, 115–19, 123,

451

Soggin, J. Alberto 158
Solomon 203–4, 209, 217, 243,
  246, 251, 256, 260, 262, 269,
  272, 274, 327
Song, C.S. 137–39, 149
Speiser, E.A. 167
Spinoza, Baruch 329, 341
Stagg, Frank 298, 306, 337
Stalin, Josef 331
Stedman, Ray 158
Stevens, William 337
Strong, Augustus 222, 253, 361,
  367
Summers, Ray 376

T

Tamar 202
Tate, Marvin 181
Tatian 20, 22, 33
Tauler, Johann 81
Teilhard, Pierre 131
Tennant, R. 28, 331, 337, 341
Terah 194
Tertullian of Carthage 29–31, 33,
  44, 297
Theodore of Mopsuestia 28–29,
  34
Theophilus 20–21, 22, 33, 44
Theresa, Mother 331
Thompson, J.A. 185
Tillich, Paul 106, 109, 124, 346
Tutu, Desmond 149

U

Unger, Merrill 382
Urban VIII 87
Uriah the Hittite 202, 250
Uytenbogaart, James 82
Uzziah — See Azariah

V

Valentinus 18
Venning, Ralph 315–16

W

Waltke, Bruce 342–43
Ward, James M. 233
Watson, John 397
Watts, John D. W. 191, 220
Weaver, David 42
Wesley, John 90–95, 106, 123
Westermann, Claus 159, 164,
  355
Whale, John 334, 341
Wieman, Henry 149
Williams, Daniel Day 131–32,
  133, 149
Williamson, Hugh 259
Woudstra, Marten 191, 193

Y

Young, Lee Jung 149

Z

Zechariah (King) 210, 243
Zechariah (the Prophet) 241,
  243, 266
Zedekiah 216, 218, 243, 272–74
Zephaniah 230–31, 243
Zerah 263
Zerubbabel 241
Zimri 205, 209
Zinzendorf, Count von 93
Zosimus 43
Zwingli, Ulrich 69–70, 79–80, 88,
  338

SCRIPTURE INDEX

459